CONTEMPT OF COURT

CONTEMPT
OF
COURT

C. J. Miller, B.A., LL.M.,
of Lincoln's Inn, Barrister at Law,
Lecturer in law, University of Leeds

Paul Elek London

First published in Great Britain 1976 by
Elek Books Limited
54–58 Caledonian Road
London N1 9RN

ISBN 0 236 31087 9

Printed in Great Britain by
Jolly & Barber Ltd
Rugby, Warwickshire

To Michèle, Anne-Marie and Mark

Preface

Contempt of court is a subject which is of considerable historical interest and yet of fundamental contemporary importance. The historical aspects of the subject have long been admirably covered in the writings of Sir John Fox. Until recent years there has, however, been no attempt to provide a statement of the modern English law of contempt. Oswald's authoritative and frequently humorous work, *Contempt of Court*, although still of considerable value in many areas, was last edited in 1910. In 1973 the gap was partly filled by Borrie and Lowe's *The Law of Contempt*, but it is felt that, notwithstanding this book's several qualities, there remains ample room for an alternative approach. Many important cases have come before the courts in the last few years including *Attorney-General* v. *Times Newspapers Ltd, Balogh* v. *Crown Court at St. Albans, Heatons Transport (St. Helens) Ltd* v. *Transport and General Workers Union* and *R.* v. *Socialist Worker Printers and Publishers Ltd.* The scope of the subject is indicated by the fact that these cases involve matters as diverse as a proposed article on responsibility for the thalidomide tragedy, an alleged attempt to release laughing gas into a court, non-observance of a labour injunction, and the purported disclosure of the identity of a witness in blackmail proceedings. In addition to such cases there has also been the report of the committee under the late Lord-Justice Phillimore, and its recommendations for reform of the law of contempt are discussed in the course of this book.

My aim in writing the book is to provide a comprehensive and critical account of the modern English law of contempt of court. It is my hope that this will be of value to all who are concerned with the many aspects of the subject, whether as students, teachers, journalists or their legal advisers, or as practitioners involved in cases where breach of a court order or undertaking is in issue. To this end I have included a certain amount of theoretical discussion as well as a reasonably full citation of the authorities. Frequent reference is made to Commonwealth decisions both for purposes of comparison and as being illustrative of general principles. The same is true of the law as it has developed in the United States of America, especially in regard to matters such as the distinction between criminal and civil contempt, punishment and the mode of trial. Contempt of Parliament has, however, been excluded as being a separate subject in its own right which is fully covered in Erskine May's *Parliamentary Practice*.

I have received considerable help and encouragement from many sources in writing the book. My pleasure in thanking them is not diminished by the thought that they may suffer guilt through association. All are entitled to the standard disclaimer and responsibility for remaining errors is mine alone. I owe a particular debt to Professor J. C. Smith of Nottingham University, who was instrumental in awakening my interest in the subject and, indeed, in law in general. More recently Professor Brian Hogan of Leeds University has helped considerably both by reading through substantial parts of the manuscript and by being readily available to talk through problems and help formulate ideas. My thanks are due to him and to Mr John Tinnion, Mrs Margaret Richards and Mr Peter Seago, who also gave me considerable assistance. Outside the university world I acknowledge and am grateful for the help I received from persons such as Mr Norman Turner, the Official Solicitor to the Supreme Court; Mr Harold Evans, editor of the *Sunday Times*; Mr R. J. Marshall and Mr B. A. Jennings of the BBC; Mr Charles Wintour, editor of the *Evening Standard*; Mr Hugh Allardyce, Barrister-at-Law, who prepared the index and the table of cases; and Joanna Evans, who helped to remove some of the worst of the infelicities of style. Finally, I acknowledge with particular gratitude the help I received from my wife, Michèle, and children, whom I am conscious of having neglected for far too long when writing the book.

I have endeavoured to state the law on the basis of the materials available to me in Leeds as at January 1st 1975, although it has been possible to take account of some subsequent developments.

C. J. Miller

Contents

Table of Statutes

TABLE OF STATUTES

Table of Cases

B

F

G

TABLE OF CASES

S

1 Introduction

Joseph Moskovitz in his notable article in the Columbia Law Review once described contempt of court as 'the Proteus of the legal world, assuming an almost infinite diversity of forms'.[1] Certainly this is no overstatement. It is, moreover, a branch of the law which is of ancient origin and yet of fundamental contemporary importance. Reference to Sir John Fox's historical text reveals the ancient origins of contempt,[2] while its diversity of forms and fundamental contemporary importance were recognised by Lord Diplock in the recent and leading case of *Attorney-General* v. *Times Newspapers, Ltd.*[3] Here his Lordship observed that:[4]

> The provision of a system for the administration of justice by courts of law and the maintenance of public confidence in it are essential if citizens are to live together in peaceful association with one another. 'Contempt of court' is a generic term descriptive of conduct in relation to particular proceedings in a court of law which tends to undermine that system or to inhibit citizens from availing themselves of it for the settlement of their disputes. Contempt of court may thus take many forms.

Since this branch of the law is concerned, therefore, to assist in the maintenance of an effective legal system for the benefit of all, it is perhaps regrettable that it should continue to be described by such an archaic and frequently misunderstood term.[5]

1 CRIMINAL AND CIVIL CONTEMPT OF COURT

Contempt of court has traditionally been divided into two main constituent parts, according to whether the contempt is criminal or civil in nature. The distinction is time honoured and of continuing importance, even though the immediate practical consequences which flow from it are now less important than formerly. These points are developed in the next chapter. Here it is sufficient to state the nature of the distinction in general terms.

---

[1] See Moskovitz, 'Contempt of Injunctions, Civil and Criminal' (1943) 43 Col. L.R. 780.

[2] See *The History of Contempt of Court* (1927), p. 1, where it is said: 'Contempt of Court (contemptus curiae) has been recognised in English law from the twelfth century to the present time.'

[3] [1974] A.C. 273; [1973] 3 All E.R. 54.

[4] [1974] A.C. 273, 307; [1973] 3 All E.R. 54, 71.

[5] *Cf. Jennison* v. *Baker* [1972] 2 Q.B. 52, 61; [1972] 1 All E.R. 997, 1001; *Morris* v. *The Crown Office* [1970] 2 Q.B. 114, 129; [1970] 1 All E.R. 1079, 1087 *per* Salmon, L. J.; *Heatons Transport (St. Helens), Ltd* v. *T.G.W.U.* [1973] A.C. 15, 27; [1972] 2 All E.R. 1214, 1229 *per* Sir John Donaldson, P. The Report of the Committee on Contempt of Court, Cmnd. 5794, 1974 (hereinafter the Phillimore Committee report) was unable to find a suitable alternative (para. 12).

Criminal contempt exists to protect many of the requirements for the due administration of justice, and its scope reflects the ways in which these requirements may be jeopardised. Thus it is, for example, a criminal contempt to disrupt proceedings in a court of law and this whether the proceedings disrupted are themselves criminal or civil in form. This needs little explanation for it is obvious that justice can only be secured within an orderly framework and against a background which lends itself to deliberation. The man who persistently interrupts proceedings interferes with the administration of justice in an immediate and readily appreciated way. Such contempts in the face of the court have sometimes been designated 'direct' contempts, while others have been termed 'constructive' or 'indirect'. These adjectives are, however, more a part of American than of contemporary English terminology.[6]

Turning to the 'indirect' forms of contempt, English law has long recognised that a criminal contempt may be committed by publishing matter, or indulging in conduct, likely to prejudice the fair trial of particular criminal or civil proceedings, whether through an effect upon the parties, the witnesses, or the tribunal itself. The affording of protection to civil litigation is indicative of the fact that the public has an interest in seeing that the requirements for the due administration of justice are observed here, no less than in a criminal prosecution. It is, of course, this branch of the law of contempt which exists to prevent the growth of 'trial' by the news media. At one stage removed, a criminal contempt may equally be committed by victimising a person for the part he has played in judicial proceedings. Again the justification is clear. If witnesses, jurors, or indeed judges or parties, could be punished in person or property others would be far less willing to come forward in future cases, and the administration of justice as a continuing process would accordingly suffer. For similar reasons it is held to be a criminal contempt to 'scandalise' a court or a judge by publishing material (such as allegations of corruption or partiality) likely to undermine public confidence in the court or judge in question. The assumptions behind this aspect of criminal contempt are, however, less readily accepted. These and other aspects of criminal contempt are discussed in some detail in later chapters.

Civil contempt has a similarly important part to play within the legal system for its role is to assist in the enforcement of court orders. As Moskovitz has so aptly put it:[7]

> It is no more than a commonplace to note that the value of a right to a litigant is no greater than the available remedy, and the remedy in equity is the injunction. This insight, however, should be worked to capacity, and we have not done so until we realize that the remedy, the injunction, is worth no more than its sanction, contempt.

Civil contempt of court exists, therefore, to provide the ultimate sanction against one who refuses to comply with the order of a properly constituted court. In English law the form of the sanction is typically committal to prison or, in the case of a corporate body, a fine or the sequestration of assets. Such coercion is usually intended to assist an individual complainant to enforce his remedy, but,

---

[6] See, e.g. 17 American Jurisprudence 2d, s. 6, which is headed 'Direct and Indirect Contempts Distinguished'.

[7] 'Contempt of Injunctions, Civil and Criminal' (1943) 43 Col. L.R. 780.

as Lord Diplock has recently recognised, there is also 'an element of public policy in punishing civil contempt, since the administration of justice would be undermined if the order of any court of law could be disregarded with impunity'.[8] This aspect of contempt has come to the forefront in this country in recent years with the reluctance of parts of the trade-union movement to obey orders of the National Industrial Relations Court.[9]

In some circumstances compliance can admittedly be secured without resort to coercion through the contempt power. For example, disobedience of an order to pay a sum of money can be effectively countered by attaching the earnings, rather than the person, of the defaulter. This is indeed the present practice.[10] Likewise failure to comply with an order of specific performance that property be conveyed can be met by the court directing that the conveyance be completed by an appointed person.[11] This is not, however, true of cases in which there is a refusal to hand over documents, or to obey an injunction enjoining the committing of a nuisance, or the association with or molesting of a particular person. Here the coercive sanctions of the law of contempt retain an obvious importance and would appear to be indispensable.

In most instances it is relatively simple to classify a given contempt as being criminal rather than civil, or vice versa. This is not, however, always true and the precise borderline between the two branches of contempt has bedevilled the law for many years. Demarcation has not been assisted by the apparent recognition of a hybrid comprised of a civil contempt which is accompanied by criminal incidents, or which 'savours of criminality'.[12] Thus at the present time there is still room for doubting the nature of the contempt committed by one who (i) procures or encourages another to act in breach of an injunction; (ii) disobeys a subpoena or refuses to answer a question put to him as a witness; (iii) interferes with a ward of court or some other person under the special protective jurisdiction of the court; (iv) disobeys a writ of habeas corpus directed to him; or (v) being a solicitor, commits a contempt when acting in his official capacity.[13]

2   CRIMINAL CONTEMPT OF COURT AND ITS RELATIONSHIP TO OTHER CRIMINAL OFFENCES

Although criminal contempt of court is a criminal offence[14] punishable by an unlimited fine or period of imprisonment, it has many characteristics which distinguish it from ordinary crimes. Indeed these characteristics are so marked

---

[8] Cf. Att.-Gen. v. Times Newspapers, Ltd. [1974] A.C. 273, 308; [1973] 3 All E.R. 54, 71.

[9] See, e.g., Heatons Transport (St. Helens), Ltd v. T.G.W.U. (above, note 5); Goad v. A.U.E.W. (No. 2) [1973] I.C.R. 42; Goad v. A.U.E.W. (No. 3) [1973] I.C.R. 108; Con-Mech Engineers, Ltd. v. A.U.E.W. [1973] I.C.R. 620.

[10] See below, p. 271 et seq.

[11] See the Judicature Act 1925, s. 47 and R.S.C. Ord. 45, r. 8. For a recent case, see Danchevsky v. Danchevsky [1974] 3 All E.R. 934, C.A.

[12] See, e.g., Wellesley v. The Duke of Beaufort (1831) 2 Russ. & M. 639, 667; 39 E.R. 538, 548 per Brougham, L.C.; Re Freston (1883) 11 Q.B.D. 545, 555 per Brett, M.R.

[13] See below, (i) p. 247; (ii) p. 56; (iii) p. 222; (iv) p. 233, note 9; (v) p. 226, note 20, respectively.

[14] Cf. Att.-Gen. v. Butterworth [1963] 1 Q.B. 696, 722; [1962] 3 All E.R. 326, 331; Balogh v. Crown Court at St. Albans [1974] 3 All E.R. 283, 289 per Lord Denning, M.R.

that criminal contempt may be said to be an offence *sui generis*.[15] Its most singular procedural characteristic is that it is tried on summary process without a jury and frequently by courts of civil jurisdiction which have no experience of dealing with criminal matters. Thus if, for example, there is a disturbance within the Chancery Division of the High Court during a wardship case the presiding judge may himself commit the offender for contempt. Moreover, any appeal will be heard by the *Civil* Division of the Court of Appeal.[16]

Equally, there are marked differences in the manner of initiating proceedings, and in the procedure adopted at the hearing itself. In particular the normal prosecution on indictment or following the issue of a summons has no place in contempt where proceedings are begun by an application for an order of committal. At the hearing itself the tradition of oral evidence in criminal cases is not observed and evidence is normally given by affidavit. These differences also continue through to the level of disposition and treatment of offenders. Thus it has been suggested that while criminal contempt may be dealt with by committal to prison, or a fine, or a binding-over order, the full range of orders available to a judge dealing with an ordinary criminal offence is not similarly available in cases of contempt. Hence it may be that a person held to have committed a contempt could not, for example, be subjected to a probation order.[17] Finally, in terms of substantive law, it will also be seen that contempt is one of the very few common law offences which embody a measure of strict, and possibly also of vicarious, liability.[18]

These points of distinction between criminal contempt of court and other criminal offences are the more noteworthy because it is now clear that it is also a common law misdemeanour punishable on indictment to pervert the course of justice, and hence to attempt, to incite another, or to conspire to do the same. Any possible doubts as to the existence of such offences have been removed by the recent decision of the Court of Appeal in *Andrews*.[19] Here it was held that A committed the offence of inciting R to pervert the course of justice by soliciting an offer of a sum of money from him (R) in consideration of his (A's) making a false statement to the police. Dismissing A's appeal, Lord Widgery, C.J. said:[20]

> . . . to produce false evidence with a view to misleading the court and perverting the course of justice is a substantive offence; an attempt so to act can be charged as such, and in our judgment an incitement so to act is also a charge known to the law and properly to be preferred in appropriate circumstances.

The relationship between this indictable offence and criminal contempt of court cannot be stated precisely. Certainly the offences are not co-extensive in scope; still less are they mutually exclusive. There are possibly certain respects

---

[15] *Cf. Morris* v. *The Crown Office* [1970] 2 Q.B. 114, 129; [1970] 1 All E.R. 1079, 1087 *per* Salmon, L.J.

[16] Under the Administration of Justice Act 1960, s. 13(2)(b)—see below, p. 38.

[17] *Cf. Morris* v. *The Crown Office* [1970] 2 Q.B. 114, 127; [1970] 1 All E.R. 1079, 1085 *per* Davies, L.J. The treatment of the offender in prison is also different in cases of contempt: see Borrie and Lowe, *The Law of Contempt* (1973), at pp. 283–284; *Halsbury*, Vol. 9, para. 116.

[18] See below, pp. 160–164, 171–177.

[19] [1973] 1 All E.R. 857. See also the Law Commission Working Paper No. 62, 'Offences Relating to the Administration of Justice', paras. 8–25 especially.

[20] *Ibid.*, at p. 859. See also *Vreones* [1891] 1 Q.B. 360; *Sharpe and Stringer* [1938] 1 All E.R. 48 and, in general, below, pp. 79–80.

in which criminal contempt covers ground not covered by the indictable offence,[1] but many others in which the indictable offence is wider in scope. This is especially true when one takes into account the many, more specific, offences which fall within the broad umbrella of the indictable offence, and which may, in appropriate circumstances, all amount to particular manifestations of it. These have been identified by the Law Commission in a recent paper as including:[2]

The concealment of crime and hampering police investigations, misconduct in office, bribery and embracery, criminal libel and blackmail (if false accusations are made), interference with evidence, perjury and subornation of perjury, and freeing persons or property from lawful custody.

This list corresponds, broadly speaking, to the lists which are to be found beneath the rubric 'Offences Against Public Justice' in standard works on criminal law.[3] It is not proposed to attempt to identify which of its component parts is capable of constituting a criminal contempt as well as a perversion of the course of justice punishable on indictment. It is clear, however, that some are not. Thus it would not, without more, be a contempt to free a person from lawful custody,[4] or to hamper police investigations.[5] Similarly, perjury through the making of false statements in judicial proceedings should be kept as distinct as possible from contempt through simply failing to reply to a question at all.[6] Likewise a contempt could not be committed on facts such as those of *Andrews*[7] since proceedings were not *pending or imminent* against R at the time when A made the unlawful approach.[8]

What is quite clear is that there is a broad area of overlap where a given act might invite either a summary committal for contempt or a prosecution for an 'ordinary' criminal offence. This would be true, for example, of a case in which there was an attempt to bribe a juror, or in which threats were directed at a party or a witness to induce him to withdraw or, as the case may be, to withhold or modify his evidence. Similarly, if a witness is victimised after the proceedings this may be dealt with summarily as a contempt or, where appropriate—and depending on the form of the victimisation—by a prosecution for assault, or for criminal damage. In theory the publication of matter which is prejudicial to a fair trial may also be charged on indictment as a perversion of the course of justice. This procedure does not, however, appear to have been adopted since the case of *Tibbits and Windust*[9] in 1902. Contempt proceedings have also been the rule in the few cases in which it has been thought necessary to deal with published matter

---

[1] *Cf.* the statutory extensions of the law of contempt which afford protection to particular bodies other than the ordinary courts of law as, e.g., Tribunals of Inquiry (see further, below, p. 33 *et seq.*). Presumably contempts in relation to such bodies could not be charged on indictment as a perversion of the course of justice.

[2] See the Law Commission Working Paper, No. 50, para. 18.

[3] See, e.g., Archbold, *Criminal Pleading, Evidence and Practice* (38th ed., 1973), Ch. 24; *Russell on Crime* (12th ed., 1964), Vol. 1, p. 291 *et seq.*; Smith and Hogan, *Criminal Law* (3rd ed., 1973), pp. 578–608.

[4] Although the position would be different if this were done in court, see below, p. 48.

[5] But *cf. Evening Standard Co., Ltd., ex p. D.P.P.* (1924) 40 T.L.R. 833.

[6] See below, p. 57.

[7] [1973] 1 All E.R. 857, above.

[8] For this requirement, see below, pp. 73–82.

[9] [1902] 1 K.B. 77.

on the basis that it scandalises the court.[10] Again, however, a prosecution for criminal libel might lie on such facts and this was indeed the usual mode of procedure in earlier years.[11]

The Phillimore Committee has recommended substantial changes in the relationship between contempt as a summarily punishable offence and its counterparts punishable on indictment. Broadly speaking, the committee recommended that both reprisals against witnesses after the termination of proceedings and scandalising the court should only be capable of being punished on indictment.[12] Likewise interference with the administration of justice *pendente lite* should only be dealt with as a contempt where: (a) the offending act does not fall within the definition of any other offence; or (b) where urgency or practical necessity require that the matter be dealt with summarily.[13] Although the changes thus proposed are mainly procedural the general approach of the committee is to be welcomed.

More recently the Law Commission has also provisionally proposed that the general common law offence of perverting the course of justice should be abolished and replaced by a simplified series of offences to be defined as precisely as possible.[14] It is proposed that these offences should cover:[15]

(1) In relation to all judicial proceedings
(a) perjury; (b) tampering with or fabricating evidence; (c) preventing witnesses from attending proceedings or inducing them to be unavailable; (d) intimidating litigants; (e) threatening or bribing a juryman or member of a court; (f) publishing material which creates a risk that the course of justice will be seriously obstructed or prejudiced, intending to pervert the course of justice; (g) impersonating a juror; (h) misconduct as a juror.
(2) In relation to criminal proceedings
(a) preventing potential witnesses from giving information to the police; (b) giving false information to the police; (c) escaping to avoid trial; (d) failing to answer bail to avoid trial; (e) agreeing to indemnify bail; (f) assisting a person believed to be guilty of an arrestable offence; (g) compounding an arrestable offence.
(3) Not necessarily related to the outcome of particular proceedings
(a) taking or threatening reprisals against witnesses, jurors or officers of a court for anything done in that capacity; (b) imputing improper or corrupt judicial conduct.

---

[10] See further, below, p. 182 *et seq.*
[11] See, e.g., *Cobbett* (1804) 29 St. Tr. 1. For a modern Canadian example of a prosecution for publishing a seditious libel, see *Boucher* [1951] 2 D.L.R. 369 (Sup. Ct. of Canada).
[12] See, respectively, paras. 155–158, and 159–167.
[13] Para 21.
[14] See Working Paper No. 62, para. 34 especially.
[15] Working Paper, para. 115.

2 Criminal and Civil Contempt of Court

The general characteristics of criminal and civil contempt of court have been noted in the previous chapter. In this chapter it is proposed to consider the nature of the distinction between these two forms of contempt in more detail and to examine the practical consequences which flow from it.

1 PUNISHMENT AND COERCION

Although criminal contempt of court differs from the 'ordinary' crimes in several significant respects, proceedings for criminal contempt are nevertheless intended to serve a *punitive* function to the same extent as proceedings for any other offence. Thus if it is alleged that a person committed an assault in court, or that he tampered with a witness, the purpose of instituting proceedings against him and of any penalty ultimately imposed is clearly the same whether the conduct is charged as a criminal contempt punishable by committal, or as an assault or attempt to pervert the course of justice punishable on indictment. In cases of civil contempt, however, where the complaint is of non-compliance with a court order or an undertaking, the purpose and intended outcome of the proceedings will typically be remedial or *coercive*. In the words of a leading American case:[1]

> It is not the fact of punishment but rather its character and purpose that often serves to distinguish between the two classes of cases. If it is for civil contempt the punishment is remedial, and for the benefit of the complainant. But if it is for criminal contempt the sentence is punitive, to vindicate the authority of the court.[2]

Although this general distinction is helpful, it may be misleading when applied to English law in that it tends to obscure the punitive element which may lie behind civil contempt proceedings. Thus it seems, according to Lord Atkinson in *Scott* v. *Scott*, that:[3]

> . . . if a person be expressly enjoined by injunction, a most solemn and authoritative form of order, from doing a particular thing, and he deliberately, in breach of that injunction, does that thing, he is not guilty of any crime whatever, but only of a civil contempt of Court.

---

[1] *Gompers* v. *Bucks Stove and Range Co.*, 221 U.S. 418, 441 (U.S. Sup. Ct., 1911). See also Goldfarb, *The Contempt Power* (1963), pp. 49–67; Moskovitz, 'Contempt of Injunctions, Civil and Criminal' (1943) 43 Col. L.R. 780, 785–786, and cases there cited.

[2] See also Sir John Fox, *The History of Contempt of Court*, p. 1; Oswald, *Contempt of Court* (3rd ed., 1910), p. 8; *Wellesley* v. *The Duke of Beaufort* (1831) 2 Russ. & M. 639, 665–668; 39 E.R. 538, 548 *per* Lord Brougham, L.C.; *Re Freston* (1883) 11 Q.B.D. 545, 552–553, C.A. *per* Brett, M.R.

[3] [1913] A.C. 417, 456, H.L.

The same point was made by Sir John Donaldson, P. when dealing with counsel's suggestion that, in adopting a policy of open non-compliance with orders of the National Industrial Relations Court, officials of the Amalgamated Union of Engineering Workers were 'as much anarchists as the members of the Angry Brigade'. Sir John responded by saying:[4]

> No official of the union would for one moment take part in or condone a criminal act, and to suggest that Mr Hugh Scanlon [General Secretary of AUEW] or any of his colleagues have anything in common with those who are responsible for actions of the type associated with the Angry Brigade is disgraceful. The policy of the union is *unlawful*, but it is in no way criminal.

Accepting that this is so it is nonetheless clear that non-compliance may be followed by a committal order or fine the purpose of which is avowedly punitive. In particular it is clearly established that a fine or committal order may be imposed as a punishment for past disobedience even though the contemnor has by then complied with the original order or undertaking.[5] The same is true of a case in which the original complainant no longer has an interest in coercing the contemnor into compliance with the order or undertaking.[6]

2 CRIMINAL SAFEGUARDS IN CIVIL CONTEMPT PROCEEDINGS

Recognition of the quasi-criminal nature of proceedings for civil contempt has led to a gradual assimilation of the two branches of contempt. This has been particularly marked in the application of criminal standards and safeguards to civil contempt proceedings. *Re Bramblevale, Ltd*[7] is a case in point. The appellant was the managing director of a property company which had gone into liquidation, and he had failed to comply with a Registrar's order calling on him to produce the company's cash book and the creditors' ledger. The case came before Megarry, J. who regarded the defendant's explanation that the books had been soaked in petrol in the boot of his car, and had then found their way into a dustbin before the deadline for producing them, as a 'cock and bull story'. He committed him to prison for an indefinite time being evidently of the opinion that the books were still in his possession. On appeal the Court of Appeal regarded this conclusion as being based on 'surmise rather than proof',[8] and ordered his immediate release. Together with the other members of the Court, Winn, L.J. based his judgment on the simple ground that:[9]

---

[4] *Goad* v. *A.U.E.W. (No. 3)* [1973] I.C.R. 108,111 (N.I.R.C.). Emphasis supplied.

[5] *Cf. Phonographic Performance, Ltd* v. *Amusement Caterers (Peckham), Ltd* [1964] Ch. 195; [1963] 3 All E.R. 493; *Steiner Products, Ltd* v. *Willy Steiner, Ltd* [1966] 2 All E.R. 387, 390–391.

[6] *Cf. Jennison* v. *Baker* [1972] 2 Q.B. 52; [1972] 1 All E.R. 997 where the tenant no longer wished to return to the flat from which he had been evicted although an injunction had been obtained restraining eviction. See also *Danchevsky* v. *Danchevsky* [1974] 3 All E.R. 934, C.A., for more general discussion.

[7] [1970] Ch. 128; [1969] 3 All E.R. 1062.

[8] [1970] Ch. 128, 137 *per* Lord Denning, M.R.

[9] *Ibid.*

. . . unless the guilt of the appellant was proved with such strictness of proof as is consistent with the test 'beyond reasonable doubt'; or [as Lord Denning M.R.] has more than once put it, consistent with such standard as the court, with its responsibility, regards as consistent with the gravity of the charge—a test which I personally prefer—the decision that he should be imprisoned for contempt of court cannot be sustained.

This application of the standard of proof normally associated with criminal proceedings to cases of civil contempt is in line with other English[10] and Commonwealth[11] decisions and is to be welcomed. A person should not be deprived of his liberty by reference to any less stringent test.

There are other respects in which proceedings for civil contempt have been held to have acquired safeguards usually associated with a criminal trial. Thus it has been held that the alleged contemnor cannot be compelled to answer interrogatories or to give evidence against himself, and that the presiding judge has a discretion to disallow cross-examination on an affidavit where this would operate unfairly.[12] Likewise it has been held that the usual inability of a court to call evidence in a civil case without the consent of the parties does not apply to a committal motion for civil contempt. A subpoena may be issued irrespective of the wishes of the parties concerned.[13] Whether one can go beyond this and infer that the other main provisions peculiar to criminal cases, such as the inability to waive the rules of evidence, the limited compellability of spouses, and the greater restrictions on admitting hearsay evidence, are similarly applicable to civil contempt is not yet clear.[14]

3 CONSEQUENCES OF THE DISTINCTION BETWEEN CRIMINAL AND CIVIL CONTEMPT[15]

In spite of this welcome tendency to assimilate the two branches of contempt the designation of a given contempt as being civil, rather than criminal, or vice versa, may continue to have certain practical consequences. Thus it may affect, inter alia, the term of imprisonment or fine which may be imposed or be ultimately

---

[10] Cf. Churchman v. Joint Shop Stewards' Committee of the Workers of the Port of London [1972] I.C.R. 222, 229; [1972] 3 All E.R. 603, 608 per Lord Denning, M.R.; Heatons Transport, Ltd v. T.G.W.U. [1973] A.C. 15, 50; [1972] 2 All E.R. 1237, 1247, C.A. per Lord Denning, M.R. See also below, p. 244.

[11] See, e.g., Tilden Rent-A-Car Co. v. Rollins (1966) 57 W.W.R. 309 (Sask. Q.B.); Imperial Oil Co., Ltd v Tanguay [1971] Que. C.A. 109. See also Moskovitz. op. cit., pp. 818–819 for a discussion of American cases.

[12] Comet Products U.K., Ltd v. Hawkex Plastics, Ltd [1971] 2 Q.B. 67; [1971] 1 All E.R. 1141, C.A.

[13] Yiani v. Yiani [1966] 1 All E.R. 231n.; [1966] 1 W.L.R. 120.

[14] In Comet Products U.K., Ltd v. Hawkex Plastics, Ltd [1971] 2 Q.B. 67, 75–76, Megaw, L. J. doubted whether a defendant in civil contempt proceedings would be entitled to make an unsworn statement as is permitted in ordinary criminal proceedings. Similar doubts were expressed in the Supreme Court of Victoria in La Trobe University v. Robinson [1972] V.R. 883, 895–896 per McInerney, J. citing Lavender v. Petherick [1960] S.A.S.R. 108.

[15] See, in general, Fischer, 'Civil and Criminal Aspects of Contempt of Court' (1956) 34 Can. Bar R. 121; Harnon, 'Civil and Criminal Contempts of Court' (1962) 25 M.L.R. 179; Beale, 'Contempt of Court, Criminal and Civil' (1908) 21 Harv. L.R. 161; Moskovitz, op. cit.; Sir John Fox, 'The Practice in Contempt of Court Cases' (1922) 38 L.Q.R. 185, 197–200; the Phillimore report, paras. 168–176.

suffered, the ability of the parties to settle the dispute, and privilege from arrest. Before discussing these matters it should be said that the consequences which flow from the distinction are much clearer where the purpose and outcome of proceedings following upon breach of an order or undertaking are avowedly *coercive* in character. Where they take on a punitive or disciplinary flavour the lines become blurred. Indeed, viewed in terms of immediate practical consequences, the distinction between criminal and civil contempt of court is now less important than a distinction in terms of whether the response of the court is predominantly punitive or coercive in the particular circumstances of the case.

(1) IMPRISONMENT

In a case of criminal contempt the superior courts have the power both to fine, impose a theoretically unlimited term of imprisonment, and to order the giving of security for good behaviour.[16] According to the decision in *Attorney-General* v. *James*[17] the imprisonment must, however, be for a fixed term although it remains open to the offender to apply thereafter for earlier release.[18] The Crown's power to pardon an offender also extends to a case of criminal contempt.[19]

Civil contempt through non-compliance with a court order may be dealt with by committal for a fixed or for an indefinite term. The form of the committal order and the duration of the term of imprisonment will depend upon the purpose for which committal is being employed. Where punishment for past disobedience is the objective, committal for a fixed term is clearly appropriate. Where, however, committal is being employed for a remedial or coercive purpose an indefinite term may be preferable as carrying the maximum incentive to comply with the original order. On compliance the contemnor could expect to be released *ex debito justitiae*.[20] Lord Denning, M.R. has recently restated the position with particular clarity in *Danchevsky* v. *Danchevsky*,[1] a case in which a husband had refused to comply with an order for the sale of the matrimonial home. According to his Lordship:[2]

> It seems to me that when the object of the committal is punishment for a *past* offence, then, if he is to be imprisoned at all, the appropriate order is a fixed term. When it is a matter of getting a person to do something in the future—and there is a reasonable

---

[16] See *Halsbury*, Vol. 9, para. 99. *Castro* (1873) L.R. 9 Q.B. 230 is a case in which an order was made for the giving of security for good behaviour. See further, below, p. 36.

[17] [1962] 2 Q.B. 637; [1962] 1 All E.R. 255, D.C.

[18] See, however, *Re B. (J.A.) (An Infant)* [1965] Ch. 1112, 1123; [1965] 2 All E.R. 168, 175 where Cross, J. suggested that a Chancery judge might have power to commit for an indefinite period even in a case of criminal contempt. Application for release is made under R.S.C. Ord. 52, r. 8(1).

[19] See *Seaward* v. *Paterson* [1897] 1 Ch. 545, 559, C.A.; *Halsbury*, Vol. 9, para. 123. It would seem that in a case of civil contempt the Crown might intervene and grant a pardon, but that it would be unconstitutional for it to do so: see Sir Charles Russell, A.-G., *arguendo*, in *In the Matter of a Special Reference from the Bahama Islands* [1893] A.C. 138, 145, P.C.

[20] *Cf. Re Freston* (1883) 11 Q.B.D. 545, 557 (Fry, L. J.); 554–555 (Brett, M. R.). On the facts the solicitor's disobedience was 'accompanied by criminal incidents' and the attachment was not mere process.

[1] [1974] 3 All E.R. 934.

[2] *Ibid.*, at p. 937.

prospect of him doing it—then it may be quite appropriate to have an indefinite order against him and to commit him until he does do it.[3]

The appropriateness of an indefinite term as an aid to coercion has likewise been emphasised in a number of American cases. In *Re Nevitt*, for example, Judge Sanborn observed that the person subjected to such a term 'carries the keys of his prison in his own pocket'.[4] In the leading case of *Gompers* v. *Bucks Stove and Range Co.* the United States Supreme Court similarly viewed a fixed term as being inappropriate as an aid to coercion, for then 'the defendant is furnished no key, and he cannot shorten the term by promising not to repeat the offence'.[5] The point does not have the same force in jurisdictions such as our own where it remains open to a contemnor to apply for release at any time whether the term originally imposed was fixed or indefinite.[6] The possibility of discharge may therefore be said to furnish the key.

(2) THE POWER TO FINE

While criminal contempt may clearly be punished by the imposition of a fine, the traditional view was that a fine was neither a permissible, nor indeed an appropriate, outcome to proceedings for civil contempt.[7] This view, which reflects the coercive function of such proceedings, was recently reiterated by the High Court of Australia in *Australian Consolidated Press, Ltd* v. *Morgan*.[8] Here the appellant newspaper had been fined the sum of $A1,500 on breach of an undertaking not to publish any Gallup Poll results of which the respondents had the copyright. On appeal to the High Court the fine was set aside as inappropriate in a case in which it was intended to mark the disapproval of the court, rather than to coerce the appellant into compliance. The High Court agreed that the position would have been different if an element of contumacy or defiance had been present for this would have been regarded as a criminal contempt.[9]

Even when allowance has been made for our different system of classifying contempts it would appear that the power to fine for disobedience of a court order is more generally available in this country. Indeed, once it is accepted that a committal order may be made as a penalty for past disobedience,[10] it must clearly follow that a court has the power to impose the lesser penalty of a fine. So much

---

[3] The case is also important as establishing that a county court judge may commit for a fixed term: see below, p. 268. For a case in which justification for continued imprisonment was discussed both in terms of punishment for past disobedience and as an aid to compliance through coercion, see *Re Barrell Enterprises* [1972] 3 All E.R. 631. For further discussion of committal for civil contempt, see below, Ch. 14, pp. 255–257 especially.

[4] 117 F. 448, 461 (1902). An expression which is criticised in Goldfarb, *The Contempt Power* (1963), pp. 59–60.

[5] 221 U.S. 418, 442 (1911).

[6] Under R.S.C. Ord. 52, r. 8(1). The Phillimore Committee has recommended (para. 172) that committals for an indefinite term should be abolished. The proposal is discussed below, p. 18.

[7] See Sir John Fox, *History of Contempt of Court*, p. 2; the report by *Justice, Contempt of Court* (1959), p. 23.

[8] (1965) 112 C.L.R. 483; (1965) 39 A.L.J.R. 32.

[9] See further, below, p. 17.

[10] See above, p. 8.

was assumed in a number of cases decided over the course of the last decade[11] until the matter was finally settled beyond doubt in *Heatons Transport (St. Helens), Ltd* v. *Transport and General Workers' Union.*[12] Here Lord Wilberforce observed, in delivering the opinion of the House of Lords reinstating fines totalling £55,000 imposed on the defendant union, that 'the effective administration of justice normally requires some penalty for disobedience to an order of a court if the disobedience is more than casual or accidental and unintentional'.[13]

In principle there would seem to be no reason why a suspended fine payable on continued disobedience after a specified period should not likewise be imposed as an aid to coercion. Certainly a suspended committal order for a fixed term is quite permissible.[14] Moreover, the suspended fine itself is well known in the United States, as can be seen from the notorious *United Mine Workers case*[15] in 1947 when the Supreme Court ordered the payment of a $2,800,000 fine if the defendant union failed to comply with a labour injunction within five days.[16] A somewhat different approach is to be seen in the English case of *Con-Mech Engineers, Ltd* v. *Amalgamated Union of Engineering Workers.*[17] Here the National Industrial Relations Court ordered sequestration of assets to the value of £100,000, but postponed a final decision on the amount of the fine which would become payable so as to give the union time for further reflection. On continued disobedience of an order of the court restraining unlawful industrial action, a fine of £75,000 was imposed. This form of judgment differs somewhat from the suspended fine in that the defendant will only know the general, rather than the precise, price of non-compliance.

(3) SETTLEMENT OF THE DISPUTE AND INSTITUTION OF PROCEEDINGS

A further difference between civil and criminal contempt lies in the ability to settle the dispute and to waive the contempt. In criminal contempt ultimate control over the proceedings lies in the hands of the Crown,[18] but in civil contempt the traditional view is that it is open to the opposing party to waive the

---

[11] See, e.g., *Phonographic Performance, Ltd* v. *Amusement Caterers (Peckham), Ltd* [1964] Ch. 195, 201; [1963] 3 All E.R. 493, 497 (Cross, J.); *Re the Agreement of the Mileage Conference Group of the Tyre Manufacturers' Conference Ltd.* (1966) L.R. 6 R.P. 49; [1966] 2 All E.R. 849; *Steiner Products, Ltd* v. *Willy Steiner, Ltd* [1966] 2 All E.R. 387; *Re W. (B.) (An Infant)* [1969] 2 Ch. 50; [1969] 1 All E.R. 594. *Re Galvanized Tank Manufacturers' Association's Agreement* [1965] 2 All E.R. 1003.

[12] [1973] A.C. 15, 78; [1972] 3 All E.R. 101, below, p. 236 and p. 259.

[13] [1973] A.C. 15, 109; [1972] 3 All E.R. 101, 117.

[14] Under R.S.C. Ord. 52, r. 7(1). For an example, see *Re W. (B) (An Infant)* [1969] 2 Ch. 50; [1969] 1 All E.R. 594, C.A. The powers of a magistrates' court are, however, limited to those conferred by the Magistrates Courts Act 1952, s. 54(3) and no provision is made for suspending a committal order: *B. (B.P.M.)* v. *B. (M.M.)* [1969] P. 103; *sub nom. B. (B.)* v. *B. (M.)* [1969] 1 All E.R. 891, below, p. 269.

[15] *United States* v. *United Mine Workers of America*, 330 U.S. 258 (1947)

[16] An avowedly punitive fine of $700,000 was also imposed. It would seem that in the United States the fine *must* be suspended in so far as it is imposed as for a civil contempt: *Doyle* v. *London Guarantee Accident Co.*, 204 U.S. 599 (1907). A fine may also be imposed with a view to compensating the plaintiff.

[17] [1973] I.C.R. 620, below, p. 241.

[18] *Newton* (1903) 19 T.L.R. 627.

breach.[19] As Lord Diplock has said, 'no sufficient public interest is served by punishing the offender if the only person for whose benefit the order was made chooses not to insist on its enforcement'.[20]

It may be the case, however, that this traditional view does not sufficiently reflect the fact that disobedience of a court order may lead to an imprisonment or fine which is intended to be punitive rather than coercive.[1] The Canadian case of *Pojé* v. *Attorney-General of British Columbia*,[2] though much criticised, is in point. Here a company had been granted an injunction restraining Pojé, a trade-union official, from picketing its works. Pojé and a number of associates acted in open defiance of the injunction and the company instituted contempt proceedings. The company later withdrew when the labour dispute was settled, but a British Columbia court, acting of its own motion, proceeded to impose fines and a period of imprisonment. A subsequent appeal to the Supreme Court of Canada was dismissed with the court stressing 'the public nature of the defiance of the order of the court'. Likewise in the *Heatons Transport*[3] case Sir John Donaldson, P. assumed that it was not open to the complainant effectively to waive the breach of an order. In his view:[4]

. . . once proceedings for contempt of court have been set in motion it is not open to the parties to settle the matter of the contempt. They can certainly settle the dispute which they may have with each other . . . But as far as the contempt of court is concerned, that is a different matter and one with which we are deeply concerned.[5]

There is likewise an element of doubt in the parallel area of entitlement to institute proceedings. A court may clearly act *ex mero motu*, that is, of its own motion, in a case of criminal contempt,[6] but the position in a case of civil contempt through non-compliance with a court order is less clear. The traditional view is again that this is a matter for the party to the proceedings. But during its existence the National Industrial Relations Court assumed a power to

[19] See, e.g., *Roberts* v. *Albert Bridge Co.* (1873) L.R. 8 Ch. App. 753; *Seaward* v. *Paterson* [1897] 1 Ch. 545, 555 *per* Lindley, L. J.; *Anon* (1808) 15 Ves. Jun. 174; 33 E.R. 720; *Woodward* v. *Twinaine* (1839) 9 Sim. 301; 59 E.R. 373; *Yianni* v. *Yianni* [1966] 1 W.L.R. 120, 124; *Halsbury*, Vol. 9, para. 56. See also Harnon, 'Civil and Criminal Contempts of Court' (1962) 25 M.L.R. 179, 182–184; *The Supreme Court Practice 1973*, Vol. 1, p. 761. See also *Adriatic Terrazzo* v. *Robinson* (1973) 4 S.A.S.R. 294 (S.A. Sup. Ct.).

[20] In *Att.-Gen.* v. *Times Newspapers, Ltd* [1974] A.C. 273, 308; [1973] 3 All E.R. 54, 71.

[1] See above, p. 8.

[2] [1953] 2 D.L.R. 785, 795–796 upholding [1953] 1 D.L.R. 385. The punishment was imposed as for a *criminal* contempt: see below, p. 17. For discussion of the case, see Carrothers, *The Labour Injunction in British Columbia* (1956), pp. 11–23, cited by Wedderburn (1974) 37 M.L.R. 187, 191. For subsequent Canadian cases, see *Re Tilco Plastics, Ltd* v. *Skurjat* (1966) 57 D.L.R. (2d) 596; affd. (1967) 61 D.L.R. (2d) 664n; *Re Att.-Gen. for Nova Scotia and Miles* (1971) 15 D.L.R. (3d) 189. *Cf.* also the judgment of Barwick, C.J. in *Australian Consolidated, Press, Ltd* v *Morgan* (1965) 112 C.L.R. 483, 489 (High Ct of Australia).

[3] [1972] 2 All E.R. 1214; [1972] I.C.R. 285.

[4] *Ibid.*, at p. 1220 and p. 298, respectively.

[5] For criticism, see Wedderburn (1974) 37 M.L.R. 187. See also *Jennison* v. *Baker* [1972] 2 Q.B. 52, 64; [1972] 1 All E.R. 997, 1004 *per* Salmon, L. J. For the position in the United States where settlement between the parties does not appear to prevent punishment as for a *criminal* contempt, see Moskovitz, *op. cit.*, p. 809 and cases there cited.

[6] See also pp. 28–9, p. 40.

issue writs of sequestration and committal orders of its own motion,[7] and Lord Denning, M.R. conceded obiter that:[8]

> It may be that in some circumstances the court may be entitled, on sufficient information being brought before it, to act on its own initiative in sending a contemnor to prison.

It is submitted that a court should have the power to act, or proceed, of its own motion following non-compliance with an order or undertaking. In certain circumstances the party at whose instance the order was granted, or the undertaking given, may genuinely feel that he is unable to proceed further—as where a landlord is continuing to harass a tenant.[9] It would be wrong if the law could not protect him. Likewise it is undoubtedly the case that open and flagrant breaches of an order would depreciate the authority of the law if they went unpunished.[10] Again a residual power to act *ex mero motu* is needed. In the typical case, however, a voluntary waiver which did not leave the law in disrepute would no doubt be the end of the matter. Influenced by such considerations the Phillimore Committee has accordingly recommended:[11]

> . . . that the court should have power of its own motion to act against a person who disobeys its order whenever it thinks fit to do so, and for this purpose it should be empowered to require any breach of its order to be reported to it by the party in whose favour the order was made[12] or, in appropriate cases, by a court official.

(4) PRIVILEGE FROM ARREST[13]

A further point of distinction between criminal and civil contempt is that certain categories of persons are privileged from arrest for civil contempt, but not where the contempt is criminal.[14] Persons enjoying the immunity include members of the House of Commons[15] and peers[16] both when Parliament is sitting, and for forty days after prorogation or dissolution and for forty days before the next appointed meeting.[17] A modern example is provided by the case of *Stourton* v.

---

[7] See *Con-Mech (Engineers), Ltd* v. *A.U.E.W.* [1973] I.C.R. 620; *Churchman* v. *Joint Shop Stewards' Committee of the Workers of the Port of London, The Times,* 15 June 1972 (N.I.R.C.).

[8] *Churchman's* case [1972] I.C.R. 222, 229; [1972] 3 All E.R. 603, 608, C.A.

[9] *Cf.,* e.g., *Jennison* v. *Baker,* above, p. 13, note 5.

[10] In *Pojé* v. *Attorney-General of British Columbia,* above, note 2, such breaches were treated and punished as for a *criminal* contempt. It is doubtful whether they would be so regarded in an English court, although an analogy might be taken with contempt through scandalising the court. See further, below, pp. 17–19.

[11] Para. 171.

[12] For the current position in this respect, see below, p. 265.

[13] See Fischer, 'Civil and Criminal Aspects of Contempt of Court' (1956) 34 Can. Bar R. 121, 151–155; *Halsbury,* Vol. 9, para. 115; *The Supreme Court Practice 1973,* Vol. 1, pp. 769–770; Oswald, *Contempt of Court,* pp. 173–190; Phillimore Committee report, para. 170.

[14] *Re The Ludlow Charities, Lechmere Charlton's Case* (1837) 2 My. & Cr. 316; 40 E.R. 661.

[15] *Catmur* v. *Knatchbull* (1797) 7 T.R. 448; 101 E.R. 1069; *Re Armstrong* [1892] 1 Q.B. 327.

[16] *Walker* v. *The Earl of Grosvenor* (1797) 7 T.R. 171; 101 E.R. 915; *Stourton* v. *Stourton* [1963] P. 302; [1963] 1 All E.R. 606.

[17] *Re Anglo-French Cooperative Society* (1880) 14 Ch. D. 533. See also Erskine May, *Parliamentary Practice* (18th ed., 1971), Ch. VII. In *Stourton* v. *Stourton* Scarman, J. appears to have agreed that the person of a peer was 'for ever sacred and inviolable' at common law, and that the privilege existed at all times: see [1963] P. 302, 306.

Stourton (Baron Mowbray, Segrave, and Stourton) [18] where Scarman, J. held that the defendant, Lord Mowbray, was privileged from arrest under a writ of attachment sought by Lady Mowbray. The writ was being sought in respect of an alleged breach of a Registrar's order calling on him to file a schedule and to deliver certain property to Lady Mowbray. Privilege having been claimed, Scarman, J. declined to look further into the merits of the case. Privilege may also be claimed by barristers and solicitors engaged in their professional duties in court, or on going to or returning from it, [19] and, it seems, by a wider class of officers and attendants upon the court, suitors, jurors and witnesses during a similar period. [20] In so far as the privilege is that of the court itself it may be waived by the court thus permitting the arrest of the contemnor. [1]

As a qualification to the position as stated above, it appears that the privilege does not attach where disobedience of a court order 'has about it some degree of criminality, some defiance of the general law'. [2] Thus in *Wellesley* v. *The Duke of Beaufort* [3] privilege was denied to a member of the House of Commons when he refused to reveal the whereabouts of a ward of court, while in *Re Freston* [4] it was denied to a solicitor who had disobeyed an order made against him in his capacity as an officer of the court. [5] More generally, it would seem that privilege from arrest cannot be successfully claimed where committal is intended as a punishment for past disobedience. [6] The Phillimore Committee recommends that privilege from arrest and committal for civil contempt should be abolished leaving the matter to be dealt with under the general law and enactments such as the Diplomatic Privileges Act 1964. [7]

(5) APPEALS

Before the passing of the Administration of Justice Act 1960 the most important result of the distinction between civil and criminal contempt undoubtedly lay in its effect on the opportunities for appeal. In cases of civil contempt, including those in which conduct calling for punitive or disciplinary measures was in issue, an appeal lay to the Court of Appeal. When, however, the contempt was criminal in nature and dealt with on summary process there was no opportunity for appeal at all. This highly anomalous position resulted from the wording of the

---

[18] [1963] P. 302; [1963] 1 All E.R. 606.

[19] *Pigot* v. *Charlewood* (1734) Barnes 200; 94 E.R. 875; *Luntly* v. *Nathaniel* (1833) 1 C. & M. 579; 149 E.R. 530; *The Case of the Sheriff of Kent* (1846) 2 Car. & K. 197; 175 E.R. 82; *The Case of the Sheriff of Oxfordshire* (1816) 2 Car. & K. 200; 175 E.R. 83.

[20] See *Pulton* v. *Farrar* (1729) 1 Barn. K.B. 251; 94 E.R. 172; *Gilpin* v. *Cohen* (1869) L.R. 4 Exch. 131; *Mountague* v. *Harrison* (1857) 3 C.B.N.S. 292; 140 E.R. 753; *Meekins* v. *Smith* (1791) 1 H. Bl. 636; 126 E.R. 363.

[1] *Re Hunt* [1959] 2 Q.B. 69; [1959] 2 All E.R. 252. See also *Cameron* v. *Lightfoot* (1778) 2 Wm. Bl. 1190, 1192; 96 E.R. 701, 702 *per* De Grey, C.J.

[2] *Stourton* v. *Stourton* [1963] P. 302, 310; [1963] 1 All E.R. 606, 610 *per* Scarman, J.

[3] (1831) 2 Russ. & M. 639; 39 E.R. 538. See also *La Trobe University* v. *Robinson* [1972] V.R. 883 (Vict. Sup. Ct.).

[4] (1883) 11 Q.B.D. 545.

[5] It is not clear in either of these cases whether the contempts were viewed as being specifically criminal in nature, or civil, but accompanied by criminal incidents.

[6] *Cf. Re Hunt* [1959] 2 Q.B. 69, 78 *per* Pearce, L.J.; *Re Freston* (1883) 11 Q.B.D. 545, 557 *per* Fry, L.J.

[7] Para. 170. The Committee adds that the position with respect to parliamentary privilege is a matter for Parliament itself to decide.

Criminal Appeal Act 1907, s. 3, which limited appeals to the Court of Criminal Appeal to cases of conviction on *indictment*, and of the Judicature Act 1925, s. 31(1)(a), which excluded appeals in any 'criminal cause or matter' from the jurisdiction of the Court of Appeal.[8]

The point was overlooked in a number of cases in the second half of the 19th century,[9] but finally settled in *O'Shea* v. *O'Shea & Parnell, ex parte Tuohy*,[10] a case which came before the Court of Appeal in 1890. Here it was held that prejudice to civil proceedings was a criminal contempt, and that there was no jurisdiction to hear an appeal against a writ of attachment issued in respect of the contempt. There the matter rested until relatively recent years when the Administration of Justice Act 1960 was enacted following the recommendations of the *Justice* Committee in their report, *Contempt of Court* (1959). By s. 13 of this Act a general right of appeal is provided in all cases of contempt dealt with on summary process, whether civil or criminal in nature. The details of the appropriate channels of appeal are discussed elsewhere.[11] At this point it is enough to note that the provision of a general system of appeal has removed one of the main practical consequences which flowed from the current system of classifying contempts.

(6) FURTHER CONSEQUENCES[12]

Apart from the points referred to above, there are certain other consequences which turn upon the distinction between criminal and civil contempt of court. These may be briefly listed as follows. One is that the writ of sequestration, being a form of civil execution, is only available in cases of civil, rather than criminal, contempt.[13] Secondly, it appears that an order for the discharge of a person committed for contempt can only be made conditional upon the payment of costs in a case of criminal, rather than civil, contempt.[14] Finally, it has been suggested that it is only in a case of criminal contempt that the officer carrying out the arrest may break open an outer door, after giving due notice, and perhaps even arrest on a Sunday.[15]

4   GENERAL CONSIDERATIONS

As is apparent from the above discussion, the immediate practical consequences of designating a given act as a criminal, rather than as a civil, contempt, or vice versa, are not far reaching. Now that civil contempt proceedings have acquired

---

[8] A similar provision was to be found in the earlier Judicature Act 1873, s. 47.

[9] See, e.g., *Hunt* v. *Clarke* (1889) 61 L.T. 343; *Re Johnson* (1887) 20 Q.B.D. 68.

[10] (1890) 15 P.D. 59. Doubts had already been expressed by Lindley, L. J. in *Jordan* (1888) 36 W.R. 797, reported *sub nom. R.* v. *The County Court Judge of the Court of Stafford* (1888) 57 L.J.Q.B. 483.

[11] See below, pp. 37–40.

[12] See Harnon, 'Civil and Criminal Contempts of Court' (1962) 25 M.L.R. 179, 181.

[13] See Oswald, *Contempt of Court*, p. 225. For sequestration generally, see below, pp. 260–264.

[14] Oswald, *op. cit.*, p. 261, citing *Jackson* v. *Mawby* (1875) 1 Ch. D. 86; *Re Jarvis* [1866] W.N. 118. See also *Re M*. (1876) 46 L.J. Ch. 24, C.A.

[15] Harnon, *op. cit.*, p. 181, citing *Harvey* v. *Harvey* (1884) 26 Ch. D. 644. But see *The Supreme Court Practice 1973*, Vol. 1, p. 769. See also *Burdett* v. *Abbot* (1811) 14 East 1, 154–155; 104 E.R. 501, 560. The Phillimore Committee recommends the abolition of this restriction: para. 173.

many of the safeguards associated with a criminal trial[16] the outstanding difference would seem to lie in the fact that committal for an indefinite term and sequestration are both available in a case of civil contempt, but not where the contempt is criminal.[17] In recent years Salmon, L.J. has characterised the classification as 'unhelpful and almost meaningless',[18] while the Phillimore Committee has recommended that it be abolished.[19]

Before considering this recommendation it should be said that the dividing line between the two forms of contempt has never been clearly drawn. Apart from certain fairly specific and well-known 'grey' areas—such as the nature of the contempt committed by one who interferes with a ward of court, or who procures another to act in breach of an injunction[20]—more general problems arise from the fact that breach of an order or undertaking may take a number of forms. Some American cases have attempted to distinguish between committal orders imposed on breach of a *prohibitory* injunction ('punitive' and thus as for a criminal contempt) and those imposed on breach of a *mandatory* injunction ('coercive' and thus as for a civil contempt). But the distinction has never been wholly convincing.[1] In Canada it seems that the open and flagrant breach of a court order may amount to a criminal contempt,[2] while in the USA criminal and civil contempt may be intermingled within the same proceedings. Thus in the *United Mine Workers case* the defendant union and its president were both fined as a punishment for past disobedience of an order (criminal contempt), and subjected to suspended fines to coerce them into future compliance (civil contempt).[3] In English law, however, it seems that such open disobedience is probably no more than a civil contempt.[4]

Against this background one may expect that the Phillimore Committee recommendation for abolishing the distinction will be received sympathetically. Yet it is open to objection both in terms of principle and probably also in terms of practical consequences. In the first place it is unclear whether the committee is proposing that all contempts should hereafter be designated 'criminal', or whether the proposal is that contempt should simply be treated as *sui generis*.[5] On the former assumption there are clearly strong objections to treating *all* breaches of a court order, or of undertakings, as being 'criminal' in any sense of the word. If the proposal is that contempt be viewed as *sui generis* then one is, in effect, required to view conduct such as an attempt to bribe or threaten a juror *pendente lite* in a different light according to whether it is charged on indictment or dealt with summarily as a contempt. At the present time criminal contempt is

---

[16] See above, pp. 8–9.
[17] See above, at pp. 10–11, and p. 16, note 13, respectively.
[18] *Jennison* v. *Baker* [1972] 2 Q.B. 52, 61.
[19] Para. 176
[20] See below at p. 222, and p. 247, respectively.
[1] See Moskovitz, 'Contempt of Injunctions, Civil and Criminal' (1943) 43 Col. L.R., 780, 791–793.
[2] *Cf. Pojé* v. *Attorney-General of British Columbia* [1953] 2 D.L.R. 785, 795–796 (Sup. Ct. of Canada).
[3] *United States* v. *United Mine Workers of America,* 330 U.S. 258 (1947).
[4] *Cf. Goad* v. *A.U.E.W. (No. 3)* [1973] I.C.R. 108, 111 Sir John Donaldson, P., cited above, p. 8.
[5] *Cf. Morris* v. *The Crown Office* [1970] 2 Q.B. 114, 129; [1970] 1 All E.R. 1079, 1087 *per* Salmon, L. J.

clearly a criminal offence in spite of the features which distinguish it from the other criminal offences[6] and it is submitted that it should so remain.

The abolition of the distinction would also have to be accompanied by the removal of the power to imprison for an indefinite term on breach of a court order. The committee so recommends.[7] Committals for a fixed term, coupled with an entitlement to apply for earlier release, would no doubt work quite adequately in the majority of cases. The contemnor who is still recalcitrant at the end of the term can be recommitted for a future breach of the order if it is still in force. This frequently happens at the present time when a person is discharged promising to obey an injunction and then later fails to do so.[8] But one wonders whether the power to commit *sine die* can be so readily dispensed with where the original order was mandatory in form, requiring, for example, the delivery up of property. Here a contemnor who resolutely refuses to comply should not, of course, be subjected to an effective term of life imprisonment.[9] But a series of committals is hardly an apt way to deal with the matter either, and it may be questioned whether the committal should spell out from the very beginning the maximum price of non-compliance. Objection might indeed be taken to this proposal on two distinct grounds. First, that committals for a fixed term are unlikely to have the same coercive power as committals *sine die*; secondly, that release before the expiry of the fixed term would be more likely to undermine the authority of the court than if no such term had been specified. An element of flexibility would accordingly be removed. In practice any such term imposed with *coercion* in mind would clearly have to be linked to the maximum term considered appropriate in the event of non-compliance.

Yet if the distinction between criminal and civil contempt is to be maintained its basis must be more clearly formulated. A person against whom proceedings are instituted is entitled to know whether a violation of the criminal law is in issue. Classification must accordingly be on an *a priori* basis, and it is not enough to look to the purpose of the penalty ultimately imposed. Nor is it sufficient to look to matters such as the identity of the person or body instituting proceedings, for this should be relevant, if at all, as a consequence of the distinction and not as a factor determining it.[10] Ultimately any such distinction must be taken at the procedural level, for just as there are no intrinsic distinguishing features of a crime so also are there no intrinsic points of distinction between a criminal and a civil contempt. If the distinction is to remain, a separate form of procedure is required. The fact that an application for a committal order is the procedure common to both branches of contempt is largely responsible for the lack of a clearer division.

In terms of substantive law it would hardly be acceptable to treat all breaches of a court order as a criminal contempt. A possible compromise solution would be to treat such a breach as a criminal contempt if the circumstances were such as to depreciate the authority of the court and undermine public confidence in the

[6] *Cf. Att.-Gen.* v. *Butterworth* [1963] 1 Q.B. 696, 722; [1962] 3 All E.R. 326, 331 *per* Lord Denning, M.R; *Balogh* v. *Crown Court at St. Albans* [1974] 3 All E.R. 283, 289.

[7] Para. 172.

[8] *Cf.* the Phillimore Committee report, para. 172 and see also *Yager* v. *Musa* [1961] 2 Q.B. 214.

[9] See *Re Barrell Enterprises* [1972] 3 All E.R. 631, below, p. 257.

[10] See Goldfarb, *The Contempt Power* (1963), pp. 56–57.

administration of justice. An anology with that aspect of criminal contempt termed scandalising the court is clearly to hand.[11] Yet this might be open to objection on the ground that the criminality of the conduct could then turn on the publicity accorded to the breach and this might be a matter over which the contemnor had little control.

[11] See below, Ch. 10, p. 182 *et seq.*

3 Procedure and Jurisdiction in Cases of Criminal Contempt

1 INTRODUCTION

The most striking feature of the procedure in cases of criminal contempt[1] undoubtedly lies in the fact that the matter is normally dealt with on summary process and hence without the assistance of a jury. Indeed where the contempt is committed *in facie curiae*, that is, in the face of the court itself, there are often no formalised proceedings as such. The offender is simply dealt with on the spot, without any specific charge being formulated, and committed to prison. As will be seen later,[2] the ability to proceed in this manner is possessed by all courts, whether superior or inferior, provided only that they are courts of record.[3] In other cases of so-called 'indirect' or 'constructive' contempts committed out of court, including contempt by publication, the proceedings are admittedly more formalised, being normally by way of an application for an order of committal, which must be moved before a superior court.[4] Even so, such proceedings are still summary in nature in the sense that the defendant is denied a jury trial. As one might expect, this state of affairs, applying as it does to a common law offence which normally carries a theoretically unlimited fine or period of imprisonment, has been criticised over the years.[5] In the light of this criticism it is interesting to note that the current summary procedure, as applied to the general range of contempt, is now accepted as being based on historical error.

2 ORIGINS OF THE SUMMARY PROCESS

The origin of the alleged error is to be found in *Almon*,[6] a case which came before Wilmot, J. in the Court of King's Bench in 1765. In this case the Attorney-General, Sir Fletcher Norton, moved for a writ of attachment following Almon's publication of a pamphlet containing passages critical of the conduct of Lord

---

[1] For the procedure in cases of civil contempt, see below, Ch. 14, pp. 255 and 261 especially.

[2] See below, pp. 23–25, 27–29.

[3] For 'courts of record', see below, pp. 25–27.

[4] Applications for leave to issue a writ of attachment appear to have been discarded under the Rules of the Supreme Court currently in force (*cf.* R.S.C. Ord. 52, r. 1). Attachment is still, however, the procedure employed in county courts to deal with breach of county court orders: see below, p. 267.

[5] See, e.g., Laski, 'Procedure for Constructive Contempt in England' (1927) 41 Harv. L.R. 1031; Campbell, 'Contemptuous Criticism of the Judiciary and the Judicial Process' (1960) 34 A.L.J. 224, 231. But *cf.*, however, Goodhart, 'Newspapers and Contempt of Court in England' (1935) 48 Harv. L.R. 885, 899; the report by *Justice, Contempt of Court* (1959), at p. 28 *et seq.*

[6] (1765) Wilm. 243; 97 E.R. 94.

Mansfield, the Lord Chief Justice, and accusing him of having acted 'officiously, arbitrarily, and illegally'. In reply, Sergeant Glynn, as counsel for Almon, conceded that attachments might properly be granted on the abuse of a process server, but he denied that this summary procedure was applicable to an alleged libelling or scandalising of a court or judge. In such a case, he argued, the prosecution should be by way of indictment or information thus leaving the matter to come before a jury. Wilmot, J. prepared a judgment which was never in fact delivered, apparently because it was later discovered that the rule nisi to attach Almon had been misentitled 'The King v. Wilkes', and Sergeant Glynn, 'as a man of honour', could not consent to its amendment.[7] Although new proceedings were begun they were later dropped following a change of government.

There the matter rested until 1802 when the judgment was published by Wilmot's son.[8] It proceeded on the assumption that the superior common law courts did have the power which had been questioned. No specific authority was cited in support of this proposition. The power was regarded as 'coeval with their [sc. the Courts in Westminster Hall] first foundation and institution', and as 'a necessary incident to every Court of Justice'.[9]

This undelivered judgment has been subjected to the most detailed and searching criticism by Sir John Fox.[10] The author's conclusion is that whereas obedience to the King's writ had indeed been enforced by attachment from time immemorial,[11] no similar claim could be substantiated in the case of criminal contempt. Even in the case of contempts committed in the face of the court itself, strangers to the proceedings were normally only punished in early years after trial in the ordinary course before a jury, unless the disruptive conduct occurred in the actual view of the justices and was not serious in nature.[12] To take but one example, Sir William Waller was indicted in 1634,[13] following an assault upon the person of Sir Thomas Reignolds near Westminster Hall at a time when the courts were sitting, 'in disturbance of justice and the law'. Sheriffs, attorneys, jurors and other officers of justice were, however, subject to a summary power of committal by virtue of the special disciplinary jurisdiction exercised over them.[14]

---

[7] *Cf.* Sir John Fox, 'The King v. Almon 1.' (1908) 24 L.Q.R. 184.

[8] The judgment had, it seems, been 'prepared for delivery, copied fair and corrected with the judge's own hand': see John Wilmot, *Memoirs of the Life of Sir John Eardley Wilmot*, 2nd. ed., p. 77.

[9] (1765) Wilm. 243, 254.

[10] See Sir John Fox, *The History of Contempt of Court* (1927). The contents of this monograph are based for the most part on the following articles by the author: 'The King v. Almon 1.' (1908) 24 L.Q.R. 184; 'The King v. Almon 2.', *ibid.*, at p. 266; 'The Summary Process to Punish Contempt 1.' (1909) 25 L.Q.R. 238; 'The Summary Process to Punish Contempt 2', *ibid.*, at p. 354; 'Eccentricities of the Law of Contempt of Court' (1920) 36 L.Q.R. 394; 'The Nature of Contempt of Court' (1921) 37 L.Q.R. 191; 'The Practice in Contempt of Court Cases' (1922) 38 L.Q.R. 185; 'The Writ of Attachment' (1924) 40 L.Q.R. 43. Further details of the historical background are to be found in Oswald, *Contempt of Court*; Frankfurter and Landis, 'Power of Congress over Procedure in Criminal Contempts in Inferior Federal Courts' (1924) 37 Harv. L.R. 1010; Nelles and King, 'Contempt by Publication in the United States' (1928) 28 Col. L.R. 401; *ibid.*, at p. 525.

[11] *Cf.* Fox, (1908) 24 L.Q.R. 184, 188.

[12] *Cf.* Fox, (1908) 24 L.Q.R. 266, 266–268; (1909) 25 L.Q.R. 238, 242–244; (1924) 40 L.Q.R. 43, 57.

[13] (1634) Cro. Car. 373; 79 E.R. 926.

[14] *Cf.* Fox, (1909) 25 L.Q.R. 238, 244–245; (1921) 37 L.Q.R. 191, 195–197.

With respect to 'constructive' or 'indirect' contempts committed out of court, the claim that attachment was sanctioned by 'immemorial usage and practice' in the common law courts has been shown to be completely without foundation. Developing his thesis Sir John Fox concedes that at the time of *Almon's* case[15] direct obstruction to the service of process had indeed been dealt with summarily for many years.[16] He maintains, however, that a general dispensing with trial by jury in contempt cases before common law courts had far more recent and questionable origins. According to the author the practice was adopted from the Star Chamber procedure of examination by interrogation, and it passed gradually into the common law on the abolition of that Court in 1641 and the transfer of its jurisdiction to the Court of King's Bench.[17] The process was aided by a series of statutes conferring summary jurisdiction on the common law courts in a number of particular cases.[18]

Although Sir John Fox was able to point to examples dating from the mid-17th century of attempts to subvert the course of justice being dealt with in the common law courts by attachment,[19] the application of this procedure to libels on the court does not appear to have come until much later. Indeed the case of *Wilkins*[20] in 1720 appears to be the earliest recorded example of a libel or slander unconnected with the service of process being tried and punished on summary process by a common law court.[1] In this case, moreover, the contempt was confessed. While several later decisions lend some support to the assumptions on which the judgment in *Almon* was based,[2] they hardly vindicate the appeal to history which was made in this leading case. Nor, it seems, is the position advanced by reference to the practice in the Court of Chancery, where the earliest recorded example of a committal of a stranger for a libel on the court does not appear to have occurred until 1736.[3]

In spite of its lack of a sound historical basis Wilmot, J.'s undelivered judgment received a generally uncritical acceptance in the first half of the 19th century.[4] It appears to have been adopted for the first time as the basis for a decision by an English judge in the case of *Clement* in 1821.[5] Thereafter its frequent citation led

[15] (1765) Wilm. 243; 97 E.R. 94.

[16] Though again the author cites some early cases in which contemptuous conduct on the service of process was punished after conviction by a jury: see (1908) 24 L.Q.R. 184, 197–198. For contempt by abusing process servers, see below, pp. 217–218.

[17] *Cf.* Fox, (1908) 24 L.Q.R. 266, 273–274; (1909) 25 L.Q.R. 354, 362 *et seq.*

[18] See Fox, (1909) 25 L.Q.R. 354, 357–362. The practice of the House of Commons may also have helped to establish the summary process in the common law courts: *cf.* Fox, (1908) 24 L.Q.R. 266, 276.

[19] See (1909) 25 L.Q.R. 354, 366.

[20] The case is referred to in Appendix E to the Report of the Select Committee of the House of Commons in *Sir Francis Burdett's case* (1810) 8 How. St. Tr. 14, 50.

[1] *Cf.* Fox, (1908) 24 L.Q.R. 184, 191.

[2] See *Anon.* (1731) 2 Barn. K.B. 43; 94 E.R. 345; *Middleton* (1723) Fort. 201; 92 E.R. 818; *Barber* (1721) 1 Stra. 444; 93 E.R. 624; *Wiatt* (1723) 8 Mod. 123; 88 E.R. 96.

[3] *Cf.* Fox (1908) 24 L.Q.R. 184, 189 referring to the case of *Dodd* (1736) Sand. Chan. Ord. 538–542. See also the *St. James's Evening Post Case* (1742) 2 Atk. 469; 26 E.R. 683.

[4] See, however, the critical comments of Fletcher, J. in *Taafe* v. *Downes* (1813) 3 Moo. P.C. 36n; 13 E.R. 15 (Common Pleas in Ireland), cited by Fox (1908) 24 L.Q.R. 184, 185–188.

[5] (1821) 4 B. & Ald. 219, 233; 106 E.R. 918, 923 *per* Holroyd, J. It had already been cited in the Report of the Select Committee of the House of Commons in *Sir Francis Burdett's case* (1810) 8 How. St. Tr. 14, 54.

to the summary procedure to punish contempt becoming firmly established in both English and Commonwealth courts.[6] Some critical comment has been voiced in more recent years,[7] and the need for restraint in exercising the jurisdiction emphasised.[8] But the procedure has nonetheless remained intact.[9] Indeed, at the present time one can say that contempt by publication seems invariably to be dealt with summarily,[10] although other forms of conduct constituting a contempt are sometimes charged on indictment as a conspiracy to pervert the course of justice or an incitement to do the same. In *Attorney-General* v. *Butterworth*[11] Pearson, L. J. gave a measure of encouragement to those who would prefer to see the procedure by indictment more generally reinstated in cases of alleged contempt. In a case in which the contempt took the form of victimising a witness who had given evidence before the Restrictive Practices Court he noted that trial on indictment before a jury might be the most appropriate way of proceeding on such facts. Likewise in the recent Australian case of *Attorney-General (N.S.W.)* v. *Mundey*[12] Hope, J. A. was of the opinion that the summary procedure was only appropriate to a case of contempt by scandalising the court where the nature of the imputation was such as to require an immediate repudiation. Again in *Balogh* v. *Crown Court at St. Albans*[13] the Court of Appeal made the somewhat different point that a judge should only act of his own motion to punish contempt when 'it is urgent and imperative to act immediately'.[14] As previously noted it is also central to the Phillimore Committee recommendations that the summary procedure should only be invoked where the offending act does not fall within the definition of any other offence or where urgency or practical necessity so requires.[15]

3   CONTEMPORARY PROCEDURE AND JURISDICTION

(1)   CONTEMPT IN THE FACE OF THE COURT

(i) *Procedure*

Where contempt is committed in the face of the court it is normally dealt with by the court itself, either by an immediate committal or summarily once the pro-

[6] See, e.g., *Davison* (1821) 4 B. & Ald. 329, 337; 106 E.R. 958, 961; *Miller* v. *Knox* (1838) 4 Bing N.C. 574, 587, 597, 606, 614, 620; 132 E.R. 915; *Ex p. Van Sandau* (1844) 1 Phil. 445, 454; 41 E.R. 701, 704; *Re Johnson* (1887) 20 Q.B.D. 68, 75; *Gray* [1900] 2 Q.B. 36, 40.

[7] See, e.g., Zelman Cowen, 'Some Observations on the Law of Criminal Contempt' (1965) Univ. Western Aus. L.R. 1, 7 and, in general, sources cited above, p. 20, note 5.

[8] See, e.g., *Re Clements and The Republic of Costa Rica* v. *Erlanger* (1877) 46 L.J. Ch. 375, 383 *per* Jessel, M.R.

[9] An unsuccessful attempt was made to reopen the question before the High Court of Australia in *James* v. *Robinson* (1963) 109 C.L.R. 593. For the development of the position in the USA, see below, p. 41 *et seq.*

[10] *Tibbits and Windust* [1902] 1 K.B. 77 appears to have been the last case in which proceedings were by way of indictment: see D.G.T. Williams [1961] Crim. L.R. 87, 93.

[11] [1963] 1 Q.B. 696, 728; [1962] 3 All E.R. 326, 334–335, C.A.

[12] [1972] 2 N.S.W.L.R. 887, 915 (N.S.W. Sup. Ct).

[13] [1974] 3 All E.R. 283.

[14] *Ibid.,* at p. 288 (Lord Denning). See also *ibid,* at p. 292 (Stephenson, L.J.), and at p. 295 (Lawton, L.J.).

[15] Para. 21, above, p. 6.

ceedings have terminated. By way of example one may cite the case of a certain Mr William Cordiner who, in November 1972, being displeased by the conduct and outcome of divorce proceedings presided over by Lord Stott, a judge of the Court of Session in Scotland, is reported as having disturbed the court by shouting: 'I will take the law into my own hands. You will find out what stabbing is. All of you people will have something to be afraid about. You will never sleep in peace. Nobody in this court will sleep in peace'. As a result of this outburst the judge ordered his immediate arrest, had him brought back into court later in the day and sentenced him to the remarkable term of three years' imprisonment for contempt. He was later released after about four months when he had made a written apology to the judge.[16] The alternative to this summary process is to proceed only after the issue of a summons or on indictment, but one suspects that this course is not frequently adopted at the present time.[17]

Where this summary procedure of committing *instanter* and without any formalised application or hearing is adopted there is room for debate as to the nature of the procedural requirements which must be observed. Certainly there is authority for the view that the alleged contemnor is entitled to be informed of the nature of the charge against him and to be given the opportunity to advance any available defence. The High Court of Australia has formulated the requirements in the following terms:[18]

> . . . it is a well-recognised principle of law that no person ought to be punished for contempt of court unless the specific charge against him be distinctly stated and an opportunity of answering it given to him.[19] The gist of the accusation must be made clear to the person charged, though it is not always necessary to formulate the charge in a series of specific allegations. The charge having been made sufficiently specific, the person accused must then be allowed a reasonable opportunity of being heard in his own defence, that is to say a reasonable opportunity of placing before the court any explanation or amplification of his evidence, and any submissions of fact or law, which he may wish the court to consider as bearing either upon the charge itself or upon the question of punishment. Resting as it does upon accepted notions of elementary justice, this principle must be rigorously insisted upon.[20]

Although this general statement does not concede the point in specific terms it is submitted that the elementary requirements of justice in a criminal case also demand that the defendant be accorded the opportunity to call and cross-examine witnesses, and to avail himself of legal representation. Yet modern English cases concerned with the imposition of binding-over orders have sanctioned minimum formality and notice where the binding over follows upon disturbances in the court itself.[1] It may be argued that there is an analogy in this

---

[16] *Cordiner* v. *Cordiner* [1973] S.L.T. 125. For critical comment, see Bernard Levin, 'Why Silence in Court is especially Golden', *The Times*, 21 November 1972.

[17] See Hansard, H.L. Deb. Vol. 222, col. 273, 24 March 1960 for an account by Lord Denning of an occasion when this course was adopted.

[18] *Coward* v. *Stapleton* (1953) 90 C.L.R. 573, 579–580.

[19] Citing *Re Pollard* (1868) L.R. 2 P.C. 106, 120; *Foster, ex p. Isaacs* [1941] V.L.R. 77, 81 (Vict. Sup. Ct.).

[20] See also *Appuhamy* [1963] A.C. 474, P.C.; *Lloyd* v. *Biggin* [1962] V.R. 593 (Vict. Sup. Ct.); *Strang* [1968] 2 C.C.C. 205; *Ex p. Stewart*; *Re Fellows* [1972] 2 N.S.W.L.R. 317.

[1] See *North London Metropolitan Magistrate, ex p. Haywood* [1973] 3 All E.R. 50. See also *Woking Justices, ex p. Gossage* [1973] 2 All E.R. 621; *Hendon Justices, ex p. Gorchein* [1974] 1 All E.R. 168.

respect between the power to bind over and the power to commit for contempt. It has also been pointed out that, apart from the requirements of English domestic law, Article 6 of the European Convention on Human Rights may also be of importance in the present context. This demands that a defendant be given 'adequate time and facilities for the preparation of his defence', and that he be entitled to avail himself of legal assistance, which should be provided free of charge when he does not have the means to pay and when the interests of justice so require.[2]

In an attempt to meet and to clarify some of the above points the Phillimore Committee has recommended that the alleged contemnor should be informed of the precise nature of his contempt, and be entitled to call and to cross-examine witnesses and to be legally represented.[3] The committee further recommended that the courts be given the power to grant legal aid on an emergency basis —a recommendation which, if implemented, would fill an important gap in the present legal aid system.[4]

(ii) *Jurisdiction*

Although it was said in the old case of *Sparks* v. *Martyn* that the Court of Admiralty might fine or imprison for contempt in the face of the court, 'tho' they are no Court of Record,'[5] it is now generally accepted that it is only courts of record which have power at common law to proceed summarily in such cases.[6] For practical purposes this means that the power is currently possessed by all *superior* courts[7] and possibly also by certain tribunals designated courts of record by the Act under which they were established.[8] Specific statutory pro-

---

[2] See D. J. Harris, 'The European Convention on Human Rights and English Criminal Law' [1966] Crim. L.R. 266, 269. The requirements are those of Art. 6(3)(b)-(c).

[3] Para. 32.

[4] *Ibid.* The recommendations also apply to pleas in mitigation of sentence (para. 33). The present lack of legal aid facilities in contempt cases was commented upon by Stephenson, L. J. in *Balogh* v. *Crown Court at St. Albans* [1974] 3 All E.R. 283, 293. He noted that a judge can always ask counsel to represent a contemnor, but thought that there were cases in which committal without legal representation would be proper. Opportunity to seek representation had been refused in the *Balogh* case itself.

[5] (1668) 1 Vent. 1; 86 E.R. 1, 2, cited with approval by Wilmot, J. in *Almon* (1765) Wilm. 243, 254; 97 E.R. 94.

[6] See Oswald, *Contempt of Court*, p. 12, where it is said: 'Courts not of Record have no jurisdiction to punish for contempt of court unless it is specially conferred by statute.' See also *McDermott* v. *British Guiana Justices* (1868) L.R. 2 P.C. 341; *Griesley's Case* (1588) 8 Co. Rep. 38a; 77 E.R. 530.

[7] See further below, p. 29. It seems that if a contempt is committed before a judge in chambers, or a master, the judge or master should bring the matter before the court: *Re Johnson* (1887) 20 Q.B.D. 68, 73, 74, C.A. See also *Halsbury*, Vol. 9, para. 5, note 2. For contempt before an official referee, see R.S.C. Ord. 36, r. 4 and accompanying annotations in *The Supreme Court Practice 1973*, Vol. 1, p. 762. The Phillimore Committee recommends (para. 38) that bankruptcy registrars should have the same powers as accorded to county courts under the County Courts Act 1959, s. 157—as to which see following text.

[8] These include a Transport Tribunal (Railways Act 1921, s. 20(1), Transport Act 1962, Sch. 10, para. 1); Iron and Steel Arbitration Tribunal (Iron and Steel Act 1949, ss. 43(1), 44(1); Iron and Steel Act 1967, s. 32); Electricity Arbitration Tribunal (Electricity Act 1947, ss. 31(1), 32(1)); Gas Arbitration Tribunal (Gas Act 1948, ss. 63(1), 64(1)).

vision superseding the common law powers[9] has now been made for county courts which, by the County Courts Act 1959, s. 157(1), may punish any person who:

(a) wilfully insults the judge of a county court, or any juror or witness, or any officer of the court during his sitting or attendance in court, or in going to or returning from the court; or (b) wilfully interrupts the proceedings of a county court or otherwise misbehaves in court.[10]

By s. 84(1) of the same Act further provision is made for the punishment of:

Any person summoned in pursuance of county court rules as a witness in a county court who (a) refuses or neglects, without sufficient cause, to appear or to produce any documents required by the summons to be produced; or (b) refuses to be sworn or to give evidence.[11]

Several local courts of record actively exercising a civil jurisdiction comparable to that of a county court were abolished by Part VI of the Courts Act 1971.[12]

Stone's Justices' Manual doubts whether magistrates' courts have the power to commit for contempt,[13] and these doubts are reinforced by decisions in other common law jurisdictions.[14] Yet magistrates' courts satisfy two of the accepted criteria of a criminal court of record in that they have the power to fine and imprison, and a record of a conviction is taken as conclusive evidence of the justices' decision.[15] Hence the position is perhaps not clear beyond doubt. Alternative procedures are, in any event, available to magistrates seeking to prevent the disruption of proceedings. The offender may be ejected from court, bound over to keep the peace with or without sureties, or have a summons served on him returnable *instanter* in cases of physical assault.[16] Similarly there is a statutory power to commit a recalcitrant witness to prison for a maximum of seven days, or to impose a £20 fine, in the event of his refusing to be sworn, to give evidence, or to produce a document.[17] If it were thought desirable to confer additional powers on magistrates this could be done by enacting a provision equivalent to those which already exist in many other common law jurisdic-

---

[9] *Cf. Lefroy* (1873) L.R. 8 Q.B. 134, 138 *per* Cockburn, C. J. discussed further below, p. 29.

[10] A maximum period of imprisonment not exceeding one month or a fine not exceeding £20 may be imposed. The Phillimore Committee recommends (para. 204) that these limits be changed to a fine of £150 or three months' imprisonment.

[11] A maximum fine of £50 may be imposed: see the Administration of Justice Act 1969, s. 11(3). See also the County Courts Act 1959, s. 30(1)—assaulting an officer of the court while executing his duty.

[12] These courts included The Mayor's and City of London Court (re-established as a county court); Tolzey and Pie Poudre Courts of the City and County of Bristol; Liverpool Court of Passage; Norwich Guildhall Court; Court of Record for the Hundred of Salford. See also the Local Government Act 1972, s. 221; Schedule 28—abolition of borough courts of record.

[13] See 105th. ed. (1973), p. 369. The basis of the doubt is an opinion of Pollock and Follett when law officers of the Crown.

[14] See, e.g., *Reece* v. *McKenna* [1953] Q.S.R. 258 (Qu. Sup. Ct); *Re Dunn* (1906) V.L.R. 493 (Vict. Sup. Ct.); *Re Rose* [1964] 1 C.C.C. 25 (Ont. H.C.).

[15] See *Tyrone Justices* [1917] 2 I.R. 437; *Chaney* v. *Payne* (1841) 1 Q.B. 712, 724; 113 E.R. 1304, 1308.

[16] *Cf. Stone's Justices Manual* (105th. ed., 1973), p. 369. See also *Butt* (1957) 41 Cr. App. Rep. 82, 84 *per* Lord Goddard, C.J., and for general discussion, below, pp. 65–67.

[17] See Magistrates' Courts Act 1952, s. 77(4).

tions.[18] The Phillimore Committee has recommended that magistrates should be empowered to deal with disruptive behaviour subject to the same limits as apply in the case of a recalcitrant witness.[19]

A similar element of doubt exists as to the status of a coroner's court. In *Jewison* v. *Dyson*[20] Lord Abinger, C.B. questioned whether such a court was a court of record, but the balance of authority both here and in other common law jurisdictions suggests that it is.[1] As Borrie and Lowe have pointed out,[2] the wording of the Coroners Act 1887 also tacitly assumes that coroner's courts have the power to punish contempt committed *in facie curiae*.[3]

(iii) *Proceeding without a formal application to commit*

In *Balogh* v. *Crown Court at St Albans*[4] B had decided to enliven a pornography case he was attending by releasing nitrous oxide, 'laughing gas', into the court. He was arrested when waiting for a suitable moment to slip up to the roof via the public gallery of the adjoining courtroom. There he had planned to release the gas into the ventilation system serving the 'pornography court'. Having been brought before Melford-Stevenson, J., the senior presiding judge who was not himself involved in the pornography case, B was sentenced to six months' imprisonment for contempt. His appeal to the Court of Appeal was allowed on the ground that his acts, though preparatory to committing a contempt, had not reached the stage when they constituted an attempt to do so, or, still less, the complete offence. As Lawton, L. J. remarked: 'Providence intervened to save him from turning his preparations into criminal action.'[5]

Whilst this was sufficient to dispose of the case the judgments in the Court of Appeal are of interest for their approach to B's alternative submission that Melford-Stevenson, J. had no jurisdiction to determine the matter summarily without there having been a formal application to commit. On this point the view which emerged was that a jurisdiction to proceed *ex mero motu* did exist whenever a criminal contempt required an immediate response to safeguard the interests of justice.[6] According to Stevenson, L. J. this might be the case when, for example, 'a witness or juror is bribed or threatened in the course of the case, whether in the court or its precincts or at any distance from it'.[7] The procedure

---

[18] See, e.g., Justices Act 1958 (Vic.), s. 211; Justices Acts 1902–1957 (N.S.W.), s. 152; Justices Acts 1886–1949 (Qu.), s. 40; Canadian Criminal Code, s. 426.

[19] Para. 37.

[20] (1842) 9 M. & W. 540, 586; 152 E.R. 228, 247.

[1] See, e.g., *Garnett* v. *Ferrand* (1827) 6 B. & C. 611, 625; 108 E.R. 576, 581 *per* Lord Tenterden, C.J.; *Thomas* v. *Churton* (1862) 2 B. & S. 475, 478; 121 E.R. 1150, 1151 *per* Crompton, J.; *Casey* v. *Candler* (1874) 5 A. J. R. 179 (Vict. Sup. Ct.); *Comyn* v. *Willshire* (1875) 9 S.A.L.R. 161 (S.A. Sup. Ct.); *Little* [1926] 2 W.W.R. 762, 46 C.C.C. 136 (Man. K.B.).

[2] *Law of Contempt* (1973), p. 275.

[3] See Coroners Act 1887, s. 19 (3). The Act also makes specific provision for the punishment of a juror who refuses to serve (s. 19(1)) and a witness who refuses to answer a question (s. 19(2)).

[4] [1974] 3 All E.R. 283, C.A.

[5] *Ibid.*, at p. 296. *Haughton* v. *Smith* [1973] 3 All E.R. 1109, H.L. was cited.

[6] *Cf. ibid.*, at p. 288 (Lord Denning), p. 292 (Stevenson, L. J.), p. 295 (Lawton, L. J.). R.S.C. Ord. 52, r. 5 makes it clear that Ord. 52 does not derogate from the power of the High Court or Court of Appeal to act of its own motion.

[7] [1974] 3 All E.R. 283, 292.

was, however, a drastic one and should not have been used against B who had already been arrested on a charge of stealing the gas cylinder. These conclusions are consistent with the earlier cases.[8]

(iv) When is a contempt committed 'in the face of the court'?

In view of the decision in *Balogh's* case, it is unlikely that an English court will be called upon to decide when exactly a contempt is committed 'in the face of the court' itself. Specific statutory provision has, moreover, been made for some of the more obvious borderline cases, such as the juror or witness who absents himself without leave.[9] Theoretically, however, the problem of delimitation could still arise since it will be seen in the following section that an inferior court of record may punish a criminal contempt if, and only if, it is committed in the face of the court itself.[10] County courts are by far the most important example of such a court and their contempt power turns on the wording of the County Courts Act 1959.[11] Coroner's courts also appear to be inferior courts of record[12] and a question of delimitation might arise in their case.

In so far as the matter has been discussed in English and Commonwealth cases there has been no discernible tendency to construe the limitation narrowly. Thus it seems that conduct in the precincts of the court may sometimes be treated as a contempt in the face of the court itself.[13] In recent years a majority of the Supreme Court of Canada has likewise regarded a barrister as having committed a contempt 'in the face of the court' by absenting himself from court, thus preventing a trial from continuing.[14] A similar view was taken by the United States Court of Appeals for the District of Columbia in *Re Gates*,[15] but there is force in the dissenting opinion of Laskin, J. in the Canadian case, who would draw the distinction according to whether all the circumstances were in the personal knowledge of the court.[16] It would seem that the choice is effectively between this 'personal knowledge' test, and a test which would require the contempt to be directly and immediately obstructive of courtroom proceedings. In *Balogh* v. *Crown Court at St. Albans* Lord Denning suggested that a contempt 'in the face of the court' was the same thing as a contempt which the court could punish of its own motion.[17] It is submitted, however, that this is not so. Con-

---

[8] See, e.g., *Moore* v. *Clerk of Assize, Bristol* [1972] 1 All E.R. 58; *Skipworth's and the Defendant's Case* (1873) L.R. 9 Q.B. 230.

[9] See further, below, p. 55 (juror) and p. 56 (witness).

[10] *Lefroy* (1873) L.R. 8 Q.B. 134. See further below, p. 29.

[11] See, in particular, s. 157(1) of the Act, above, p. 26.

[12] *Cf.* above, p. 27.

[13] *Ex p. Burrows* (1803) 8 Ves. 535; 32 E.R. 462; *Wigley* (1835) 7 C. & P. 4; 173 E.R. 3; *Halsbury*, Vol. 9, para. 5, note 2. But *quaere* whether these cases decide more than that such conduct may be punished by a superior court?

[14] *McKeown* (1971) 16 D.L.R. (3d) 390. Contrast *Vallieres* (1974) 47 D.L.R. (3d) 378 (Quebec C.A.)—sending insulting letter to judge in chambers not a contempt in the face of the court.

[15] 478 F. 2d 998 (1973). The case turned on whether this was a contempt committed in the 'actual presence of the court' for the purposes of the Federal Rules of Criminal Procedure, r. 42(a). See also *Re Farquhar*, 492 F. 2d 561 (1973), and *cf. U.S.* v. *Delahanty*, 488 F. 2d 396 (1973). See further, below, p. 43.

[16] (1971) 16 D.L.R. (3d) 390, 408.

[17] [1974] 3 All E.R. 283, 287.

tempts committed in the face of the court may certainly be punished *ex mero motu*. But it does not follow that because a contempt may be punished in this way it is *therefore* a contempt committed in the face of the court itself.[18] There is no necessary equivalence between the ability to dispense with a formal application to commit and the place where the contempt is committed. If there were it would presumably follow that an inferior court of record could punish as for a contempt committed *in facie curiae* when a witness is victimised in respect of evidence already given.[19] No such jurisdiction would appear to exist.

(2) CONSTRUCTIVE OR INDIRECT CONTEMPTS

(i) *General considerations*

As has been noted above, jurisdiction to punish for 'constructive' or 'indirect' contempts committed out of court is vested solely in the *superior* as opposed to inferior courts. Thus in the English domestic system the power is possessed by the House of Lords, Court of Appeal,[20] High Court of Justice,[1] Crown Court,[2] Restrictive Practices Court[3] and the Courts-Martial Appeals Court.[4] An inferior court of record may only punish a contempt in the face of the court itself.[5]

The main modern authority establishing the limits to the contempt jurisdiction of inferior courts is *Lefroy*.[6] Here an application was made to the Court of Queen's Bench to prevent a county court judge from proceeding against the publisher of a letter which was critical of his conduct. In the course of his judgment granting the writ of prohibition Cockburn, C. J. relied as much on the common law rules as on the implied limits to the powers of county courts set out in the legislation under which they were constituted.[7] With respect to the former he said:[8]

> [Though] this power [*sc.* to punish for contempts committed out of court] is recognised in the superior courts, it is nowhere said that an inferior court of record has any power to proceed for contempt out of court; and there is an obvious distinction between the superior courts and other courts of record.

This statement of principle may be taken to be of general application.

It is important to note, however, that this limitation does not mean that out-of-court publications or other forms of conduct which interfere with the due

---

[18] Thus in both *Moore* v. *Clerk of Assize, Bristol* [1972] 1 All E.R. 58 (victimising a witness) and *Skipworth's Case* (1873) L.R. 9 Q.B. 230 (prejudicial public speech) proceedings were taken *ex mero muto*.

[19] As in *Moore* v. *Clerk of Assize, Bristol* [1972] 1 All E.R. 58. Yet curiously Lord Denning suggested that this was a contempt committed in the face of the court: [1974] 3 All E.R. 283, 288.

[20] See Judicature Act 1925, s. 26(1): Criminal Appeal Act 1966, s. 1.

[1] See Judicature Act 1925, s. 18(1).

[2] Courts Act 1971, s. 4(1).

[3] Restrictive Trade Practices Act 1956, s. 2(3).

[4] Courts-Martial (Appeals) Act 1968, s. 1(2).

[5] See above, p. 28 for discussion of the meaning of the term.

[6] (1873) L.R. 8 Q.B. 134.

[7] See the County Courts Act 1846, ss. 113–114. See now the County Courts Act 1959, s. 157, and above, p. 26.

[8] (1873) L.R. 8 Q.B. 134, 137.

administration of justice before inferior courts remain wholly immune. On the contrary it has long been clear that they may be punished either on indictment,[9] or even summarily before a Divisional Court of the Queen's Bench Division. This latter point was established in *Davies, ex parte Hunter,*[10] where a newspaper had published material prejudicial to the fair trial of an accused on charges of abandoning a child and attempted murder. The former charge would normally have been tried at quarter sessions, which was an inferior court. Wills, J. was nonetheless clear that the King's Bench Division had power to punish the offending editor on summary process for his interference with the cause pending before that inferior court. In the result a fine of £100 was imposed.

Authority for this view was admittedly sparse, and the conclusion was supported more by reference to principle than to existing cases. Thus having referred to the general supervisory function exercised by the King's Bench over the inferior courts through the prerogative orders, Wills, J. felt able to infer:[11]

> . . . that it is no departure from principle, but only its legitimate application to a new state of things, if others whose conduct tends to prevent the due performance of their duties by those Courts have to be corrected as well as the Courts themselves.

The connection between a power to correct and a duty to protect may not be regarded as obvious,[12] but, in any event, the decision and the reasoning behind it have been followed both in this country and elsewhere.[13] In *Daily Mail (Editor), ex parte Farnsworth,*[14] a case involving alleged interference with proceedings pending before a court-martial, Avory, J. was accordingly able to say with reference to the decision in *Davies* that:[15]

> The result of that judgment is to show that wherever and whenever this Court has power to correct an inferior court, it also has power to protect that court by punishing those who interfere with the due administration of justice in that court.

(ii) *Jurisdiction of and procedure before particular courts*

(a) *Divisional Courts of the Queen's Bench Division.* R.S.C. Ord. 52, r. 1(2) confers a wide ranging and (within the sphere of its application and subject to what is said below) *exclusive* jurisdiction to make committal orders on Divisional Courts of the Queen's Bench Division. With the exception of contempt of the Court of Appeal, it covers all cases where contempt of court:

(a) is committed in connection with
   (i) any proceedings before a Divisional Court of the Queen's Bench Division, or

---

[9] *Cf. Tibbits and Windust* [1902] 1 K.B. 77.

[10] [1906] 1 K.B. 32.

[11] *Ibid.,* at p. 43.

[12] *Cf. Packer* v. *Peacock* (1912) 13 C.L.R. 577, 585–586 *per* Griffith, C. J. (High Ct. of Australia). The existence of any such jurisdiction had been denied by Holroyd, J. in *Re Syme, ex p. Worthington* (1902) 28 V.L.R. 552 (Vict. Sup. Ct.).

[13] See, e.g., *John Fairfax and Sons Pty Ltd* v. *McRae* (1954) 93 C.L.R. 351 (High Ct. of Australia); *McKinnon* (1911) 30 N.Z.L.R. 884 (N.Z. Sup. Ct.) and, in general, cases cited below, p. 31, notes 17–1.

[14] [1921] 2 K.B. 733.

[15] *Ibid.,* at p. 752.

(ii) criminal proceedings, except where the contempt is committed in the face of the court or consists of disobedience to an order of the court or breach of an undertaking to the court, or

(iii) proceedings in an inferior court, or

(b) is committed otherwise than in connection with any proceedings.

To amplify the above provision it may be said that the first sub-heading, (a)(i), is primarily directed towards cases of non-compliance with orders issued by Divisional Courts of the Queen's Bench Division, such as orders of mandamus, prohibition or certiorari. The point does not need to be developed further at this stage. The second sub-heading, (a)(ii), would typically cover cases where, for example, criminal proceedings pending in the Crown Court have been allegedly prejudiced. In the unlikely event of contempt proceedings being based upon prejudice to a criminal appeal pending before a Divisional Court of the Queen's Bench Division, the application would again be made to a Divisional Court, whether under the present heading or the former heading (a)(i). Alleged prejudice to a criminal appeal pending before the Court of Appeal may be dealt with by an application to a Divisional Court or to the Court of Appeal itself. The third sub-heading, (a)(iii), which refers to 'proceedings in an inferior court' obviously builds upon the jurisdiction assumed to exist in *Davies*.[16] The jurisdiction has been applied to allegations of interference with proceedings in a court of quarter sessions,[17] a court-martial,[18] county court,[19] consistory court,[20] and other inferior courts.[1] In all such cases, therefore, applications for committal orders must be made to a Divisional Court of the Queen's Bench Division. The extent of the jurisdiction envisaged by rule 1(2)(b) is not so clear. Presumably, however, contempts committed 'otherwise than in connection with any proceedings' would include contempts through scandalising a court or judge, and possibly also through victimising a witness or juror.

It may also be noted that, although the present rule is expressed as conferring on Divisional Courts of the Queen's Bench Division an *exclusive* jurisdiction to grant committal orders in the case of contempts falling into the above categories, it must clearly be read subject to any relevant statutory provisions. In particular the Restrictive Trade Practices Act 1956 provides that no person may be punished for contempt of the Restrictive Practices Court, which is itself a superior court of record,[2] except by or with the consent of a judge who is a member of that court.[3] Thus it would seem that applications for committal orders should generally be moved before the Restrictive Practices Court itself. Whether this is equally so where the contempt is committed 'otherwise than in connection with any proceedings'—as, for example, by scandalising the

---

[16] [1906] 1 K.B. 32.

[17] As in *Davies* itself.

[18] *Daily Mail (Editor), ex p. Farnsworth* [1921] 2 K.B. 733; *Gunn, ex p. Att-Gen.* [1954] Crim. L.R. 53.

[19] *Edwards, ex p. Welsh Church Temporalities Commissioners* (1933) 49 T.L.R. 383.

[20] *Daily Herald, ex p. The Bishop of Norwich* [1932] 2 K.B. 402.

[1] *Cf. Clarke, ex p. Crippen* (1910) 103 L.T. 636, 641 *per* Lord Coleridge (coroner's court).

[2] See the Restrictive Trade Practices Act 1956, s. 2(3).

[3] See Sch., para. 12 of the Act. For a case discussing the general application of the law of contempt to the court, see *Re The Cement Makers' Federation's Agreement* [1961] 2 All E.R. 75, 96 (R.P.C., Diplock, J.).

Restrictive Practices Court—or whether Ord. 52, r. 1(2)(b) then envisages an application to a Divisional Court after obtaining the *consent* of a judge of the Restrictive Practices Court is unclear.[4]

The procedure governing applications to a Divisional Court for an order of committal is set out in Ord. 52, rules 2 and 3 and in broad outline it may be summarised as follows. By Ord. 52, r. 2 the person seeking a committal order must initially seek leave to apply through an *ex parte* application, which must itself normally be made to a Divisional Court.[5] The application must be accompanied by a statement setting out, inter alia, the grounds on which the committal order is sought, and it must be supported by an affidavit verifying the facts relied on.[6] If leave to apply is granted the application will be by motion,[7] notice of which must generally be served personally on the person whom it is sought to commit. Under Ord. 52, r. 3(3) the service of the notice of motion must also be accompanied by a copy of the statement and affidavit supporting the original application for leave.[8] The alleged contemnor's reply or defence will likewise be by affidavit, though Ord. 52, r. 6(4) entitles him to support his defence at the hearing by giving oral evidence if he expresses a wish to do so. The actual hearing of the application will generally take place in open court,[9] but Ord. 52, r. 6(1) makes provision for a limited number of cases in which it may be conducted in private.[10] The overall procedure appears to be convenient, subject always to the major point of contention as to whether a jury trial should be denied in cases of criminal contempt.

(b) *Single judges of the High Court.* Jurisdiction in cases of alleged contempt committed in connection with civil litigation pending in the High Court is governed by Ord. 52, r. 1(3). The effect of this rule is that where the contempt is committed in connection with proceedings assigned or transferred to the Chancery Division or the Family Division committal orders may *only* be made by single judges of these respective Divisions.[11] Since 1965 a similar jurisdiction to make committal orders has likewise been conferred by rule 1(3) upon single judges of the Queen's Bench Division in cases of interference with litigation

---

[4] In *Att.-Gen.* v. *Butterworth* [1963] 1 Q.B. 696; [1962] 3 All E.R. 326, C.A., the application for committal orders following the victimisation of a witness who had given evidence before the court was made to the Restrictive Practices Court itself. *Quaere*, however, whether this would be a contempt committed 'otherwise than in connection with any proceedings' for the purposes of Ord. 52, r. 1(2)(b)?

[5] R.S.C. Ord. 52, r. 2(2) makes provision for an application to a judge in chambers during the vacation.

[6] *Ibid.* The grounds thus stated cannot be departed from at the hearing unless the Court gives leave: see Ord. 52, r. 6(3).

[7] Ord. 52, r. 3(1). Both the application for leave and the motion may now be moved by litigants in person: see *The Supreme Court Practice 1973*, Vol. 1, p. 766 and sources there cited.

[8] Ord. 52 r. 3(4) permits service of the notice of motion to be dispensed with by the court where this is thought just. See *The Supreme Court Practice 1973*, Vol. 1, p. 767 for further details.

[9] Ord. 52, r. 6(1).

[10] As, for example, where the application arises out of proceedings relating to the wardship or adoption of an infant: Ord. 52, r. 6(1)(a). If a committal order is made certain basic details (as, e.g., the name of the person and the general nature of the contempt committed) must be stated in open court: see r. 6(2).

[11] For an example of an application to the Chancery Division, see *Vine Products, Ltd* v. *MacKenzie and Co. Ltd* [1966] Ch. 484; [1965] 3 All E.R. 58.

pending there. This jurisdiction is not, however, expressed as being exclusive, and it seems that an application may equally well be made to a Divisional Court as in *Attorney-General* v. *London Weekend Television Ltd.*[12]

By Ord. 52, r. 1(4) a committal order may also be made by a single judge of the Queen's Bench Division:

> Where by virtue of any enactment the High Court has power to punish or take steps for the punishment of any person charged with having done any thing in relation to a court, tribunal or person which would, if it had been done in relation to the High Court, have been a contempt of that Court . . .

As will be seen below,[13] there are a number of enactments providing for reference to the High Court in such cases of which the most important is the Tribunals of Inquiry (Evidence) Act 1921, s. 1(2).

Ord. 52, r. 4 lays down a similar procedure for applying to a single judge for a committal order as in applications to a Divisional Court, except that there is no requirement of an initial *ex parte* application for leave to apply. Application is again by motion, notice of which must generally be served in person on the person sought to be committed, together with a copy of the supporting affidavit.[14]

(c) *Other superior courts.* In cases falling outside Ord. 52, r. 1 applications for committal orders would be made to the appropriate superior courts. Thus on an alleged contempt of the Court of Appeal the application may be made to that Court,[15] and, as was noted above,[16] contempts of the Restrictive Practices Court, would normally be dealt with by that court, and would, in any event, require the consent of a judge of the court before proceedings were taken.[17] Application is again by motion after notice to the person whom it is sought to commit in accordance with the procedure laid down by Ord. 52, r. 4.

(3) CONTEMPT OF TRIBUNALS AND OF SIMILAR BODIES

Certain statutory provisions extend the law of contempt to cover bodies other than the ordinary courts of law. A notable example is furnished by the Tribunals of Inquiry (Evidence) Act 1921. Under this Act ad hoc tribunals may be set up following a resolution of both Houses of Parliament in order, as the Royal Commission on Tribunals of Inquiry put it, 'publicly to establish the truth when there is a nation-wide crisis of confidence about matters of urgent public importance'.[18] Recent examples of such tribunals have included the Vassall Tribunal in 1962, the Aberfan Tribunal in 1966 and the tribunal conducted by Lord Widgery,

---

[12] [1972] 3 All E.R. 1146.

[13] See following text, pp. 33–34.

[14] See Ord. 54, r. 4(2). Rule 4(3) again permits the Court to dispense with service of the notice of motion if it thinks it just to do so. According to *The Supreme Court Practice 1973*, Vol. 1, p. 767: 'Personal service has in practice been required save in exceptional cases, e.g., where the respondent evades service.'

[15] See, e.g., *Metropolitan Police Commissioner, ex p. Blackburn (No. 2)* [1968] 2 Q.B. 150; [1968] 2 All E.R. 319, C.A.

[16] At p. 31.

[17] See the Restrictive Trade Practices Act 1956, s. 2(3), Sch., para. 12.

[18] Cmnd. 3121, November 1966, para. 45.

C. J. in 1972 to inquire into the causes of the deaths in Northern Ireland on what
came to be known as 'Bloody Sunday'. By s. 1(2) of the 1921 Act:

> If any person:
> (a) on being duly summoned as a witness before a tribunal makes default in
> attending; or
> (b) being in attendance as a witness refuses to take an oath legally required by the
> tribunal to be taken, or to produce any document in his power or control legally
> required by the tribunal to be produced by him, or to answer any question to which
> the tribunal may legally require an answer; or
> (c) does any other thing which would, if the tribunal had been a court of law having
> power to commit for contempt, have been contempt of that court;
> the chairman of the tribunal may certify the offence of that person under his hand to the
> High Court, or in Scotland to the Court of Session, and the court may thereupon
> inquire into the alleged offence and . . . punish or take steps for the punishment of that
> person in like manner as if he had been guilty of contempt of the court.

S. 1(2)(b) of this Act was invoked at the time of the Vassall Tribunal to punish
certain journalists who had refused to answer questions on the ground that to do
so would disclose their sources of information.[19] There seems little doubt,
moreover, that s. 1(2)(c) of the Act is wide enough to encompass other types of
contempt ranging from disruptive conduct during the hearing of the tribunal, to
conduct which prejudices the ability of the tribunal to get at the truth or which
undermines public confidence in its impartiality.[20]

Similar provisions are contained in a number of other Acts. These include the
Army Act 1955, the Air Force Act 1955 and the Naval Discipline Act 1957, all of
which enable the president of a court-martial to certify as offences any acts done
in relation to the court-martial which would have been punishable as a contempt
if done in relation to a court of law.[1] Certification is not, however, a condition
precedent to the ability of the High Court to commit for contempt of a court-
martial.[2] Likewise the Parliamentary Commissioner Act 1967 effectively extends
the law of contempt through a similar process to cover investigations held by the
Commissioner under the Act,[3] while equivalent provisions cover the case of
inspectors directed to inquire into dangerous occurrences at nuclear installations
under the Nuclear Installations Act 1965, and persons appointed to inquire into
pipe-line accidents under the Pipe Lines Act 1962.[4]

These specific extensions of the law of contempt have apparently been adopted
on a purely random basis, rather than as part of a coherent pattern. Hence it must
be asked whether, in the absence of such a provision, the law of contempt is
capable of being applied to protect the deliberations of other decision-making

---

[19] See *Att.-Gen.* v. *Mulholland and Foster* [1963] 2 Q.B. 477; [1963] 1 All E.R. 767 discussed below,
p. 58.

[20] See the *Report of the Interdepartmental Committee on the Law of Contempt as it Affects Tribunals
of Inquiry*, Cmnd. 4078, June 1969, para. 12.

[1] See, respectively, the Army Act 1955, s. 101; Air Force Act 1955, s. 101; Naval Discipline Act
1957, s. 65(2). Courts-martial themselves have certain powers to punish persons subject to military
etc. law: see Borrie and Lowe, *Law of Contempt* (1973), p. 312.

[2] *Cf. Daily Mail (Editor), ex p. Farnsworth* [1921] 2 K.B. 733.

[3] See the Parliamentary Commissioner Act 1967, s. 9(1).

[4] See, respectively, the Nuclear Installations Act 1965, s. 22(5) and Sch., para. 7; the Pipe Lines Act
1962, Sch. 5, para. 7.

agencies which are not courts of law in the narrow sense. The general assumption certainly seems to be that it is not. Yet if this is correct the line delimiting the scope of the law of contempt is drawn at a singularly arbitrary point. There are, after all, few, if any, distinguishing features between 'courts' and 'tribunals'.[5] It is largely a matter of the terminology employed in the Act under which the body is constituted. Thus while the Restrictive Practices Court is specifically designated a 'superior court of record',[6] the Lands Tribunal Act 1949, s. 1 provides that that body shall be a 'tribunal'. Yet the importance of the decisions of the Lands Tribunal is such as to give it a status equivalent to most courts of law, and the same is true of other administrative tribunals which form an integral part of the machinery for adjudication in this country.[7]

If it were thought desirable to extend the scope of the law of contempt to protect the deliberations of such bodies this might theoretically be done under the present law by calling in aid the decision in *Davies*,[8] to which reference was made above. In this case the Divisional Court justified its assumption of jurisdiction to punish contempts committed in relation to inferior courts on the ground that this was a corollary of its power to supervise and correct those courts through the prerogative orders. Since control through the prerogative orders also extends (broadly speaking) to all bodies which exercise a 'judicial' or 'quasi-judicial' function (including administrative tribunals),[9] it might be argued that the contempt power of the Divisional Court can likewise be employed to protect the deliberations of such bodies.[10]

A more limited extension might be achieved by regarding the bodies protected by the law of contempt as being coextensive with those which are engaged in 'judicial proceedings' for the purposes of the Perjury Act 1911, that is bodies which have by law 'power to hear, receive, and examine evidence on oath'.[11] Alternatively, an analogy might perhaps be drawn with the position which has developed in the law of defamation. There the absolute privilege which attaches to statements made by persons taking part in court proceedings is recognised as extending to the proceedings of other bodies which exercise functions *equivalent to those of an established court of justice*. According to Devlin, L. J. in *Lincoln* v. *Daniels*,[12] 'the overriding factor' in a case of doubt 'is whether there will emerge from the proceedings a determination the truth and justice of which is a matter of public concern'. In this leading case the privilege was held to attach to disciplinary proceedings before Benchers of an Inn of Court, while in *Addis* v. *Crocker*[13] it was similarly held to attach to proceedings before the Disciplinary Committee of the Law Society.

[5] For a discussion of the characteristics of courts of law, see *United Engineering Workers' Union* v. *Devanayagam* [1968] A.C. 356, P.C.

[6] By the Restrictive Trade Practices Act 1956, s. 2(3).

[7] *Cf.* the *Report of the Committee on Administrative Tribunals and Enquiries*, Cmnd. 218, July 1957, para. 40.

[8] [1906] 1 K.B. 32, above, p. 30.

[9] See *Halsbury*, Vol. 1, para. 65 and sources there cited. The leading case is *Ridge* v. *Baldwin* [1964] A.C. 40.

[10] Yet in spelling out the jurisdiction of Divisional Courts R.S.C. Ord. 52, r. 1(2)(a)(iii) refers to 'proceedings in an inferior *court*' (emphasis supplied).

[11] See the Perjury Act 1911, s. 1(2).

[12] [1962] 1 Q.B. 237, 255–256; [1961] 3 All E.R. 740, 748, C.A.

[13] [1961] 1 Q.B. 11; [1960] 2 All E.R. 629, C.A.

(4) PUNISHMENT FOR CRIMINAL CONTEMPT[14]

Criminal contempt of court may be punished in the superior courts by committal for a fixed[15] but theoretically unlimited period of imprisonment, or by an unlimited fine, or by the taking of security for good behaviour.[16] In *Morris* v. *The Crown Office*,[17] where a group of young people had interrupted proceedings and had been sentenced to terms of imprisonment of up to three months, the Court of Appeal held that the then mandatory provisions relating to suspended sentences in criminal proceedings[18] had no application to criminal contempt of court.[19] Davies, L. J. suggested, moreover, that the general range of methods for dealing with offenders in criminal cases (including probation orders and detention centres) was likewise unavailable in a case of criminal contempt.[20] This suggestion must clearly carry considerable weight, but it may be noted that American courts have seen no obstacle to imposing probation orders in such cases.[1]

Theoretically certain inferior courts of record would also possess the same powers of unlimited imprisonment where a contempt is committed in the face of the court. In the case of county courts, however, the common law powers have been superseded by limited statutory powers. Thus the wilful interruption of proceedings in a county court may only be punished by a maximum term of imprisonment of one month or a fine not exceeding £20.[2] Equally where a contempt in relation to superior courts has been singled out for special statutory treatment the maximum penalty provided by the statute will, for practical purposes, be the maximum penalty for that offence. There can hardly be any question of continuing to deal with it as for a common law contempt. Examples falling within this category would include jurors or witnesses who fail to attend court in disobedience of an appropriate summons or order.[3]

The Phillimore Committee has proposed that the power to imprison for contempt should be limited to a maximum period of two years[4] but that no limit should be placed upon any fine which may be imposed.[5] In the case of county courts it further recommended that the present limits should be changed to a term of three months' imprisonment or a fine of £150.[6] Provision should also be made

---

[14] See also above, p. 10.

[15] *Att.-Gen.* v. *James* [1962] 2 Q.B. 637; [1962] 1 All E.R. 255.

[16] See *Skipworth's and the Defendant's Case* (1873) L.R. 9 Q.B. 230.

[17] [1970] 2 Q.B. 114; [1970] 1 All E.R. 1079.

[18] Under the Criminal Justice Act 1967, s. 39. See now the Powers of Criminal Courts Act 1973, s. 22.

[19] A committal order *may*, however, be suspended by the court in the exercise of its discretion: see R.S.C. Ord. 52, r. 7(1).

[20] [1970] 2 Q.B. 114, 127; [1970] 1 All E.R. 1079, 1085.

[1] See, e.g., *Frank* v. *U.S.*, 395 U.S. 147, 151–152 (1969).

[2] See the County Courts Act 1959, s. 157, above, p. 26.

[3] See the Juries Act 1974, s. 20 (jurors)—discussed below, p. 55; Criminal Procedure (Attendance of Witnesses) Act 1965, s. 3 (witnesses in criminal cases before the Crown Court)—discussed below, p. 56.

[4] Para. 201. The same limit is also suggested for the proposed statutory offences of taking reprisals against jurors or witnesses, noted below, p. 207.

[5] Para. 202.

[6] Para. 204. For the recommendation with respect to magistrates' courts, see above, pp. 26–27 and para. 37 of the report.

for dealing with the mentally disordered, as by an order under the Mental Health Act 1959, s. 60.[7]

At a more general level it should also be noted that since a committal order envisages the seizure of the offender's person by a tipstaff, who is a court official, and his conveyance to prison, it is obvious that a corporation or a similar body cannot itself be committed. As Darling, J. observed in *J. G. Hammond and Co. Ltd*,[8] 'the officer of the Court would not be able to put his hand upon that which has no corporeal existence'. On the other hand, there is no impediment to fining such a body or ordering it to pay the costs of the proceedings. An order to this effect may, moreover, be enforced by a writ of sequestration seizing the corporate property, or the personal property of the directors or officers, or ultimately by the committal of the director or officer himself.[9] Hence there is no lack of effective sanctions.

Even in the absence of any physical impediment to imprisoning an offender, English courts have not often found it necessary in recent years to resort to this extreme course, especially in the case of contempts committed by the news media. The usual outcome is either that no separate order is made against an individual such as an editor, or that a fine is imposed; or an order made for the payment of costs. Any committal order would normally be granted subject to the condition that its execution be suspended pending the payment of a fine within a given period of time. Sentences of imprisonment have admittedly been imposed in the past,[10] and threats of imprisonment have been made.[11] Nonetheless, it is felt that the *Justice* committee was somewhat overstating its case in agreeing in its report *The Law and the Press* (1965) that the danger of a prison sentence was a 'very real factor to be taken into consideration.[12] Committals to prison are admittedly more likely where a witness or juror has been threatened or victimised,[13] or where a contemnor has indulged in violent or obstructive behaviour in court.[14]

(5) APPEALS[15]

Provisions for appeal in cases of criminal contempt were introduced by the Administration of Justice Act 1960. During the second reading debate in the House of Lords opposition was expressed, notably by Lord Goddard, to the extension of the right of appeal to cases of contempt in the face of the court.[16] In the result the opposition did not prevail and this form of contempt was included

[7] Para. 203.

[8] [1914] 2 K.B. 866, 867.

[9] See R.S.C. Ord. 45, r. 5 and, in general, below, p. 242 *et seq.*

[10] *Cf. Bolam, ex p. Haigh* (1949) 93 Sol. Jo. 220; *Wilkinson, The Times*, 16 July 1930; *Higgins* v. *Richards* (1912) 28 T.L.R. 202.

[11] See, e.g., *Evening Standard (Editor), ex p. D.P.P.* (1924) 40 T.L.R. 833; *Surrey Comet, ex p. Baldwin* (1931) 75 Sol. Jo. 311.

[12] At p. 11.

[13] See *Re B (J.A.) (An Infant)* [1965] Ch. 1112; [1965] 2 All E.R. 168; *Moore* v. *Clerk of Assize, Bristol* [1972] 1 All E.R. 58.

[14] See *Morris* v. *The Crown Office* [1970] 2 Q.B. 114, and the cases of Mr William Cordiner (above, p. 24), and Mr David Crowley (below, p. 49).

[15] See also above, p. 15.

[16] See Hansard, H.L. Deb. Vol. 222, col. 277, 24 March 1960.

within the general provisions of the Act.[17] The system of appeal provided by s. 13 of the 1960 Act thus applies to all categories of contempt dealt with on summary process.[18] It may conveniently be summarised at this point.

(i) Appeals to a Divisional Court of the High Court

By the Administration of Justice Act 1960, s. 13(2)(a), an appeal lies to a Divisional Court of the High Court[19] 'from an order or decision of any inferior court', other than a court from which appeals generally lie to the Court of Appeal for which provision is made by s. 13(2)(b). The scope of s. 13(2)(a) is extended by defining the word 'court' to include 'any tribunal or person having power to punish for contempt'.[20] Appeals against committal for disobeying an order made by a magistrates' court under the Magistrates' Courts Act 1952, s. 54(3) lie to a Divisional Court of the Family Division.[1] Otherwise appeal lies to a Divisional Court of the Queen's Bench Division.[2] Clearly s. 13(2)(a) was primarily intended to provide for an appeal from a court of quarter sessions and since the abolition of these courts its scope has been considerably diminished. Indeed apart from appeals against orders made under s. 54(3) of the 1952 Act it is now singularly unlikely that there would be an appeal under s. 13(2)(a) at all. Appeals might, however, lie from a committal by a coroner's court.[3]

(ii) Appeals to the Court of Appeal

By s. 13(2)(b) of the 1960 Act, as amended, an appeal lies to the Civil Division of the Court of Appeal:[4]

. . . from an order or decision of a county court[5] or any other inferior court from which appeals generally lie to the Court of Appeal, and from an order or decision of . . . a single judge of the High Court, or of any court having the powers of the High Court or of a judge of that court . . . or (bb) from an order or decision of the Crown Court . . .[6]

---

[17] The avenue of appeal in such a case was used in *Morris* v. *The Crown Office* [1970] 2 Q.B. 114; [1970] 1 All E.R. 1079, and in *Balogh* v. *Crown Court at St. Albans* [1974] 3 All E.R. 283.

[18] S. 13(1) of the Act provides that in relation to appeals from orders or decisions of a court in the exercise of jurisdiction to punish for contempt the section 'shall have effect in substitution for any other enactment': see *Re Rudkin-Jones (a bankrupt)* [1964] 3 All E.R. 750n. By virtue of s. 13(6) of the Act, as amended, appeals against conviction or sentence in cases dealt with on *indictment* are subject to the provisions of Part I of the Criminal Appeal Act 1968. For a general discussion of the 1960 Act, see D. G. T. Williams, 'The Administration of Justice Act 1960' [1961] Crim. L.R. 87, 97–99.

[19] For the procedure on appealing, see R.S.C. Ord. 55, r. 3; Ord. 109, r. 2(4)(5). *Halsbury*, Vol. 9, para. 109.

[20] See s. 13(5) of the 1960 Act; Courts Act 1971, s. 56, Sch. 8, para. 40.

[1] R.S.C. Ord. 109, r. 2(2). S. 54(3) of the 1952 Act is concerned with penalties for disobedience of orders to do an act (other than the payment of money) or to abstain from doing an act.

[2] Ord. 109, r. 2(1).

[3] There might also possibly be an appeal from any such local inferior court of record as has survived the reforms introduced by the Courts Act 1971 and the Local Government Act 1972 and for which there was no general provision for an appeal to the Court of Appeal: see D. G. T. Williams, *op cit.*, p. 98.

[4] For the procedure when appeal lies to the C.A., see R.S.C. Ord. 59, r. 20(1); and, r. 19 (appeals from county courts), *Halsbury*, Vol. 9, para. 108.

[5] Made under the County Courts Act 1959, ss. 30, 127, 157, and (in so far as they confer jurisdiction in respect of contempt of court), ss. 74 and 195, but not under any other section: see Administration of Justice Act 1960, s. 13(5).

[6] For the amendment introducing (bb) see the Courts Act 1971, s. 56(1); Sch. 8, Part II, para. 40(1).

The reference to 'any other inferior court [apart, that is, from a county court] from which appeals generally lie to the Court of Appeal' would appear to be of little practical significance today. This is especially so since the abolition by the Courts Act 1971[7] of a number of local courts which had actively exercised a jurisdiction equivalent to that of county courts. Secondly, the provision for appeal to the Court of Appeal from an order of a single judge of the High Court obviously refers to appeals from fines or committal orders imposed by judges of the Queen's Bench Division, Chancery Division and Family Division.[8] Equally included within this category, however, are cases in which a single judge of the High Court is enpowered to punish as a contempt conduct which obstructs the administration of justice in certain designated tribunals such as a Tribunal of Inquiry appointed under the 1921 Act.[9] Thirdly, the reference to 'any court having the powers of the High Court or of a judge of that Court' includes the Restrictive Practices Court, and the Lord Chancellor and nominated judges acting under part VIII of the Mental Health Act 1959.[10]

(iii) Appeals to the House of Lords

By the Administration of Justice Act 1960 s. 13(2)(c), as amended,[11] provision is made for an appeal to the House of Lords from: 'an order or decision of a Divisional Court or the Court of Appeal (including a decision of either of those courts on an appeal under this section), and from an order or decision of the Courts-Martial Appeal Court . . .' Leave to appeal is required from either the House of Lords or the court below.[12] Where the appeal is from a decision of a Divisional Court or the Court of Appeal in the exercise of its *appellate* jurisdiction under s. 13(2)(a) or s. 13(2)(b), above, there is the further requirement that:[13]

> . . . such leave shall not be granted unless it is certified by the court below that a point of law of general public importance is involved in the decision and it appears to that court or the House of Lords, as the case may be, that the point is one which ought to be considered by that House.

Since the Divisional Court has by far the most extensive original jurisdiction in cases of criminal contempt of court, this direct right of appeal to the House of Lords is potentially of considerable significance. It is a curious paradox that in the years which have now elapsed since the Act came into force neither of the two appeals which have gone to the House of Lords have done so by virtue of this extension of the right of appeal. In the one case, *Heatons Transport (St. Helens) Ltd* v. *Transport and General Workers' Union*,[14] civil contempt was involved and provisions for appeal in such cases existed before 1960.[15] In the other case,

---

[7] Sections 42, 43.
[8] As in *Morris* v. *The Crown Office* [1970] 2 Q.B. 114; [1970] 1 All E.R. 1079.
[9] See further above, pp. 33–34.
[10] See the Restrictive Trade Practices Act 1956, s. 2(4), Sch., para. 10 and, in general, D. G. T. Williams, *op cit.*, p. 98.
[11] Criminal Appeal Act 1966, s. 1(6)(a).
[12] S. 13(4).
[13] S. 1(2); s. 13(4).
[14] [1973] A.C. 15, at p. 78; [1972] 3 All E.R. 101.
[15] *Cf.* above, p. 15.

Attorney-General v. *Times Newspapers, Ltd,*[16] the proceedings were by way of an *injunction* to restrain the publication of matter which would have constituted a criminal contempt. An appeal from a decision to grant or to deny an injunction would likewise have existed before 1960.[17]

Finally, the point may be made that in all cases falling under s. 13(2)(a), (b) or (c) an appeal lies at the instance of both the defendant and, 'in the case of an application for committal or attachment', the applicant.[18] The appeal court is empowered by s. 13(3) of the Act to 'reverse or vary the order or decision of the court below, and make such other order as may be just'. Provision is also made for releasing the appellant on bail on his giving security for his appearance.[19] The Phillimore Committee considered whether it should recommend the amendment of the 1960 Act so as to remove the applicant's present right of appeal, but decided against making such a recommendation.[20]

(6) THE INSTITUTION OF PROCEEDINGS

In so far as the actual institution of proceedings for criminal contempt is concerned, it is clear that no one body has a monopoly in the field. Thus leave to apply for a committal order may, for example, be sought by the party to the proceedings allegedly prejudiced,[1] or by a witness allegedly subjected to pressure to change her testimony.[2] Alternatively, it seems that it may equally be sought by an ordinary member of the public with no especial interest in the matter.[3] It has also been seen that a court may act *ex mero motu*, that is, of its own motion, in all cases of criminal contempt, and not only in cases of contempt committed in the face of the court itself where, of course, it would typically do so.[4]

The predominant role where contempt is committed in relation to criminal proceedings is, however, played by the Law Officers of the Crown. Indeed it has been suggested that criminal contempt of court should be included among those offences which can *only* be proceeded against by or with the consent of a Law Officer. Thus in *Hargreaves, ex parte Dill,*[5] where there was an unsuccessful application to commit the editor of the magazine *Lilliput*, Lord Goddard, C.J. is reported as saying that he had, 'always taken the view that it would be a good change if these actions were moved only by a Law Officer or on the instructions of

[16] [1974] A.C. 273; [1973] 3 All E.R. 54.

[17] Thus the case went via the Court of Appeal to the House of Lords and a certificate was not required.

[18] Administration of Justice Act 1960, s. 13(2). See, however, *Hoffman-la Roche & Co., Att-Gen.* v. *Sieczko* [1968] R.P.C. 460, 466, C.A.

[19] Administration of Justice Act 1960, s. 13(3), R.S.C. Ord. 59, r. 20(2)-(3)-(4); Ord. 109, r. 3(1)-(2); *Halsbury*, Vol. 9, para. 111.

[20] Para. 189.

[1] See, e.g., *Duffy, ex p. Nash* [1960] 2 Q.B. 188; [1960] 2 All E.R. 891; *Vine Products, Ltd* v. *MacKenzie and Co., Ltd.* [1966] Ch. 484; [1965] 3 All E.R. 58.

[2] *Re B. (J.A.) (An Infant)* [1965] Ch. 1112; [1965] 2 All E.R. 168.

[3] *Metropolitan Police Commissioner, ex p. Blackburn (No. 2)* [1968] 2 Q.B. 150; [1968] 2 All E.R. 319.

[4] Cf. *Skipworth's and the Defendant's Case* (1873) L.R. 9 Q.B. 230; *Fletcher, ex p. Kisch* (1935) 52 C.L.R. 248, 258 *per* Evatt, J. (High Ct. of Australia). See also R.S.C. Ord. 52, r. 5, which expressly preserves the power of the High Court and the Court of Appeal to act *ex mero motu*. The question is discussed further above, pp. 13, 28–29.

[5] [1954] Crim. L.R. 54; *The Times*, 3, 4, November 1953.

the Attorney-General, because the object is to punish an editor who has committed contempt, not to assist the defence'. Recommendations to the same effect were contained in two subsequent reports by committees of *Justice*.[6]

A different suggestion was advanced by Lord Denning, M.R. in delivering his judgment in the Court of Appeal in *Attorney-General* v. *Times Newspapers, Ltd.*[7] In his opinion, Lord Goddard's remarks were to be understood as referring to contempts committed in relation to *criminal* proceedings alone. Where civil proceedings were concerned it was, on the contrary, he thought, preferable to revert to the old practice of leaving the party aggrieved to move the court at his own expense and risk as to costs, unless the case was a very plain one. Phillimore, L.J. agreed with this opinion.[8] In the House of Lords, however, support for Lord Denning's distinction was markedly absent, and Lord Diplock summarised his own view, which corresponded with the view of the House as a whole, in the following terms:[9]

> My Lords . . . unlike the Court of Appeal, so far from criticising I commend the practice which has been adopted since 1954 as a result of the observations of Lord Goddard, C.J. in *R.* v. *Hargreaves, ex parte Dill*, whereby the Attorney-General accepts the responsibility of receiving complaints of alleged contempt of court from parties to litigation and of making an application in his official capacity for committal of the offender if he thinks this course to be justified in the public interest. He is the appropriate public officer to represent the public interest in the administration of justice.

It is submitted that the view of the House of Lords is to be preferred, reflecting, as it does, the fact that the public as a whole has an interest in seeing that the requirements for the due administration of justice are protected in civil proceedings as well as in criminal prosecutions. The Phillimore Committee took the same view while declining to adopt representations suggesting that the Attorney-General should have an exclusive jurisdiction to proceed in contempt cases. The Committee also believed it was desirable that the attention of the Attorney-General should be drawn to the matter before private proceedings were instituted.[10]

4 THE RECEPTION OF THE SUMMARY PROCESS INTO THE UNITED STATES AND SUBSEQUENT DEVELOPMENTS

(1) HISTORICAL BACKGROUND

By way of contrast with the relatively settled position in this country, the power to punish contempt summarily has had a particularly chequered history in the United States. This may be conveniently outlined at this stage as it is at least worthy of consideration whether some of the more recent developments could not be profitably adopted in this country.

---

[6] See, respectively, *Contempt of Court* (1959), p. 34; *The Law and the Press* (1965), para. 55.

[7] [1973] 1 Q.B. 727, 737–738; [1973] 1 All E.R. 815, 820–821.

[8] *Cf. ibid*, at p. 742 and p. 824.

[9] [1974] A.C. 273, 311; [1973] 3 All E.R. 54, 74.

[10] See paras. 184–187. The problems of entitlement to proceed were also discussed in the House of Commons in 1969. See Hansard, H.C. Deb. Vol 776, col 1727, 31 January 1969.

The writings of Blackstone, who had himself read the judgment of Wilmot, J. in *Almon*, were responsible for the initial reception of the summary process into the United States in the late 18th century. His influence can be clearly seen in the early case of *Respublica* v. *Oswald*[11] in 1788, where M'Kean, C. J. was called on to consider the jurisdiction of Pennsylvanian courts to punish imputations of partiality made against them. Having been referred by counsel to *Blackstone's Commentaries* and to *The St James's Evening Post Case*[12] he entertained no doubt that the jurisdiction existed.[13]

The existence of a power to proceed on summary process in Federal courts was also recognised by Congress in enacting s. 17 of the Judicature Act 1789, which provided: 'That all the said courts of the United States shall have power to . . . punish by fine or imprisonment, at the discretion of said courts, all contempts of authority in any cause or hearing before the same.' The power is generally regarded as having been abused, most notably in the famous *Peck-Lawless* case,[14] which led directly to the enactment of the statute forming the basis of the present Federal law. The background was that Judge Peck's adjudication in an important test case involving Missouri land claims was followed by the publication in a newspaper of what purported to be 'a concise statement of some of the principal errors' into which he had fallen. One Luke Lawless, an adventurer of Irish origins and one of the counsel involved in the litigation, was the person responsible. Believing, no doubt, that the publication would create an atmosphere of pronounced bias in cases which were still outstanding, Judge Peck held him guilty of contempt. He sentenced him summarily to one day's imprisonment, and suspended him from practice for eighteen months. Lawless thereafter promoted proceedings to impeach Peck; his charges were eventually taken up by the House of Representatives, and articles of impeachment were duly presented to the Senate. Peck was, in the result, acquitted by the narrowest of margins, though mainly, it appears, as a concession to his old age and infirmity.[15]

(2) LIMITATIONS IMPOSED BY LEGISLATION AND THE FEDERAL RULES OF CRIMINAL PROCEDURE

In the immediate aftermath of the *Peck-Lawless* case Congress passed the Federal contempt statute of 1831.[16] This Act, which was expressed as being declaratory of the common law, was modelled on Pennsylvania and New York legislation and it severely limited the scope of the summary power to punish contempt in Federal courts. With some modifications in terminology since the original, the Act provides in its present form in 18 U.S.C. s. 401 that:

[11] 1 Dallas 319 (1788). For a discussion of the case, see Nelles and King, 'Contempt by Publication in the United States' (1928) 28 Col. L.R. 410, 409–415. See also *Bayard and Petit* v. *Passmore*, 3 Yeates 439 (Pa. 1802); *Respublica* v. *Passmore*, 3 Yeates 441 (1802).

[12] (1742) 2 Atk. 469; 26 E.R. 683.

[13] See 1808–1809 Pa. Acts, c. 78, p. 146 for the subsequent curtailment of the power.

[14] For the background to the case, see Nelles and King, *op. cit.*, pp. 423–430; Frankfurter and Landis, 'Power of Congress over Procedure in Criminal Contempts in Inferior Federal Courts' (1924) 37 Harv. L.R. 1010, 1024–1029.

[15] The record of the impeachment proceedings is contained in Stansbury, *Report of the Trial of James H. Peck* (1833). Twenty-one senators voted for conviction and twenty-two for acquittal.

[16] For the text, see Frankfurter and Landis, *op. cit.*, at pp. 1031–1032; Nelles and King, *op. cit.*, at pp. 430–431.

A court of the United States shall have power to punish by fine or imprisonment, at its discretion, such contempt of its authority, and none other, as

(1) Misbehaviour of any person in its presence or so near thereto as to obstruct the administration of justice;

(2) Misbehaviour of any of its officers in their official transactions;

(3) Disobedience or resistance to its lawful writ, process, order, rule, decree, or command.

Obstruction to the administration of justice falling outside s. 401, as subsequently limited by further enactments,[17] is punishable, if at all, on indictment and is not susceptible to summary punishment as a contempt.[18]

In *Nye* v. *United States*[19] the Supreme Court held, overruling an earlier decision,[20] that the crucial 'so near thereto' phrase as used in the first sub-section of s. 401 should be construed in a narrow and geographical, rather than in a causative, sense. Thereby the court ensured that effect was given to the intent of the legislature, and that the summary method of procedure was confined within very narrow bounds in Federal law. In particular it was held to have no application to a contempt by publication.

The power of a court to subject an alleged contemnor to immediate committal, without the benefit of a formalised evidentiary hearing, is further restricted by the Federal Rules of Criminal Procedure. Rule 42 (a) provides that this course may only be followed if,

. . . the judge certifies that he saw or heard the conduct constituting the contempt and that it was committed in the actual presence of the court.

Otherwise rule 42 (b) requires the contempt to be prosecuted on notice, which must state the essential facts constituting the criminal contempt charged, grant the defendant a reasonable time for the preparation of his defence, and enable him to present and cross-examine witnesses.

Subsequent developments in recent years have placed still further limits on the power of a trial court judge to deal with a contemnor personally and without the benefit of an evidentiary hearing. Thus in *Mayberry* v. *Pennsylvania*,[1] the facts of which are mentioned below,[2] the Supreme Court held that a judge who has been

---

[17] A jury trial may be demanded as of right although the case would otherwise have come under s. 401 if the proceedings fall within the provisions of 18 U.S.C., s. 3692 (Norris-La Guardia Act—labour dispute cases) or s. 402 (Clayton Act). For a discussion of these provisions, see *U.S.* v. *Barnett*, 376 U.S. 681 (1964). See also the Civil Rights Act of 1957, 42 U.S.C., s. 1995; the Civil Rights Act of 1964, 42 U.S.C., s. 200hl and, in general, Goldfarb and Kurzman, 'Civil Rights and Civil Liberties: The Jury Trial Issue' 12 U.C.L.A.L. Rev. 486 (1965).

[18] Of particular importance is 18 U.S.C., s. 1503 which is closely modelled on s. 2 of the original Federal Act and which covers attempts to influence or injure officers, jurors or witnesses generally. See also 18 U.S.C., s. 201 (bribery of public officials and witnesses); s. 1501 (assault on process server); s. 1504 (influencing juror by written communication); s. 1509 (interference with Federal court orders).

[19] 313 U.S. 33 (1941).

[20] *Toledo Newspaper Co.* v. *U.S.*, 247 U.S. 402. See also *In re Independent Publishing Co.*, 240 Fed. 849 (1917); *U.S.* v. *Sanders*, 290 Fed. 428 (1923).

[1] 400 U.S. 455 (1971). See Note, 'Disqualification of Judge in Contempt Proceedings' (1971) 85 Harv. L.R. 293. See also *In re Dellinger*, 461 F. 2d 389 (1972); *Grizzell* v. *Wainwright*, 481 F. 2d 405 (1973).

[2] At p. 51.

subjected to personal vilification and abuse must disqualify himself from dealing with the contempt if he waits to act until after the end of the trial. As the court explained with reference to the facts of the case, this was required as a matter of due process because, '[A] judge, vilified as was this Pennsylvania judge, necessarily becomes embroiled in a running, bitter controversy. No one so cruelly slandered is likely to maintain that calm detachment necessary for fair adjudication.'[3] It seems, however, that notwithstanding his subjection to abuse, a judge may still deal with a contemnor personally, provided that he acts *instantly* and does not postpone the matter until the trial is over.[4] This distinction could be justified on the ground that the need to maintain order overrides other considerations.

It is not wholly clear whether a judge may commit summarily under rule 42 (a) after the trial has been completed where this element of personal insult or embroilment is absent. A clear affirmative answer was given by the Supreme Court in *Sacher* v. *United States*,[5] where it was held that if the conduct of the defendants warranted immediate summary punishment 'no possible prejudice to them can result from delaying it until the end of the trial if the circumstances permit such delay'.[6] A different view was, however, adopted in *Harris* v. *United States*[7] where the Supreme Court held that committal under rule 42 (a) was reserved for cases where there was such a 'serious threat to orderly procedure that instant and summary punishment, as distinguished from due and deliberate procedures . . . was necessary'.[8] On the facts of the case the court reversed the summary post-trial committal of a witness who had refused to testify and held that he was entitled to an evidentiary hearing under rule 42 (b). This latter view would appear to be more consistent with the rationale of the Federal Rules and it is supported by recent cases.[9]

Finally, it may also be noted that, although the above limitations do not impinge directly on the power of state courts in the United States, most state legislatures have themselves adopted similar constraints from the mid-19th century.[10] Moreover, many of the limitations would, in any event, be binding on the states as a part of the due process requirement posited by the Fifth Amendment. *Mayberry* v. *Pennsylvania*[11] itself provides a good illustration of this point.

---

[3] 400 U.S. 455, 465.

[4] *Cf. Mayberry* v. *Pennsylvania, ibid.*, at p. 463. See also *U.S.* v. *Seale*, 461 F. 2d 345, 351 (1972); *U.S.* v. *Meyer*, 462 F. 2d 827, 843 (1972). In *U.S.* v. *Marra*, 482 F. 2d 1196 (1973) it was emphasised that summary committal under rule 42(a) was only permissible where there had been a 'flagrant defiance of the person and presence of the Judge'.

[5] 343 U.S. 1 (1951).

[6] *Ibid.*, at p. 10. The case involved contempt by attorneys whose immediate committal might well have prejudiced their clients in the eyes of the jury.

[7] 382 U.S. 162 (1965).

[8] *Ibid.*, at p. 165. See also *Cooke* v. *U.S.*, 267 U.S. 517 (1925).

[9] See, e.g., *U.S.* v. *Meyer*, 462 F 2d 827 (1972). But see *Weiss* v. *Burr*, 484 F 2d 973 (1973) where a distinction is taken between the *citation* for contempt and the sentence—which, it is said, may be delayed. See also *U.S.* v. *Camil*, 497 F. 2d 225 (1974); *Groppi* v. *Leslie*, 404 U.S. 496 (1972).

[10] See Nelles and King, *op. cit.*, pp. 533–536. See also [1967] Duke L.J. 632, 654–655.

[11] 400 U.S. 455 (1971), above. See also *Johnson* v. *Mississippi*, 403 U.S. 212 (1971).

(3) CONSTITUTIONAL REQUIREMENTS

This is a convenient point to turn to the overriding requirements of the United States Constitution. Of particular importance to the question of jurisdiction and procedure is the right to a jury trial guaranteed by Article III, s. 2 of the Constitution and by the Sixth Amendment[12] and the prohibition, noted above, against depriving any person of 'life, liberty or property, without due process of law'. This due process requirement binds Federal and state courts alike by virtue of the Fifth and Fourteenth Amendments. Control over contempt by publication also has to contend with the substantive limitations imposed by the First Amendment guarantee of freedom of speech and of the press.

To trace the historical development in broad outline one can say that until comparatively recent years contempt of court was regarded as falling outside the protection afforded by the Constitution. In *United States* v. *Barnett*[13] the proceedings were fought against the background of an attempt by the negro student James Meredith to enter the University of Mississippi. A policy of deliberate non-compliance with court orders on the part of the governor of Mississippi led to a contempt citation in respect of which the Supreme Court eventually held that the petitioner was not entitled to a jury trial. The decision was that of a bare majority of the court, and doubts were expressed by members of the majority as to whether penalties in excess of those provided for petty offences could be imposed without affording an opportunity for a jury trial.[14] These doubts were later seized upon by the Supreme Court in *Bloom* v. *Illinois*[15] in 1968 as a preliminary to re-examining the issue. In this case the petitioner was alleged to have filed a forged will entitling a nurse whose patient had died to a substantial share of the estate. The offence was charged as a criminal contempt and an Illinois state court denied a request for a jury trial. A sentence of twenty-four months imprisonment was imposed on conviction. On a subsequent appeal to the Supreme Court, White, J., delivering the opinion of the court, agreed with the decision in *Barnett* in so far as it held that:[16]

> Criminal contempt, intrinsically and aside from the particular penalty imposed, was not deemed a serious offense requiring the protection of the constitutional guarantees of the right to jury trial.

He added, however,[17]

> . . . that the traditional rule is constitutionally infirm insofar as it permits other than petty contempts to be tried without honoring a demand for a jury trial . . . [In] our view, dispensing with the jury in the trial of contempts subjected to severe punishment represents an unacceptable construction of the Constitution.

[12] This binds state courts under the Fourteenth Amendment: see *Duncan* v. *Louisiana*, 391 U.S. 145 (1968) and following text.

[13] 376 U.S. 681 (1964). See also *Green* v. *U.S.*, 356 U.S. 165 (1958) and, in general, Frankfurter and Landis, 'Power of Congress over Procedure in Criminal Contempts in Inferior Federal Courts' (1924) 37 Harv. L.R. 1010.

[14] *Ibid.*, p. 695, note 12.

[15] 391 U.S. 194 (1968). See Note, 'Right to Jury Trial in Criminal Contempt Proceedings' (1968) 82 Harv. L.R. 153; Davis, 'The Contempt Power: The Barnett Dictum has Matured in Bloom, But is the Hybrid Viable?' (1969) 11 Arizona L.R. 501.

[16] 391 U.S. 194, 197.

[17] *Ibid.*, at p. 198.

Since a sentence of twenty-four months' imprisonment was regarded as a *severe* punishment Bloom's appeal was allowed.

In the result, therefore, it appears that summary proceedings are now only permissible in cases of criminal contempt coming before either state or Federal courts to the extent that they are sanctioned by the historical exception to entitlement to jury trial covering *petty* offences.[18] The point of demarcation between 'petty' and 'serious' offences is not a precise one, but within the Federal system a petty offence would generally be regarded as carrying a maximum of six months' imprisonment.[19] In state courts the dividing line is not so clear. Indeed in *Duncan* v. *Louisiana* the Supreme Court expressly declined to 'settle the exact location between petty offences and serious crimes' in this area.[20] Where no statutory maximum punishment is provided, as in the case of s. 401 of the present Federal Act, then one is required, in the words of White, J. in *Bloom* v. *Illinois*, 'to look to the penalty actually imposed as the best evidence of the seriousness of the offense'.[1] This solution may be open to theoretical objection on the ground that it requires the court to exercise what is, in effect, a prosecutorial function of designating the alleged contempt as 'petty' or 'serious' before proceeding to deal with it. Nonetheless it appears to represent a sensible and workable compromise in what has been a protracted debate.

The decision in *Bloom* v. *Illinois* has inevitably left several loose ends to be resolved. It has already been necessary to decide that the six month limitation does not prevent a contemnor from being subjected to a suspended sentence and period of probation in excess of six months.[2] At some stage the courts will have to resolve the question of whether the limitation is to be applied in cases of *civil* contempt where the court seeks to coerce the defendant into compliance through the imposition of an indefinite period of imprisonment. Finally, there is the problem of whether the six month limitation can be effectively bypassed by dealing with disruptive conduct in the face of the court as comprising a number of *distinct* offences warranting the imposition of separate short sentences to run *consecutively*, and total more than six months in all. This was the course adopted by Judge Hoffman in the notorious Chicago Conspiracy trial, which is discussed in more detail in the following chapter.[3] On appeal, however, the Court of Appeals reversed this decision and held that where a judge waits to act until the end of the trial, consecutively imposed sentences for contemptuous conduct occurring during the course of the preceding trial must be cumulated to de-

---

[18] Although *Bloom* v. *Illinois* arose out of the due process clause of the Fourteenth Amendment the same limitations would clearly apply to Federal courts under the Fifth and/or Sixth Amendments. In *Cheff* v. *Schnackenberg*, 384 U.S. 373 (1966) the Supreme Court had already indicated that it would limit the length of summary punishment for criminal contempt through the exercise of its general *supervisory* power to review proceedings in Federal courts.

[19] See 18 U.S.C., s. 1(3) and *Callan* v. *Wilson*, 127 U.S. 540 (1888); *Cheff* v. *Schnackenberg*, 384 U.S. 373, 379–380 (1966).

[20] 391 U.S. 145, 161–162 (1968).

[1] 391 U.S. 194, 211 (1968).

[2] See *Frank* v. *U.S.*, 395 U.S. 147, 151–52 (1969).

[3] See below, p. 52, and, in general, Clavir and Spitzer, *The Conspiracy Trial* (1971); Note (1971) 69 Mich. L.R. 1549.

termine the defendant-contemnor's right to a jury trial.[4] This aggregation principle would appear to more apt to give effect to the ruling of the Supreme Court in *Bloom* v. *Illinois* than was the course adopted at first instance. On the other hand the court also added that: '. . . where contemptuous conduct is cited and punished instantly, we think the punishment assessed for that conduct may be considered separately in determining the right to a jury trial.'[5]

Any anomalies created by this distinction might be justified by the need to avoid a situation in which an accused, intent on disrupting a trial, could rapidly use up the six month limit, and so deprive the trial court judge of all effective use of the contempt power. In any event, it must be emphasised, aggregate sentences in excess of six months are perfectly permissible in the United States if imposed after a jury trial has been held.

[4] See *U.S.* v. *Seale*, 461 F. 2d 345, 356 (1972). See also the companion case, *In re Dellinger*, 461 F. 2d 389, 397; *Matthews* v. *Florida*, 422 F. 2d 1046, 1048 (1970); *James* v. *Headley*, 410 F. 2d 325, 329 (1969), and, for a general discussion, see Dobbs, 'Contempt of Court: A Survey' (1971) 56 Cornell L.R. 183, 234.

[5] 461 F. 2d 345, 355 (1972). There is also the very considerable problem of determining what is a *distinct* contempt ((as opposed to a single continuous course of contemptuous behaviour) for present purposes: see *Yates* v. *U.S.*, 355 U.S. 66 (1957); *In re Oliver*, 452 F. 2d 111 (1971).

4 Contempt in the Face of the Court

1 INTRODUCTION

There is general agreement that a court of law must possess the ability to maintain an atmosphere conducive to judicial proceedings within the confines of the court itself. A case must be conducted within an orderly framework if justice is to be secured. In English law it is the law of contempt which has played the predominant role in achieving this goal, enabling, as it does, all courts of record to treat as a contempt conduct which interferes with the administration of justice in the court itself. The meaning of the term 'court of record', and the nature of the punishment which may be imposed have already been discussed in earlier chapters.[1] This chapter is intended to provide a number of examples of this aspect of the offence, and to discuss some of the issues raised by particular categories of potential offenders. It is also proposed to consider the desirability of the current summary procedure for dealing with contempts in the face of the court, and to note some of the other means which may be employed to maintain order.

2 EXAMPLES OF CONTEMPT IN THE FACE OF THE COURT[2]

(1) DISRUPTIVE BEHAVIOUR

One of the oldest examples of committal following the disruption of proceedings is to be found in an incident involving Gascoigne, C.J. and Prince Hal. It appears that the Prince, annoyed by the fact that one of his favoured servants had been arraigned before the Court of King's Bench, armed himself and appeared before the bar of the court in an attempt to secure his release. There he is said to have been met by an impassive Chief Justice who charged him to, 'desiste of your wilfulnes and unlaufull entreprise, and from hensforth gyue good example to those whiche hereafter shall be your propre subiectes'. Thereafter it seems that Gascoigne, C.J. committed the Prince to prison until the King's wishes were known, and that the Prince went as commanded. This story may or may not be authentic,[3] but it is certainly clear that any such disruption of proceedings, whether or not accompanied by an attempt to rescue a prisoner,[4] would constitute a contempt.

---

[1] *Cf.* above, pp. 25–27 and pp. 36–37 respectively.

[2] The section which follows is taken in part from an article by the author entitled 'Eggs, Tomatoes and the Welsh Language Demonstrators' [1970] Crim. L.R. 527. See also *Halsbury*, Vol. 9, para. 6.

[3] See Oswald, *Contempt of Court*, pp. 39–41 and sources cited.

[4] See also *The Earl of Thanet's Case* (1799) 27 State Tr. 821, for another attempt to rescue a prisoner.

(i) *Throwing missiles at or otherwise assaulting judges in court*

Another early and much cited example occurred in 1631 when a condemned felon appearing before Richardson, C.J. at Salisbury Assizes is reported as having 'ject un Brickbat a le dit Justice que narrowly mist'. The unfortunate man had the offending hand cut off in accordance with what was for many years the standard punishment for such an offence. It was then affixed to a gibbet on which he was subsequently hanged in the presence of the court as a punishment for the earlier felony.[5] In later years the punishment in respect of similar incidents has happily been less drastic, but the general principle remains intact. Any conduct which is seriously disruptive of court proceedings is likely to be punished as a contempt.

A further well known example involved an American citizen by the name of Robert Cosgrave who, in March 1877, threw an egg at Vice-Chancellor Malins as he was sitting in court.[6] Precisely what happened thereafter is not wholly clear. According to the version of the facts preferred by *Oswald's* leading historical work on the law of contempt, Malins is said to have remarked that 'the present must have been intended for his brother Bacon, V.-C.'. Sir John Fox believes that it is unlikely that a judge 'could have perpetrated such an unseemly jest from the bench'. His preferred version is that Malins simply asked, 'What was that?', and that Glasse, Q.C. informed him, 'An egg.' Thereafter, Sir John believes, the learned judge further inquired, 'Where did it come from?', to which Glasse responded, 'A hen, I presume.' It may be that 'unseemly jests' can be more readily imputed to a Queen's counsel than a Chancery judge, but, whatever the truth of the matter, Cosgrave was committed to Holloway prison. He was discharged some five months later to return to New York. As for Malins, V.-C., he emerged from the incident unscathed, which was especially fortunate since Cosgrave was later found to have been carrying a loaded pistol at the time.

Similar incidents have occurred in more recent years, though they rarely raise points of law, and hence are not normally reported. To take one or two examples. Lord Goddard recounted during the House of Lords debates on the Administration of Justice Bill in 1960 how a dissatisfied litigant had been committed to prison for six weeks after throwing tomatoes at members of the Court of Appeal.[7] He was, however, eventually released after some fifteen days. In March 1973 a somewhat more serious incident occurred in the Court of Appeal when one David Alfred Crowley responded to the dismissal of his appeal by leaping from the dock and attacking Mr Justice Brabin, whose wig and glasses were knocked off. He was brought back into court two hours later and sentenced to an additional nine months' imprisonment.[8] Less serious perhaps was the incident in February 1970 when a lady who had conducted her case in person reacted to the

---

[5] *Anon.* (1631) 2 Dyer 188bn; 73 E.R. 416. See also the similar incident involving one James Williamson, reported *sub nom. Anon.* (1634) Chester Docket Book (1603–1652) fo. 166, and cited in Oswald, *op. cit.*, at p. 42.

[6] *Re Cosgrave* (1877), Seton, *Judgments and Orders* (7th ed.) Vol. 1, p. 457 – discussed in Oswald, *op. cit.*, p. 42 and by Sir John Fox, 'The Practice in Contempt of Court Cases' (1922) 38 L.Q.R. 185–186.

[7] Hansard, H.L. Deb. Vol. 222, col. 277. See also Lord Denning, *ibid.*, col. 273, and Megarry, *Miscellany-at-Law* (1955), p. 295 for further incidents.

[8] See *The Times*, 2 March 1973. See also *The Times*, 18 November 1972, and 7 March 1973 for a similar incident involving one William Cordiner—discussed above, p. 24.

dismissal of her appeal by throwing her law books at the members of the Court of Appeal as they departed. Lord Denning, M.R. and his colleagues did not make an issue of the matter, but left the court with carefully measured tread.[9]

(ii) Assaulting other persons in court

All of the above cases have involved assaults of varying degrees of seriousness directed against judges. It is clear, however, that it may similarly be a contempt to assault or threaten any other person within the confines of the court, whether he be a juror, witness, party, advocate, official or a member of the general public. This was brought home to an accused in the case of *Craddock*[10] in a particularly poignant manner. Having secured an acquittal he turned to a fellow prisoner in the dock and said, 'I will give it you for this splitting on me'. He was thereupon sentenced to one year's imprisonment for contempt.[11]

(iii) Other forms of disruptive behaviour in court

Apart from conduct of this nature, other forms of disturbance, whether by outsiders or by parties to the proceedings, may equally constitute a contempt. There are several examples in the older cases of persons being dealt with for contempt following applause or other misconduct in the public gallery.[12] A more recent example of a less spontaneous disturbance is provided by the case of *Morris* v. *The Crown Office*.[13] Here a group of students from the University College of Wales at Aberystwyth travelled to London and entered Mr Justice Lawton's court at a time when he was hearing a libel action, which had attracted the attention of the press. There they sought to advance the cause of the Welsh Language Society, and to protest against an order imposed upon one of its leaders, by shouting slogans, scattering pamphlets, singing songs and breaking up the hearing. Order was eventually restored, and those who subsequently apologised were fined £50 and required to enter into recognisances to keep the peace. Those who felt unable as a matter of principle to do so were sentenced to three months' imprisonment for contempt of court.

On appeal to the Court of Appeal this sentence was regarded as being both permissible in terms of the existing legislation governing the sentencing of offenders,[14] and not unduly excessive having regard to the seriousness of the case. In the event, though, the Court decided to order the immediate release of the appellants, subject to a twelve month binding over order. This course was regarded as appropriate in view of the lack of any element of 'violence, vice or dishonesty' on their part, and the fact that this was the first time that such an incident had occurred in recent years. The Court nonetheless recognised that courts of law constituted convenient and well-publicised arenas for protests or

[9] *The Times*, 12 February 1970.

[10] *The Times*, 18 March 1875, cited in *Oswald, op. cit.*, at p. 45.

[11] See also *Wigley* (1835) 7 C. & P. 4; 173 E.R. 3 (party); *Purdin* v. *Roberts* (1910) 74 J.P. Jo. 88 (witness); *Carlion's Case* (1345) 2 Dyer 188b; 73 E.R. 416 (juror).

[12] See, e.g., *Stone* (1796) 6 T.R. 527; 101 E.R. 684, *Fox* v. *Wheatley* (1893) unreported, cited in Oswald, *op. cit.*, at p. 53.

[13] [1970] 2 Q.B. 114; [1970] 1 All E.R. 1079.

[14] See above, p. 36.

demonstrations, and would-be imitators were severely discouraged. As Salmon, L.J. noted:[15]

> Everyone has now been warned. If this sort of conduct is repeated by anyone in the future, whatever their motives, no excuse will be accepted, and a sentence of three months' or even six months' imprisonment should not, in my view, be regarded as in any way excessive.[16]

(2) INSULTING AND DISRESPECTFUL BEHAVIOUR

Direct interference with the administration of justice may be occasioned by some of the more extreme instances of insulting, as opposed to physically obstructive, behaviour. It was, however, emphasised by the Privy Council in *Parashuram Detaram Shamdasani* v. *King Emperor*[17] that the summary jurisdiction should only be invoked in extreme cases. In this case the High Court of Bombay had committed the appellant for contempt after he had responded to a suggestion that he was misleading the court when presenting his own case by saying, 'My fault is that I disclose everything, unlike members of the Bar, who are in the habit of not doing so and misleading the court'. On appeal the Privy Council had no hesitation in quashing the order. The words, though directed at the opposing counsel, clearly did not have the necessary tendency to interfere with the administration of justice. The opposite conclusion was reached in the old case of *Davison*[18] in 1821, where the Court of King's Bench upheld the imposition of fines imposed on a defendant who had attacked the Christian religion when defending himself on a charge of publishing a blasphemous libel. The language employed would hardly be regarded as insulting today,[19] but it was no doubt so regarded at the time.

Happily the reported English cases are but a pale reflection of some of their American counterparts. A notable example is provided by the case of *Mayberry* v. *Pennsylvania*.[20] Here the defendant in a criminal trial in a Pennsylvania state court displayed a certain monotony of language, and a penchant for canine epithets, by repeatedly insulting the presiding judge and calling him a 'dirty sonofabitch', 'dirty tyrannical old dog', 'stumbling dog' and a fool. He was sentenced summarily to the remarkable total of twenty-two years' imprisonment for contempt. The United States Supreme Court eventually reversed the decisions of the courts below on the basis of the important constitutional holding noted in the preceding chapter[1] that the trial court judge should have disqualified himself from dealing with the contempt since he had been subjected to personal insults.

---

[15] [1970] 2 Q.B. 114, 130; [1970] 1 All E.R. 1079, 1087.

[16] For another recent case, see *Balogh* v. *Crown Court at St. Albans* [1974] 3 All E.R. 283, C.A., above, p. 27.

[17] [1945] A.C. 264, P.C.

[18] (1821) 4 B. & Ald. 329; 106 E.R. 958.

[19] A fine of £40 was imposed following the observation: 'The Bishops are generally sceptics'. For further examples, see *Skinner* (1772) Lofft. 54; 98 E.R. 529; *Rogers* (1702) 7 Mod. Rep. 28; *Nuns* (1712) 10 Mod. Rep. 186.

[20] 400 U.S. 455 (1971).

[1] See above, p. 43.

Another notorious example is provided by the Chicago Conspiracy trial.[2] In August 1968 a group of several thousand demonstrators gathered in Chicago at the time of the Democratic National Convention which was being held to choose the Democratic presidential candidate. Their purpose was to protest against the Vietnam war, and the manner in which the convention was conducted. The week which followed was filled with violent clashes between the demonstrators and the police, and in its aftermath eight persons were indicted before Mr Justice Julius Hoffman on charges of incitement to riot. The trial lasted six weeks and its earlier stages were marked by the insistence of one of the defendants, Bobby Seale, that he should be entitled to represent himself in the absence of his chosen counsel, who was too ill to attend. He was denied the right to do so, Mr Justice Hoffman insisting that he was being represented by Mr Kunstler, who was acting for some of the other defendants. Seale's reaction to this denial led to his being eventually gagged and shackled in court, and to his referring to the judge as a 'racist, a fascist and a pig'. At the end of the trial some 175 separate contempt citations had been recorded against the several defendants and their counsel. A subsequent appeal succeeded in obtaining a reversal of the contempt sentences on the grounds that the judge should again have disqualified himself, and that he could not, in any event, impose aggregate sentences in excess of six months without affording an opportunity for a jury trial.[3] Both of these matters, which are peculiar to the law in the United States, have been discussed in more detail in the previous chapter.[4]

Extreme cases of non-verbal disrespect may also be regarded as having the necessary tendency to interfere with the administration of justice. An example is provided by the conduct of one of the accused in the Chicago trial who entered the courtroom dressed in judicial robes, which he later proceeded to remove, throw on the floor and wipe his feet on. He was sentenced to seven days' imprisonment for this conduct.[5] A similar sentence was imposed by the English Court of Appeal in *Gohoho* v. *Lintas Export Advertising Services,*[6] when an unsuccessful litigant expressed his feelings by undressing himself and prostrating himself naked before the court. Clearly where disrespect and a lack of decorum is in issue there can be no absolute standards, and the limits of permissible conduct will vary from time to time and from place to place. In recent Australian cases, for example, the raising of the right hand with clenched fist as a gesture of political solidarity has been held to be capable of constituting a contempt,[7] whilst a simple refusal to recognise the authority of the court has not.[8] A borderline case is presented by an accused who makes a point of refusing to stand on the judge's entry into court. This repeatedly occurred in the Chicago trial and was treated by Mr Justice Hoffman as a contempt.[9] A similar view was taken by the British

[2] *U.S.* v. *Dellinger, U.S.* v. *Seale*, No. 69 C.R. 180 (N.D. Ill., Feb. 14–15 1970). See, in general, Clavir and Spitzer, *The Conspiracy Trial* (1971).

[3] *U.S.* v. *Seale*, 461 F 2d 345; *In re Dellinger*, 461 F. 2d 389 (1972). In subsequent proceedings Judge Ginoux refrained from imposing a prison sentence on the contemnors: 357 F. Supp. 949 (1973) affd. 502 F.2d 813 (1974).

[9] See above, pp. 41–47.

[5] *Cf.* Clavir and Spitzer, *op. cit.*, at p. 613.

[6] *The Times*, 21 January 1964.

[7] See *Ex p. Tuckerman; Re Nash* [1970] 3 N.S.W.R. 23 (N.S.W. Sup. Ct., C.A.).

[8] See *O'Hair* v. *Wright* [1971] S.A.S.R. 436 (S.A. Sup. Ct.). See also *Royle* v. *Gray* [1973] S.L.T. 31.

[9] The same conclusion was reached in subsequent proceedings: see *In re Dellinger*, 502 F. 2d 813, 817 (1974).

Columbia Supreme Court in *Hume, ex parte Hawkins,*[10] where the conduct of the accused was characterised as a 'marked insult to the Court'. On the whole it would seem that the administration of justice can function without insisting that such courtesies be followed, and that the dignity of the court would normally be better served by refusing to make an issue of the matter.

Finally reference may be made to an incident involving Mr Justice Lawson and a certain Mr Bangs which occurred in May 1973. It was related by Bernard Levin in his own inimitable style as follows:[11]

> Mr Bangs has recently had his rates increased, and is, understandably enough, displeased in consequence. When, therefore, a large and official-looking car passed him, in which he saw a gentleman in colourful, not to say ridiculous, clothes, he suited his action to his feelings and extended the first and second fingers of his right hand, knuckles outwards, in its direction, believing that the gorgeously-caparisoned traveller was the Mayor. In this, it speedily appeared, he was mistaken, for the man at whom he had made his rude gesture was not only blameless in the matter of the rates; he was Mr Justice Lawson, on his way to clock in for the morning shift at Teesside Crown Court.

Mr Bangs was, it appears, taken along to the Crown Court and brought before Lawson, J. some two hours later to be informed that it was a serious matter and that there was jurisdiction to send him to prison. He was thereafter released. The incident has, perhaps, a more serious side for even assuming that Mr Bangs had intended to direct his time-honoured gesture at a person whom he knew to be a judge[12]—and this seems likely for a similar occurrence had apparently taken place the previous day—it would seem quite wrong to treat such conduct as a contempt. Any action which was considered necessary might be taken under the Public Order Act 1936, s. 5[13] or through invoking the binding-over procedure.

(3) CONTEMPT BY ADVOCATES

Acute problems may be posed in cases in which it is sought to hold an advocate in contempt in respect of his conduct in court. Here one of the most celebrated of all cases centred on the conduct of Erskine when acting for the defence in the case of the *Dean of St. Asaph* in 1784. The case arose out of a prosecution for publishing an allegedly seditious libel entitled 'A Dialogue between a Gentleman and a Farmer', the object of which was to promote parliamentary reform. After an eloquent speech by Erskine to the jury on the importance of the liberty of the press, and his conception of their role in such cases, Mr Justice Buller directed them that their sole function was to determine whether or not the defendant had published the tract. The question of 'libel or no libel' was for him to decide. The jury returned a verdict of 'Guilty of Publishing only', which the learned judge was not prepared to accept, but which Erskine insisted should be recorded in that form. After the jury had made it clear in response to questions that they intended

---

[10] [1966] 3 C.C.C. 43; *sub. nom. Re Hawkins' Habeas Corpus Appln.* (1965) 53 W.W.R. 406. See also *U.S.* v. *Malone*, 412 F. 2d 848 (1969)—nuns refusing to stand held in contempt; *In re Chase*, 468 F. 2d 128 (1972).

[11] See 'Two Fingers and the Long Arm of the Law', *The Times*, 24 May 1973.

[12] For *mens rea*, see below, pp. 62–63.

[13] Insulting conduct likely to cause a breach of the peace. But *quaere* as to the likelihood of a breach of the peace?

the verdict to mean that the defendant had published the tract, but no more, the following exchange took place:

> Erskine: 'The jury do understand their verdict.'
> Buller, J.: 'Sir, I will not be interrupted.'
> Erskine: 'I stand here as an advocate for a brother citizen, and I desire that the word *only* may be recorded.'
> Buller, J.: 'Sit down, Sir; Remember Your Duty, or I shall be obliged to proceed in another manner.'
> Erskine: 'Your Lordship may proceed in what manner you think fit; I know my duty as well as your Lordship knows yours. I shall not alter my conduct.'

Mr Justice Buller did not repeat his threat of committal, and Erskine's conduct has frequently been cited as illustrating the need for an independent and courageous Bar.[14] While it would be difficult to overstate the importance of this principle, it is nevertheless clear that in extreme cases an advocate may be regarded as going beyond commendable firmness and as indulging in contemptuous conduct. Thus in *Ex parte Pater*[15] the Court of Queen's Bench refused to interfere when a court of quarter sessions had imposed a £20 fine on counsel for imputing bias to the foreman of the jury. The presiding judge had taken the view that the conduct was deliberately insulting and went beyond a legitimate attempt to protect his client's interests. Similarly, and in more recent years, the Supreme Court of New South Wales has refused to interfere where the chairman of Sydney quarter sessions had fined a counsel whom he believed was misconducting himself in an attempt to get himself expelled from court, thus having the jury dismissed and securing a retrial. The Court summarised the position in the following terms:[16]

> If the words were harsh and disrespectful to the judge, although in breach of good manners, they may have been within the legal right and privilege of counsel. Counsel may, for instance, in appropriate circumstances and in a proper manner request the judge to refrain from interfering with his cross-examination at what he honestly believes to be a critical point. But if his words took the form of insults to the judge or of setting at defiance his ruling as to the discharge of the jury, or if the manner of their utterance was insulting and offensive, then they could amount to an abuse of a barrister's privilege and the judge might treat the utterances as contempt and deal with them accordingly.

The borderline between an expression of firmness or mere discourtesy, on the one hand, and, on the other, a contempt through direct and substantial interference with the administration of justice, is inevitably a difficult one to draw. In modern Commonwealth cases advocates have been held in contempt through a persistent refusal to accept a court's ruling,[17] and through absenting themselves

---

[14] *Cf.* Campbell. *The Lives of the Lord Chancellors*, 4th ed. (1857), Vol. VIII, p. 277.

[15] (1864) 5 B. & S. 299; 122 E.R. 842. See also *Carus Wilson's Case* (1845) 7 Q.B. 984; 115 E.R. 759; and cases cited in *Halsbury*, Vol. 9, para. 6.

[16] *Ex p. Bellanto; Re Prior* (1963) 63 S.R. (N.S.W.) 190, 203 (N.S.W. Sup. Ct.). See also *Re Shumiatcher*, Q.C. [1969] 1 C.C.C. 272; (1968) 64 W.W.R. 743 (Saskatchewan C.A.). Leading American cases include *In re Halliman*, 459 P. 2d 255; 81 Cal. Rptr. 1 (1969); *U.S.* v. *Schiffer*, 351 F. 2d 91 (1965); *In re McConnell*, 370 U.S. 230 (1962); *U.S. ex rel. Robson* v. *Oliver*, 470 F. 2d 10 (1972).

[17] *Cf. Lloyd* v. *Biggin* [1963] V.L.R. 593 (Vict. Sup. Ct.) where, however, the verdict was set aside on procedural grounds.

from court without excuse or justification.[18] The apparent absence of recent English cases suggests that professional etiquette, coupled with a recognition by the judiciary of the importance of an independent Bar, work together to minimise the possibility of confrontation.

A barrister or solicitor who so conducts a case as knowingly to become a party to fraud, or to deceiving the court, may be dealt with for contempt as well as finding himself subjected to professional discipline.[19] Likewise some of the older cases provide examples of contempts being committed through the drawing up or signing of pleadings which were regarded as scandalous or frivolous. In *Everet* v. *Williams*,[20] for example, it seems that solicitors were attached and fined after filing a bill in the Court of Exchequer whereby one highwayman sought an account of partnership profits from another. The same fate was suffered by a person who pleaded infancy as a defence to an action of ejectment when it was found 'by sufficient proof, by oath, and by examination of the church book, that he was of the age of 63 years'.[1]

(4) CONTEMPT BY JURORS

It is also clear that jurors may commit a contempt. *Oswald* recounts several examples,[2] ranging from cases in which the jury determined its verdict by 'hustling halfpence in a hat'[3] to cases of jurors eating sugar candy in court,[4] and absenting themselves from court without leave. Within this latter category the author relates an incident involving Mr Justice Gould when he was trying a case at York. It appears that whilst the case was still in progress he noticed that there were only eleven persons in the jury box, and that on asking the foreman where the twelfth might be the latter disarmingly replied: 'Please, my Lord, the other has gone away about some business he had to do, but he has left his verdict with me.'[5] In a more recent Canadian case[6] a juror was committed to prison for some thirty days after he had arrived at court intoxicated having drunk two quarts of beer.

The general principles of contempt no doubt retain a residual importance in such cases in English law, but most incidents would be dealt with under s. 20(1) of the Juries Act 1974.[7] This section provides that,

(a) if a person duly summoned under this Act fails to attend (on the first or on any subsequent day on which he is required to attend by the summons or by the appropriate officer) in compliance with the summons, or

[18] *McKeown* (1971) 16 D.L.R. (3d) 390 (Sup. Ct. of Canada). *Cf. Izuora* [1953] A.C. 327, P.C.
[19] See, e.g., *Linwood* v. *Andrews and Moore* (1888) 58 L.T. 612; *Weiz* [1951] 2 K.B. 611. See also *Abraham* v. *Jutson* [1963] 2 All E.R. 402, 404 *per* Lord Denning, M.R.
[20] (1725): see (1893) 9 L.Q.R. 197 and Megarry, *Miscellany-at-Law* (1955), at p. 76 *et seq.*
[1] *Lord* v. *Thornton* (1614) 2 Bulst. 67; 80 E.R. 965. See, in general, *Oswald, op. cit.,* at pp. 61–62; *Halsbury*, Vol. 9, para. 43 and cases there cited.
[2] *Contempt of Court*, pp. 67–70.
[3] *Langdell* v. *Sutton* (1737) Barnes 32; 94 E.R. 791.
[4] *Weleden* v. *Elkington* (1578) Plowd. 516, 518a; 75 E.R. 763. See also *Burdett* (1697) 1 Ld. Raym. 148; 91 E.R. 996. (Jury taking evidence with them, without the consent of the court, when retiring.)
[5] *Op. cit.,* at p. 69. See also *Rhoder, The Times,* 12 February 1894 cited in *Halsbury*, Vol. 9, para. 44, para. 6(6).
[6] *Rodgers, Re Reynolds* (1952) 103 C.C.C. 168.
[7] This provision effectively reproduced the earlier s. 38(1) of the Courts Act 1971.

(b) if a person, after attending in pursuance of a summons, is not available when called on to serve as a juror, or is unfit for service by reason of drink or drugs,

he shall be liable to a fine not exceeding £100. By s. 20(2) such conduct may be punished either following conviction in a magistrates' court, or as if it were a criminal contempt committed in the face of the court itself. Provision is also made in s. 20(4) of the Act for the juror who can show 'some reasonable cause for his failure to comply with the summons, or for not being available when called on to serve'.[8]

It is also an offence punishable on indictment or summarily as a contempt to impersonate a juryman and to act in his stead. So much was decided in *Clark*,[9] where the defendant, a farm bailiff, took the oath in the name of his employer to save him the trouble of appearing. Likewise a juror will commit an offence in consenting to embracery, that is, to an attempt to persuade him to reach a verdict otherwise than on the basis of evidence and argument adduced in open court.[10]

(5) CONTEMPT BY WITNESSES[11]

(i) *Failure to attend court or to produce documents*

Witnesses may also commit a contempt in various different ways. They may, for example, fail to attend court or to produce a document, without circumstances of justification, and in disobedience of a subpoena *ad testificandum*, a subpoena *duces tecum* or a county court summons. In the former case there is no theoretical limit to the punishment which may be imposed, but disobedience of a county court summons is punishable by a maximum fine of £50.[12] In a criminal case a contempt may be committed through disobedience of a witness order or a witness summons requiring attendance before the Crown Court. In this eventuality s. 3 of the Criminal Procedure (Attendance of Witnesses) Act 1965, as amended,[13] provides for summary punishment by that court as if the contempt had been committed in the face of the court itself. A maximum term of three months' imprisonment may be imposed.

(ii) *Refusal to be sworn or to answer questions*

A contempt may equally be committed by a witness who, being compellable, refuses to be sworn,[14] or who refuses to answer a question which a court, or a body possessed of the necessary statutory powers,[15] may lawfully require him to

[8] For contempt by a juror in refusing to be sworn or to give a verdict, see 2 Hawk P.C. (8th ed.), c. 22, s. 115.

[9] (1918) 82 J.P. 295 (Avory, J.). See also *Levy* (1916) 32 T.L.R. 238, D.C., where such conduct was dealt with summarily as a contempt.

[10] See further, below Ch. 7, p. 94. For attempts to exert improper influence upon a fellow juror, see *Re M.M. and H.M.* [1933] I.R. 299.

[11] See Borrie and Lowe, pp. 24–32; Oswald, pp. 63–66; *Halsbury*, Vol. 9, paras 6 and 70.

[12] See the County Courts Act 1959, s. 84(1) and the Administration of Justice Act 1969, s. 11(3). It seems that: 'Failure to attend the court in civil proceedings will only amount to a contempt if full conduct money has been tendered with the subpoena': *Halsbury*, Vol. 9, para. 70.

[13] By the Courts Act 1971, s. 56, and Sch. 8 Part II, para. 45(1).

[14] *Hennegal* v. *Evance* (1806) 12 Ves. 201; 33 E.R. 77.

[15] As, e.g., a tribunal of inquiry appointed under the Tribunals of Inquiry (Evidence) Act 1921. See further *Halsbury*, Vol. 9, para. 70, note 1.

answer,[16] or who remains in court after being ordered to leave.[17] A detailed discussion of the various grounds on which a witness may claim to be privileged against answering a question, or disclosing a document, falls outside the scope of this work,[18] although the particular problem of the journalist who seeks to protect his sources of information will be considered below.[19]

(iii) *Contempt and perjury*

There is also a difficult borderline to be drawn in this area between a contempt through a refusal to answer a question, and perjury through the making of a statement known by the witness to be false, or not believed by him to be true.[20] Here it may be said at the outset that an answer to a question may be so evasive as to be regarded as a simple refusal to reply and hence a contempt. This approach may be especially appropriate in bankruptcy proceedings or proceedings to wind up a company, where the coercive power of the law of contempt is well suited to assist in the discovery of assets.[1] On the other hand it would be equally wrong for a court to treat a witness as being in contempt simply on the basis that it is convinced he is lying. The point was emphasised by the High Court of Australia in *Coward* v. *Stapleton,*[2] where it was said that it was 'essential not to lose sight of the sharp distinction that exists between a false answer and no answer at all'. The court added:[3]

> Of course a purported answer may be so palpably false as to indicate that the witness is merely fobbing off the question. . . . In such cases it may well be right to say that the witness refuses to answer the question,[4] but it cannot be too clearly recognised that the remedy for giving answers which are false is normally a prosecution for perjury or false swearing, and not a summary committal for contempt.

The need to draw this distinction and to keep the contempt power within its proper confines has likewise been recognised in a series of American cases.[5] Thus in *Re Michael,*[6] for example, the Supreme Court reversed the decision of a District Court which had held the petitioner in contempt after he had willingly and unequivocally given what the court took to be false answers to questions put by a grand jury. As Mr Justice Black observed, deliberate falsehoods did not

---

[16] *Ex. p. Fernandez* (1861) 10 C.B. (N.S.) 3; 142 E.R. 349; *Att.-Gen.* v. *Clough* [1963] 1 Q.B. 773. *Semble* that the contempt thus committed is criminal in nature. Magistrates' courts are empowered by the Magistrates' Courts Act 1952, s. 77(4) to commit the recalcitrant witness for a maximum term of seven days. For county courts, see County Courts Act 1959, s. 84(1)(b).

[17] *Chandler* v. *Horne* (1842) 2 Mood & R. 423; 174 E.R. 338.

[18] See Cross, *Evidence*, 4th ed., 1974, Ch. XI. *Quaere* whether D has committed a contempt if he has refused to answer a question and privilege has been wrongly denied? *Cf. Ex p. Fernandez* (1861) 10 C.B. (N.S.) 3, 40 *per* Willes, J; *Boyes* (1861) 1 B. & S. 311, 121 E.R. 730.

[19] At p. 58 *et seq.*

[20] The offence of perjury is defined in the Perjury Act 1911, s. 1(1).

[1] For the procedure in such cases, see, respectively, The Bankruptcy Rules 1952 (S.I. 1952 No. 2113), r. 83 and The Companies (Winding-Up) Rules 1949 (S.I. 1949 No. 330), r. 73. See also *Halsbury*, Vol. 9, para. 72 and 73, respectively.

[2] (1953) 90 C.L.R. 573.

[3] *Ibid.*, at pp. 578–79.

[4] *Cf. U.S.* v. *Appel*, 211 F. 495, 495–496 (1913) *per* Learned Hand., J.

[5] Reviewed by Dobbs, 'Contempt of Court: A Survey' (1971) 56 Cornell L.R. 183, 194–200.

[6] 326 U.S. 224 (1945). See also *Ex p. Hudgings*, 249 U.S. 378 (1919).

obstruct the administration of justice to the same extent as a simple refusal to answer. A court is equipped to deal with the former, and to sift the true from the false with the aid of the process of cross-examination. It is not equipped to deal with the witness who fails to give what can be regarded as a reasonably full reply.[7]

(iv) *Journalists and their sources of information*

The position of a journalist who refuses to answer a question or to disclose a document on the ground that he is protecting his sources of information was considered by the Court of Appeal in *Attorney-General* v. *Mulholland and Foster*.[8] The case arose out of the conviction of an Admiralty clerk, William Vassall, on charges of communicating secret information to the Russians. Vassall's trial had been surrounded by adverse publicity for the Admiralty and the security service because it was widely suggested that he had lived in a way which should have marked him out as an obvious security risk. Partly to allay the public disquiet the Home Secretary set up a tribunal of inquiry under the chairmanship of Lord Radcliffe and with widely drawn terms of reference. It was to inquire, inter alia, into any allegations which reflected upon the honour and integrity of persons who, as ministers, naval officers or civil servants were concerned in the case, and into any neglect of duty by persons who were responsible for Vassall's conduct and his employment on security work.

During the course of its deliberations the tribunal called upon several journalists, who had written articles on Vassall, to disclose their sources of information. Desmond Clough, the defence correspondent of the *Daily Sketch*, Reginald Foster, a freelance writer retained by the same newspaper, and Brendan Mulholland of the *Daily Mail* all declined. Their conduct was certified by Lord Radcliffe to the High Court in accordance with the provisions of the Tribunals of Inquiry (Evidence) Act 1921,[9] and they were sentenced to terms of imprisonment of up to six months. Clough, who had written that, 'Vassall's spying led to Russian trawler spying fleets turning up with uncanny accuracy in the precise area of the secret N.A.T.O. sea exercises' had the good fortune to be released after a few days when his informant, an Admiralty employee, came forward to give evidence to the tribunal himself. Mulholland, who had asserted that, 'it was the sponsorship of two high-ranking officials which led to Vassall avoiding the strictest part of the Admiralty's security vetting' was less lucky, and he appealed, together with Foster, to the Court of Appeal. There they sought to establish, inter alia, that they enjoyed a privilege as journalists to refuse to disclose sources of information which had been given to them in confidence. The court had no difficulty in holding that it was relevant to the tribunal's inquiry to elicit the sources of such information and, moreover, that no privilege against disclosure existed.

There can be no doubt that this decision creates problems for the press and the

---

[7] *Cf.* however, *Smith* v. *Bond* (1845) 13 M. & W. 594, 596, 153 E.R. 248 where Alderson, B. is reported as saying, *arguendo,* 'Persons giving false testimony in Court are frequently committed for contempt.' See also *Apted* v. *Apted and Bliss* [1950] P. 246, 263 *per* Lord Merrivale, P.

[8] [1963] 2 Q.B. 477; [1963] 1 All E.R. 767. See, in general, Tapper (1963) 26 M.L.R. 571; Goodhart (1963) 79 L.Q.R. 167.

[9] See above, Ch. 3, pp. 33–34.

other news media and that it places the journalist in an invidious position. He must either run the risk of committal for contempt, or act in breach of what is accepted, rightly or wrongly, as a basic tenet of the code of ethics applicable to his profession. The point was well expressed in a leading article in *The Times* commenting on a sentence of four days' imprisonment for contempt imposed by a Belfast court on Mr Bernard Falk, a BBC television reporter. Mr Falk had refused to identify a man who had appeared in the *Twenty-Four Hours* programme and who was claimed to be a member of the IRA. *The Times* commented:[10]

> Had Mr Falk not promised to keep secret the identity of those appearing on the programme he would no doubt have been unable to persuade members of the IRA to take part. Had he given such an undertaking and then broken it under pressure from the court his act would not only have been a breach of personal faith but would also have been harmful to the practice of good journalism in the future. . . . The principle does matter. Without it serious reporting would be impossible. The graver the abuse that is under scrutiny the more likely it is that nobody will reveal discreditable facts unless he can be sure that his identity will be kept absolutely secret. . . . In politics the whole system of information depends on the respect for confidences.

Only the profoundest sceptic would dismiss this view as being based entirely on special pleading. Yet it is difficult to see how the court could have reached the opposite conclusion. Clergymen, doctors and bankers can all be required to divulge confidences where this is considered to be essential to the due administration of justice, and the case for according privilege to a journalist cannot realistically be pitched at a higher level. This certainly does not mean that disclosure will be required as a matter of course. As Lord Denning explained in the *Mulholland* case: 'The judge will respect the confidences which each member of these honourable professions receives in the course of it, and will not direct him to answer unless not only it is relevant but also it is a proper and, indeed, necessary question in the course of justice to be put and answered.' His Lordship added, however, that at the end of the day:[11]

> A judge is the person entrusted, on behalf of the community, to weigh these conflicting interests—to weigh on the one hand the respect due to confidence in the profession and on the other hand the ultimate interest of the community in justice being done or, in the case of a tribunal such as this, in a proper investigation being made into these serious allegations.

A more recent incident arose out of a successful claim for damages for personal injuries suffered during the Windsor Great Park Pop Festival in August 1974. Judge Duveen had ordered ITN to produce all of the film taken over the three days of the festival and the order had been disobeyed. In subsequent proceedings[12] the Court of Appeal confirmed the existence of a general power to require the production of news film (whether transmitted or not) when it was likely that it

---

[10] *The Times*, 5 May 1971.
[11] [1963] 2 Q.B. 477, 489–90; [1963] 1 All E.R. 767, 771. See also *Att.-Gen.* v. *Clough* [1963] 1 Q.B. 773, 792; [1963] 1 All E.R. 420, 427–428, *per* Lord Parker, C.J.
[12] *Senior* v. *Holdsworth, ex p. ITN* [1975] 2 W.L.R. 987.

would play an important or useful part in the proceedings. In the result, however, ITN's appeal was allowed on the ground that the order was too wide and oppressive.[13]

The same conclusion denying privilege has also been reached in other common law jurisdictions including Australia[14] and, in more recent years, the United States. The leading American decisions are *Branzburg* v. *Hayes* and the two companion cases of *United States* v. *Caldwell* and *In re Pappas*.[15] The background to the former case was that Paul Branzburg, a newspaper reporter from Kentucky, was responsible for the publication of an article depicting the manufacture of hashish in Jefferson County. The article was accompanied by a photograph of a pair of hands working with a substance described as hashish, and a statement that he had promised not to reveal the identity of those involved. Branzburg subsequently refused to act in breach of this undertaking when subpoenaed to appear before a grand jury investigating the manufacture and use of drugs in the area. Caldwell, a *New York Times* reporter covering the activities of the Black Panther Party and other militant groups, had been ordered to appear before a grand jury in California and to bring with him notes and tape recordings of interviews with spokesmen of the Black Panthers. The grand jury was investigating alleged offences including attempts to assassinate the President. Caldwell, like Branzburg, refused to appear and to divulge his sources. The *Pappas* case arose out of a similar background.

Dealing with the claims to privilege in these cases the United States Supreme Court held that journalists did not enjoy an absolute privilege against disclosing their sources to a grand jury, whether at common law or as an integral part of the constitutional protection of the First Amendment guaranteeing freedom of the press. Neither, in the view of a majority of the court, did they enjoy a qualified privilege whereby the government was compelled to show an overwhelming reason for requiring the information, and that it could not be obtained in other ways less destructive of First Amendment rights. All that the majority of the court was prepared to concede was that privilege should be accorded where the investigation was 'instituted or conducted other than in good faith', or in furtherance of a policy of 'harassment of the press undertaken not for the purposes of law enforcement but to disrupt a reporter's relationship with his news sources'.[16]

This denial of privilege has generally been received critically and not only by the news media, as one would expect, but also by commentators in the leading law journals.[17] It appears, however, that disclosure is not being ordered as a matter of course at least in civil cases as opposed to grand jury criminal in-

---

[13] For editorial comment, see (1975) New Law Jo. 54.

[14] See *McGuinness* v. *Att.-Gen. of Victoria* (1940) 63 C.L.R. 73, at pp. 102–103 especially, *per* Owen Dixon, J. (High Ct. of Australia).

[15] 408 U.S. 665 (1972).

[16] *Ibid.*, at 707–708.

[17] For a general discussion of the issues involved, see Blas, 'The Newsman's Privilege: An Empirical Study (1971) 70 Mich. L.R. 229; Note, 'Reporters and Their Sources: The Constitutional Right to a Confidential Relationship' (1970) 80 Yale L.J. 317. Note, 'Newsmen's Privilege to Withhold Information from Grand Jury' (1972) 86 Harv. L.R. 137.

vestigations.[18] Moreover legislation granting a privilege has been enacted in a number of states.

(6) PHOTOGRAPHS, PORTRAITS AND SKETCHES IN COURT[19]

A brief reference may also be made to the provisions of the Criminal Justice Act 1925 which cover the taking of photographs and the making of sketches in court. By s. 41(1) of the Act, no person shall:

(a) take or attempt to take in any court[20] any photograph, or with a view to publication make or attempt to make in any court any portrait, or sketch, of any person, being a judge[1] of the court or a juror or a witness in or a party to any proceedings before the court, whether civil or criminal; or

(b) publish any photograph, portrait or sketch taken or made in contravention of the foregoing provisions of this section or any reproduction thereof; . . .

A maximum fine of £50 may be imposed on summary conviction for each offence.

Whatever the precise limits of this prohibition (and these are by no means clear), s. 41(2)(c) of the Act extends them to cover both photographs and sketches taken 'in the building or in the precincts of the building in which the court is held', and photographs and sketches of persons entering and leaving the court or its precincts. Such photographs and sketches are deemed to have been taken or made in the court itself. This latter provision seems to be honoured more in the breach than in the observance, in view of the appearance every day of newspaper photographs and television shots of accused persons entering court, frequently with blankets over their heads.

As has been intimated, s. 41 poses difficulties of interpretation and its overall objective is far from clear. Portraits and sketches are only prohibited if two conditions are satisfied, namely (i) that they are made of a judge, juror, witness or party; and (ii) that they are made with a view to publication. Hence sketching a member of the general public in court is not an offence under the Act, even though done 'with a view to publication'. Neither is it an offence under the Act to sketch the presiding judge etc., unless this is done 'with a view to publication'.[2] Even the subsequent publication of such a sketch would not be an offence under s. 41(1)(b) since there was no intention to publish at the time it was made and this sub-section is so worded as to be restricted to the publication of material obtained in contravention of s. 41(1)(a). Likewise the offence will clearly not be committed by drawing the judge or jury from memory *outside* court. Indeed the *Sunday Times* regularly publishes such sketches.

The position with respect to photographs is open to doubt. Under s. 41(1)(a) the offence may still be committed even though the photograph is not taken with

---

[18] See, e.g., *Baker* v. *F & F Investment*, 470 F. 2d 778 (1972) (Federal class action involving alleged racial discrimination in sale of houses); *Democratic National Committee* v. *McCord*, 356 F. Supp. 1394 (1973) (civil actions arising out of the Watergate break-in).

[19] See also Borrie and Lowe, *Law of Contempt* (1973), pp. 18–20; Halsbury, *Laws of England* (3rd ed.), Vol. 30, para. 1067; Phillimore Committee report, paras. 41–43.

[20] Defined by s. 41(2)(a) to mean 'any court of justice, including the court of a coroner'.

[1] Defined by s. 41(2)(b) to include a 'recorder, registrar, magistrate, justice and coroner'.

[2] Presumably publication to one other person would suffice, and publication in a newspaper etc. would not be required.

a view to publication. This particular limit only applies to portraits or sketches. What is more debatable is whether the subsequent qualification in terms of subject matter—that is a judge, juror, witness etc.—applies to photographs as well as to sketches. It will be seen that the wording of the section is unclear on this point. The qualification can equally well be construed as applying solely to portraits or sketches, or as referring back to photographs as well. In favour of the former interpretation it may be sensible to construe the sub-section as embodying a total prohibition against photographing *anyone in the court itself*, including members of the general public. Yet against this view one can point to the absurdities which would result when s. 41(1)(a) is taken in conjunction with s. 41(2)(c). A would, for example, commit the statutory offence by taking a photograph of his girl friend, B, within the precincts of the court (perhaps sitting on the steps by the ubiquitous lion), since the photograph would be deemed by s. 41(2)(c) to have been taken in the court itself.[3] To avoid such a singularly odd conclusion it would seem preferable to construe the qualification as applying to photographs no less than to portraits or sketches. On this basis the statutory offence would not be committed by photographing a member of the general public in court, although this may still amount to a *contempt* if it is seriously disruptive of court proceedings.

In so far as is known s. 41 has given rise to very few incidents. In October 1970 Durham police acted with dubious propriety in taking photographs of students and young people who were entering a magistrates' court to attend the hearing of a drugs charge. The photographs were subsequently destroyed and no further action appears to have been taken.[4] In any event it seems unlikely that an offence would have been committed, unless those photographed included parties or witnesses. More recently in February 1973 the underground newspaper *IT* published a picture purporting to come from a photograph taken in the Central Criminal Court of the judge and jury in the 'Nasty Tales' obscenity trial. The chief clerk of the court referred the matter to the Director of Public Prosecutions, who subsequently instituted proceedings. It is understood that the photographer and editor were each fined £10 and the publishers £30 and £30 costs.

3 MENS REA[5]

The nature of the mental element which must be established before a contempt can be held to have been committed in the face of the court is not a matter which appears to have been discussed in English cases. In spite of the general tendency to discount the need for *mens rea* in cases of criminal contempt[6] it is submitted

[3] It is frequently unclear how far the 'precincts' of a court extend, and the Phillimore Committee has recommended (para. 41) that whenever practicable a map or plan should be displayed indicating what will normally be treated as the precincts of the court in question for the purposes of s. 41. The committee also discusses the position with respect to tape recorders in court (para. 42–43).

[4] See *The Times*, 22 October 1970, and (1970) 134 J.P. 839.

[5] The term is used throughout this book to denote intent or recklessness as to all the elements of the *actus reus*: see Glanville Williams *Criminal Law: General Part*, 2nd ed., 1961, Ch. 2; Smith and Hogan, *Criminal Law*, Ch. 4, p. 42 *et seq.*

[6] See, e.g., *Odhams Press, Ltd.* [1957] 1 Q.B. 73; [1956] 3 All E.R. 494, and, in general, below, Ch. 9.

that the position should be construed as follows. In the first place liability must clearly depend on establishing that the alleged contemnor's act was volitional and that none of the general defences to criminal liability are available to him. For example, duress is a defence to a charge of perjury[7] and it must equally be a defence to a witness allegedly in contempt through refusing to answer a question.

Secondly, liability should not be incurred unless D intends his conduct to disrupt proceedings, or he consciously runs the risk of this occurring. The County Courts Act 1959, s. 157 refers to one who *wilfully* interrupts the proceedings' in a county court,[8] and this requirement should be implied as a matter of course. Although the word 'wilful' is not a term of art it should be regarded as inconsistent with liability that D acted under an honest but mistaken belief in the existence of circumstances which would justify disruptive conduct.[9] Similar principles should apply to insulting behaviour and again the County Courts Act, s. 157 refers to one who 'wilfully insults' the judge etc. of such a court. As an example of a lack of intent or recklessness in this regard a person from an underprivileged background might employ a turn of phrase without realising that it would be regarded as insulting by those to whom it was addressed. An extreme example is provided by an American case in which a New Jersey court declined to hold in contempt a person who had expressed his disapproval of a court ruling by using what the court termed 'an epithet descriptive of excrement'.[10] Attempts by American courts to distinguish between 'clearly blameworthy' and less serious conduct, and to require a specific finding of wrongful intent in the latter case, do not appear to have been particularly fruitful.[11]

4   REFORMING THE SUMMARY PROCESS

It would probably be true to say that there has been no sustained movement in this country for a reform of the procedure adopted to deal with contempts in the face of the court. The protracted debate which has taken place in the United States,[12] and the fine distinctions which have been drawn there have, for the most part, passed by unnoticed. Yet the fact remains that the summary procedure which we currently employ must be open to serious objection.

In *Balogh* v. *Crown Court at St. Albans*[13] the Court of Appeal emphasised that summary committal should only be adopted 'when it is urgent and imperative to act immediately'. In similar vein the Phillimore Committee believed that the

---

[7] *Hudson* [1971] 2 Q.B. 202; [1971] 2 All E.R. 244.

[8] Emphasis supplied. See above, p. 26 for the wording of s. 157.

[9] As where he throws an object in the belief that he is forestalling an act of violence by another. For a case in which an issue of *mens rea* might have been raised, see the incident involving a Mr Bangs discussed above, p. 53. See, in general, *Morgan* [1975] 2 All E.R. 347, H.L.

[10] *State of New Jersey* v. *Jones,* 105 N.J. Super 493; 253 A. 2d 193 (1969).

[11] See, e.g., *Offut* v. *U.S.,* 232 F. 2d 69, 72 (1956) and, in general, Dobbs, *op. cit.,* at pp. 263–265. In *U.S.* v. *Seale,* 461 F. 2d 345, 368 (1972) it was said that: 'The minimum requisite intent is better defined as a volitional act done by one who knows or should reasonably be aware that his conduct is wrongful.'

[12] See above, pp. 41–47.

[13] [1974] 3 All E.R. 283, 288 *per* Lord Denning, M.R. See also, above, p. 23 and p. 27.

contempt jurisdiction should be invoked only 'where urgency or practical necessity require that the matter be dealt with summarily'.[14] The committee also recommended that certain defence opportunities be clearly established (including provision for legal aid);[15] that the more serious cases be generally left to the 'slower process of the ordinary criminal law';[16] and that a maximum term of two years' imprisonment for contempt be adopted.[17] Beyond this it also recommended that a period of delay should be interposed between determination of the issue of contempt and the imposition of the penalty.[18] Generally, however, the committee favoured the retention of the basic position whereby the presiding judge deals with the contempt himself and of his own motion.[19]

A number of considerations are normally advanced in support of the status quo. First, it is said that the judge, having heard or seen the incident and being aware of the context in which it arose, will be the person best placed to deal with it.[20] The facts are rarely in dispute and a formalised hearing before another judge is unnecessary. None of the strands of this argument is particularly convincing and they would hardly be advanced in any other context. Contempt may raise issue of fact like any other offence; convenience does not generally provide a sufficient reason for dispensing with the ordinary criminal process, and personal knowledge of the circumstances would generally be a reason for a judge to step down, rather than a reason for him to hear the case. No one would seriously contend that an ordinary trial should be denied to the assassin who stabs his victim in front of a large audience which immediately overpowers him. Still less would it be suggested that a judge forming part of that audience should preside at the hearing.

A further justification frequently advanced is that the summary process is necessary to preserve order in the courtroom, or (as a variation) that the threat of immediate punishment is a more effective *deterrent* than drawn-out criminal proceedings elsewhere.[1] These reasons have more validity. But the argument in terms of practical necessity can only apply with full force to persons such as an accused, juror, or witness, whose continued presence in court serves to promote the due administration of justice. Moreover it only applies to contemnors dealt with during the course of the proceedings for when the proceedings are over the immediate need to preserve order will, *ex hypothesi*, have passed. Whether the allegedly greater deterrent effect of immediate punishment is a sufficient reason for retaining the status quo may be doubted.

In the light of such considerations it is submitted that reform should proceed along the following lines. First, the summary contempt procedure should not be applied to persons such as members of the general public whose presence in court can be conveniently dispensed with. Secondly, the summary procedure should not be employed after the termination of the proceedings which have been disrupted, but only (at the very most) when it is considered to be imperative to act

[14] Para. 21.
[15] Paras. 32–33. See further, above, p. 25.
[16] Para. 34.
[17] Para. 201.
[18] Para. 33. There is a saving for a case in which no more than a small fine is being imposed.
[19] Para. 30.
[20] *Cf.* the Phillimore Committee report, para. 30.
[1] *Ibid.*

during the course of the proceedings themselves. Failing this a judge who has been subjected to personal abuse or attack should in any event be required to step down if he waits until the case is over.[2] A second judge may well find it necessary to deal with the matter more severely.[3] But it is important that justice should be *seen* to be done. Adoption of this proposal would not mean that the trial judge would have to give evidence in subsequent proceedings. The incident would almost invariably have been seen by others, including court officials, and their evidence could be supplemented by extending the process of certification which now applies in proceedings before tribunals of inquiry.[4]

The more difficult question is whether the summary power should be retained when the presiding judge considers it necessary to take immediate action against a person whose presence cannot be conveniently dispensed with. On balance it is thought that there is a sufficiently strong case for retaining a limited deterrent power here. A short statutory maximum term of perhaps one month's imprisonment might be appropriate. If the circumstances are considered to warrant more severe punishment resort should be had to the ordinary criminal process, thus giving the alleged contemnor the opportunity of a jury trial.[5] Sentences for distinct acts of contempt imposed so as to run consecutively should be aggregated for this purpose, notwithstanding the objection that a person who is intent on disrupting a trial can thereby rapidly deprive the court of an effective contempt power.[6] Such cases are extremely rare; the deterrent effect of a subsequent lengthy sentence has not been dispensed with, and order can be restored in other ways.

5 OTHER MODES OF DEALING WITH DISRUPTIVE BEHAVIOUR

As was mentioned above, there are other ways of dealing with disruptive conduct apart from, and in addition to, holding the person responsible in contempt. If a person so conducts himself as to give the presiding judge grounds for fearing a future breach of the peace, he may be bound over to keep the peace. If he commits an assault a summons may be served on him returnable *instanter*.[7] Similarly, he may be removed from court. This latter course does not normally create any difficulty, except perhaps in the instance of an accused, where two alternative courses are then open to the presiding judge. If the case is being heard with a jury, he may decide it is preferable to order a retrial to avoid the prejudice to the accused which might otherwise be occasioned. This course was adopted by Park,

---

[2] *Cf. Mayberry* v. *Pennsylvania*, 400 U.S. 455 (1971), above, pp. 43–44.

[3] *Cf.* the Phillimore Committee report, para. 30.

[4] *Cf.* the *Justice* report, *Contempt of Court* (1959), at p. 30. For tribunals of inquiry, see above, p. 33. Difficulty might be created when an alleged contemnor sought to compel the presiding judge to give evidence in his defence.

[5] *Cf.* the limitation of six months established in American cases, above pp. 45–47.

[6] *Cf. U.S.* v. *Seale*, 461 F. 2d 345 (1972), above p. 46. In the United States, However, the aggregation principle only appears to be applied where the sentence is imposed *after* the termination of the trial.

[7] *Cf.* the suggestion of Lord Goddard, C.J. in *Butt* (1957) 41 Cr. App. Rep. 82, 84, and see further, above, p. 26.

J. sitting in Winchester Crown Court in October 1972, when he was attacked by
an accused, who had been indicted on a charge of attempting to murder a fellow
inmate of Parkhurst prison.[8] Alternatively, he may order the hearing to continue
in the prisoner's absence. *Browne*[9] provides a leading example of a case in which
this latter course was adopted. Here the defendant had sought to obstruct her
trial on charges of obtaining certain garments by false pretences by screaming,
shouting and throwing herself down in the dock. The recorder proceeded to hear
the case in her absence after satisfying himself as to her sanity and citing a passage
in Stephen's *Digest of Criminal Procedure* where it was said: 'If a prisoner so
misconducts himself as to make it impossible to try him with decency, the court, it
seems, may order him to be removed and proceed in his absence.' Any difficulty
which there might have been in adopting the same procedure in cases of felony
was removed by s. 1 of the Criminal Law Act 1967, which abolished the
distinction between felonies and misdemeanours, and provided that the practice
previously applicable to misdemeanours shall be applicable in all cases. As a
result an accused may even be removed from court on a charge of murder. Indeed
this occurred during the Barn Restaurant trial in 1973 when Melford-Stevenson,
J. ordered that George Henry Ince be removed from the court while a witness was
giving evidence.[10] Ince was subsequently acquitted in a retrial after the jury in the
first trial had failed to reach a verdict. Another recent example is provided by the
case of *Jones*.[11] Here the trial was allowed to continue in the absence of the
defendant who had jumped bail and disappeared at the end of the case for the
prosecution. Not surprisingly the Court of Appeal dismissed an application for
leave to appeal some ten months out of time when Jones was eventually arrested
in Denmark, and brought to England in custody.[12]

Alternative means of maintaining order have been adopted in the United
States, though their employment is in no sense advocated here. In the Chicago
Conspiracy trial, for example, one of the defendants, Bobby Seale, was bound
and gagged in court, although this did not apparently succeed in silencing him.[13]
In *Illinois* v. *Allen*[14] the Supreme Court upheld the propriety of removing from
court a defendant who had persisted in interrupting the proceedings, and stated
that 'no person should be tried whilst shackled and gagged except as a last resort'.
As the court noted in a masterly understatement: 'Not only is it possible that the
sight of shackles and gags might have a significant effect on the jury's feelings
about the defendant, but the use of this technique is itself something of an
affront to the very dignity and decorum of judicial proceedings that the judge

---

[8] See *The Times*, 28, 31 October 1972.

[9] (1906) 70 J.P. 472. See also *Berry* (1897) 104 L.T. Jo. 110 (Northampton Assizes)—defendant
tore off his clothing, struggled with warders and uttered loud, incomprehensible cries; *Abrahams*
(1895) 21 V.L.R. 343, 348 (Vict. Sup. Ct.).

[10] See *The Times*, 5 May 1973.

[11] *Jones (R.E.W.) (No. 2)* [1972] 2 All E.R. 731.

[12] More questionable was the Court of Appeal's agreement that counsel had been right to
withdraw from the case and not to call witnesses it had been proposed to call: [1972] 2 All E.R. 731,
733. *Cf.* Zellick, 'Defendant's Misbehaviour in Court' (1972) 122 New Law Jo. 1139.

[13] *U.S.* v. *Dellinger*, *U.S.* v. *Seale*, No. 69 C.R. 180 (N.D. Ill., Feb. 14–15 1970); reversed and
remanded on appeal, 461 F. 2d 345 (1972): see further above, pp. 52.

[14] 397 U.S. 337 (1970), and see Note (1970) 84 Harv. L.R. 90.

is seeking to uphold.'[15] One trusts that in this country the line will be firmly drawn at handcuffing, and that any temptation to bind and gag even 'as a last resort' will be firmly resisted.

[15] 397 U.S. 337, 344 (1970). For a general discussion of the position in the United States, see the American College of Trial Lawyers' Report and Recommendations on Disruption of the Judicial Process (1970) 16 Catholic Lawyer 242.

5 Contempt through Infringing the Sub Judice Rule[1]

1 INTRODUCTION

The most important function associated with the law of criminal contempt is that of prohibiting conduct likely to interfere with the due administration of justice in proceedings which are *sub judice*. Such conduct may clearly take a variety of forms. The most obvious, is, perhaps, an attempt to bribe or intimidate a judge, juror or witness, all of which may be dealt with either summarily as a contempt, or as an indictable offence.[2] Equally, however, the offence may be committed through publishing matter carrying the same attendant risk, whether the publication be in the press, as will usually be the case, or through any other medium of communication. Thus radio and television broadcasts, cinema films, public speeches, sermons, theatrical performances, and even posters and wax models have all given rise to contempt proceedings in the past.[3]

2 THE REQUIREMENTS FOR THE DUE ADMINISTRATION OF JUSTICE

The requirements for the due administration of justice, which provide the background against which this branch of the law of contempt operates, have recently been analysed by Lord Diplock in *Attorney-General* v. *Times Newspapers, Ltd.* According to his Lordship:[4]

> The due administration of justice requires *first* that all citizens should have unhindered access to the constitutionally established courts of criminal or civil jurisdiction for the determination of disputes as to their legal rights and liabilities; *secondly*, that they should be able to rely upon obtaining in the courts the arbitrament of a tribunal which is free from bias against any party and whose decision will be based upon those facts only that have been proved in evidence adduced before it in accordance with the

---

[1] The contents of this and the four following chapters are based, in part, on an article by the author entitled, 'Contempt of Court: The Sub Judice Rule' [1968] Crim. L.R. 63–70, 137–150, 191–202.

[2] See e.g., *Martin's Case* (1747) 2 Russ. & M. 674; 39 E.R. 551, and below, p. 105 (judge); *Re Dunn* [1906] V.L.R. 493 (Vict. Sup. Ct), and below, p. 93 (juror); *Re B. (J.A.) (An Infant)* [1965] Ch. 1112; [1965] 2 All E.R. 168, and below, p. 100 (witness). See also below, p. 136 *et seq.*

[3] See, e.g., *Att.-Gen.* v. *London Weekend Television, Ltd* [1972] 3 All E.R. 1146 (television); *Hutchison, ex p. McMahon* [1936] 2 All E.R. 1514 (news film); *Onslow's and Whalley's Case* (1873) L.R. 9 Q.B. 219 (speech); *Re South Meath Election Petition, Fay's Case* (1892) 30 L.R. Ir. 659 (sermon); *Williams* (1823) 2 L.J. (O.S.) K.B. 30 (theatrical performance); *Daily Herald, ex p. Rouse* (1931) 75 Sol. Jo. 119 (poster); *Gilham* (1827) M. & M. 165; 173 E.R. 1118 (wax model).

[4] [1974] A.C. 273, 309; [1973] 3 All E.R. 54, 72.

procedure adopted in courts of law; and *thirdly* that, once the dispute has been submitted to a court of law, they should be able to rely upon there being no usurpation by any other person of the function of that court to decide it according to law. Conduct which is calculated to prejudice any of these three requirements or to undermine the public confidence that they will be observed is contempt of court.

The first requirement of unhindered access to the courts would typically be violated by subjecting a party to proceedings to threats or improper pressure, or by holding him up to public vilification and abuse. The second requirement of a tribunal which is free from bias, and which reaches its decision solely on the basis of evidence properly adduced in court, will likewise be violated by conduct which impairs the impartiality of a juror or which exerts an improper influence on a witness. The third requirement that there be no usurpation of the function of the court seems to require that other persons desist from prejudging the issues which the court will be called upon to determine. All of these matters will be developed in more detail in the chapters which follow.

3 THE TEST OF LIABILITY

The test of liability for conduct warranting summary punishment as a contempt has undergone changes over the years. Before the latter part of the 19th century the courts had not discouraged the widespread use of the contempt power to punish comment upon civil and criminal proceedings. A more restrictive approach was achieved through distinguishing between 'technical' contempts[5] and contempts which were deserving of punishment. Thus in *Hunt* v. *Clarke*,[5] a case which arose from newspaper comment upon a civil action involving company fraud, Cotton, L.J. agreed that: 'It does technically become a contempt if pending a cause, or before a cause even has begun, any observations are made or published to the world which tend in any way to prejudice the parties in the case. . . .'[6] But both he and the other members of the Court of Appeal emphasised that jurisdiction to punish contempt should not be invoked lightly and in respect of such technical contempts. It was to be reserved, rather, for conduct calculated (that is, likely) to cause substantial prejudice to a party in the conduct of an action and hence to the due administration of justice.

Similar sentiments were expressed by Lord Russell, C.J. in *Payne and Cooper*[7] and they have been frequently reiterated in recent years. Thus in *Duffy, ex parte Nash*[8] Lord Parker, C.J. emphasised, in delivering the judgment of a strong Divisional Court, that there must be 'a real risk, as opposed to a remote possibility, that the article was calculated to prejudice a fair hearing'. In similar vein Russell, J. stressed in *Carl-Zeiss-Stiftung* v. *Rayner & Keeler, Ltd*[9] that 'a finding of contempt of court must be based on a solid view of the likelihood of such interference and not on fanciful notions'. Likewise in the Divisional Court in *Attorney-General* v. *Times Newspapers, Ltd.* Lord Widgery, C.J. said that 'the

---

[5] (1889) 58 L.J.Q.B. 490.
[6] *Ibid.*, at pp. 491–492.
[7] [1896] 1 Q.B. 577, 580.
[8] [1960] 2 Q.B. 188, 200; [1960] 2 All E.R. 891, 896.
[9] [1960] 3 All E.R. 289, 293.

test of contempt is whether the words complained of create a serious risk that the course of justice may be interfered with'.[10] On the other hand, the speeches in the House of Lords in this leading case suggest that the test of liability is not a stringent one. Thus Lord Reid agreed that there must be a real risk as opposed to a remote possibility of prejudice, but he added:[11]

> That is an application of the ordinary de minimis principle. There is no contempt if the possibility of influence is remote. If there is some but only a small likelihood, that may influence the court to refrain from inflicting any punishment. If there is a serious risk some action may be necessary.

On this basis it would appear that at least a technical contempt will have been committed where the possibility of influence is other than 'remote'. Lord Diplock expressed himself as being in agreement with Lord Reid on this point,[12] whilst of the other speeches it is only that of Lord Morris which is couched in less restrictive terms.[13] It will also be seen later that this case establishes a general prohibition against prejudging the issues in pending proceedings.[14]

All of the above formulae place the emphasis upon the seriousness or triviality of the risk of interference, rather than upon the *degree* of interference. The Phillimore Committee believes that this is wrong and that the law should aim at preventing serious prejudice, not serious risks. It proposes a new statutory definition whereby, 'The test of contempt is whether the publication complained of creates a risk that the course of justice will be seriously impeded or prejudiced.'[15] Subject to one point this formula should meet with widespread acceptance. The present law does not sufficiently emphasise that the risk must be of substantial interference, nor, indeed, that the interference must take a form which is *improper*.[16] It is submitted, however, that the word 'serious' should qualify both the degree *and* the risk of prejudice, and that it would not be right to treat as a contempt conduct which carries no more than a small likelihood of serious prejudice.

A further point to note is that liability for contempt does not depend on prejudice to a fair trial having actually occurred. The offence is concerned, rather, with the *potential* effect of conduct viewed in the light of the circumstances existing at that time. *Re B. (J.A.) (An Infant)*[17] illustrates the point. Here there had been an ineffectual attempt to prevent a witness from giving evidence in pending Chancery proceedings. In holding the person responsible in contempt, Cross, J. noted that, 'the mere fact that no harm has been done in this particular case is neither here nor there'.[18] Such conduct was intrinsically likely to pose a serious threat to the administration of justice, and that was sufficient. A similar

---

[10] [1973] 1 Q.B. 710, 725; [1972] 3 All E.R. 1136, 1145.
[11] [1974] A.C. 273, 299; [1973] 3 All E.R. 54, 63.
[12] [1974] A.C. 273, 312; [1973] 3 All E.R. 54, 75.
[13] *Cf.* [1974] A.C. 273, 303; [1973] 3 All E.R. 54, 67.
[14] See below, pp. 126–130.
[15] Para. 113.
[16] See further, below, pp. 136–141 for examples of cases in which it would be quite permissible to influence a party to proceedings.
[17] [1965] Ch. 1112; [1965] 2 All E.R. 168.
[18] [1965] Ch. 1112, 1123; [1965] 2 All E.R. 168, 175.

point was made by McInerney, J. in a modern Australian case[19] which arose out of a newspaper article referring to the previous conviction for murder of a person currently charged with driving offences. The learned judge noted that:[20]

Whether that article had a tendency to prejudice the fair trial of [the defendant] must be determined at the time of its publication and on a perusal of that article in the context of the pendency of the charges brought against [him]; and on the probabilities then existing. It is not to be determined in the light of what subsequently happened at the trial.

Given that the concern is ultimately with the potential effect of the publication at the time when it appeared it would be unwise to assume that a contempt depends upon a person having at some stage come before a court. In November 1974 when a warrant had been issued for the arrest of Lord Lucan on a charge of murder there was a good deal of speculation in the press as to his possible motives.[1] If proceedings against him were 'pending or imminent' at *that* time[2] it should not excuse a publisher to plead three months later that the prejudice was now spent, that Lord Lucan had still not been arrested or, indeed, that he might never be arrested.

It will also be seen later that what is in a sense the obverse of the above proposition is equally true. An attempt improperly to interfere with the due administration of justice will constitute a contempt even though it may be safely assumed from the outset that it had absolutely no chance of succeeding. Such cases are rare, but a clear example is provided by an attempt to bribe a judge. This would be singularly unlikely to affect his decision in the case; yet it is certainly a contempt.[3]

In the light of the above considerations one may say that subject to any additional requirement of *mens rea* or negligence being satisfied[4] conduct may warrant summary punishment as a contempt of the present category if it (i) publicly prejudges the issues in a case; (ii) has the potential for creating a serious risk of improper interference with the due administration of justice;[5] or (iii) is intended to have this effect. It seems, however, that a 'technical' contempt not deserving of punishment may be committed by something less than this, provided that there is *some* risk of interference going beyond a remote possibility.[6] The main practical consequence of retaining the concept of the technical contempt is that it may affect the incidence of costs since liability to pay the costs of the opposing party will, it seems, only accrue if an offence has been committed. It will not, however, necessarily do so. The court may at its discretion simply make

[19] *Regal Press Pty., Ltd* [1972] V.R. 67 (Vict. Sup. Ct).

[20] *Ibid.,* at p. 73.

[1] See (1974) 124 New Law Jo. 1069 for critical editorial comment on the conduct of the press. The argument is also supported by *Davies* [1906] 1 K.B. 32 where prejudice to a charge which was later dropped was one of the grounds on which a contempt was held to have been committed: see below, p. 74.

[2] This requirement is discussed in the following chapter.

[3] See *Martin's Case* (1747) 2 Russ. & M. 674; 39 E.R. 551, and below, p. 105 and p. 136.

[4] See below, Ch. 9, pp. 158–168.

[5] *Quaere* whether under the present law as opposed to the Phillimore Committee proposals (noted above) the risk must be one of *serious* interference?

[6] *Cf. Att.-Gen.* v. *Times Newspapers, Ltd* [1974] A.C. 273, 312 (Lord Diplock), p. 321 (Lord Simon).

no order as to costs, or even require the opposing party to pay the contemnor's costs if it feels that the contempt is so trivial that the application should not have been brought.[7] Beyond this the consequences of retaining the 'technical contempt' are less tangible but no less important. As in other areas of the law where proceedings may end in an absolute discharge of the offender, the decision that he has nonetheless technically committed what amounts to a criminal offence may leave him with a sense of grievance and a feeling that a stigma has attached.[8]

The following four chapters will discuss the several prerequisites of liability in this branch of the law of contempt in some detail. The first problem to be discussed in the next chapter is that of when proceedings are *sub judice* for the purposes of the offence. The two chapters which follow discuss the types of conduct which are likely to be regarded as prejudicial to the fair trial of criminal and civil proceedings respectively. Finally, it is proposed to consider the extent to which liability depends upon an element of *mens rea* or negligence, and the various categories of persons who may be held to have committed a contempt.

---

[7] *Cf. Att.-Gen.* v. *Times Newspapers, Ltd* [1974] A.C. 273, 312 *per* Lord Diplock.

[8] The Phillimore Committee suggests that adoption of its proposed test for contempt would have the advantage of doing away with the concept: para. 113. But this assumes that the creation of a minor risk of serious prejudice would be more than a 'technical' contempt if its proposal were enacted.

6   Contempt through Infringing the Sub Judice Rule: the Requirement that Proceedings be Sub Judice.

1   INTRODUCTION

One of the most difficult problems in the law of contempt is to determine when proceedings are *sub judice* so that an act or publication which is alleged to prejudice their conduct or outcome may give rise to the commission of the offence. The problem may arise in both criminal and civil proceedings and in proceedings before bodies such as tribunals of inquiry. In practice, however, it is in the case of criminal proceedings that the problem has proved to be especially acute. Traditionally the solution has been sought by asking whether the proceedings allegedly prejudiced were 'pending' or perhaps 'imminent' at the material time. Both these terms have proved to be extremely elastic and not susceptible of precise definition.

2.   CRIMINAL PROCEEDINGS

(1)   WHEN ARE PROCEEDINGS PENDING?

At the end of the 19th century it would probably have been true to say that criminal proceedings were only regarded as pending in a court possessed of the necessary jurisdiction to punish for contempt once an accused had been committed to a superior court for trial. While it was not necessary that the trial should have actually commenced,[1] the line was, it seems, drawn at the pre-committal stage. Certainly this was the view of Holroyd, J. in *Re Syme, ex parte Worthington*,[2] a case which came before the Supreme Court of Victoria sitting at Melbourne in 1902.

The following decade saw a trilogy of important English cases which brought about a considerable extension in the law. In *Parke, ex parte Dougal*[3] articles had been published in the *Star* newspaper which were prejudicial to the fair trial of one Dougal on charges of forgery. At the time of publication Dougal had been remanded in custody by the examining magistrates, but not yet committed to assizes for trial. The Divisional Court nonetheless held that the case was pending

---

[1] See *Onslow's and Whalley's Case* (1873) L.R. 9 Q.B. 219, 227 *per* Cockburn, L.C.J.
[2] (1902) 28 V.L.R. 552.
[3] [1903] 2 K.B. 432.

in the assize court even though it was unclear at the time of publication that matters would proceed thus far. A contempt was accordingly held to have been established. Delivering the judgment of the court, Wills, J. preferred to leave open the wider question of whether a contempt could equally have been held to have been committed because of the prejudice to the case when it was pending in the magistrates' court itself.[4]

The question left open in *Parke* was considered further some three years later in *Davies, ex parte Hunter*.[5] Here one Henrietta Hunter had been arrested and remanded in custody on a charge of abandoning a child and her arrest was followed by a series of highly prejudicial articles in the *South Wales Daily Post*. A charge of attempted murder of the same child was later substituted for the original charge, and Hunter was, in the result, committed to Glamorgan assizes for trial on this latter charge. The Divisional Court held that a contempt had been committed on the ground, inter alia, that the articles, when published, might have been prejudicial to the original charge which would typically (though not invariably) have been heard at quarter sessions. A fine of £100 was imposed. As has been noted in an earlier chapter, jurisdiction to punish interference with the administration of justice in an inferior court such as quarter sessions was viewed as a corollary of the supervisory functions exercised by the King's Bench over such courts.[6] Parity of reasoning would accordingly suggest that a contempt may be committed through prejudicing proceedings which can *only* be heard by an inferior court such as a magistrates' court. This indeed was the conclusion reached by the High Court of Australia in *John Fairfax and Sons Pty, Ltd* v. *McRae*.[7]

Clarke, ex parte Crippen,[8] the third of the trilogy of cases mentioned above, established that proceedings may be regarded as pending at an earlier point in the criminal process. In July 1910 human remains had been found in Crippen's home in London and a warrant was issued for his arrest on a charge of murder. He was arrested in Quebec some two weeks later whereupon the *Daily Chronicle* published a highly prejudicial article suggesting that he had confessed to responsibility for the death of his wife. Crippen was subsequently brought back to London in custody. On August 27th 1910 he appeared at the Bow Street Magistrates' Court on a charge of murder and was later committed for trial. In the ensuing contempt application the defence argued that at the time of publication matters had gone no further than an arrest and that a contempt could not be committed until such time as the suspect had been brought before a court. The submission failed, the Divisional Court being unanimously of the opinion that criminal proceedings were certainly pending from the time when a suspect was arrested under a warrant.

It was also suggested *obiter* in this case that it would be sufficient that a warrant had been issued for the arrest of a suspect since, as Lord Coleridge, C.J. explained: 'The issue of the warrant is an act of a magistrate not merely min-

---

[4] *Cf. ibid.*, at pp. 443–444.

[5] [1906] 1 K.B. 32.

[6] See above, p. 30.

[7] (1954) 93 C.L.R. 351. (The material was not, however, prejudicial on the facts.) See also *McKinnon* (1911) 30 N.Z.L.R. 884 (N.Z. Sup. Ct).

[8] (1910) 103 L.T. 636.

isterial, but involving the exercise of a judicial discretion.'[9] In similar vein Pickford, J. said: 'There is ample authority for holding that the prosecution has begun at the time, at any rate, when the warrant is issued.'[10] Lord Coleridge was equally prepared to envisage that proceedings might be pending at a still earlier point because he expressly declined to 'express any opinion as to whether [contempt] proceedings could be taken when the sole thing that has been done was the swearing of an information upon which no further steps had been taken'.[11] Similar considerations presumably apply to the laying of an information preceding the issue of a summons. Of course if these views represent the law, proceedings may be technically pending a very considerable time before they actually get under way in a court. The warrant may take months or even years to execute. On the whole it would seem preferable to draw the line at the point where the suspect is arrested or the charge preferred.

Where a person is arrested without a warrant commonsense would suggest that proceedings may again be regarded as pending forthwith. Support for this view is, moreover, to be found in the leading Australian case of *James* v. *Robinson*, where the High Court agreed that: 'The proposition that proceedings are pending in criminal cases after a person has been arrested and charged is firmly established.[12] Since the suspect in that case was ultimately arrested without a warrant it seems fair to assume that the court had this situation in mind. Yet in such a case one cannot point to any act involving the exercise of judicial discretion or say that a court is otherwise seized of the matter. There is simply an obligation to bring the suspect before a magistrates' court as soon as practicable which means within twenty-four hours unless the offence is a 'serious' one.[13] If, as seems likely, proceedings are nonetheless to be regarded as pending for the purposes of the law of contempt, the same clearly cannot be said of a case in which the suspect is 'assisting the police with their inquiries', and is technically free to leave. Still less can proceedings be said to be pending where the suspect is being pursued, and no warrant for his arrest has been issued. The question remains, however, whether it is essential for the purposes of the offence that they should be, or whether it is sufficient that they were 'imminent'.

(2) CONTEMPT THROUGH PREJUDICE TO IMMINENT PROCEEDINGS

(i) *Authorities favouring the wider view*
Although there is no binding authority directly in point there is now substantial support for the view that a contempt may be committed even though the proceedings which were prejudiced were not technically pending at the time of publication, provided only that they were imminent. Frequently cited in this

---

[9] *Ibid.,* at p. 641.

[10] *Ibid.,* at p. 640. See also *ibid.,* at p. 639 (Darling, J.).

[11] *Ibid.,* at p. 641. For further discussion in a different context of when proceedings commence, see *Hull* (1860) 2 F. & F. 16; 175 E.R. 939; *Hancock* v. *W. Angliss & Co., Ltd.* [1961] V.R. 590 (Vict. Sup. Ct).

[12] (1963) 109 C.L.R. 593, 606.

[13] This is the effect of the Magistrates' Courts Act 1952, s. 38. Some of the uncertainties in the law in this area are noted in editorial comment in [1974] Crim. L.R. 330. The comment was prompted by the 'Land Deals' or Milhench affair.

context is a statement of Wills, J. in *Parke*,[14] where it was suggested that the emphasis in the earlier authorities on the need for proceedings to be pending merely 'accentuates the fact, not that the case has been begun; but that it is not at an end. That', Wills, J. added, 'is the cardinal consideration. It is possible very effectively to poison the fountain of justice before it begins to flow. It is not possible to do so when the stream has ceased.'[15]

Further support for this view is to be found in *Savundranayagan*,[16] where Salmon, L.J., delivering the judgment of the Court of Appeal, stressed *obiter* that:[17]

> It must not be supposed that proceedings to commit for contempt of court can be instituted only in respect of matters published after proceedings have actually begun. No-one should imagine that he is safe from committal for contempt if, knowing or having good reason to believe that criminal proceedings are imminent, he chooses to publish matters calculated to prejudice a fair trial.

The possibility of committing a contempt through prejudicing imminent proceedings was also tacitly assumed by both Lord Reid and Lord Diplock in *Attorney-General* v. *Times Newspapers, Ltd.*[18] The same view has also been expressed by Professor Goodhart,[19] Lord Parker,[20] and by the committee under Lord Justice Salmon in its report on the law of contempt as it affects tribunals of inquiry.[1] The Scottish case of *Stirling* v. *Associated Newspapers, Ltd*[2] is also said to be in point but it is of little value in ascertaining the position in English law. At the time when the Scottish *Daily Mail* published the prejudicial article Stirling had, it seems, been arrested on a warrant issued some time previously.[3] In any event the High Court of Justiciary apparently regarded newspapers as being at risk as soon as criminal investigations were in progress and this is certainly not the law in England.

(ii) *The effect of the Administration of Justice Act 1960, s. 11*

A further dimension to the problem in English law is created by the wording of s. 11 of the Administration of Justice Act 1960. S. 11(1) provides as follows:

> A person shall not be guilty of contempt of court on the ground that he has published any matter calculated to interfere with the course of justice in connection with any proceedings *pending or imminent* at the time of publication if at that time (having taken

---

[14] [1903] 2 K.B. 432, 437–438.

[15] Cited *obiter*, though with apparent approval, by Lord Hewart, C.J. in *Daily Mirror ex p. Smith* [1927] 1 K.B. 845, 851.

[16] [1968] 3 All E.R. 439.

[17] *Ibid.,* at p. 441.

[18] *Cf.* [1974] A.C. 273, 301; [1973] 3 All E.R. 54, 65 (Lord Reid); *ibid.,* at p. 308, and p. 71 (Lord Diplock). See also below, pp. 85–86.

[19] (1964) 80 L.Q.R. 166. See also Zelman Cowen, 'Some Observations on the Law of Criminal Contempt' [1965] Univ. Western Aus. L.R. 1, at pp. 22–28.

[20] 39th Report of Judicial Council of Massachusetts, 1963 referred to by Goodhart, *op. cit.*

[1] Cmnd. 4078, para. 22.

[2] [1960] S.L.T. 5.

[3] But see [1960] Crim. L.R. 251. He had in any event been 'detained' by the police as a preliminary to taking him back to Scotland. For suggestions that proceedings are 'pending' once a warrant has been issued, see above, p. 74.

all reasonable care) he did not know and had no reason to suspect that the proceedings were *pending,* or that such proceedings were *imminent*, as the case may be. (Emphasis supplied.)

This provision was intended to establish a limited defence based upon the absence of negligence where one had not existed at common law.[4] Nevertheless, the natural inference from its wording is that an offence *will* be comitted where prejudicial comment relates to proceedings which were either pending or *imminent*, and the publisher cannot bring himself within the terms of the statutory defence.

This indeed was the view taken by the High Court in Northern Ireland in *Beaverbrook Newspapers, Ltd.*[5] In this case an article was published in the *Daily Express* referring in detail to the previous criminal record of Robert McGladdery, who was described as the 'No 1 suspect' in relation to the murder of one Pearl Gamble. At the time of publication McGladdery was under constant surveillance with police officers guarding the front and rear of his house. This fact was clearly known to the *Daily Express* reporter, but no objection was taken to his entering the house accompanied by a photographer. McGladdery was arrested the following day and charged with the girl's murder. In the ensuing motion to commit for contempt, it was submitted that the offence had not been committed as proceedings against McGladdery were not pending at the time of publication. Furthermore, it was said, s. 11 of the 1960 Act should not be construed as extending the common law when its purpose was clearly to do no more than establish a limited defence. These submissions did not meet with success. Delivering the main judgment of the Northern Ireland court, Sheil, J. was content, in effect, simply to point to the wording of the Act. 'Applying that section to the present case', he asked, 'how can it be said that there was no reason to suspect that proceedings were imminent, having regard to the material contained in the publication?'[6]

This decision is far from satisfactory for it assumes the possibility of committing a contempt once proceedings are imminent simply from the wording of the 1960 Act. There is no inquiry into the position at common law, or the possible effect of the Act on the common law. As to the latter, Windeyer, J. suggested in *James* v. *Robinson* that the Act might have extended the law by an 'indirect approach',[7] but the better view is surely that it should not be so construed. As Professor Goodhart has observed, it is difficult to believe that a draftsman would have introduced a positive amendment extending the law by the use of negative terms in a section which was designed to afford a defence. Granted that this is so, then, as Goodhart remarks: '. . . the only importance of the 1960 Act in regard to imminent proceedings is that it furnishes strong evidence that Parliament must have assumed that in using the word "imminent" it was describing the then existing law.'[8] If Parliament was incorrect in its assumptions (and this is still a

---

[4] See below, p. 164 *et seq.*
[5] [1962] N.I.L.R. 15.
[6] *Ibid.,* at p. 21.
[7] (1963) 109 C.L.R. 593, 618. (High Ct of Australia).
[8] (1964) 80 L.Q.R. 166, 168.

matter for debate), general principles of statutory interpretation would require the section to be construed restrictively so as not to alter the common law.[9]

(iii) *Australian decisions*

As against this considerable array of authority, which is persuasive but less than conclusive, there are Australian decisions which point in the opposite direction. The most important is *James* v. *Robinson*.[10] In this case a West Australian Sunday newspaper had published articles which were admitted to be prejudicial to the fair trial of one Brian Robinson on charges of murder. They recounted how he had killed two named persons, and threatened others, before seeking to hide in a pine plantation near Perth, where an intensive 'manhunt' was being conducted. Robinson was arrested soon afterwards, and he was charged and remanded in custody within two days of the articles appearing. Against this background the High Court of Australia held that a contempt had not been committed since proceedings were not pending at the time of publication and it was not sufficient that they might be said to have been imminent. This latter conclusion was supported by reference to the many English and Commonwealth cases in which the courts had examined how far the proceedings ultimately prejudiced had progressed at the time of publication. The inference drawn by the High Court was that:[11]

> [If] the imminence of proceedings were to be regarded as sufficient foundation for applications for attachment for contempt in matters of this character—which would, of course, introduce many difficulties and much uncertainty—then there was no reason why the courts should have taken the trouble, as they have done in the many cases mentioned, to examine the significance of the laying of an information or the making of a charge and subsequent arrest.

Although none of the cases goes so far as to decide that proceedings *must* be pending before a contempt can be committed the approach of the High Court clearly represents the most natural interpretation of them.

This point apart, the High Court also held that the 'ultimate reason' behind its decision was that the contempt power had been assumed by the courts to protect persons aggrieved in their capacity as parties to proceedings. Such persons were under the protection of the court and were not, in the words of Lord Erskine, 'to be driven to other remedies against libels upon them in that respect'.[12] No such protection was afforded at an earlier stage when it was a matter for speculation whether the person aggrieved would become a party to proceedings. This is less convincing, for the same objection could be raised to extending the protection of the law of contempt back to the time when the suspect is arrested, and this the law

---

[9] *Cf.* Maxwell, *The Interpretation of Statutes* (12th ed., 1969), at pp. 116–123. Any doubts as to the possible effect of s. 11 might have been removed when the Bill was in its Committee stage in the House of Lords where Lord Chorley dropped a proposed amendment designed to ensure that the section was not interpreted as extending the law: see Hansard, H.L. Deb. Vol. 223, col. 583.

[10] (1963) 109 C.L.R. 593. See also the decision of the High Court in *Porter, ex p. Yee* (1926) 37 C.L.R. 432, 444 *per* Isaacs, J.; *Crew and Ipec Australia Ltd* [1971] V.R. 878 (Vict. Sup. Ct).

[11] (1963) 109 C.L.R. 593, 607.

[12] *Ibid.* citing *Ex p. Jones* (1806) 13 Ves. 237, 238; 33 E.R. 283. Lord Erskine was, in turn, citing Lord Hardwicke, L.C. in *The St. James's Evening Post Case* (1742) 2 Atk. 469, 471; 26 E.R. 683.

has clearly done. Certainly no violence would be done to the historical basis of the modern law of contempt if it were to be regarded as applying to proceedings which were imminent.

(iv) *Further considerations and conclusions*

Before drawing any conclusions from the above discussion two further points must be noted. The first is that the extension of the law of contempt to protect 'imminent' proceedings can only be done at the expense of uncertainty in the law and at the risk of hampering the legitimate activities of investigative journalism. The Savundra affair provides a good example of the genuine conflict of interests which may arise. Emil Savundra was convicted in March 1968 on charges of conspiring to defraud persons who had taken out insurance policies with his company. His appeal to the Court of Appeal was later dismissed.[13] As is common in such cases, the precarious financial state of his company was suspected by the press for some time before criminal proceedings were instituted. In July 1966, when people were continuing to pour money into the company, a campaign was mounted against him pointing out his past criminal record and warning off would-be insurers. At this stage there was no suggestion that criminal proceedings were contemplated and hence no question of a contempt being committed. Indeed Salmon, L.J. later agreed during the hearing of Savundra's appeal against conviction that the conduct of the press in this period was very much in the public interest.[14]

A wholly different attitude was, however, adopted towards a television interview by David Frost in February 1967. This interview with Savundra was regarded as deplorable because at the time of the programme 'it must surely have been obvious to everyone that he was about to be arrested and tried on charges of gross fraud'.[15] Apart altogether from the fact that Frost had apparently contacted the Board of Trade and other sources to ensure that proceedings were not contemplated in the immediate future,[16] the Court of Appeal's attitude was perhaps less than fair. Certainly it was important that Savundra should have received a fair trial. Equally, however, it was in the interest of the public that it should be warned against placing further sums of money with Savundra's company. In the absence of something concrete—such as an arrest and charge—it is by no means clear that the former interest is the more worthy of protection. As it turned out Savundra was not in fact arrested until several months had passed and his trial did not begin until eleven months after the interview.

The second consideration is that the choice under the existing law cannot simply be described in terms of whether prejudice to imminent proceedings should be punished as a contempt, or not at all. As Windeyer, J. noted in *James* v. *Robinson*: 'The common law misdemeanour constituted by conduct tending to

---

[13] *Savundranayagan and Walker* [1968] 3 All E.R. 439. See further C. J. Miller, 'The Freedom of Publication (Protection) Bill' [1969] Crim. L.R. 177, 180–182; Hansard, H.C. Deb. Vol. 776, col. 1711, 31 January 1969, and, in general, below, pp. 145–149, 150–154.
[14] [1968] 3 All E.R. 439, 441.
[15] *Ibid.*
[16] See the letter by David Frost in *The Times*, 18 July 1968.

pervert the course of justice does not, it has been held, depend upon there being proceedings presently pending'.[17] The reference is to the decision of the Court of Criminal Appeal in *Sharpe and Stringer*.[18] Here it was held to be an offence punishable on indictment for A and B to conspire together to conceal and destroy evidence and to persuade a third party to make a false statement to the police. This was so although proceedings were not pending at the time when the agreement was reached.[19] The more recent decision of the Court of Appeal in *Andrews*[20] suggests that the same act would constitute an offence if done by one person acting alone. In any event it is theoretically possible to indict those responsible for publishing a newspaper on a charge of conspiring to pervert the course of justice.[1] In all such cases, however, liability will depend on establishing an *intent* improperly to interfere with the administration of justice[2] and, as will be seen later, no such requirement exists in summary proceedings for contempt.[3]

In the light of the above discussion any conclusions as to the state of English law must necessarily be tentative. Section 11 of the Administration of Justice Act 1960 may be regarded as indicative of parliament's assumptions as to the scope of the offence, but not as having itself extended the law. As for the common law authorities English cases and opinion clearly favour the wider approach. But *James* v. *Robinson*[4] is the only case in which the issues have been squarely faced. Given the respect which is always accorded to the decisions of the High Court of Australia it is persuasive authority for the narrow approach whereby a contempt will only be committed if proceedings were pending and not simply imminent at the time of publication. It must be said, however, that it is doubtful whether the decision would be followed in an English court.

(v)   *When are proceedings imminent?*

Assuming, therefore, that conduct prejudicial to imminent proceedings may be punished as a contempt the question remains as to when this limited requirement will be satisfied. The word 'imminent' does not lend itself to precise definition though various suggestions have been made over the years. Thus during the House of Lords debates on the Administration of Justice Bill in 1960 Viscount Kilmuir, L.C. suggested that: 'Proceedings may be imminent for example, when no one has yet been charged with a crime but an arrest is hourly expected.'[5] This test would, no doubt, be satisfied on the facts of cases such as *James* v. *Robinson*

---

[17] (1963) 109 C.L.R. 593, 618. The same point was noted in the composite judgment of Kitto, Taylor, Menzies and Owen, JJ: *ibid.*, at p. 607.

[18] [1938] 1 All E.R. 48.

[19] *Cf. ibid.*, at p. 51 (Du Parcq, J.). See also the Phillimore Committee report, Appendix II, paras. 5–11. The committee notes that the indictable offence is capable of being committed as from the moment when a crime is committed; para. 9.

[20] [1973] 1 All E.R. 857, C.A., above, p. 4. See also *Vreones* [1891] 1 Q.B. 360, and Zelman Cowen, *op. cit.*, at pp. 32–35.

[1] *Tibbits and Windust* [1902] 1 K.B. 77.

[2] Certain passages in the judgment of the Court for Crown Cases Reserved in *Tibbits and Windust*, above, suggest that criminal intent may be imputed to the publisher: *cf.* [1902] 1 K.B. 77, at p. 88. But the position is now governed by the more stringent requirements of the Criminal Justice Act 1967, s. 8.

[3] See below, pp. 158–159.

[4] (1963) 109 C.L.R. 593, above, p. 78.

[5] Hansard, H.L. Deb. Vol. 222, col. 252, 24 March 1960.

(where the suspect was being pursued within the limited area of a pine plantation), and *Beaverbrook Newspapers, Ltd* (where the police had surrounded the suspect's house to carry out an arrest).[6] In this latter case Sheil, J. himself suggested that the word imminent means 'impending' or 'threatening',[7] which is indeed the standard dictionary definition. Equally Viscount Kilmuir's test would be satisfied where a person whose trial was prejudiced was 'helping the police with their inquiries' at the time of publication. Substantially the same test was advanced by Sir Elwyn Jones when, speaking as Attorney-General, he suggested that he would not 'expect proceedings for contempt to be begun or successfully concluded save in cases in which the newspaper ought reasonably to have been aware of the likelihood of a very early arrest'.[8] In similar vein the *Report of the Interdepartmental Committee on the Law of Contempt As It Affects Tribunals of Inquiry*, having agreed that it was impossible to define the word 'imminent' with precision, added: 'There are cases, however, in which it is obvious that a certain individual is on the point of being arrested on a serious criminal charge—perhaps in 24 hours, perhaps in seven or eight days; it is impossible to lay down a precise scale.'[9] Lest it be thought that there is any inevitability in such developments it is worth recalling that Lord Salmon, the chairman of the committee, had suggested in the *Savundra* case that it was 'obvious' at the time of the Frost interview that Savundra was about to be arrested.[10] In fact several months elapsed before an arrest was carried out.

Elsewhere the concept of imminency has been expressed in still wider terms. Thus it has been suggested that the press and broadcasting authorities publish at their peril once the police have issued their 'wanted to assist in investigations' notices, or once they have a suspect in mind.[11] If this is correct, proceedings may, of course, be imminent many months before they are actually instituted. The suspect may succeed in avoiding capture by whatever means, as is currently the case with Lord Lucan; or the investigating authorities may take months to assimilate sufficient evidence to warrant a decision to prosecute, as in the Poulson case. The greater the time lag between publication and trial the less likely it is that there will be a real risk of prejudice. But one may still have to decide whether proceedings were imminent at that time since this is a separate constituent element of the offence.

A further difficulty was noted by Windeyer, J. in *James* v. *Robinson,* when he observed that: 'it seems uncertain whether the imminence of the event is determinable solely by what was expected at the time of publication, or is to be judged by what in fact occurred'.[12] It is submitted that it is the position as at the time of publication which is important. Thus it is clear that if subsequent unforeseen developments create an element of prejudice which was not intrin-

---

[6] See, respectively (1963) 109 C.L.R. 593, and [1962] N.I.L.R. 15.

[7] [1962] N.I.L.R. 15, 21.

[8] Hansard, H.C. Deb. Vol. 776, col. 1728, 31 January 1969.

[9] Cmnd. 4078, 1969, para. 22.

[10] [1968] 3 All E.R. 439, 441.

[11] *Cf.* Street, *Freedom, The Individual and The Law* (3rd ed. 1972), p. 164. See also *Stirling* v. *Associated Newspapers, Ltd* [1960] S.L.T.R. 5, 8 *per* Lord Clyde, where it is apparently suggested that a contempt may be committed as from the moment when a *crime* has been suspected.

[12] (1963) 109 C.L.R. 593, 618.

sically likely or intended at the time of publication no liability will be incurred.[13] Equally, however, it is submitted that D would not be liable when he publishes material prejudicial to the ultimate fair trial of P where P's arrest was *apparently* imminent, although not so as a matter of reality. Hence if, for example, the suspect had, contrary to all expectations, not been in the house which was surrounded by the police no contempt would be committed.[14] If, however, he was in the house, but managed to escape through the ineptitude of the police and to remain at large for a period of months, the position would be different. Here proceedings may be said to have been imminent at the time of publication even though, as events turned out, the likelihood of a very early arrest was not translated into reality. In the latter case the situation (viewed objectively) was substantially likely to result in criminal proceedings in the immediate future. In the former case it was not. There is, of course, no requirement that the proceedings should *remain* pending or imminent through to the moment of trial; nor indeed that the case should actually come to trial. A contempt might be committed though the proceedings were ultimately dropped,[15] or if the suspect died before trial or, indeed, if, having escaped, he was never subsequently caught.

(vi) *The Phillimore Committee proposals*[16]

There are two main ways in which one might seek to ease the constraints which the *sub judice* rule imposes upon the press. One is to provide for a broad-based defence of counterbalancing public interest under which the prejudice to a fair trial might be viewed as offset by some other public benefit advanced by the publication. It will be submitted later that such a defence should be introduced.[17] Here it is sufficient to note that its main disadvantage lies in the element of uncertainty which would necessarily accompany it. The Phillimore Committee favoured the second approach of limiting the ambit of the law of contempt by reference to a fixed point in the criminal process. Their conclusion was that 'the right point in England and Wales is the moment when the suspected man is charged or a summons served'.[18] Comment published before this point could not be a contempt though it might be punished on indictment in the unlikely event that an intent to interfere with the administration of justice could be established.

It is, of course, easy to point to the anomalies and disadvantages of this proposal. Indeed they are fairly rehearsed in the report itself. On the facts of cases such as *James* v. *Robinson*[19] and *Beaverbrook Newspapers, Ltd*[20] there are strong and obvious arguments against removing the sanctions of the law of contempt from those who would publish grossly prejudicial material perhaps a matter of hours before a charge is preferred. Again under the 1960 Act the publisher will, in

---

[13] *Lawson, ex p. Nodder* (1937) 81 Sol. Jo. 280; Phillimore Committee report, para. 74.

[14] The position might conceivably have arisen in *Beaverbrook Newspapers, Ltd* [1962] N.I.L.R. 15.

[15] *Cf. Davies* [1906] 1 K.B. 32 where one ground for holding the publisher in contempt was the prejudice to the charge of abandoning the child and this charge was not proceeded with.

[16] See paras. 115–132.

[17] See below, pp. 150–154.

[18] Para. 123.

[19] (1963) 109 C.L.R. 593.

[20] [1962] N.I.L.R. 15.

any event, be safe if he has exercised reasonable care and had no reason to suspect that proceedings were pending or imminent.[1] Yet when such points have been made the fact remains that the doctrine of 'imminency' does create insuperable problems for journalists and their legal advisers.[2] The 1960 Act provides no more than limited assistance, because the typical difficulty is not so much a lack of knowledge as that of deciding what inferences to draw from the known facts. Moreover the risk of prejudice can clearly be overstated. According to the Phillimore Committee, there is an average delay in London of some 22 weeks between committal by the magistrates and trial in the Crown Court, plus, of course, a further period between arrest and committal.[3] The committee made the point as a preliminary to concluding that restrictions on publicity during this period are justifiable. Equally, it may be said that with such delays it will only be in an exceptional case that prejudice is likely to carry over to the trial. It is submitted that it is preferable on balance to remove editorial uncertainty by fixing a readily ascertainable point for the start of the *sub judice* period. It seems right, however, to have a restraint operating from the moment of arrest, as opposed to the moment when a charge is preferred which may be some hours later.[4] It will also be submitted later that a defence of counterbalancing public interest would be desirable (though rarely successful) even if the Phillimore proposals (or a variation) were adopted.[5]

(3) WHEN DO PROCEEDINGS CEASE TO BE PENDING?

The problem of delimitation also exists at the opposite end of the criminal process, but since a contempt is unlikely to be committed once the trial has concluded one may dispense with detailed discussion of the cases. In *Delbert-Evans* v. *Davies and Watson*[6] it was held that a criminal case remains *sub judice* during the period when it is open to the accused to appeal against conviction or sentence. More recently in *Duffy, ex parte Nash*[7] Lord Parker, C.J., delivering the judgment of the Divisional Court, similarly agreed that: '. . . a criminal case remains *sub judice* at any rate until the time has expired within which notice of appeal to the Court of Criminal Appeal may be given, or, in the event of such notice being given, until the appeal has been heard and determined.'[8] He also noted the possibility of a subsequent appeal to the House of Lords.[9] In neither of these two cases, however, was a contempt held to have been committed because the possibility of prejudice was remote or non-existent.

[1] Administration of Justice Act 1960, s. 11(1), discussed further below, pp. 164–166.

[2] A balanced criticism was advanced by Harold Evans in the 1974 Granada Guildhall Lecture printed in the U.K. *Press Gazette*, No. 424 (March 1974).

[3] Para. 122.

[4] Against this view the Committee notes that 'an arrest may not, for good reasons, be immediately announced by the police': para. 123. This is true but the same point might be made with respect to the charge which will follow.

[5] See below, pp. 150–154.

[6] [1945] 2 All E.R. 167.

[7] [1960] 2 Q.B. 188; [1960] 2 All E.R. 891.

[8] *Ibid.*, at p. 196, and at p. 893 respectively.

[9] A point which was probably overlooked by Humphreys, J. in the *Delbert-Evans* case when he said: 'I think a criminal case may be said to be finally over when the Court of Criminal Appeal has heard and determined the appeal': *ibid.*, at p. 174.

In principle it is clear that criminal proceedings by way of indictment remain pending until they are concluded by an acquittal, or until the time for appealing or for seeking leave to appeal (whether to the Court of Appeal or to the House of Lords) has expired,[10] or until any such application or appeal has been disposed of.[11] Summary proceedings would similarly remain pending until time for appealing or for seeking leave to appeal has expired, or until any such appeal or application (whether to the Crown Court, a Divisional Court, or the House of Lords) has been disposed of. The possibility of a court hearing an appeal out of time also needs to be kept in mind. In such a case proceedings would presumably become *sub judice* again once an extension of time had been granted, and possibly also once notice had been given. Similarly, proceedings would no doubt remain pending where a jury has failed to agree upon a verdict,[12] at least until the prosecution intimates that it does not intend to proceed further. The same is true where the Court of Appeal has ordered a retrial on the basis that fresh evidence is available,[13] or where it is held that there has been a mistrial warranting a *venire de novo*.[14] Beyond this it is important to note the possibility that distinct, but connected, proceedings may be pending or imminent either against one of the defendants to the original charge or against another defendant who has been separately charged. Difficulties caused by inter-connected proceedings have recently been highlighted by the Poulson affair.[15]

On a related point the decision in *Attorney-General* v. *Times Newspapers, Ltd*[16] appears to have established that proceedings are only protected by the law of contempt to the extent that they are being actively pursued.[17] There is no reason to doubt that this requirement applies to criminal proceedings as well as to civil proceedings. Thus in future the press and broadcasting agencies may not feel themselves to be subject to the same constraints as at the time of the Kray trial, when several charges were adjourned *sine die* and there was widespread belief that discussion of those aspects of the Krays' alleged activities which related to the adjourned charges (e.g. fraud, long firms and bond stealing) was not permissible.

The Phillimore Committee has recommended that the law of contempt should cease to apply once the trial has been concluded and sentence passed.[18] It is unlikely that this proposal will be controversial, bearing in mind that it will remain an offence punishable on indictment to attempt improperly to induce a person to refrain from appealing. The committee further recommended that if a

[10] For the time limit for appeals, see Criminal Appeal Act 1968, ss. 18(2), 34(1).

[11] Support for this statement is also to be found in *Ex. p. Att.-Gen., Re Truth and Sportsman, Ltd* (1961) 61 S.R. (N.S.W.) 484 (N.S.W. Sup. Ct); *Att.-Gen.* v. *Crisp and Truth (N.Z.), Ltd* [1952] N.Z.L.R. 84 (N.Z. Sup. Ct).

[12] *Re Labouchere, ex p. The Columbus Co., Ltd* (1901) 17 T.L.R. 578; *O'Dogherty* (1848) 5 Cox C.C. 348.

[13] See Criminal Appeal Act 1968, ss. 7, 23.

[14] See, in general, Michael Knight, *Criminal Appeals* (1970), Ch. 9.

[15] The point is discussed further below, p. 117 *et seq.*

[16] [1973] 1 All E.R. 815, C.A.

[17] *Cf. ibid.*, p. 822 (Lord Denning), and see also *ibid.*, at p. 827 (Scarman, L.J.) and at p. 825 (Phillimore, L.J.). On appeal the House of Lords did not appear to question that the requirement existed.

[18] Para. 132.

trial ends in disagreement of the jury, or without a verdict reached, restrictions should continue unless and until it is clear that there will be no further trial. Similarly, restrictions should apply again once a new trial has been ordered. Both proposals are probably in line with the present law. Where there is an appeal against conviction from a magistrates' court to the Crown Court the law of contempt should, it is suggested, apply 'from the moment the appeal is set down'.[19]

3   CIVIL PROCEEDINGS

(1)   WHEN DO PROCEEDINGS BECOME SUB JUDICE?

Although there is little authority in point, it seems clear in principle that civil proceedings will become pending once a writ or originating summons is issued, or some other appropriate step (such as the presentation of a petition) is taken, to set the law in motion.[20] It is not necessary that the case should have been set down for trial.[1]

Equally it seems clear that proceedings are not *pending* before this time. This view is supported by the judgment of North, J. in *Re Crown Bank*.[2] Here a series of articles had been published in the *Star* newspaper before the presentation of a petition for winding up the bank. A further article followed soon after the petition had been presented. This latter publication was held to be a gross contempt, but, by way of contrast, North, J. agreed that: 'So far, however, as the earlier paragraphs published before the petition was presented are concerned, their publication might be the subject of an action for libel, but could be no contempt of Court.'[3]

Re Crown Bank was decided in 1890 and there have been significant developments since then. In particular it now seems that the law of contempt applies to proceedings which are imminent no less than to those which are pending.[4] The point has generally been discussed with comment on criminal proceedings in mind, but the same rule must be presumed to apply to civil proceedings. Indeed in *Attorney-General* v. *Times Newspapers, Ltd* Lord Reid said that: 'There is no magic in the issue of a writ or in a charge being made against an accused person. Comment on a case which is imminent may be as objectionable as comment after it has begun.'[5] Similarly, Lord Diplock was of the view that: 'To constitute a contempt of court that attracts the summary remedy, the conduct complained of must relate to some specific case in which litigation in a court of law is actually

---

[19] *Ibid.*

[20] *Cf.* Oswald, *Contempt of Court*, p. 97; Borrie and Lowe, *Law of Contempt* (1973), p. 148 *et seq.*, *Dunn* v. *Bevan* [1922] 1 Ch. 276, 284.

[1] *Cf. Att.-Gen.* v. *Times Newspapers, Ltd* [1974] A.C. 273, 323; [1973] 3 All E.R. 54, 84 *per* Lord Cross. For the relevance of this point of time to the parliamentary convention governing discussion of matters *sub judice*, see below, p. 155. For the Phillimore Committee recommendations, see below, p. 87.

[2] (1890) 44 Ch. D. 649.

[3] *Ibid.*, at p. 651.

[4] See above, p. 75 *et seq.*

[5] [1974] A.C. 273, 301; [1973] 3 All E.R. 54, 65.

proceeding or is known to be *imminent*.'[6] Although neither of the above statements was made with the present point directly in mind (Lord Reid was concerned, rather, to deny the efficacy of a 'gagging' writ), both may come to be
regarded as persuasive authority if the problem is squarely posed in a future case.
It may also be added that the practical difficulties of determining when civil
proceedings are imminent are, if anything, more acute than in the case of criminal
proceedings. In the latter case the police may intimate that an early arrest is
expected, whereas in the former there may be no warning that a writ is to be
issued or an equivalent step taken.[7]

(2) WHEN DO PROCEEDINGS CEASE TO BE SUB JUDICE?

In principle civil proceedings should remain technically pending at least until
time for appealing has expired, or any such appeal or application for a new trial
has been disposed of. The authorities directly in point do not, however, support
this view. Thus in *Metzler* v. *Gounod*[8] it was sought to attach the agent of an
unsuccessful defendant to an action for breach of contract following the publication of comment supporting the defendant's case. The application was dismissed, Keating, J. saying:[9]

> The trial had taken place, and the plaintiff had obtained a verdict, and the defendant
> had leave to move for a nonsuit or a new trial on technical grounds. The motion may or
> may not be made; the time has not expired; but it does not matter whether it is made or
> not, nothing is now pending before the court;

A similar view was taken in *Dallas* v. *Ledger*[10] where the proceedings had gone
somewhat further in that the unsuccessful defendant to a libel action had given
notice of an application for a new trial although the application had not yet been
heard. In this case, though, the chance of any resultant prejudice to a new trial
was understandably regarded as extremely remote. No consideration was given
to the question whether the *application* itself was pending since it was not
suggested that this might have been prejudiced. On the basis of these cases one
might conclude that civil proceedings will be regarded as terminating (at least
temporarily) once a judgment has been entered at first instance, and even though
time for appealing has not expired. Presumably they would become pending once
more when notice of appeal had been given.

Again, however, it is significant that these 19th-century cases were decided well
before the modern English authorities establishing that criminal proceedings
remained *sub judice* at least during the period when it is open to an accused to
appeal.[11] There is no reason why a different rule should apply in civil proceedings, although the Supreme Court of New South Wales has admittedly declined

---

[6] *Ibid.*, at p. 308, and at p. 71 respectively. Emphasis supplied.

[7] Consequently the defence afforded by the Administration of Justice Act 1960, s. 11(1) may be
more readily satisfied. See further below, pp. 164–166.

[8] (1874) 30 L.T. 264.

[9] *Ibid.*

[10] (1888) 4 T.L.R. 432. See also *Glasgow Corporation* v. *James Hedderwick & Sons, Ltd* (1918) S.C.
639 – Scotland.

[11] See *Delbert-Evans* v. *Davies and Watson* [1945] 2 All E.R. 167; *Duffy, ex p. Nash* [1960] 2 Q.B.
188; [1960] 2 All E.R. 891 and, in general, above pp. 83–84.

to extend the law by analogy in a modern case.[12] It is accordingly submitted that civil proceedings remain technically pending during the period when it is open to a party to appeal and until any such appeal (including an appeal to the House of Lords) has been determined. Equally, it seems clear that fresh proceedings will be pending if a jury has failed to agree,[13] or if the Court of Appeal has ordered a new trial. It would, however, remain unlikely that a contempt would be committed in practice through the possibility of prejudicing a pending appeal or of exerting improper pressure upon a party to induce him to refrain from appealing.[14]

(3) THE PHILLIMORE COMMITTEE PROPOSALS

The Phillimore Committee has put forward proposals for curtailing the period within which the law of contempt operates. According to the committee the restrictions should only begin to apply once the case has been set down for trial, this being the latest convenient and ascertainable date under existing procedures.[15] In the case of county courts it should apply from six weeks before the date fixed for the hearing with a similar period for civil proceedings in magistrates' courts.[16] In the only note of dissent to the report Mr Robin Day advocated the adoption of a period even closer to the trial.[17] Having referred to Lord Denning's evidence to the committee stating that there is presently a delay of up to twelve months between setting down and hearing,[18] he proposed the establishment of a *sub judice* list of cases coming up for trial within one or two weeks. Lord Denning had himself suggested that the period of quarantine should perhaps begin 'when the case comes into the term's list for hearing'.[19] While there is considerable scope for debate as to where the line might be drawn it is thought that the general approach of the committttee is correct. As with the parallel proposal for criminal proceedings[20] it is easy to point to the anomalies which might arise in borderline cases. But these are more than compensated by the desirable element of certainty which would be introduced into the law. Again, as in the case of criminal proceedings, it is recommended that the contempt restrictions should cease to apply once the first instance hearing has been concluded.[1] Intentional interference with the administration of justice thereafter would, of course, be punishable as an indictable offence.

---

[12] *Ex. p. Dawson; Re Australian Consolidated Press, Ltd* (1958) 61 S.R. (N.S.W.) 573.

[13] *Cf. Re Labouchere, ex p. The Columbus Co., Ltd* (1901) 17 T.L.R. 578.

[14] See further below, p. 107 *et seq.* where the point is discussed in relation to criminal cases.

[15] See paras. 124–132. This is also the period adopted for the purposes of the parliamentary *sub judice* convention (see below, p. 155).

[16] Para. 131. For the recommendation for interlocutory proceedings, see para. 129.

[17] Mr Day's note is printed on pp. 98–100 of the report.

[18] Para. 3 of the dissenting note.

[19] *Ibid.*

[20] See above, p. 82.

[1] Para. 132 of the main report. If a new trial is ordered restrictions would apply again when it was set down for trial.

(4) LITIGATION MUST BE ACTIVELY PURSUED

As was mentioned earlier it appears that litigation is only protected by the present law of contempt to the extent that it is being actively pursued. Thus in *Attorney-General* v. *Times Newspapers, Ltd* Lord Denning, M.R. stated that:[2]

> Our law of contempt does not prevent comment before the litigation is started, nor after it has ended. Nor does it prevent it when the litigation is dormant and is not being actively pursued . . . . No person can stop comment by serving a writ and letting it lie idle: nor can he stop it by entering an appearance and doing nothing more. It is active litigation which is protected by the law of contempt, not the absence of it.

In Lord Denning's opinion the requirement of active litigation was not met on the facts of the case where the actions between the thalidomide children and Distillers 'have gone soundly to sleep and have been asleep for these last three or four years'.[3] On appeal the House of Lords did not appear to question that the requirement existed so much as to draw markedly different inferences from the facts. According to Lord Diplock it was 'wholly unrealistic to take the view, expressed in the judgments of the Court of Appeal, that the existence of the actions can be ignored because they are "dormant" pending the complicated negotiations for settlement.'[4] As to the merits of these views one can only say that while twelve years had lapsed since the drug thalidomide was taken off the market the case was admittedly exceptional in terms of the legal issues raised and the number of people concerned in any settlement.

4   PROCEEDINGS BEFORE TRIBUNALS AND OTHER BODIES

The question of when the limitations imposed by the law of contempt should begin to apply to tribunals of inquiry appointed under the 1921 Act was discussed by the Salmon Committee in its report published in June 1969. The committee concluded that:[5]

> We do not consider that the law of contempt should apply as soon as the government of the day has announced its intention of establishing a Tribunal of Inquiry. This we think would be giving too much power to the executive. On the other hand we would not postpone its application until the Tribunal sits. We recommend that the law of contempt should apply only as from the date of the instrument appointing a Tribunal under the Act of 1921. There would thus be no uncertainty as to when anyone was at risk.

This seems to represent a sensible compromise solution. A law whereby a contempt could be committed when the appointment of a tribunal might be considered 'imminent' would place intolerable restrictions upon the press and broadcasting agencies. Discussion of matters which are creating a nationwide crisis of confidence would in practice be severely curtailed even though there was

---

[2] [1973] 1 Q.B. 710, 740; [1973] 1 All E.R. 815, 822, C.A.
[3] *Ibid.*, at p. 738, and at p. 821. See also Phillimore, L.J. *ibid.*, at p. 744 and at p. 825 respectively.
[4] [1974] A.C. 273, 311. See also *ibid.*, at p. 301 (Lord Reid), p. 306 (Lord Morris), p. 317 (Lord Simon), and p. 324 (Lord Cross).
[5] Cmnd. 4078, para. 24.

no real certainty that a tribunal would be ultimately appointed. Pressure to hold an inquiry might be resisted, or it might be decided to hold an inquiry, but not under the 1921 Act.[6] Moreover, as the committee noted, there is no administrative reason for a delay once the government of the day has decided to set up a tribunal under the Act. The composition of the tribunal can be arranged, the necessary instrument of appointment prepared in draft, and the resolutions of both Houses of Parliament secured within a short space of time.[7]

The views of the Salmon Committee do not, of course, constitute law. Neither have their recommendations been implemented by an amendment to the 1921 Act or otherwise. Accordingly there is room for debate on the current state of the law. Speaking in the House of Commons when a resolution was being moved to establish a tribunal of inquiry into the collapse of the Vehicle and General Insurance Company in April 1971, Mr Edward Heath, then prime minister, assumed that the committee's recommendations accurately reflected the present law.[8] This may be so. But the committee itself did not make any such claims, and since it now seems likely that a contempt may be committed in relation to criminal proceedings which are no more than imminent[9] it is at least arguable that the same is true of tribunals of inquiry. Similar considerations apply to those tribunals and decision-making agencies which are not courts of law, but whose deliberations are protected by the law of contempt. Examples include courts-martial and the Parliamentary Commissioner in the performance of his duties under the Parliamentary Commissioner Act 1967.[10]

---

[6] Para. 23. The Flixborough disaster was e.g. followed by a court of inquiry, rather than a tribunal appointed under the 1921 Act.

[7] Para. 25.

[8] Hansard, H. C. Deb. Vol. 816, col. 436, 28 April 1971.

[9] See above, p. 75 et seq.

[10] See further above, pp. 33–35.

7 The Sub Judice Rule:
Conduct Prejudicial to the
Fair Trial of Criminal Proceedings

1 INTRODUCTION

The determination of liability in criminal proceedings should clearly be as free as possible from extraneous influences and proceed solely upon the basis of evidence and argument adduced in open court. Many different aspects of English law have a part to play in achieving this end. These include the tradition of judicial independence, the rules of natural justice, the power to direct that a case be heard at a different venue to avoid local prejudice, the ability to challenge a juror peremptorily or for cause, and the restrictions on the reporting of committal proceedings imposed by the Criminal Justice Act 1967.[1] Of particular importance, however, is the general requirement of the law of contempt that persons desist from conduct which may interfere with the administration of justice in proceedings which are pending or imminent.

No doubt in the majority of contempt cases the courts will be concerned with conduct likely to interfere with a fair trial in a way which is adverse to the interests of an accused. It is clear, though, that this need not invariably be so and that alleged interference with the immediate interests of the prosecution may equally form the basis of contempt proceedings. This point was made very clearly by McRuer, C.J. in the Canadian case of *Bryan*.[2] Having referred to the right of an accused person to have a fair and unprejudiced trial, he continued: 'There is an equal right—that the prosecution is entitled to have the case for the Crown dealt with in a fair and unprejudiced manner on the evidence given in the witness-box, and on that alone.'[3] In short, society has an interest in securing the conviction of the guilty as well as the acquittal of the innocent. Both considerations are embodied within the concept of a 'fair trial'. Equally it is quite immaterial for present purposes whether the assertions which form the subject matter of the contempt proceedings are true or false.[4] An accused who is factually guilty is as entitled to a fair trial as an accused who is factually innocent, and the due administration of justice may be improperly interfered with in either case.

As was noted in an earlier chapter the law of contempt is primarily concerned with the *potential* effect of conduct and liability may be incurred even though, in

---

[1] The provisions of the 1967 Act are discussed below, pp. 112–116.

[2] [1954] 3 D.L.R. 631 (Ontario High Ct).

[3] *Ibid.,* at p. 632. See also *Att.-Gen.* v. *Noonan* [1956] N.Z.L.R. 1021; *Att.-Gen.* v. *Tonks* [1934] N.Z.L.R. 141 (N.Z. Sup. Ct).

[4] *Cf. Skipworth and Castro's Case* (1873) L.R. 9 Q.B. 230, 234.

the result, no interference with the administration of justice has materialised.[5] It follows that there is no necessary inconsistency between a decision holding the publisher of an article in contempt, and a subsequent refusal to quash a conviction on the ground that prejudice to a fair trial was not in fact occasioned. In *Thomson Newspapers, Ltd, ex parte Attorney-General*,[6] for example, the proprietors of the *Sunday Times* were fined for contempt following references to the discreditable background of one Michael Abdul Malik, who was then awaiting trial on charges under the Race Relations Act. Delivering the judgment of the Divisional Court, Lord Parker C.J. was clear that, '. . . to say of a man that he has had an unedifying career as a brothel-keeper, procurer and property racketeer, is undoubtedly something which is likely to prejudice the fair trial of that person before a jury'.[7] Yet Malik's subsequent appeal against conviction and sentence on the ground, inter alia, that his trial had been prejudiced by the article was dismissed. Lord Parker, C.J. (presiding this time over the Court of Appeal) viewed the conviction in the light of the totality of the evidence, and concluded that: 'It was quite inevitable, as it seems to this court, that the jury must come to that conclusion; and in those circumstances there could be no possible prejudice affecting the result of the trial.'[8] Similarly, Savundra's appeal against conviction was dismissed in spite of a television interview by David Frost which was criticised in the Court of Appeal on the ground that it was highly prejudicial.[9]

While inconsistency of approach is not necessarily involved, the extreme reluctance of the courts to quash convictions in such cases gives English law the appearance of being somewhat schizophrenic in this respect.[10] The case of *Dyson*[11] in 1943 appears, in fact, to provide the only modern recorded instance of a conviction being quashed because of prejudicial publicity in the period before the trial. Goldfarb, a leading American writer on contempt, has accordingly commented:[12]

> The greatest failure of English contempt law is its disrelation with its most valuable object—protection of fair trials. It is of little service to an accused person who is written into jail by a prejudiced press that the publisher or editor is fined or imprisoned. His victory is a hollow one unless the conviction is reversed. The contempt vehicle is only indirectly curative of unfair trials, if at all, though this is its most valuable purpose.

It is of interest to note that in the United States the position is, in effect, exactly the reverse from that which exists in this country. State courts have been denied the power to punish for contempt by publication unless there has been a 'clear and present danger' to the administration of justice.[13] This formula has, more-

---

[5] *Cf.* above, Ch. 5, pp. 70–71.
[6] [1968] 1 All E.R. 268.
[7] *Ibid.,* at p. 269.
[8] *Malik* [1968] 1 All E.R. 582, 585.
[9] *Savundranayagan and Walker* [1968] 3 All E.R. 439. See also above, p. 79.
[10] *Cf.* Goodhart (1964) 80 L.Q.R. 13 commenting on *Box* [1963] 3 W.L.R. 696, where the Court of Criminal Appeal had refused to quash a conviction even though one of the jurors had a detailed prior knowledge of the accused's past disreputable conduct.
[11] (1943) 29 Cr. App. R. 104. *Cf. Armstrong* (1952) 35 Cr. App. R. 72.
[12] See *The Contempt Power* (1963), at p. 88.
[13] The effect of the statutory provision contained in 18 U.S.C. s. 401 is to prevent Federal courts from punishing contempt by publication on summary process at all: see *Nye* v. *U.S.,* 313 U.S. 33 (1941) and, in general, above, p. 43.

over, been interpreted very restrictively[14] with the result that the contempt power
has been said to constitute 'a negligible device for protecting a defendant's right
to a fair trial'.[15] The result is to be seen in cases such as *Sheppard* v. *Ohio*,[16] where
the Supreme Court of Ohio described the trial for murder of Dr Samuel
Sheppard as having taken place in an 'atmosphere of a "Roman Holiday" for
the news media'. As Justice Clark later observed:[17]

> Much of the material printed or broadcast during the trial was never heard from the
> witness stand, such as the charges that Sheppard had purposely impeded the murder
> investigation and must be guilty since he had hired a prominent criminal lawyer; that
> Sheppard was a perjurer; that he had sexual relations with numerous women; that his
> slain wife had characterised him as a 'Jekyll-Hyde'; that he was a 'bare-faced liar'
> because of his testimony as to police treatment; and, finally, that a woman convict
> claimed Sheppard to be the father of her illegitimate child.

Conversely the United States Supreme Court has been relatively willing to
reverse convictions on the ground of denial of due process when they have been
obtained against a background of overwhelming pre-trial publicity. Indeed
Sheppard himself finally succeeded on an application for habeas corpus some
twelve years after his original conviction, the Supreme Court taking the view that
he had been denied a fair trial through prejudicial publicity and disruptive
behaviour by the press within the courtroom itself.[18] Further protection to the
accused in the United States is afforded through the jury selection process, which
may last an inordinate length of time, postponement of the trial and change of
venue, sequestration of the jury, and exhortations to persons concerned in the
case not to release prejudicial material.[19] The overall effect of this approach is
that it is apt to produce a situation in which a person who has been found guilty
will go free, or at least be entitled to a retrial, because of prejudicial pre-trial
publicity which the courts have denied themselves the power to control.[20] It is
hoped that one may safely express a clear preference for the approach of the
English courts without being thought unduly chauvinistic.

While it is not proposed to speculate as to when the more stringent English
approach became firmly established, it may be noted in passing that prejudicial
press comment accompanied some of the leading criminal trials in the early 19th
century, though it was controlled by the end of the century. An example is to be
found in the trial in 1824 of Thurtell and Hunt for the murder of a man named
Weare. It seems that in the months preceding the trial:[1]

[14] See, e.g., *Bridges* v. *California,* 314 U.S. 252 (1941); *Wood* v. *Georgia,* 370 U.S. 375 (1962)—U.S.
Sup. Ct.

[15] *Cf.* Donnelly and Goldfarb, 'Contempt by Publication in the United States' (1961) 24 M.L.R.
239, 245.

[16] 165 Ohio St. 293, 294; 135 N.E. 2d 340, 342; cert. denied, 352 U.S. 910 (1956). See also *Stroble* v.
California, 343 U.S. 181 (1951).

[17] In *Sheppard* v. *Maxwell,* 384 U.S. 333, 356–357 (1966).

[18] See *Sheppard* v. *Maxwell,* above. See also *Rideau* v. *Louisiana,* 373 U.S. 723 (1963); *Estes* v.
Texas, 381 U.S. 532 (1965).

[19] For a useful brief survey, see *Freedom of the Press and Fair Trial* (1967)—being the final report of
the New York Bar Association.

[20] *Cf.* Zelman Cowen, 'Some Observations on the Law of Criminal Contempt' (1965) Univ. W.
Aus. L.R. 1, 20.

[1] See *The Trial of Thurtell and Hunt* (Notable British Trials Series), p. 29.

. . . the daily and weekly press teemed with allusions to the case. Anecdotes of the early lives of the prisoners and of their victim, and of all associated in any way with the case, flooded the newspapers. . . . All sorts of crimes actually executed or merely contemplated were attributed to the prisoner John Thurtell.

Following representations by counsel for Thurtell, Mr Justice Park adjourned the trial for a month, 'urging all persons "within the sound of his voice" to "disclaim and withhold such publications" as had been set out in the affidavits on the prisoners' behalf'.[2] This appears to have put an end to the prejudicial comment.[3]

A further example is provided by the conduct of the press at the time of the trial of the banker Henry Fauntleroy, again in 1824, in respect of forgeries which deceived the Bank of England on a colossal scale. It has been said in relation to the trial that:[4]

The attitude of *The Times* towards the unhappy banker is a black record in its history. Although the man was a great criminal, it is not creditable to British journalism of those days that a leading newspaper should take infinite pains to rake up every scandal of his past life and to prejudice the public mind against him *before* he was brought to trial. A more deliberate attempt to condemn a man unheard has never been made in the press.

Again:[5]

The most intimate details of Fauntleroy's past life were revealed by the newspapers. *The Times* of 24th September [1824] contained an exhaustive biography that was both merciless and untrue. Not only was the forger depicted as a heartless voluptuary, but he was declared to be a gamester and a spendthrift, who had squandered most of his ill-gotten gains upon women and play.

In the remainder of this chapter it is proposed to consider the various types of conduct currently likely to be prohibited by the law of contempt on the ground that they are prejudicial to the fair trial of criminal proceedings. For convenience of exposition the discussion is divided into three main headings according to whether the conduct occurs (i) before or during the trial, (ii) when an appeal is pending or (iii) after the final termination of proceedings.

2 CONTEMPT IN RELATION TO PROCEEDINGS BEFORE AND DURING THE TRIAL

(1) EXPOSING A JUROR TO IMPROPER INFLUENCES

In both English and Commonwealth cases it is the danger of exposing a juror to improper and extraneous influences which is most frequently used to justify the invoking of the power to punish for contempt. This is readily understandable since a juror's lack of legal training leaves him particularly susceptible to influence. Such influence may take a multiplicity of forms. Before discussing some of the more important, one point of a general nature should be noted. This is that

[2] *Ibid.,* at p. 32.
[3] For an unusual contempt incident arising out of the case, see below, p. 95.
[4] See *The Trial of Henry Fauntleroy* (Notable British Trials Series), p. 145.
[5] *Ibid.,* at p. 19.

in the period preceding a trial it is frequently uncertain whether a jury will ultimately be involved in the case. Many offences are hybrid in nature, and may be tried either on indictment or summarily.[6] Likewise many indictable offences may be tried summarily with the consent of the accused,[7] while, conversely, an accused generally has the right to require trial before a jury if the offence charged carries more than three months' imprisonment.[8] The nature of the offence charged will clearly affect the likelihood of a jury trial, and so, logically, the likelihood of prejudice through this medium. On the other hand, nice calculations along these lines are unlikely to be encouraged by the courts, and there remains, in any event, the possibility of committing a contempt through improperly influencing a witness, or even the presiding judge or the parties themselves.

(i) Direct approaches to jurors

Direct approaches to jurors, accompanied by either threats or promises, may be punished either on indictment as constituting the offence of embracery, or summarily as a contempt.[9] In *Russell on Crime* the general principle is stated as follows:[10]

> Any attempt whatsoever to corrupt or influence or instruct a jury in the cause beforehand, or in any way to incline them to be more favourable to the one side than to the other, by money, promises, letters, threats, or persuasions, except only by the strength of the evidence and the arguments of counsel in open court, at the trial, is an act of embracery.

Where the juror himself consents to the improper approach both may be charged with conspiring to pervert the course of justice. Thus in one recent case a certain David Bowden was sentenced at the Central Criminal Court to three years' imprisonment for this offence after he had been paid a bribe of £50 to secure the acquittal of a prisoner. In passing sentence Kilner Brown, J. is reported as saying:[11]

> Such conduct strikes at the whole system of fair trial by jury established over the centuries. This type of offence goes back hundreds of years but I am informed that so far as this court is concerned there has been no trace of it for 200 years. But in case anyone in these days might be tempted to revive a course of conduct which was no doubt prevalent in medieval times a judge has a duty to pass such a sentence as will deter others.

(ii) Prejudging the merits of a case

A discussion of the merits of a case which prejudges its outcome, or states an opinion as to the guilt or innocence of an accused, is also likely to be viewed as a

---

[6] As, e.g., dangerous and reckless driving, contrary to the Road Traffic Act 1972, s. 2.

[7] As, e.g., theft, contrary to the Theft Act 1968, s. 1.

[8] See the Magistrates' Courts Act 1952, s. 25(1), as amended by the Children and Young Persons Act 1969, s. 6(2).

[9] See *Re Dunn* [1906] V.L.R. 493 (Vict. Sup. Ct).

[10] 12th ed., 1964, Vol. 1, p. 357 citing 1 Hawk. c. 86, ss. 1,5; 4 B1. Comm. 140.

[11] See *The Times*, 27 June 1972.

contempt, both because of its probable effect upon a juror and also because trial by the news media is 'intrinsically objectionable' and usurps the function of the court.[12] So also is a publication which seeks to discredit a witness or an item of evidence. Thus in *Balfour, Re Stead*[13] the publisher of the *Review of Reviews* was fined £100 in respect of the following comment:

> Another rare rogue in the shape of Jabez Balfour was a good deal before the Courts last month. He will reappear at the Old Bailey, and then we may expect to hear no more of him for some time to come. Nemesis has leaden feet, but even justice comes to him who knows how to wait.

This was regarded as a contempt because, in the words of Wills, J.: 'The writer here had thrown his contribution into the stream of prejudice against the person to be tried, and was anticipating the result of the trial, which was an illegal and improper thing to do.'[14]

The old case of *Williams and Romney*[15] provides a further and unusual example arising out of the trial of John Thurtell to which reference was made above.[16] Thurtell had been committed for trial for the murder of a gambler named Weare when a play was staged at the Surrey Theatre representing the subject matter of the proceedings in a way which suggested that Thurtell was guilty. Addressing the Court of King's Bench on a motion for a criminal information against the proprietor of the theatre Mr Chitty described the performance as an 'atrocious and monstrous indecency'.[17] The information was granted, the Court saying that: 'Any attempt whatever to prejudge a criminal case, whether by a detail of the evidence, or by a comment, or by a theatrical exhibition, is an offence against public justice, and a serious misdemeanour.[18]

Modern English examples of such blatant attempts to prejudge the guilt or innocence of an accused are happily rare, but the case of *Bolam, ex parte Haigh*[19] provides a striking exception. Here, Silvester Bolam, the editor of the *Daily Mirror*, was imprisoned for three months, and the proprietors fined £10,000, for publishing material highly prejudicial to the fair trial of John George Haigh. Haigh was later found by the jury to have disposed of his victims with the aid of acid in what proved to be one of the most notorious murder trials of the century. The offending publication not only described him as a 'vampire', but it also stated that he had committed other murders in the past and named the victims. 'In the long history of the present class of case', said Lord Goddard, C.J. in delivering the judgment of the Divisional Court, 'there had never, in the opinion

---

[12] *Cf. Attorney-General* v. *Times Newspapers, Ltd* [1974] A.C. 273; [1973] 3 All E.R. 54, discussed below, pp. 127–130.

[13] (1895) 11 T.L.R. 492.

[14] *Ibid.*, at p. 493.

[15] (1823) 2 L.J. (O.S.) K.B. 30.

[16] At p. 92.

[17] See *The Trial of Thurtell and Hunt*, at p. 190.

[18] (1823) 2 L.J. (O.S.) K.B. 30, 31. See also *Parnell* (1880) 14 Cox C.C. 474 (High Court in Ireland); *Ex p. Higgs; Re Smith's Newspapers, Ltd* (1927) 28 S. R. (N.S.W.) 85; *Auburn* v. *Reading* (1924) 26 W.A.L.R. 134; *McKay* (1927) Q.S.R. 230—Australia.

[19] (1949) 93 Sol. Jo. 220. See Charles Wintour, *Pressures on the Press* (1973), p. 131.

of the court, been one of such gravity as this, or one of such a scandalous and wicked character'.[20]

(iii) Publications containing tacit assumptions of guilt

Questions of contempt may also be involved when publications contain a tacit assumption rather than a direct assertion of guilt. An example is provided by the case of *Hutchinson, ex parte McMahon*.[1] Here a news film had been distributed to some 263 cinemas depicting the arrest of a man following an incident which occurred while the King was riding in a procession down Constitution Hill. It seems that a revolver, which fell close to the King's horse, was either thrown by or knocked from the hands of the man who was subsequently arrested. He was later charged with the unlawful possession of firearms. The film was held to be a contempt because of the damaging assumption implicit in the accompanying caption worded, 'Attempt on the King's life'. The distributors, Gaumont British Distributors, Ltd, were fined £50 and ordered to pay the costs of the proceedings. A similar slip led to the institution of proceedings in the Australian case of *Pacini*.[2] Here a contempt was held to have been committed when it was suggested in a radio broadcast that the arrest of a particular suspect constituted a successful conclusion to police investigations.

The likelihood of resultant prejudice will, however, ultimately depend upon the circumstances of individual cases. According to Windeyer, J. in *James* v. *Robinson* it would not, for example, be a contempt for a newspaper to state: 'that two persons had been seen to be shot dead, that the man who shot them was—the fact being beyond dispute—a named person who was at large and sought for by the police.' Neither would matters be advanced if the victims were described as having been 'murdered', rather than 'shot', for the word would be understood as a description of an event rather than an accusation of a crime.[3] The same might have been true of the incident involving Princess Anne in the Mall in March 1974 which was widely described in the press the following day as an 'Assassination Attempt'.

(iv) Publications espousing the case of the accused.

A contempt may also be committed through conduct which is intended or intrinsically likely to influence a jury in favour of the accused. In *Onslow's and Whalley's Case*[4] a man known as Castro or Orton was awaiting trial for perjury and forgery in respect of his claim to the title and estate of Sir Roger Tichborne. His cause was taken up by two members of parliament, Guildford Onslow and

---

[20] See also *Odhams Press, Ltd., ex p. Att.-Gen.* [1957] 1 Q.B. 73; [1956] 3 All E.R. 494, below, p. 161.

[1] [1936] 2 All E.R. 1514. See also *Daily Herald (Editor, Printers and Publishers), ex p. Rouse* (1931) 75 Sol. Jo. 119.

[2] [1956] V.L.R. 544 (Vict. Sup. Ct.).

[3] (1963) 109 C.L.R. 593, 611 (High Ct of Australia). See also *Packer* v. *Peacock* (1912) 13 C.L.R. 577, 588 *per* Griffith, C.J.

[4] (1873) L.R. 9 Q.B. 219. For further details of the background to this case, see below, p. 132. On the general point, see also *Mason, ex p. D.P.P., The Times*, 7 December 1932; *Bottomley, The Times*, 19 December 1908; *Nield, The Times*, 27 January 1909; *Davis* v. *Baillie* [1946] V.L.R. 486.

George Whalley, who called a series of meetings charging that he was the victim of a conspiracy. At one such meeting Whalley secured the passing of a resolution:

> That this meeting declares its opinion, in common with the country at large, that the prosecution of the claimant at the public cost was uncalled for, and in the absence of explanation which has been refused, wholly unjustifiable, and demands public reprobation; and that the support and sympathy of the British public are justly due to the claimant.

Holding both Onslow and Whalley in contempt, Lord Cockburn, C.J. stated that such conduct was 'calculated to interfere most seriously with the course of public justice'.[5] Some nine days later the Court of Queen's Bench was called upon to deal with one Skipworth together with Castro (or Orton) himself in respect of their comments on the case against Onslow and Whalley. Holding that a contempt had again been committed Blackburn, J. said the important question was whether the defendants had sought to 'prejudge the question by what is called appealing to the public, so as to prejudice the minds of the jurors who may come to try the case'.[6]

(v) Publishing matter likely to be inadmissible in evidence

(a) *Previous convictions or misconduct.* A risk of interference with the administration of justice may also be seen to be present where matter is published which may be inadmissible in evidence in subsequent criminal proceedings. Of particular importance in this context is the rule which generally precludes the prosecution from adducing evidence of an accused's previous convictions or misconduct.[7] This prohibition is designed to avoid prejudice to an accused and it is clearly apt to be circumvented by out-of-court publications which refer to his discreditable past. Certainly the risk of prejudice can be overstated and there have been a number of striking examples in recent years of cases in which a jury has acquitted in spite of its knowledge of previous convictions.[8] But while the assumption that juries are likely to be prejudiced continues to underpin much of the law of criminal evidence it is clearly right that juries should not learn out of court that which they are prevented from knowing in court itself.[9]

Publications referring to an accused's discreditable past have been held to be a contempt on numerous occasions. Thus in *Parke*[10] an article in the *Star* newspaper stating that a person currently charged with forgery had a previous conviction for the same offence was held to be a contempt. Similarly the offending article in *Beaverbrook Newspapers, Ltd*[11] detailed the criminal record of one Robert McGladdery who was about to be arrested on a charge of murder. More recently it was a description of Michael Malik as a person who had had an

---

[5] (1873) L.R. 9 Q.B. 219, 226.
[6] See *Skipworth's and Castro's Case* (1872) L.R. 9 Q.B. 230, 234.
[7] As to which, see Cross, *Evidence*, 4th ed., 1974 Ch. XIV.
[8] Notably the *Kray* and *Janie Jones* trials, below, p. 117.
[9] The matter is discussed in the Phillimore Committee report, para. 50.
[10] [1903] 2 K.B. 432—see above, p. 73. See also *Davies* [1906] 1 K.B. 32; *Tibbits and Windust* [1902] 1 K.B. 77; *Re Thomas* [1928] S.A.S.R. 210; *Davies v. Baillie* [1946] V.L.R. 486; *Queensland Newspapers Pty, Ltd, ex p. Shannon* [1962] Q.W.N. 50—Australia.
[11] [1962] N.I.L.R. 15—see above, p. 77.

'unedifying career as brothel-keeper, procurer and property racketeer', which formed the basis of the contempt proceedings in *Thomson Newspapers, Ltd.*[12] Delivering the judgment of the Divisional Court in this latter case Lord Parker, C.J. explained that such statements must clearly be viewed as a serious contempt, 'when one realises that, except in special circumstances, a jury is not entitled to know anything of the prisoner's bad character, if he has a bad character'.[13]

Statements suggesting that a person charged with an offence is currently serving a prison sentence, or has been to prison in the past, will obviously convey the same damaging impression. The Canadian case of *Bochner and Ruby*[14] provides an example. Here the offence was held to have been committed through the publication of an article during the trial of one McDonald on charges of armed robbery and kidnapping. The offending article referred to his 'legendary exploits in the world of crime' and to the fact that he was then 'serving $2\frac{1}{2}$ years in the penitentiary'.

(b) *Confessions.* A publication may also be a contempt if it states or infers that an accused has confessed to committing the offence charged or otherwise admitted incriminating facts. Here the risk of interference would normally arise from the fact that the confession may not be offered in evidence or may be held to be inadmissible as being involuntary. *Clarke, ex parte Crippen*[15] is the leading English example. In this case the *Daily Chronicle* was held to have committed a contempt in publishing a statement from a special correspondent suggesting that 'Crippen admitted in the presence of witnesses that he had killed his wife, but denied that the act was murder'. Further examples stressing the element of prejudice to an accused in such publications are to be found in other common law jurisdictions.[16]

(c) *Hearsay, opinion etc.* Such cases apart it is true to say that any account of the circumstances surrounding a crime which goes beyond a statement of the bare undisputed facts[17] may carry an attendant danger of contempt proceedings. For example, statements purporting to be a verbatim account of the events as seen by a potential witness may contain matters which will be subsequently held to be inadmissible in evidence as hearsay or mere opinion.[18]

No doubt this is one of the reasons why the courts have sought to discourage the notion that criminal investigation is one of the functions of the press. The leading English case arose out of the well-publicised 'Crumbles' case in 1924 when a sales manager, Patrick Mahon, murdered and dismembered the body of

[12] [1968] 1 All E.R. 268.

[13] *Ibid.,* at p. 269.

[14] [1944] 3 D.L.R. 788 (Ontario High Ct).

[15] (1910) 103 L.T. 636—see above, p. 74.

[16] See, e.g., *Ex p. Senkovitch* (1910) 10 S.R. (N.S.W.) 738. *Ex p. Norton; Re John Fairfax and Sons Pty. Ltd* (1952) 69 W.N. (N.S.W.) 312; *Pacini* [1956] V.L.R. 544; *West Australian Newspapers, Ltd* (1958) 60 W.A.L.R. 108—Australia; *Wills and Pople,* (1913) 9 D.L.R. 646, 651 (Manitoba King's Bench).

[17] *Cf. Packer* v. *Peacock* (1912) 13 C.L.R. 577, 588 *per* Griffith, C.J.

[18] See, e.g. *Ex p. Kear; Re Consolidated Press, Ltd* (1954) 54 S.R. (N.S.W.) 95; *Ex p. Jane Smith* (1901) 1 S.R. (N.S.W.) 55—(N.S.W. Sup. Ct); *cf. Att.-Gen.* v. *Mathison* [1942] N.Z.L.R. 302 (N.Z. Sup. Ct).

Emily Kaye. Three leading newspapers, which had published the results of their investigations into the circumstances surrounding the death, were brought before the Divisional Court and fined for contempt.[19] In caustic terms Lord Hewart, C.J. sought to disabuse them of the idea that, 'it had come to be somehow for some reason the duty of newspapers to employ an independent staff of amateur detectives', who were free 'to conduct their investigation unfettered, to publish to the whole world from time to time the result of these investigations'. Pointing to the dangers involved, he added:[20]

> It was not possible even for the most ingenious mind to anticipate with certainty what were to be the real issues, to say nothing of the more difficult question what was to be the relative importance of different issues in a trial which was about to take place. . . . It was impossible to foresee what was important.

On the facts of the 'Crumbles' case Lord Hewart's observations were, no doubt, entirely justified. On the other hand investigative journalism clearly serves a useful function in other areas (notably in exposing fraud), and cannot sensibly be condemned without qualification.[1]

(d) *Prejudicing the prosecution.* Publications drawing inadmissible evidence to the attention of the jury, or affecting the weight accorded to admissible evidence, may exceptionally constitute a contempt as being prejudicial to the immediate interests of the prosecution. In *Ruse* v. *O'Sullivan*,[2] for example, a person charged with attempting to obtain money by false pretences sought to invite a prosecution witness to open a small brown box which he handed to him in court. The trial court judge did not permit disclosure of the contents of the box. An evening newspaper thereafter enlightened the jury by stating that it contained $A20,000 in cash and that it was the accused's contention that his access to such a sum tended to negative any dishonest intent. The Supreme Court of Western Australia held that the publication constituted a contempt.

A further example is provided by another Australian case, *Consolidated Press, Ltd* v. *McRae*.[3] Here the Sydney *Daily Telegraph* had published an article reporting a suspect's allegation that he had been, 'violently assaulted by police officers at a police station with a view to obtaining confessional statements from him'. In subsequent contempt proceedings the High Court of Australia agreed:[4]

> It may readily be conceded that . . . if a question to be determined by the judge at a trial of any of the charges would be whether such a statement was voluntary in character so as to be admissible, then the publication in the newspaper in advance of the trial . . . of the defendant's detailed allegations that they were extorted by violence would constitute contempt of court.

In the result, however, liability for contempt was not established.

[19] See *Evening Standard, ex p. D.P.P.* (1924) 40 T.L.R. 833. See also *Surrey Comet, ex p. Baldwin* (1931) 75 Sol. Jo. 311, D.C.; *Ex p. Higgs; Re Smith's Newspapers, Ltd* (1927) 28 S.R. (N.S.W.) 85, 93 (N.S.W. Sup. Ct).
[20] (1924) 40 T.L.R. 833, 835.
[1] See further, above, p. 79, and below, pp. 145–149, 150–154.
[2] [1969] W.A.R. 142.
[3] (1955) 93 C.L.R. 325.
[4] *Ibid.,* at p. 333 (Dixon, C.J., Kitto, Taylor, JJ.).

It is submitted that the High Court's view is correct in principle, and that allegations of police brutality may be regarded as affecting the weight which a jury will ultimately attach to an alleged confession. It is doubtful, however, whether such allegations would affect the preliminary issue of admissibility which is determined by the judge. Equally, it may be argued that references to alleged confessions or to previous misconduct may prejudice the case for the prosecution by providing a ground for reversal on appeal.[5]

(2) EXPOSING A WITNESS TO IMPROPER INFLUENCES

Interference with the administration of justice may likewise be occasioned through conduct which is either intended, or substantially likely, to influence a witness in an improper manner. Such conduct may take a variety of different forms, some of which have already been discussed in the previous section. Thus just as the detailing of an accused's discreditable past, or of the fact that he has made a confession, may be seen as being likely to prejudice the jury against him, so also may it be seen as likely to deter witnesses from coming forward to give evidence on his behalf, or to modify the evidence which they would otherwise have given. Since most of the cases emphasising this latter danger have arisen in civil proceedings, they will be discussed in the following chapter.[6]

(i) *Direct approaches to witnesses.*

In *Russell on Crime* it is said that:[7]

> It is an offence at common law to use threats or persuasion to witnesses to induce them not to appear or give evidence in courts of justice, even if the threats or persuasion fail, or to endeavour to persuade a witness to alter the evidence already given by him.

As in the case of direct approaches to jurors, attempts to intimidate, bribe, or otherwise improperly influence an actual or potential witness may be punished either on indictment or summarily as a contempt. The same is true of an attempt to induce an actual or potential witness not to give evidence at all. An example of proceedings being taken by way of indictment is to be found in a recent case which arose out of allegations in the *News of the World* that certain BBC employees had been bribed to play records on their programmes in return for sexual and other favours. The resultant proceedings against Miss Janie Jones and others included charges of attempting to pervert the course of justice by interfering with witnesses and inducing them by threats and intimidation not to give evidence.[8] *Re B. (J.A.) (An Infant)*[9] provides a modern example of summary

---

[5] As was noted above, p. 91, however, English courts have proved reluctant to quash convictions in such cases.

[6] See below, at pp. 131–133.

[7] 12th ed., 1964, Vol. 1, p. 312. See also Archbold, *Criminal Pleading, Evidence and Practice*, (38th ed., 1973), para. 3451.

[8] See the report of the committal proceedings in *The Times*, 10 July 1973. See also *Andrews* [1973] 1 All. E.R. 857, C.A.; *Greenberg* (1919) 121 L.T. 288. *Lawley* (1731) 2 Str. 904; *Steventon* (1802) 2 East 362. For the protection afforded to witnesses appearing before a wide range of inquiries which are not courts of law, see the Witnesses (Public Inquiries) Protection Act, 1892.

[9] [1965] Ch. 1112; [1965] 2 All E.R. 168. See also *Lewis v. James* (1887) 3 T.L.R. 527; *Shaw v. Shaw* (1861) 2 Sw. & Tr. 517; 164 E.R. 1097; *Wellby v. Still* (1892) 8 T.L.R. 202; *Re Hooley, Rucker's Case* (1898) 79 L.T. 306; Archbold, *op cit.*, para. 3481.

proceedings for contempt following upon an improper approach to a witness. In this case certain persons were seeking to make their infant daughter a ward of court and an injunction to restrain one John Woodall from associating with her. Woodall threatened a witness that he would inform the principal of the college where she was a student teacher that she had had an illegitimate child by him unless she refrained from giving evidence against him. The threat was ineffectual but, having regard to the potential danger involved in such conduct, Cross, J. committed Woodall to prison for four weeks for contempt.

Inducements aimed at persuading a witness not to give evidence, to give false evidence, or to retract evidence which is true do not normally pose any particular difficulty for legal analysis. The more difficult question is whether it may similarly be a contempt to offer an inducement, monetary or otherwise, to persuade a known witness to give evidence in a particular sense when such evidence would represent the truth, or to persuade him to retract false evidence. In *Re Hooley* Wright, J. referred *obiter* to an earlier unreported case in which he had held in contempt one who had offered money to a witness to secure the withdrawal of an admittedly false statement.[10] This might seem an odd conclusion. But it is submitted that it is correct in principle. Certainly there can be little doubt that a person may be held liable if threats, intimidation, or means which are otherwise improper are employed to induce evidence which is factually true. Likewise, it is submitted, promises of sums of money beyond the normal reimbursement of expenses might equally be a contempt if directed towards the same end. The same is true of other forms of inducement going beyond straightforward persuasion. It will be submitted later that it is no less a contempt because the threat is to do something which one would otherwise be at liberty to do.[11] Here it is submitted that the truth or falsity of the evidence solicited cannot be made the ultimate test of liability either. A substantial monetary or other inducement to give evidence in *any* particular sense may properly be viewed as interfering with the administration of justice.[12]

(ii) *Payment for exclusive stories etc.*

At the time of the Moors murder trial in 1966 there was discussion as to the propriety of an agreement to pay a sum of money to a witness at the end of the trial in return for his exclusive story. It was suggested that the *News of the World* might have entered into an agreement with one David Smith, the chief witness for the prosecution, whereby he was to receive a sum of money which would vary according to whether or not the accused, Ian Brady, was convicted. The newspaper, however, denied that payment was contingent upon a conviction and, in the result, the Attorney-General was not satisfied that there was sufficient

---

[10] (1898) 79 L.T. 306, 307. The question is further examined by Lanham, 'Payment to Witnesses and Contempt of Court' [1975] Crim. L.R. 144—discussing the recent case of *Kwan Cheuk-Yin* (Cr. App. No. 75 of 1973 in the Sup. Ct of Hong Kong Appellate Division).

[11] See below, pp. 137–141.

[12] Some support for this view may be found in *Kellett* [1974] Crim. L.R. 552 (Plymouth Crown Ct, Lord Widgery, C.J.); *The Times,* 21 June 1975, C.A., below, p. 141.

evidence to warrant the institution of contempt proceedings.[13] There would be widespread agreement that on proof of such facts those responsible would commit a contempt. To provide a witness with a financial or other incentive in securing a conviction must (as in the case of a bribe) be regarded as likely to prejudice a fair trial.

Where payment to a witness for an exclusive story is not made contingent upon a conviction there is no reason to suppose that an offence would be committed. This would presumably not happen very frequently in practice because of the obvious danger of libel proceedings. Lord Hewart, C.J. likewise disapproved of this feature of 'cheque-book journalism' in the 'Crumbles' case in 1924, where he is reported as saying: 'With unlimited enterprise and wealth, we may reach a time when witnesses on both sides will be bound by contract and lodged by this or that newspaper.'[14] In this case, however, prejudicial material was published while the trial was pending. Moreover, a possible witness had apparently been spirited away to stay with the wife of one of the sub-editors of the *Evening Standard*, there being doubt as to whether she would resist the wiles of other newspapers.

The related question of the legality of advertisements which call for witnesses to come forward with a promise of reward has typically arisen in civil proceedings and is discussed in the following chapter.[15]

(iii) *Interviewing of witnesses.*

In recent years there has been discussion as to the extent to which the conducting of interviews with potential witnesses may fall foul of the law of contempt. The question arose at the time of the Aberfan disaster in October 1966 when a slag heap collapsed onto and engulfed a school in a Welsh mining village. In the immediate aftermath of the tragedy a resolution was passed by both Houses of Parliament setting up an inquiry under the Tribunals of Inquiry (Evidence) Act 1921. Sir Elwyn Jones, the Attorney-General, then issued a general warning as to the undesirability, 'that any comments should be made either in the Press or on the radio or on television on matters which it will be the express function of the Tribunal to investigate'.[16] He added that such comment might constitute a contempt. This threat or warning was criticised at the time as being too sweeping, but it seems from the terms in which it was subsequently defended by the Prime Minister and the Lord Chancellor that Sir Elwyn had in mind the specific danger of a witness's evidence becoming warped or distorted through a television interview which was accorded widespread publicity. As Mr Harold Wilson, the prime minister, put it: 'Once statements have been elucidated by television interviewers under non-judicial procedures, they are on the

---

[13] See Hansard, H.C. Deb., Vol. 728, cols. 400–403, 11 May 1966. See also *The Times,* 23 April 1966; Goodman, *The Trial of Ian Brady and Myra Hindley* (1973), pp. 36–38. The general question is also discussed by the Phillimore Committee which recommends that an inquiry be carried out into the prevalence of the practice: paras. 78–79.

[14] See *Evening Standard, ex p. D.P.P.* (1924) 40 T.L.R. 833, 834. See also Street, *Freedom, the Individual and the Law* (3rd ed., 1972), p. 169; *Observer,* 24 April 1966.

[15] See below, pp. 141–142.

[16] Hansard, H.C. Deb. Vol. 734, col. 1316, 27 October 1966.

record in a form which could hinder the Tribunal's ability to get at the truth.'[17]

The Salmon Committee which was subsequently appointed to report on the law of contempt as it affects tribunals of inquiry appears to have accepted this view. Thus while the committee agreed that it was part of a journalist's legitimate function to interview witnesses for the purposes of preparing an article to be published after the proceedings,[18] it saw different considerations as being applicable to publications (and especially live interviews) when proceedings were pending. It is submitted that there is indeed a realistic danger involved. A witness may feel a psychological pressure to defend a statement made under such circumstances or, alternatively, the fact that he departs from the statement may detract from the value accorded to his testimony.[19] Beyond this the potential witness may refer to matters which would be inadmissible in evidence, or the interviewer may leave his audience with the impression that an accused in a criminal case is guilty.[20]

A further danger was suggested in the Australian case of *Ex parte Kear; Re Consolidated Press, Ltd.*[1] A man had died in a Sydney hospital following an exchange of blows at a restaurant during a New Year's Eve party. His assailant was arrested, and the following day the Sydney *Daily Telegraph* published a description by an eye witness of the events leading up to the incident. The Supreme Court of New South Wales held this to be a contempt on the ground, inter alia, that other potential witnesses would inevitably read the article with close attention, and their recollection of events would be coloured by what they had read. This case illustrates once more the danger run by the news media when they go beyond a straightforward statement of such facts as would not be in dispute in subsequent proceedings.

(iv) *Publishing photographs of an accused*

Interference with the administration of justice may sometimes occur where a photograph of a suspect is published at a time when a question of identity is likely to arise in future proceedings. The leading English case is *Daily Mirror, ex parte Smith.*[2] Here the *Daily Mirror* had published a photograph of one Edgar Smith on the morning of an identification parade at which potential witnesses were to be called on to identify Smith as the person responsible for the attempted murder of a police officer. The photograph was accompanied by a caption indicating that he had been remanded in custody on the charge. On these facts the Divisional Court held that a contempt had been committed even though none of the witnesses in fact saw the photograph, and though an issue of identity was not in the event raised at the trial. As Lord Hewart, C.J. pointed out, such a publication created a danger that a witness would approach the difficult task of identification,

---

[17] *Ibid.*, Vol. 735, col. 256, 1 November 1966. See also Hansard, H.L. Deb. Vol. 277, col. 528 (Lord Gardiner, L.C.), and, in general, *The Aberfan Inquiry and Contempt of Court* (Press Council, 1967).

[18] See the *Report of the Interdepartmental Committee on the Law of Contempt as it Affects Tribunals of Inquiry*, Cmnd 4078, June 1969, para. 29.

[19] *Cf. ibid.*, para. 31. See also the Phillimore Committee report, para. 55.

[20] *Cf.* the Savundra incident, discussed above, p. 79.

[1] (1954) 54 S.R. (N.S.W.) 95.

[2] [1927] 1 K.B. 845. See also *Beaverbrook Newspapers, Ltd* [1962] N.I.L.R. 15; *Lawson, ex p. Nodder* (1937) 81 Sol. Jo. 280.

'with his mind prejudiced by the knowledge that this particular person has been arrested and is in the hands of the police'.[3] A witness who saw the photograph would, in other words, know who he was expected to pick out. Bearing in mind the accepted impropriety of a police officer showing a photograph to a witness prior to an identification parade,[4] Lord Hewart's reasoning would appear to be entirely sound. A similar danger was seen to exist in a Scottish case involving the *Daily Record* newspaper, which had published the photograph of a well-known Scottish footballer who had been arrested on a charge of indecent exposure.[5]

In theory it is only when identity is likely to be a live issue at the trial that a question of contempt will arise in such cases. Certainly there are situations in which this requirement cannot realistically be said to have been satisfied—as where an assailant attacks his victim in front of eye witnesses and is immediately overpowered, or a thief is caught by fellow employees with his hand in the till.[6] But the cases suggest that speculation as to a suspect's probable line of defence is a hazardous occupation. Thus in *Attorney-General* v. *Noonan*[7] a contempt was committed despite the fact that the solicitor for the accused had informed the defendant newspaper editor that his client would plead guilty at the trial. Henry, J. agreed that this was relevant to the question of whether identity was likely to be in issue, but he did not accept that it excluded such a likelihood. The accused was quite entitled to change his mind. Similarly in the Australian case of *Ex parte Auld; Re Consolidated Press, Ltd*[8] Jordan C.J. went out of his way to 'repel the suggestion that, because a journalist has learnt from the police that an alleged confession has been made, or fingerprints found, he may assume that identity cannot come in question'. He added that it was equally a misconception to think, 'that a junta of police officers and journalists can hold a sort of preliminary settling of the issues likely to be tried at the hearing, and that this Court ought not lightly to interfere with their rulings as to the probability of identity being raised'.[9]

Although a publication of this nature would normally be claimed to be detrimental to the accused, it can also be seen as prejudicial to the immediate interests of the prosecution. Indeed in *Attorney-General* v. *Noonan*[10] the court was invited to consider the publication solely from this standpoint.[11] Holding that a contempt had been committed Henry, J. noted that the publication of the photograph enabled defence counsel to challenge the soundness of the victim's

---

[3] [1927] 1 K.B. 845, 849.

[4] This practice led to the quashing of convictions in cases such as *Dwyer* [1925] 2 K.B. 799 and *Haslam* (1925) 19 Cr. App. R. 59.

[5] See the *Manchester Guardian*, 13 February 1959, and Wintour, *Pressures on the Press* (1973), at p. 133. See also *Stirling* v. *Associated Newspapers, Ltd* [1960] S.L.T. 5. Do the television authorities run a similar risk of being held in contempt when they publish close up pictures of persons taking part in riotous behaviour during a demonstration?

[6] Cf. *James* v. *Robinson* (1963) 109 C.L.R. 593, 611 per Windeyer, J.

[7] [1956] N.Z.L.R. 1021 (N.Z. Sup. Ct).

[8] (1936) 36 S.R. (N.S.W.) 596 (N.S.W. Sup. Ct).

[9] *Ibid.*, at p. 598. See also *Pacini* [1956] V.L.R. 544, 547–548 per Lowe, J. (Vict. Sup. Ct); *Att.-Gen. for N.S.W.* v. *Mirror Newspapers, Ltd* (1961) 62 S.R. (N.S.W.) 421 (N.S.W. Sup. Ct).

[10] [1956] N.Z.L.R. 1021.

[11] It was conceded that reliance could not be placed on the possible prejudice to the accused since he had himself supplied the photograph for publication: *sed quaere?*

evidence in identifying the assailant. Similar reasoning was adopted by Blair, J. in the earlier New Zealand case of *Attorney-General* v. *Tonks*.[12] Alternatively, it might be argued that the publication might provide a ground for reversal of a verdict of guilty on appeal.

A further point to note is that the news media frequently publish a photograph, or an 'identikit' or 'photophit' impression, of a wanted person at the request of the police. It appears that an automatic immunity from successful contempt proceedings is not assumed and that an independent judgment as to the desirability and legality of publishing is exercised.[13] In the majority of cases there would be no question of a contempt being committed in that proceedings might not be pending or imminent, or identity would be unlikely to be in issue. There remains, however, a residue of cases in which a satisfactory solution is only to be found through recognising that prejudice to a fair trial may sometimes have to give way to some competing interest. The *Justice* committee took as an example a case in which a newspaper published a photograph of a violent criminal who was being sought by the police. The committee concluded that 'it would be nothing short of folly to label as "contempt" publication of his name and photograph, and the crimes he is suspected to have committed, with a view to securing his arrest and protecting the public meanwhile'.[14] Few would disagree. But it appears from the recent decision of the House of Lords in *Attorney-General* v. *Times Newspapers, Ltd*[15] that the newspaper would not be able to plead the public benefit advanced by the warning if the wanted man later instituted contempt proceedings.[16]

(3) EXPOSING A JUDGE TO IMPROPER INFLUENCES

A contempt of court may also be committed through conduct which is either intended or likely to prejudice the fair trial of criminal proceedings through its effect upon a judge.

The clearest example is again provided by a direct approach to a judge with the intention of influencing his decision in a given case. In Oswald on *Contempt* it is rightly said of such conduct that:[17]

> It is a grave contempt of Court to communicate with, or to seek in any way to influence, a Judge upon the subject of any matter which he has to determine . . . . The contempt is the same whether the communication be accompanied by abuse or by a bribe or not.

The fact that there appears to be a paucity of modern English examples in point no doubt testifies to the high reputation for incorruptibility which English judges enjoy. Nowadays it is difficult to envisage anyone following the example of one Thomas Martin who, in 1747, finding himself the defendant to a suit in Chancery, wrote a letter to the Lord Chancellor with a bank-note for £20 enclosed. The

---

[12] [1934] N.Z.L.R. 141, 153.

[13] Support for the overall legality of such publications might, however, be derived from *Lawson, ex p. Nodder* (1937) 81 Sol. Jo. 280. See also *Stirling* v. *Associated Newspapers Ltd* [1960] S.L.T. 5, 8; *James* v. *Robinson* (1963) 109 C.L.R. 593, 611.

[14] *Contempt of Court* (1959), p. 11. See also *The Law and the Press* (1965) para. 43.

[15] [1974] A.C. 273; [1973] 3 All E.R. 54.

[16] See further below, pp. 150–154.

[17] At p. 48.

money was ordered to be, 'applied and distributed for the relief of such of the poor prisoners in the Fleet prison as are the most proper objects of charity'. Martin was fortunate not to join them, but his apparent contrition, coupled with his recent appointment as Mayor of Great Yarmouth, saved him from this fate.[18]

These extreme cases apart, it is singularly unlikely that a finding of contempt would be based on the possibility of prejudicing a judge of the Crown Court—whether a High Court judge, circuit judge, or a recorder. It now seems to be generally accepted that their professional experience enables them to discount that which might affect a jury.[19] The decisions in point are, however, mainly concerned with either civil proceedings[20] or criminal proceedings pending on appeal.[1] They are accordingly discussed at a later stage.

Different considerations may apply where criminal proceedings are pending before magistrates' courts, for here it is not so unrealistic to regard at least a lay, if not a stipendiary, magistrate as being susceptible to improper influences. The recent Australian case of *Regal Press Pty, Ltd*[2] provides some support for this view. One John Kerr was awaiting trial in a stipendiary magistrates' court on a number of charges arising out of a driving incident when the *Melbourne Observer* published an article recalling that he had previously served a sentence for murder. McInerney, J., sitting in the Supreme Court of Victoria, held that a contempt had been committed and imposed a fine of $A500. No distinction appears to have been taken as between a stipendiary and a lay magistrate, but the authority of the case is weakened by the fact that the court speaks in terms of the magistrate being 'embarrassed' by the information,[3] and this should not be sufficient to constitute a contempt.[4] More recently, Lord Diplock has also said *obiter* that: 'Laymen, whether acting as jurymen or witnesses *(or, for that matter, as magistrates)*, were regarded by the judges as being vulnerable to influence or pressure'.[5] Indirect support for this view may also be found in the fact that magistrates are not generally informed of an accused's previous convictions and background until after they have found him guilty of the offence charged. The fact that publications such as those in the *Regal Press* case are apt to circumvent this rule also suggests that they may constitute a contempt.

(4) EXERTING IMPROPER PRESSURE ON PARTIES TO PROCEEDINGS

Conduct may also constitute a contempt if it is either intended or substantially likely to interfere with the administration of justice through exerting improper

[18] See *Martin's Case* (1747) 2 Russ & M. 674; 39 E.R. 551. See also *Re Dyce Sombre (A Lunatic)* (1849) 1 Mac. & G. 116; 41 E.R. 1207; *Lechmere Charlton's Case* (1837) 2 My. & Cr. 316; 40 E.R. 661; *Macgill's Case* (1748) 2 Fowler Exch. Pr. 404.

[19] See the Salmon Committee report, para. 26; Phillimore Committee report, para. 49. For a decision of the High Court of Ireland, see *Att.-Gen.* v. *Connolly* [1947] I.R. 213.

[20] As, e.g., *Vine Products, Ltd* v. *Mackenzie & Co., Ltd* [1966] 1 Ch. 484; [1965] 3 All E.R. 58, below, p. 124.

[1] *Duffy, ex p. Nash* [1960] 2 Q.B. 188; [1960] 2 All E.R. 891. *Cf. Delbert-Evans* v. *Davies and Watson* [1945] 2 All E.R. 167, below, pp. 107–109.

[2] [1972] V.R. 67. *Cf. Re Depoe and Lamport* (1967) 66 D.L.R. (2d) 46 (Ontario High Court).

[3] *Cf.* [1972] V.R. 67, 79–80.

[4] See further, below, p. 109.

[5] See *Att.-Gen.* v. *Times Newspapers, Ltd* [1974] A.C. 273, 309; [1973] 3 All E.R. 54, 72—Emphasis supplied.

pressure on a party to proceedings.[6] This danger would normally only be considered to be present in civil proceedings where the parties are more susceptible to pressure. In principle, however, there is no reason why the exerting of improper pressure on parties to criminal proceedings should not equally constitute a contempt. This might occur where, for example, an attempt was made through threats or a bribe to induce a prosecutor to offer no evidence in pending proceedings, or to induce an accused to plead guilty to an offence. The matter is discussed further below, both in the context of criminal cases pending on appeal, and, more fully, in the context of prejudicing civil proceedings.[7]

3 CONTEMPT IN RELATION TO PROCEEDINGS PENDING ON APPEAL

(1) INTRODUCTION

It has already been seen that even though proceedings in the trial court have been concluded a criminal case remains technically *sub judice* until time for appealing has expired, or a final appeal has been ultimately disposed of.[8] The Phillimore Committee has recommended that the law of contempt should cease to apply once the trial has been concluded.[9] But pending the possible adoption of this recommendation there is a risk of committing a contempt in the post-trial period. At this stage in the criminal process, however, the position differs radically from the position which obtains in the period before and during the trial. An appeal will be heard without a jury. Hence one can discount the possibility of prejudice through this medium. It is unlikely that the bare possibility of a *venire de novo*, or a new trial, being ordered will be regarded as a sufficient basis for a finding of contempt.[10] The position would, however, be different once the Court of Appeal had made such an order, or if the jury in the original trial had failed to reach a verdict.[11] Again, it may be said that any possible effect upon a witness can generally be discounted in the post-trial period although it is open to the Court of Appeal to receive evidence in certain circumstances.[12]

The discussion which follows will consider the further grounds on which it might be argued that a publication after a trial or hearing may constitute a contempt as infringing the *sub judice* rule.

(2) EFFECT ON APPELLATE JUDGES

A divergence of views emerges from the two main English cases which have considered post-trial publications from the viewpoint of their possible effect on

---

[6] *Cf. Re The William Thomas Shipping Co., Ltd* [1930] 2 Ch. 368, 376 *per* Maugham, J.

[7] See below, pp. 109–110, 133–136, 137–141.

[8] See above, pp. 83–84.

[9] Para. 132.

[10] But see *Delbert-Evans* v. *Davies and Watson* [1945] 2 All E.R. 167, 171 *per* Humphreys, J. *Cf.*, however, *Duffy, ex p. Nash* [1960] 2 Q.B. 188, 198; [1960] 2 All E.R. 891, 895.

[11] See *Re Labouchere, ex p. The Columbus Co., Ltd* (1901) 17 T.L.R. 578; *O'Dogherty* (1848) 5 Cox C.C. 348.

[12] Under the Criminal Appeal Act, 1968, s. 23(1).

appellate judges. In the earlier case of *Delbert-Evans* v. *Davies and Watson*[13] a medical practitioner had been convicted on charges of procuring abortion when the *News of the World* and the *Daily Telegraph* newspapers published accounts of his earlier criminal background. At the time of publication it was open to Delbert-Evans to appeal to the Court of Criminal Appeal, and he did in fact subsequently appeal against conviction, though without success. He also sought orders of attachment for contempt against the editors of the newspapers concerned. In the result the application failed, but mainly, it seems, because the appeal was against conviction alone and only raised points of law, while the matter published went, rather, to sentence.[14] Both Humphreys and Oliver, JJ. were, however, apparently prepared to countenance the possibility of an appellate judge being both embarrassed and improperly affected by newspaper publications of this nature. According to Oliver, J. it was 'absurd to suggest that judges' minds could not be affected by prejudice'.[15]

This view was followed in the Australian case of *Ex parte Attorney-General; Re Truth and Sportsman Ltd.*[16] Here a newspaper described a driver, who had been convicted after his car had knocked over and killed two young children, as a 'monster', adding that: 'It was one of the most inhuman road killings on record in New South Wales.' The Supreme Court of New South Wales justified the imposition of a fine for contempt on the ground, inter alia, that: 'If comment and criticism of the nature dealt with in these proceedings were permitted while an appeal is pending, prejudice would undoubtedly be likely to be created, and in any event the court could be seriously embarrassed.'[17]

In *Duffy, ex parte Nash,*[18] the second of the two English cases directly in point, a different approach was adopted by a strong Divisional Court. Here an article had been published in the *Daily Sketch* newspaper the day after one Nash had been convicted on charges of causing grievous bodily harm. It contained the following passage:

> A C.I.D. officer pointed a finger in an East End pub and said 'That man will end up in the dock on a charge of violence'. That was a year ago and the finger pointed to a vicious-looking man who was sipping a grapefruit and was surrounded by admiring young tear-aways and adoring street-girls. Jimmy Nash was his name—the twenty-eight-year old muscle-man jailed for five years yesterday for causing grievous bodily harm to Soho club manager Selwyn Keith Cooney. . . . This, then, is the villain of the piece. A man who, until he stepped into the Pen Club just after midnight on Feb. 6, was just an obscure thug.

Nash later applied for leave to appeal against conviction and sentence, and instituted contempt proceedings against those responsible for the publication. Delivering the judgment of the Divisional Court dismissing the proceedings,

---

[13] [1945] 2 All E.R. 167.

[14] *Cf. ibid.,* at p. 173 (Humphreys, J.); p. 175 (Oliver, J.). Yet presumably it was still open to the accused at the time of publication to appeal against sentence as well.

[15] *Ibid.,* at p. 174. See also Humphreys, J., *ibid.,* at p. 172.

[16] (1958) 61 S.R. (N.S.W.) 484.

[17] *Ibid.,* at p. 495. The decision was not, however, followed on this point in *Att.-Gen. (N.S.W.)* v. *Mundey* [1972] 2 N.S.W.L.R. 887. See also *Att.-Gen.* v. *Crisp and 'Truth' (N.Z.), Ltd* [1952] N.Z.L.R. 84 (N.Z. Sup. Ct); *Editor and Publisher of the People, ex. p. Hobbs* (1925) 69 Sol. Jo. 494, D.C.

[18] [1960] 2 Q.B. 188; [1960] 2 All E.R. 891.

Lord Parker, C.J. emphasised that liability for contempt required an intention to prejudice, or a real risk of prejudicing, a fair hearing. It was not sufficient, as the *Delbert-Evans* case appeared to suggest, that a judge had been 'embarrassed' by the material, in the sense that it had imposed on him 'quite unnecessarily, the task of dismissing the offending matter from his mind'.[19] Applying the more stringent test, Lord Parker concluded that:[20]

> Even if a judge who eventually sat on the appeal had seen the article in question and had remembered its contents, it is inconceivable that he would be influenced consciously or unconsciously by it. A judge is in a very different position to a juryman. Though in no sense superhuman, he has by his training no difficulty in putting out of his mind matters which are not evidence in the case. This indeed happens daily to judges on assize.

It is submitted, with respect, that Lord Parker's view is entirely realistic. Even if one can overcome the difficulty of imagining a senior appellate judge reading the *Daily Sketch* at breakfast time, it would seem singularly unlikely that he would be prejudiced, consciously or otherwise, by its contents. The same reasoning would apply to a judge of the Divisional Court hearing an appeal by way of case stated on a point of law and, *a fortiori*, to a Law Lord sitting in the House of Lords. Again, however, different considerations may arguably be applicable to appeals, or committals for sentence, pending before the Crown Court where lay magistrates will typically sit alongside a circuit judge or a recorder.[1]

Finally, it should be emphasised that not all comments which are intended or even likely to influence a judge necessarily amount to a contempt. The influence must clearly be in a manner which is *improper*, and, in principle, some forms of influence ought to be perfectly permissible. This point is developed in more detail in the following chapter.[2]

(3) EFFECT ON THE PARTIES

As has been noted above,[3] conduct may amount to a contempt if it carries a serious risk of exerting improper pressure on the parties to the proceedings. This principle has been recognised in the context of civil proceedings,[4] and there is no reason, in theory, why it should not equally apply to criminal cases which are pending on appeal. Support for this view is to be found in the Australian case of *Ex parte Attorney-General; Re Truth and Sportsman, Ltd*[5] the facts of which have already been mentioned. According to the Supreme Court of New South Wales: 'If [a convicted person] were aware that a campaign of vilification was in progress against himself and that newspapers were urging that his sentence was inadequate, this would be calculated to cause him to hesitate before instituting an appeal.'[6] In *Duffy, ex parte Nash*, however, Lord Parker, C.J. appears to have

---

[19] [1960] 2 Q.B. 188, 200; [1960] 2 All E.R. 891, 896.
[20] *Ibid.*, at p. 198 and at p. 895, respectively.
[1] *Cf.* above, p. 106, and see also C. K. Allen, (1960) 76 L.Q.R. 497, 498.
[2] See below, at p. 136.
[3] See p. 106.
[4] See, e.g., *Re The William Thomas Shipping Co., Ltd* [1930] 2 Ch. 368; *Att.-Gen.* v. *Times Newspapers, Ltd* [1974] A.C. 273; [1973] 3 All E.R. 54, and, in general, below, pp. 133–136, 137–141.
[5] (1958) 61 S.R. (N.S.W.) 484, above, p. 108.
[6] *Ibid.*, at p. 496.

discounted this consideration when saying, 'the effect of such an article may well be that the prisoner will, however wrongly, think that he will be or has been prejudiced in his appeal. That, however, is not a relevant consideration for this court, which is only concerned with whether a contempt of court has been committed.'[7]

It is submitted that the view of the Australian court is to be preferred, and that some of the more extreme publications which denigrate an accused's character after the trial may be regarded as a contempt on the ground that they are likely to deter him from appealing. In any event they are likely to leave him with the impression that his appeal has been prejudiced. To deny that this is relevant is to give a very narrow meaning to the concept of a fair trial.

(4) UNDERMINING PUBLIC CONFIDENCE IN THE ADMINISTRATION OF JUSTICE

In the New Zealand case of *Attorney-General* v. *Tonks*[8] a further ground was advanced for treating post-trial publications as a contempt. In this case one Town had been remanded to the New Zealand Supreme Court for sentence when the *New Zealand Truth* newspaper published the following comment:

> The revolting nature of Town's offence against this helpless innocent demands that he should meet with the upmost rigour of the law when he comes up for sentence. This is due to the community for the sake of the protection of little children.

The publication was held to be a contempt, not because it was likely to have any effect upon the actual sentence imposed, but because it was likely, rather, to undermine public confidence in the administration of justice. As Myers, C.J. explained: 'If the Court imposed that sentence, it might well be assumed by the readers of the paper that the Court had been influenced by the newspaper's demand. If, on the other hand, a lesser sentence were imposed, the article was calculated in anticipation to arouse resentment against the Court.'[9] This reasoning is normally employed to justify that branch of the law of contempt known as scandalising the court,[10] but it is submitted that it is also appropriate in the present context. In *Attorney-General* v. *Times Newspapers, Ltd*[11] substantially similar dangers were seen by the House of Lords as accompanying the public abusing of parties to civil proceedings.

(5) ATTEMPTS TO 'DICTATE' DECISIONS TO APPELLATE COURTS

An alternative way of justifying the imposition of liability in cases such as *Attorney-General* v. *Tonks*[12] is to categorise the publication as an attempt to 'dictate' a decision to an appellate court. As such, it may be viewed as a contempt because a person who acts with the *intention* of interfering with the administration of justice will commit the offence, even though there is absolutely no likelihood of his achieving this objective. The point is developed in more detail in

---

[7] [1960] 2 Q.B. 188, 200; [1960] 2 All E.R. 891, 896.
[8] [1939] N.Z.L.R. 533.
[9] *Ibid.*, at p. 537.
[10] See below, p. 182.
[11] [1974] A.C. 273; [1973] 3 All E.R. 54.
[12] [1939] N.Z.L.R. 533.

a later chapter when discussing the mental element needed to ground liability in contempt.[13] At present it is sufficient to note that Lord Parker, C.J. agreed in *Duffy, ex parte Nash* that a contempt may be committed, 'where the article in question formed part of a deliberate campaign to influence the decision of the appellate tribunal.'[14] Hence there is authority establishing the illegality of such a campaign in this country.[15]

(6) FURTHER PROCEEDINGS BEFORE A JURY STILL PENDING

Although a given case is pending on appeal, it is, of course, quite possible that *other* proceedings connected with it are still at the trial court or the pre-trial stage. Where this is so there is every likelihood of a contempt being committed if the news media publish matter which goes beyond a fair and accurate report of the original trial.[16] This occurred in the Canadian case of *Thomas*.[17] Here a newspaper commented on the completed trial of a group of persons jointly charged with rape when proceedings were still in progress against another member of the group who had been separately charged. The publishers were ordered to pay the costs of the ensuing contempt application. Since such separate trials are an everyday occurrence, the danger is clearly one which the news media would be well advised to keep in mind. Occasionally a specific warning is issued, as at the time of the 'Great Train Robbery', when the Metropolitan Police Commissioner adopted this course.[18]

As a variation on the problem a similar danger exists where separate proceedings are still outstanding against a person who was himself the subject of the original charge. An example is provided by the notorious *Kray* case where the trial of the original charge of murdering one McVitie was fully publicised with accompanying background articles, and then followed within a month by a second trial on a charge of murdering another man, Mitchell. Lawton, J. was required to give a ruling on whether defence counsel could challenge jurors as to their bias against Ronald Kray, and in the exceptional circumstances of the case he permitted this course. No question of contempt was involved. But the learned judge agreed that a danger of a juror being prejudiced might certainly exist, 'when newspapers, knowing that there is going to be a later trial, dig up from the past of the convicted who have to meet further charges discreditable allegations which may be either fact or fiction and those allegations are then publicised over a wide area'.[19] Parity of reasoning and general principles would both suggest that the publication of such discreditable allegations may amount to a contempt if it goes beyond a fair and accurate report of the original trial, and the subsequent proceedings are pending or imminent.

---

[13] See below, at pp. 159–160.

[14] [1960] 2 Q.B. 188, 197; [1960] 2 All E.R. 891, 894.

[15] Contrast the position in the United States as seen in *Times Mirror Co.* v. *California*, 314 U.S. 252 (1941).

[16] For the legality of such reports, see below, p. 112 *et seq.*

[17] [1952] 3 D.L.R. 622 (Ontario High Ct).

[18] See *The Lawyer*, Vol. 7, No. 2, p. 13 (1964).

[19] (1969) 53 Cr. App. R. 412, 415.

(7) CONCLUSIONS

It may be said by way of conclusion that there are clearly various grounds on which a publication which appears when an appeal is pending may be viewed as a contempt. A contempt is, however, relatively unlikely to be committed at this stage by anything less than a systematic campaign aimed at influencing the decision of an appellate court. This notwithstanding, one occasionally comes across cases in which the courts have criticised the news media for having discussed the background of a prisoner at a time when his appeal was pending. The BBC, for example, was criticised by Edmund-Davies, L.J. in 1968 when an edition of Twenty-Four Hours contained an item on Charles Richardson who had recently acquired some notoriety in the so-called 'torture' trial of that year.[20] Yet it would be regrettable if the news media felt constrained to desist from responsible comment on the verdicts and sentences of criminal courts.[1] Such comment benefits the administration of justice and it can only be made effectively at the conclusion of a trial when public interest is at its height. Only a limited number of persons sustain an interest in a case until all the channels of appeal have been exhausted.[2]

4   THE POSITION WHERE PROCEEDINGS HAVE TERMINATED

Once proceedings in a given case have finally terminated, there is, of course, no question of a contempt being committed through prejudicing the proceedings in question. On the other hand, care should be taken to ensure that further proceedings are not pending, whether against the same person, or against another person who has been separately charged with an offence arising out of the original incident.[3] Equally, a contempt may still be committed through a publication which scandalises the court—as through the imputation of improper motives to the trial court judge—or which victimises a witness or anyone else involved in the proceedings. These aspects of contempt are developed in more detail in later chapters.

5   REPORTS OF COURT PROCEEDINGS[4]

(1) COMMITTAL PROCEEDINGS

(i) *The background to the statutory restrictions*

The legality of reporting committal proceedings held to determine whether there is a case against an accused warranting his trial on indictment has undergone

---

[20] See *The Times*, 27, 28 March 1968.

[1] In 1967 the then Attorney-General refused to introduce legislation to curb such comment: see Hansard, H.C. Deb. Vol. 750, col. 31 (W.A.) 10 July 1967.

[2] *Cf.* the *Justice* report, *The Law and the Press* (1965), para. 28.

[3] *Cf. Thomas* [1952] 3 D.L.R. 622 (Ontario High Ct) and above, p. 111.

[4] The section which follows is based on an article by the author entitled, 'Reporting Committal Proceedings' in (1973) 123 New Law Jo. 1119–1121; *ibid.*, 1129–1131.

marked changes over the years in English law. Since it is the normal practice for an accused to reserve his defence until the trial itself, the overall picture presented by this preliminary hearing tends to be somewhat lopsided. This led judges in the early 19th century to adopt the view that the reporting of such proceedings was unlawful at common law. As Lord Ellenborough, C.J. put it in the case of *Fisher* in 1811:[5]

> The publication of proceedings in courts of justice, where both sides are heard, and matters are finally determined, is salutary, and therefore it is permitted. The publication of these preliminary examinations has a tendency to pervert the public mind, and to disturb the course of justice; and it is therefore illegal.

This view did not, however, prevail and subsequent cases appear to have established that a fair and substantially accurate report of committal proceedings was lawful notwithstanding any resultant prejudice to an accused.[6]

In the opinion of many the immunity thus accorded produced indefensible anomalies in the law. The press could, for example, quite lawfully publish references to an accused's previous convictions or alleged confession, either of which might subsequently not be offered or admitted in evidence at the trial itself.[7] Of course, if such matters had been written up other than as a report of committal proceedings the publisher would in all probability have committed a contempt.[8] Yet the risk of prejudicing a jury was the same in both cases. Matters finally came to a head in the trial for murder of Dr John Bodkin Adams in April 1957, when the prosecution led evidence at the committal proceedings of earlier deaths which they claimed were attributable to Dr Adams, but did not offer the evidence at the trial itself. In the meantime certain sections of the press had published the details in a way which apparently prompted Mr Percy Hopkins of the *Daily Express* to say: 'This man, at this moment is being sent to the gallows on trial by newspaper.'[9] Dr Adams was fortunately acquitted notwithstanding the publicity, but the anomaly highlighted by the case still remained.

(ii) *The Criminal Justice Act 1967, s. 3*

In the immediate aftermath of the *Adams* case the Tucker Committee was set up, and in its report published in 1958 it recommended that severe restrictions be placed upon the publication of committal proceedings.[10] The report was shelved for far too long, but substantial changes in the law were finally introduced in the Criminal Justice Act 1967. By s. 3 of the Act it is generally unlawful to publish a

---

[5] (1811) 2 Camp. 563, 570; 170 E.R. 1253. See also *Fleet* (1818) 1 B. & Ald. 379; 106 E.R. 140.

[6] See, e.g., *Gray* (1865) 10 Cox C.C. 184; *Kimber* v. *The Press Association, Ltd* [1893] 1 Q.B. 65; *The Evening News, ex p. Hobbs* [1925] 2 K.B. 158; *Hudson; ex p. Gaskell and Chambers, Ltd* [1936] 2 K.B. 595.

[7] In *Sanderson* (1915) 31 T.L.R. 447 Low, J. described this as 'an extremely undesirable practice', but did not suggest that it was unlawful. See also *Armstrong* [1951] 2 All E.R. 219, C.C.A.

[8] Cf. *Thomson Newspapers, Ltd* [1968] 1 All E.R. 268, above, p. 97 (previous misconduct); *Clarke; ex p. Crippen* (1910) 103 L.T. 636, above, p. 98 (confession).

[9] Cf. Hansard, H.C. Deb. Vol. 776, cols. 1752–1753, 31 January 1969 (Michael Foot).

[10] See the *Report of the Departmental Committee on Proceedings before Examining Justices*, Cmnd 479, 1958.

report of committal proceedings before examining magistrates[11] which goes beyond the following basic details listed in s. 3(4):

(a) the identity of the court and the names of the examining justices;

(b) the names, addresses and occupations of the parties and witnesses and the ages of the defendant or defendants and witnesses;

(c) the offence or offences, or a summary of them, with which the defendant or defendants is or are charged;

(d) the names of counsel and solicitors engaged in the proceedings;

(e) any decision of the court to commit the defendant or any of the defendants for trial, and any decision of the court on the disposal of the case of any defendants not committed;

(f) where the court commits the defendant or any of the defendants for trial, the charge or charges, or a summary of them, on which he is committed and the court to which he is committed;

(g) where the committal proceedings are adjourned, the date and place to which they are adjourned;

(h) any arrangements as to bail on committal or adjournment;

(i) whether legal aid was granted to the defendant or any of the defendants.

These restrictions operate from the time when the magistrates begin to hear the case as examining justices, and s. 35 of the 1967 Act makes it clear that this is as from the moment when a person charged with an indictable offence 'appears or is brought before the court'. The appearance may, of course, be quite brief and be followed by a remand in custody. The restrictions cease to apply once the trial on indictment has been completed,[12] but it is safe to assume that the proceedings would normally have lost all news value by then. Neither do the restrictions apply if the magistrates' court decides not to commit for trial,[13] or to try the case summarily,[14] and once it has so decided. Furthermore, the restrictions do not operate where there is an application 'by the defendant or one of the defendants' for the reporting restrictions to be lifted.[15] This latter provision was included for the benefit of an accused who believed, or was advised, that full reporting was, on balance, beneficial to him because the publicity might, for example, induce witnesses to come forward in his defence. Regrettably, however, the provision was so drafted as to require examining magistrates to lift the restrictions *entirely* whenever one defendant makes an application, and irrespective of the wishes of other defendants who are being proceeded against at the same hearing.[16]

It should also be noted that s. 3(7) of the Act makes it clear that the restrictions

---

[11] The statutory restrictions would appear to have no application to proceedings in a coroner's court, even though it has the power to commit for trial.

[12] See s. 3(3)(b) of the 1967 Act.

[13] Sec. 3(3)(a).

[14] Sec. 3(3).

[15] Sec. 3(2).

[16] *Cf. Russell, ex p. Beaverbrook Newspapers, Ltd* [1969] 1 Q.B. 342; [1968] 3 All E.R. 695; *Blackpool Justices, ex p. Beaverbrook Newspapers, Ltd* [1972] 1 All E.R. 388.

on reporting operate 'in addition to, and not in derogation from, the provisions of any other enactment with respect to the publication of reports and proceedings of magistrates' and other courts'. The enactments in question include provisions designed to shield children from publicity,[17] to prevent the reporting of indecent matter,[18] and to permit cases to be heard in camera.[19]

On conviction for an offence under the 1967 Act editors and publishers of newspapers and periodicals, together with their counterparts in broadcasting, are liable to a maximum fine not exceeding £500 for each offence.[20] This, on the face of it, is a relatively modest sum when compared with the fine of £5,000 for contempt imposed on the proprietors of the *Sunday Times* newspaper in *Thomson Newspapers, Ltd.*[1] Hence it is important to bear in mind the relationship between the statutory offence and contempt of court.[2] This may be summarised by saying that a report of committal proceedings may constitute a contempt (as well as a statutory offence under the 1967 Act) if it is likely to prejudice the fair trial of the accused and at the same time fails to meet the common law prerequisites of legality as by being inaccurate or unfair. If it does meet these prerequisites but still contains items not permitted by s. 3 of the 1967 Act, the statutory offence alone will be committed. The contents of the common law requirements of legality are examined in more detail below.[3]

Thus far it seems that there have been four prosecutions under the 1967 Act. According to Sir Peter Rawlinson, the bare details of the first three were as follows:[4]

(1) 12th September, 1968. The BBC and two of its editors pleaded guilty on each of two counts. The BBC was fined £500. The two editors were discharged. (2) 7th October, 1968. *Bicester Advertiser Ltd* and the editor pleaded guilty on one count. The editor was fined £75, the company was fined £50. (3) 28th July, 1972. The editor of *Kosmos* pleaded guilty on one count. He was fined £25.

In the first case involving the BBC, the prosecution followed upon the transmission of items in two separate news broadcasts on the radio programme 'The World at One' and the television evening news. Both contained the same offending matter, namely a reference to the fact that a police officer, on applying for a remand in custody on a charge of taking away a child, had said that 'sticking plaster had been stuck over the mouth of a girl and that she had been assaulted'. Clearly this statement could not be reported under the 1967 Act and the corporation was fined £250 on each of the resultant summonses.[5]

---

[17] See the Children and Young Persons Act 1933, s. 39(1), s. 49(1) as amended by the Children and Young Persons Act 1963, s. 57, discussed below, p. 210.

[18] See the Judicial Proceedings (Regulation of Reports) Act 1926, discussed below, p. 211.

[19] As, e.g., proceedings under the Official Secrets Act 1911. See also Criminal Justice Act 1967, s. 6.

[20] See s. 3(5)(c) of the 1967 Act.

[1] [1968] 1 All E.R. 268.

[2] The point is also important because whereas s. 3(6) of the Act provides that proceedings in respect of the statutory offence may only be brought by or with the consent of the Attorney-General, there is no such limitation in the case of contempt of court.

[3] See p. 119.

[4] See Hansard, H.C. Deb. Vol. 859, cols. 437–438 (W.A.), 13 July 1973.

[5] See *The Times*, 13 September 1968, p. 2. See also the *Birmingham Post*, 13 September 1968; and the *Wolverhampton Express & Star*, 13 September 1968.

The fourth and most recent prosecution, which was also the first defended case, involved the *Eastbourne Herald* newspaper. Here the paper had published an article based on committal proceedings against a man charged with unlawful sexual intercourse. Exception was taken to the following matters which appeared within the article: (a) a headline reading 'New Year's Day Bridegroom Bailed'; (b) a description of the offence charged as being 'serious'; (c) a description of the alleged offender as 'bespectacled and dressed in a dark suit'; (d) a note to the effect that he had been 'married at St. Michael's Church on New Year's day'; and (e) a reference to the way in which the prosecuting solicitor had handled the case. The editor and proprietors were found guilty by the Eastbourne magistrates on the five counts relating to these different passages and were each fined a total of £200 and ordered to pay £37·50 costs.[6]

This decidedly strange result stems from the fact that liability may be incurred under the 1967 Act where a report of committal proceedings contains *any* details other than those permitted by s. 3(4), and quite irrespective of whether or not the details are potentially prejudicial in nature. Indeed, all that is required of the prosecution is to show (i) that D published a report of committal proceedings to which the restrictions apply and (ii) that the report contained matters for which no specific provision is made in s. 3(4). Thus it was an offence under the Act to describe unlawful sexual intercourse as a 'serious' offence, for s. 3(4) (c) permits of no such qualifying adjective. Equally, it was an offence to describe the defendant as 'bespectacled and dressed in a dark suit', for s. 3(4)(b) only provides for a reference to his name, address and occupation. So also would it be an offence to report that the examining magistrate was wearing a pin-striped suit and that he spoke in a high-pitched voice, for s. 3(4)(a) sanctions no more than a reference to his name.

It would seem, moreover, that the general prohibition goes even further than this and that it covers references to matters of general knowledge, or of background information, even though they are not brought out during the course of the proceedings themselves. It is not apparently necessary for the prosecution to show that the offending item purported to be an account of what transpired in court provided only that it is contained within a report of committal proceedings. Thus the Eastbourne magistrates held that it was an offence to refer to the fact that the defendant had been married at St Michael's Church on New Year's Day, although it is not clear that this fact was adduced as evidence in court. Likewise it would seem that the offence would be committed by a report which describes the defendant as (say) an ex-prime minister or foreign secretary,[7] and irrespective of whether this matter of general knowledge is actually brought out in evidence in the case itself.

Such results are obviously absurd. It would have been preferable to have enacted a simple provision whereby it was no longer to be a defence to the publisher of prejudicial matter to show that the publication was a fair and accurate report of committal proceedings. There is no reason to prohibit the dissemination of material which could not conceivably be described as prejudicial.

[6] See *The Times*, 12 June 1973, p. 4.
[7] This is hardly an 'occupation' within s. 3(4)(b) of the Act: see (1973) Vol. 137 J.P. 387.

(2) CRIMINAL TRIALS

The restrictions introduced by the 1967 Act do not, of course, apply to the reporting of the actual trial itself. Indeed this is as it should be for there is a clear difference between committal proceedings and the criminal trial in this respect. The latter should, in so far as possible, always take place in open court and with full attendant publicity. Yet fair and accurate reports of the trial may occasionally prejudice further proceedings which are still pending—whether against one of the defendants to the original trial, or against another person who is to be separately tried for an offence arising out of the same incident.[8] In this context Professor Street mentions a case in 1960 involving one Albert Jones, who was convicted on a charge of raping a girl guide and then charged within three months with the murder of another girl, Brenda Nash. The original trial was fully publicised and featured prominently in the Sunday press. As Street observes, 'It is plain that the risk of the jury being prejudiced against Jones because of his preceding trial was much greater than was the risk in many of the convictions for contempt . . . . Yet the conduct of the police, the Press, and the broadcasting agencies did not infringe the law of contempt.'[9] A substantially similar situation occurred during the *Kray* case which was discussed earlier.[10] Again it may be thought that jurors in the subsequent trial on the charge of murdering Mitchell would have needed a remarkable degree of detachment if they were to approach their task with an open mind. Lawton, J., the presiding judge, was more sanguine and believed that: 'the mere fact that a newspaper has reported a trial and a verdict which was adverse to a person subsequently accused ought not in the ordinary way to produce a case of probable bias against jurors empanelled in a later case'.[11] The fact that Ronald Kray was subsequently acquitted on the later charge arguably provides some support for this view. The same may be said of the acquittal of Miss Janie Jones on charges of blackmail in spite of the publicity accorded to the earlier colourful trial in the 'Payola' case.

A further unusual example occurred in the period before the trial of Frederick Sewell when a certain Mrs Jermain was charged under the Criminal Law Act 1967, s. 4 with assisting him to evade arrest. The charge against her alleged that:

> At Blackpool on 23rd August 1971 after Frederick Joseph Sewell had committed an arrestable offence, *namely had murdered Gerald Irving Richardson*, knowing or believing that Frederick Joseph Sewell had committed the offence she did assist him by driving him out of Blackpool in the boot of a motor car with intent to impede his apprehension or prosecution. (Emphasis supplied.)

At the time Sewell was being sought by the police in connection with this murder, but he had not yet been arrested. To the extent that publicity was accorded to the evidence in the Jermain case establishing that he did commit the murder, it is arguable that his own subsequent trial on a charge of murder was thereby prejudiced.

---

[8] As in the Canadian case of *Thomas* [1952] 3 D.L.R. 622 (Ontario High Ct).

[9] See *Freedom, the Individual and the Law* (3rd ed., 1972), p. 166. The appeal against conviction on the latter charge was reported *sub nom Jones* v. *D.P.P.* [1962] A.C. 635, H.L.

[10] See above, p. 111.

[11] (1969) 53 Cr. App. Rep. 412, 414.

It may also happen that press reports of proceedings which are not themselves criminal in nature may carry a contingent danger of prejudicing a subsequent criminal trial. Thus at the trial of Mr John Poulson at Leeds Crown Court in 1974 on charges of corruption defence counsel was clearly concerned that the jury might have been prejudiced against Poulson by the publicity which had accompanied Poulson's earlier public examination in bankruptcy. In opening the defence of the former architect he is reported as saying that, in this respect, Poulson was 'in a worse position than almost anyone else in recent criminal history'.[12]

(3) ORDERS TO POSTPONE REPORTING

One way of avoiding prejudice in the cases considered above would be through a court ordering that publication of the original proceedings be postponed until a later date. The old case of *Clement*[13] in 1821 suggests that such a power exists at least where a number of persons have been jointly charged on the same indictment, and a successful application has been made for separate trials. On the facts of the case Abbott, C.J. made an order prohibiting the publicising of the trials of two persons for high treason in the Cato Street conspiracy until separate proceedings against other persons charged with the same offence had been concluded. The *Observer* newspaper then published a fair, true, and impartial account of the proceedings and was fined £500 for contempt for having acted 'contrary to the order of this Court, and to the obstruction of public justice'.[14] The fine was subsequently upheld by the Court of King's Bench.

Assuming that this case still represents the law,[15] it is by no means clear that a similar power exists in other cases—as, for example, where quite distinct proceedings are pending against one of the defendants to the original trial.[16] The fact that the obstruction of justice envisaged in *Clement* was not prejudice to the accused, but the creation of a situation in which witnesses in the later trials would be able to trim their evidence in the light of what they had read,[17] might be thought to suggest that it does not. So also does the fact that the separate trials were regarded, in effect, as being one entire proceeding. No doubt the news media would normally accede to a request to delay reporting, but this is not the same thing as being under an obligation to do so.[18]

The trial of John Poulson provides a recent example of a case in which publicity was restrained. During his examination-in-chief Poulson had referred to his association with another man against whom separate proceedings in conjunction with Poulson himself were still outstanding. Waller, J., the presiding judge, is reported as having said[19]

---

[12] *The Times*, 3 January 1974, p. 2.

[13] (1821) 4 B. & Ald. 218; 106 E.R. 918.

[14] *Ibid.*, at p. 220.

[15] It was cited without apparent disapproval by Lord Atkinson in *Scott* v. *Scott* [1913] A.C. 417, 453–454. But see Goodhart, 'Newspapers and Contempt of Court' (1935) 48 Harv. L. R. 885, 904.

[16] As in cases such as *Jones* and *Kray* noted above.

[17] *Cf.* (1821) 4 B. & Ald. 218, 230 *per* Bayley, J.

[18] See *The Report of the Departmental Committee on Proceedings before Examining Justices*, Cmnd 479, 1958, para. 59.

[19] See *The Times*, 4 January 1974.

I do not see myself how the press can properly report this evidence without running the risk of being in contempt of this other trial. When we are dealing with someone who is subject to another trial, things have been said here which might be highly prejudicial to that trial, and therefore must not be published.

The Times report of the day's proceedings carried a note stating that it had 'not been able to report fully Mr Poulson's evidence because of Mr Justice Waller's request'.[20] Again, however, it must be said that it is far from clear that there is in fact a power to order that reporting be postponed until the hearing of the subsequent connected proceedings. Subject to this central point, the procedure adopted by Waller, J. at the trial was both helpful and well suited to keep restrictions on reporting to a minimum. He directed that counsel should give advance warning of possible prejudice at the time when the questions were going to be asked and then ruled after the evidence had been given as to whether its publication might prejudice a subsequent trial. The system of advance warning by counsel was designed to ensure that the press did not send off details for publication before the ruling was made.

(4) REPORTS WHICH ARE NOT ACCURATE AND FAIR

It was noted above that reports of judicial proceedings are, in any event, only lawful for the purposes of the law of contempt if they are substantially accurate and fair. No such protection is granted to reports which fail to meet these requirements and which are prejudicial to further pending proceedings. This limitation is of general application and it remains important even in the case of reports of committal proceedings.[1]

The leading English case discussing what constitutes a fair and accurate report of judicial proceedings for the purposes of the law of contempt is *Evening News, ex parte Hobbs.*[2] Here one William Hobbs had been charged with conspiring to defraud an oriental Rajah by the name of Sir Hari Singh of his property. On the evening after his appearance before the grand jury the *Evening News* published the following statement:

NO DOUBT PARTY TO A MONUMENTAL FRAUD

'There can be no doubt, I should say, that Hobbs was a party to a gigantic fraud. It was as monumental and as impudent a fraud as, perhaps, has ever been perpetrated in the course of our criminal history.' These words were used by the Recorder, Sir Ernest Wild K.C., in his charge to the grand jury at the Old Bailey today. He was referring to William Cooper Hobbs, aged 60, accountant, who was indicted for conspiring to defraud Sir Hari Singh.

The report was not in fact a precise verbatim rendering of the recorder's charge to the jury, since it omitted a parenthesis in which he had added: 'It is for you to decide.' Nonetheless it conveyed the *substance* of what was itself a highly improper direction and, in the judgment of the Divisional Court, it was accordingly to be regarded as fair and accurate. As Lord Hewart, C.J. observed, the

[20] See *The Times*, 3 January 1974.
[1] *Cf.* the position as to maximum penalties and entitlement to institute proceedings, above, p. 115.
[2] [1925] 2 K.B. 158.

responsibility for any prejudice to Hobbs's fair trial lay with the recorder's charge, and not with the report.[3]

On the other hand a report which contains substantial inaccuracies may well constitute a contempt if it is prejudicial to a fair trial. The case of *Evening Standard Co., Ltd, ex parte Attorney-General*[4] illustrates the point and the dangers involved. In this case George Forrest, a reporter on the *Evening Standard*, had been attending the trial for murder of a man named Kemp. He telephoned a message through to his office which formed the basis for a report which read in part as follows:

TRUNK TRIAL STORY OF MARRIAGE OFFER

Mrs. Gertrude Darmody, of Spitalfields, Norwich, said at the assizes here today that a man accused of murdering his wife asked her to marry him. Mrs. Darmody said she met Kemp in a public house in September last year.

The report continued by citing a statement purportedly made by Mrs Darmody that:

He told me he was not married. After I had seen him in the same public house again and he had asked me to marry him, I asked him to show me his army pay book.

In fact no such statement had been made by Mrs Darmody, and the supposition was that Forrest had mistakenly attributed to her evidence which he had heard another witness, a Miss Briggs, give at the earlier committal proceedings. Evidence by Miss Briggs of the offer allegedly made to her by Kemp had, moreover, been held to be inadmissible at the trial as being unduly prejudicial and irrelevant. A fine of £1,000 for contempt was imposed on the proprietors to mark the danger of such misreporting.[5]

A recent Australian case may also be cited as giving some indication of the meaning of the requirement that the report be *fair* as well as accurate. In *Minister for Justice* v. *West Australian Newspapers, Ltd*[6] one Albert Virtyo had been remanded in custody and subsequently committed for trial on a charge alleging the murder by shooting of a Perth shopkeeper. He had also been committed for trial on a number of breaking and entering charges (including one involving the stealing of a rifle and ammunition), and sentenced on summary conviction on pleading guilty to the unlawful use of motor vehicles. The *Daily News* published an account of the proceedings in the magistrates' court beneath a heading in bold type stating, 'Youth on murder charge gaoled on car counts.' The article read in part as follows:

A youth, charged with having wilfully murdered East Perth shopkeeper Stephen Walter Hobbs (53) on August 28, was remanded for eight days when he appeared in Perth Police Court today. He was also gaoled for a total of 15 months when he pleaded guilty to three charges of unlawful use of motor vehicles. On four other charges of breaking and entering, including one where he allegedly stole a ·22 calibre rifle and 1000 rounds of ammunition, he was remanded for eight days.

[3] *Ibid.*, at p. 170. The recorder's direction was hardly improved by the fact that he referred to the accused as 'these clever scoundrels'.
[4] [1954] 1 Q.B. 578; [1954] 1 All E.R. 1026. See also pp. 160–161, 169–170.
[5] See also *Daily Worker, ex p. Goulding* (1934) 78 Sol. Jo. 860.
[6] [1970] W.A.R. 202.

The Supreme Court of Western Australia held that the article constituted a contempt because, as Jackson, C.J. explained, 'although it was largely a report of court proceedings it was neither fair nor uncoloured and it had a real and practical tendency to prejudice Virtyo on his trial for wilful murder'.[7] The learned judge also pointed out that:[8]

> A report may be accurate as far as it goes, but unfair either in its mode of presentation or in stressing unfavourable aspects of the proceedings or in accurately reporting some parts but omitting other parts of the proceedings.

Applying these considerations to the facts of the case Jackson, C.J. concluded that the article was highly *selective*, and placed undue emphasis on the charge of stealing the rifle and ammunition which it linked in a footnote with the victim being shot through the head. The effect would be to lead the ordinary reader to the conclusion, 'not only that the accused is a criminal but that the shooting probably was linked with the offence of stealing the rifle and ammunition'.[9] But for this selectivity and emphasis Virtue, S.P.J. would not have regarded the report as unfair simply because it enumerated the convictions on the car offences, and the committals on the breaking and entering offences. Burt, J., the third of the judges in the West Australian court, also noted that the manner, as well as the contents, of the publication will often be of decisive importance in such a case.[10]

It is not wholly clear whether there are further prerequisites of legality apart from those of substantial accuracy and fairness. It would seem that at common law the report of the proceedings must also have been published in good faith, and that an objectively fair report would not enjoy any immunity if its publication was in fact actuated by malice or an improper motive.[11] It may be, however, that the common law has been superseded in this respect by the Law of Libel Amendment Act 1888, s. 3. This section provides that:

> A fair and accurate report in any newspaper of proceedings publicly heard before any court exercising judicial authority shall, if published contemporaneously with such proceedings, be privileged: provided that nothing in this section shall authorise the publication of any blasphemous or indecent matter.

This provision has been generally assumed to confer an absolute privilege which is not defeasible on proof of bad faith.[12] But it is perhaps not clear beyond doubt that the statutory privilege protects against contempt as well as libel, given that the headnote to the Act reads: 'An Act to amend the Law of Libel'. If it does, then both newspaper and radio and television reports[13] of judicial proceedings will

---

[7] *Ibid.*, at p. 208.

[8] *Ibid.*, at p. 207.

[9] *Ibid.*, at p. 208.

[10] For other Australian cases, see *Ex p. Terrill; Re Consolidated Press* (1937) 37 S.R. (N.S.W.) 255; *Ex p. Fisher; Re Associated Newspapers, Ltd* (1941) 41 S.R. (N.S.W.) 272; *West Australian Newspapers, Ltd, ex p. Minister for Justice* (1958) 60 W.A.L.R. 108; *Cassidy* v. *Mercury Newspapers Pty. Ltd* [1968] Tas. S.R. 198.

[11] *Cf.* the defence of fair comment in defamation proceedings and *McQuire* v. *Western Morning News* [1903] 2 K.B. 100, C.A.

[12] *Cf.* Street, *The Law of Torts* (5th ed., 1972), p. 309; Clerk & Lindsell, *Torts* (13th ed., 1969), para. 1792, note 24; Gatley, *Libel and Slander* (16th ed., 1974), para. 650 and cases there cited.

[13] The statutory defence was extended to radio and television broadcasts by the Defamation Act 1952, s. 9(2).

fall within the protection of this absolute privilege provided that they are objectively fair and published contemporaneously with the proceedings. It is generally assumed that the qualified privilege existing outside the 1888 Act does not depend upon the requirement of contemporaneity,[14] but there would seem to be room for debate on this point.

Finally, the point may be made that the Phillimore Committee has recommended that: 'It should be provided by statute that it is a defence to contempt proceedings to show that the publication was a fair and accurate report of legal proceedings in open court published contemporaneously and in good faith.'[15] This recommendation is designed to remove the uncertainty highlighted by the ruling of Waller, J. in the Poulson hearing. It will be observed that the wording of the suggested defence is substantially similar to that of the Libel Amendment Act 1888, s. 3, except for the explicit requirement that the report be published in good faith.[16]

[14] See, e.g., Street, *op cit.*, p. 316. Such a requirement is not mentioned in *Gatley*.
[15] Para. 141. The general issues are discussed in paras. 134–142 of the report.
[16] The requirement of contemporaneity would probably represent a restriction on the scope of the common law defence. See above, note 14 and corresponding text.

8 The Sub Judice Rule: Conduct Prejudicial to the Fair Trial of Civil Proceedings and Proceedings in Tribunals

1 CIVIL PROCEEDINGS

(1) INTRODUCTION

Although the restrictions imposed by the *sub judice* rule are primarily associated with criminal proceedings, it has long been clear that they apply to civil proceedings as well. Indeed *The St. James's Evening Post Case*,[1] perhaps the *locus classicus* of contempt, followed upon the abusing of litigants in civil proceedings.[2] Thereafter the law reports until the latter part of the 19th century include a substantial number of civil cases which were accompanied by an application to commit or attach for contempt. Since then the number of applications has decreased markedly, but the recent and leading case of *Attorney-General* v. *Times Newspapers, Ltd*[3] suggests that it would be plainly wrong to assume that comment upon pending civil litigation can no longer constitute a contempt. In reimposing an injunction enjoining the *Sunday Times* from publishing an article on the thalidomide tragedy the House of Lords reversed the less restrictive trend of recent cases and sounded a clear warning to all concerned.

In the discussion which follows many of the considerations which were noted as being relevant to contempt through prejudicing criminal proceedings will be seen to be equally applicable to civil proceedings. So if, for example, a judge were to be threatened with physical violence were he to decide a case in a particular way the liability of the person offering the threat will clearly not vary according to whether the case is a civil or a criminal one. Separate treatment of criminal and civil proceedings is convenient, however, because, notwithstanding the points of similarity, there remain substantial differences between them, both in terms of the type of problem typically posed and in terms of the reasons typically advanced to substantiate an allegation of contempt.

(i) *The importance of the composition of the court*

The likelihood of a court being prejudiced by a particular publication or course of conduct will clearly depend upon a variety of factors. The paramount

---

[1] (1742) 2 Atk. 469; 26 E.R. 683.
[2] *Cf. ibid.*, at p. 471, *per* Lord Hardwicke, L.-C.
[3] [1974] A.C. 273; [1973] 3 All E.R. 54.

consideration, however, is undoubtedly the composition of the court itself. Maugham, J. recognised this point very clearly in a case which came before him in the Chancery Division in 1930. As his Lordship observed:[4]

> There is an atmosphere in which a common law judge approaches the question of contempt somewhat different from that in which a judge who sits in this Division has to approach it. The common law judge is mainly thinking of the effect of the alleged contempt on the mind of the jury and also, I think, he has to consider the effect or the possible effect of the alleged contempt in preventing witnesses from coming forward to give evidence. In these days, at any rate, a judge who sits in this Division is not in the least likely to be prejudiced by statements published in the press as to the result of cases which are coming before him.

(a) *Judges not generally susceptible to influence.* In subsequent cases it has likewise been assumed that a High Court judge is not to be regarded as susceptible to improper influence. Thus in *Vine Products, Ltd* v. *Mackenzie & Co., Ltd*[5] Buckley, J., although prepared to countenance the possibility that a publication might theoretically influence a judge, nonetheless agreed that:[6]

> It has generally been accepted that professional judges are sufficiently well equipped by their professional training to be on their guard against allowing [a prejudging of the issues] to influence them in deciding the case.

This assumed immunity from improper influence is also supported by statements in cases involving alleged prejudice to criminal proceedings which were discussed in the last chapter.[7] Subject to the exceptions which were then noted,[8] these cases do not, on balance, suggest that a 'professional' judge is likely to be more than embarrassed by a publication which sets out to discuss a defendant's discreditable past. To 'embarrass' a judge does not constitute a contempt.[9]

Although the point does not appear to have arisen for discussion, it is further submitted that a county court judge may, by virtue of his background, be similarly regarded as immune from influence from improper sources. On the other hand different considerations may apply to lay magistrates sitting in civil cases for it seems realistic to regard them as being vulnerable to influence or pressure which might impair their impartiality.[10]

(b) *The incidence of jury trials.* The other side of the coin is, of course, that juries are certainly assumed to be open to improper influences in civil as well as in

---

[4] *Re The William Thomas Shipping Co., Ltd* [1930] 2 Ch. 368, 373.
[5] [1966] Ch. 484; [1965] 3 All E.R. 58.
[6] *Ibid.*, at p. 496 and at p. 62 respectively.
[7] See, e.g., *Duffy, ex p. Nash* [1960] 2 Q.B. 188; [1960] 2 All 891 and, in general, above, p. 107.
[8] *Cf. Delbert-Evans* v. *Davies and Watson* [1945] 2 All E.R. 167.
[9] *Cf. Duffy, ex p. Nash* (above, n.7).
[10] *Cf.* the remarks of Lord Diplock in *Att.-Gen.* v. *Times Newspapers, Ltd* [1974] A.C. 273, 309; [1973] 3 All. E.R. 54, 72. See also *Regal Press Pty., Ltd* [1972] V.R. 67 (Vict. Sup. Ct). It has been said that the risk of prejudicing the lay members of a tribunal of inquiry is minimal: see the *Report of the Interdepartmental Committee on the Law of Contempt as it Affects Tribunals of Inquiry*, Cmnd. 4078, June 1969, para. 26.

criminal cases. However, jury trials in civil cases are now comparatively rare.[11] The position in this regard may be briefly summarised as follows. By s. 6(1) of the Administration of Justice (Miscellaneous Provisions) Act 1933 a jury trial *must* be ordered on the application of either party to an action for libel, slander, malicious prosecution or false imprisonment, and at the instance of a party against whom a charge of fraud has been levelled, unless the court is of the opinion that the trial requires 'any prolonged examination of documents or accounts or any scientific or local investigation which cannot conveniently be made with a jury'.[12] Where such cases involving a person's reputation or liberty are pending a publisher must clearly take the possibility of a jury trial into account.

In other cases falling outside this provision a court has a general *discretion* as to whether to order a jury trial. In *Ward* v. *James*,[13] however, a full Court of Appeal made it clear that this discretion should only be exercised in favour of ordering a jury trial in a personal injury case in the most exceptional of circumstances. The same is no doubt equally true of other cases in the Queen's Bench Division not falling within s. 6(1) of the 1933 Act. In modern times jury trials in the Chancery Division are unknown and if this mode of trial were to be considered appropriate in a particular case the action would be transferred to the Queen's Bench Division.[14] Likewise a jury trial in the Family Division of the High Court would only occur very rarely,[15] and the same is true of cases pending in the county courts.[16] It is accordingly submitted that in all such cases the possibility of committing a contempt through improperly influencing a jury may be safely discounted, at least until such time as successful application for a jury trial has in fact been made.

(ii) *Some further general considerations*

Apart from the composition of the court, the incidence of liability for contempt by publication may also depend in part on factors such as the timing of the publication and its volume and area of circulation. Thus, other things being equal, a publication is generally less likely to constitute a contempt if it has a limited circulation, or if it appears immediately after the issue of a writ rather than during the course of the actual trial itself.[17] As with all generalisations, however, this one is likely to break down in practice. A limited circular to the jurors in a case may obviously be more prejudicial than an article conveying the same ideas in the popular press. Equally the proceedings against the Distillers Company were technically, as Lord Cross observed,[18] still at an early stage when

[11] In 1972 only 23 (or 2·04 per cent) of Queen's Bench Division actions in London and only four county court actions in the whole country were heard with a jury: Phillimore Committee report, para. 47.

[12] For a recent discussion of this provision, see *Rothermere and Others* v. *Times Newspapers, Ltd* [1973] 1 All E.R. 1013, C.A.

[13] [1966] 1 Q.B. 273; [1965] 1 All E.R. 563.

[14] *Cf. The Supreme Court Practice 1973* Vol. 1, p. 548.

[15] *Cf.* Rayden on *Divorce* (11th ed., 1971), p. 474 and M.C.R. 1971, rule 48.

[16] *Cf.* Jackson, *The Machinery of Justice in England* (6th ed., 1972), p. 33, and p. 92.

[17] *Cf. Dallas* v. *Ledger* (1888) 4 T.L.R. 432, 434 *per* Stephen, J. See also *Ex p. The Standard, The Times*, 28 January 1907.

[18] See *Att.-Gen.* v. *Times Newspapers, Ltd* [1974] A.C. 273, 323; [1973] 3 All E.R. 54, 84.

the *Sunday Times* wished to publish its article assessing the company's alleged responsibility for the thalidomide tragedy. This did not, however, prevent the House of Lords from reimposing an injunction restraining the publication of the article.

Against the background of such general considerations it is now proposed to examine the types of conduct which may constitute a contempt as being likely to prejudice civil proceedings. In some instances the conduct should be regarded as equally capable of amounting to a contempt whether it occurs during the first instance hearing, or when the case is pending on appeal.[19] Examples of such conduct include the public abuse of a party, and the directing of improper threats and persuasion at the court or at the parties themselves. In other instances as where the complaint is of conduct likely to affect a juror or witness, the danger will only exist at the earlier point of time. Once the proceedings are finally over a contempt of the kind presently under discussion cannot, in the nature of things, be committed through allegedly prejudicing those particular proceedings. The possibility of scandalising the court[20] or of victimising a person involved in the proceedings[1] should, however, be borne in mind.

(2) EXAMPLES OF CONDUCT WHICH MAY CONSTITUTE A CONTEMPT

(i) *Prejudging the merits of a case*

A publication which prejudges the likely outcome of a case, or which otherwise canvases its merits, may be regarded as creating a serious risk of interference with the administration of justice. A clear warning to this effect is to be found in the judgment of Cotton, L.J. in *Hunt* v. *Clarke*.[2] In this case a paragraph in the *Star* newspaper had referred to an action involving alleged company fraud which was to come on for trial in the special jury list. Cotton, L.J. commented:[3]

> If any one discusses in a paper the rights of a case or the evidence to be given before the case comes on, that, in my opinion, would be a very serious attempt to interfere with the proper administration of justice. It is not necessary that the Court should come to the conclusion that a Judge or a jury will be prejudiced, but if it is calculated to prejudice the proper trial of a cause, that is a contempt.

On the actual facts of the case, however, the contempt was a purely technical one[4] and the publisher was only penalised to the extent that he was required to pay his own costs in the Court of Appeal.

A number of 19th-century decisions have similarly held a canvasing of the merits of cases pending in Chancery, where there is no jury, to constitute a contempt.[5] A somewhat different attitude was, however, taken by Buckley, J. in

---

[19] But see above, p. 86 for a discussion of cases doubting whether a contempt can be committed through prejudicing civil proceedings pending on appeal.

[20] See below, p. 182.

[1] See below, p. 198.

[2] (1889) 58 L.J.Q.B. 490.

[3] *Ibid.*, at p. 492. See also *Re The Finance Union* (1895) 11 T.L.R. 167; *Re Robbins, ex p. Green* (1891) 7 T.L.R. 411.

[4] For 'technical' contempts, see above, p. 69.

[5] See, e.g., *Re Crown Bank, Re O'Malley* (1890) 44 Ch.D. 649; *Daw* v. *Eley* (1868) L.R. 7 Eq. 49.

Vine Products, Ltd v. *Mackenzie & Co., Ltd.*[6] Here an action was pending in the Chancery Division of the High Court to determine whether the word 'sherry' was only appropriately used to describe a wine coming from Jerez and surrounding districts in Spain, or whether it could equally be applied to wine from other countries such as South Africa. The *Daily Telegraph* thereupon published a leading article referring to a similar test case involving champagne in which it had been held that the word 'champagne' meant a wine produced in the Champagne district of France, and nothing else.[7] The *Daily Telegraph* commented beneath the heading 'The Truth of Labels':

> If the Sherry Shippers' Association intend, as is reported, to bring a test case in defence of their own name, their position must be fundamentally the same. Sherry, to be fully entitled to the name, should come from Jerez (or the closely adjoining wine field of San Lucar which makes Manzanilla). To speak of South African or Cypriot sherry is as anomalous as to speak of Spanish champagne.

These comments clearly amounted to an endorsement of the views of one of the parties to the litigation, but Buckley, J. did not regard them as a contempt. In his Lordship's opinion it had not been shown that they created a real risk of interference with the administration of justice, whether through an effect upon a Chancery judge, the witnesses, or the parties themselves. He accordingly dismissed the application to commit the publishers for contempt, and ordered the applicants to pay the costs of the proceedings.

Although the view of Buckley, J. commends itself to common sense, the recent decision of the House of Lords in *Attorney-General* v. *Times Newspapers, Ltd*[8] indicates that wider considerations may be involved and indeed suggests that *any* prejudging of the merits of a case is to be regarded as a contempt. This is a convenient place to set out the facts of this leading case as a preliminary to examining the attitude of the House of Lords to this particular issue. The effect of the decision on other aspects of the law of contempt either has been, or will be, considered elsewhere in the book.

The background to the case was that in 1958 Distillers (Biochemicals), Ltd began to market a sedative called 'Distaval' containing the drug thalidomide, the main ingredient of which was glutamic acid. When taken by pregnant women the sedative had tragic results, for it caused gross malformation of the foetus in the womb. A substantial number of babies were consequently born with the most serious deformities, frequently without arms and legs. The sedative was eventually withdrawn by Distillers in 1961.

Between 1962 and 1968 some 70 writs were issued on behalf of the deformed children claiming damages against Distillers on the ground of their alleged negligence in marketing the drug. The proceedings thus instituted posed formidable legal problems, both in terms of whether it was possible to found a cause of action on pre-natal injuries, and of establishing negligence on Distillers' part. In February 1968 these claims were settled on the basis that Distillers should pay £1 million by way of compensation without in any way admitting

---

[6] [1966] 1 Ch. 484; [1965] 3 All E.R. 58. See also *Carl-Zeiss-Stiftung* v. *Rayner & Keeler, Ltd* [1960] 3 All E.R. 289, below, p. 142.

[7] See *Bollinger* v. *Costa Brava Wine Co., Ltd* [1960] Ch. 262; [1959] 3 All E.R. 800.

[8] [1974] A.C. 273; [1973] 3 All E.R. 54.

liability. Leave to issue writs out of time was subsequently granted in respect of some 266 children, and altogether some 389 claims were outstanding after the 1968 settlement. Distillers proposed that these claims should be settled by their paying £3·25 million to trustees for the benefit of the children, again without admitting liability. They insisted, however, that *all* claimants should agree to the terms of this settlement. Five parents refused to accept and resisted the moral (and legal) pressure[9] which was brought to bear on them as a result. There the matter remained from the spring until the autumn of 1972. Over ten years had passed since the origins of the tragedy had first come to light.

On September 24, 1972 the *Sunday Times* published a lengthy article headed 'Our Thalidomide Children: A Cause For National Shame'. Its avowed purpose was to put pressure on Distillers to get them to increase their offer.[10] Distillers made a formal complaint to the Attorney-General and contended that this article was a contempt of court. The Attorney-General asked the editor of the *Sunday Times*, Harold Evans, for his observations and then declined to institute proceedings. The *Sunday Times* thereafter planned to publish a further article which, it seems, was to contain a detailed examination of the issue of Distillers' legal liability as well as imposing further pressure towards a better offer. They sent an advance copy of the proposed article to the Attorney-General at his request. The Attorney-General responded by seeking an injunction restraining publication and this was granted by a Divisional Court presided over by Lord Widgery, C.J.[11] The order was discharged on appeal to the Court of Appeal,[12] which took the view that the proceedings were 'dormant',[13] and that there was, in any event, an overwhelming public interest to be served by airing the issues involved.[14] On a further appeal to the House of Lords the injunction was reimposed.[15]

In delivering their respective speeches in favour of allowing the Attorney-General's appeal, two members of the House of Lords committed themselves to the proposition that *any* public prejudgment of the issues in pending litigation constituted a contempt even though it was not contended that it would have any immediate effect upon the litigation in question. In the opinion of Lord Reid, public prejudgment was tantamount to trial by newspaper and, as such, was 'intrinsically objectionable'.[16] Lord Cross agreed and spelt out the full implications of this view, and the dangers which he regarded as inherent in such prejudgment, in the following terms:[17]

---

[9] It was sought unsuccessfully to have the parents removed as next friend of the children to be replaced by the Official Solicitor: see *Re Taylor's Application* [1972] 2 Q.B. 369; [1972] 2 All E.R. 873.

[10] An extract from the article is set out below, p. 134 where contempt through imposing improper pressure on the parties is discussed.

[11] [1973] 1 Q.B. 710; [1972] 3 All E.R. 1136.

[12] [1973] 1 Q.B. 710, at 727; [1973] 1 All E.R. 815 (Lord Denning, M.R., Phillimore and Scarman, LL.JJ.).

[13] See above, p. 88.

[14] See below, p. 151.

[15] [1974] A.C. 273; [1973] 3 All E.R. 54. The passages which follow are reproduced with some minor modifications from an article by the author, 'Contempt of Court: The Sunday Times Case' [1975] Crim. L.R. 132.

[16] [1974] A.C. 273, 300; [1973] 3 All E.R. 54, 65.

[17] [1974] A.C. 273, 322; [1973] 3 All E.R. 54, 84.

It is easy enough to see that any publication which prejudges an issue in pending proceedings ought to be forbidden if there is any risk that it may influence the tribunal—whether judge, magistrates or jury, or any of those who may be called on to give evidence when the case comes to be heard. But why, it may be said, should such a publication be prohibited when there is no such risk? The reason is that one cannot deal with one particular publication in isolation. A publication prejudging an issue in pending litigation which is itself innocuous enough may provoke replies which are far from innocuous but which, as they are replies, it would seem unfair to restrain. So gradually the public would become habituated to, look forward to, and resent the absence of, preliminary discussions in the 'media' of any case which aroused widespread interest. An absolute rule—though it may seem to be unreasonable if one looks only to the particular case—is necessary in order to prevent a gradual slide towards trial by newspaper or television.

The other members of the House of Lords were perhaps less unequivocal on the point, but appear to have agreed that prejudgment should be absolutely prohibited. Lord Simon, for example, agreed with both Lord Reid and Lord Cross that the *Daily Telegraph* article in the *Vine Products* case was technically a contempt (though not one deserving of punishment) because it prejudged the issues.[18]

Whether such an absolute rule is in fact desirable, especially in the case of civil proceedings where it is likely to have more practical repercussions, may be doubted. Certainly there is force in Lord Morris's view that the courts 'owe it to the parties to protect them either from the prejudices of prejudgment or from the necessity of having themselves to participate in the flurries of pretrial publicity.[19] But it is submitted that the Phillimore Committee was right not to support an absolute prohibition and to leave individual cases to stand or fall under their general proposed test of whether the publication 'creates a risk that the course of justice will be seriously impeded or prejudiced.'[20] Thus far we have managed to avoid the spectre of trial by newspaper without the rule.

Until such time as the law is changed it is necessary to determine the limits of the prohibition. Here it may be said that the term 'prejudgment' is clearly being used to cover publications which suggest what a court ought to decide as well as those which predict what it will *in fact* decide. Beyond this the rule would also preclude any canvasing of the merits of a case, or attempt to assess the weight of the evidence advanced by the opposing parties. Indeed this appears to have been the form taken by the proposed article in the *Sunday Times*, which was described by Lord Morris as going too far because, while not asserting a settled conclusion, it 'conveyed the message to all who could read . . . that an examination of the issue as to negligence showed that there was a considerable case that could be presented against Distillers.'[1] A simple setting out of the issues to be decided is clearly not a prejudgment. Yet when this is done by someone whose views are well known, as were those of the editor of the *Sunday Times*, it will be difficult to avoid inviting the reader to draw inferences thus bringing oneself within the

[18] [1974] A.C. 273, 321; [1973] 3 All E.R. 54, 83. See also Lord Diplock: *ibid.*, at p. 310, and at p. 73 respectively.

[19] [1974] A.C. 273, 304; [1973] 3 All E.R. 54, 68.

[20] Paras. 106-111. The preferred test is set out in para. 113 and discussed above, p. 70.

[1] [1974] A.C. 273, 307; [1973] 3 All E.R. 54, 71.

scope of the prohibition. Whether the authority and influence of the person expressing the opinion will be determinative of liability may be doubted. As the Phillimore Committee notes in a memorable phrase, 'A dictum of Ulpian will carry more weight from its origin alone than a dozen judgments of as many long-forgotten but doubtless worthy praetors'.[2] But even the praetor may prejudge the issue and, as the extract from Lord Cross's speech clearly indicates, it will not then avail him to plead his lack of influence.

There is also room for doubt whether the absolute prohibition was intended to apply to the prejudgment of issues of *law* as well as to the prejudgment of issues of fact. Certainly Lord Cross referred to the illegality of prejudging issues 'whether of fact or of law.'[3] But it is hoped that the case will not come to be regarded as authority for this wide proposition. Lord Simon accepted that 'scholarly discussion in the legal journals of decisions which may be the subject of appeal could not appropriately be described as interference with the due course of law'.[4] The same must be true of discussion elsewhere and this—assuming, at least, that prejudice through a juror or witness is not in issue—irrespective of whether the case is pending on appeal or is still before a first instance judge. Had the *Sunday Times* confined its proposed discussion to the specifically legal issues raised by the thalidomide tragedy (as, for example, the ability to sue for prenatal injury) it would have been absurd to have forbidden publication. Reasoned submissions on points of law do not fall within the proper ambit of the law of contempt any more than do reasoned criticisms of sentences passed in criminal cases.[5]

(ii) *Publishing inadmissible evidence.* In civil proceedings the exclusionary rules of evidence are less important than they are in criminal proceedings.[6] The danger of committing a contempt through publishing inadmissible evidence is accordingly less marked. Yet it is still possible to envisage circumstances in which a realistic danger clearly exists. Suppose, for example, that A is suing B for libel and that B maintains that A's reputation is such that he should be awarded no more than nominal damages. On such facts B would be entitled to lead evidence of A's bad reputation, but he may not lead evidence of specific instances of past misconduct tending to show no more than that a good or neutral reputation is undeserved.[7] If a newspaper were to supply the details in a case involving a jury there would clearly be a risk that the fair trial of the issue of damages might be impaired.

A similar risk of prejudice may exist if a publication were to disclose the fact that a defendant had paid money into court under R.S.C. Order 22. Order 22 is designed to promote out-of-court settlements. The mechanics are briefly that the defendant may pay a sum of money into court which it is then open to the plaintiff to take out in settlement of his claim. If he chooses not to do so then he is, in effect, required to gamble on the damages ultimately awarded exceeding the amount paid in, for if they do not he will be required to pay all the costs of the proceedings from the date of payment in. Ord. 22, r.7 provides that:

[2] Para. 111.
[3] [1974] A.C. 273, 322; [1973] 3 All E.R. 54, 84.
[4] [1974] A.C. 273, 321; [1973] 3 All E.R. 54, 83.
[5] As to which, see below, p. 188 *et seq.*
[6] *Cf.* above, pp. 97–100.
[7] See *Plato Films, Ltd* v. *Speidel* [1961] A.C. 1090; [1961] 1 All E.R. 876, H.L.

. . . the fact that money has been paid into court . . . shall not be pleaded and no communication of that fact shall be made to the Court . . . until all questions of liability and of the amount of debt or damages have been decided.

This has obvious implications for the law of contempt. If a publication were to disclose the simple fact that money had been paid in, this, of itself, might prejudice a jury against the defendant in that they might regard the payment as tantamount to a concession that the plaintiff had at least a very strong case. It is unlikely that a similar risk of prejudice could be assumed if the case were being heard by a judge sitting alone.[8] If the publication went further and disclosed the *amount* paid in, then the risk of prejudicing the jury in their assessment of damages would be even clearer.[9]

(iii) *Publicly abusing parties or witnesses*[10]

(a) *Effect on the court.* Public abuse or disparagement of a party or witness may be regarded as a contempt because of its tendency to distort the attitude which a court will adopt to the party or witness in question. Naturally the danger will be greater where a jury is involved than where a judge is sitting alone. In *Higgins* v. *Richards*[11] the chief constable of Neath had instituted libel proceedings against the editor of the *Neath News* following the publication of an article stating that he had behaved with gross impropriety when putting down local rioting. The paper responded to the issue of the writ by publishing a series of articles under the pseudonym 'Quill' in which the writer recounted how he had persuaded his editor to return to the topic and to expose what he called, 'the disgraceful carryings on of certain members of the borough police force'. One such article suggested that public feeling was strongly in support of the editor and the stand he was taking. In holding that a serious contempt had been committed Bray, J. said that: 'It mattered not that the jury who would try the case might not come from Neath itself or from the neighbourhood. The editor boasted of the extended circulation of his paper, and it was almost certain that at least some of the jury would read some of the articles.'[12] The editor was sent to prison for six weeks for having created a serious danger that they might be prejudiced by them.

(b) *Effect on witnesses.* In other cases hostile criticism of parties or witnesses has been held to constitute a contempt because of its likely effect upon the witnesses themselves. It may, for example, deter a particular witness, or witnesses in general, from coming forward to give evidence on behalf of a party, or colour the evidence which they would otherwise have given. *Hutchinson* v. *Amalgamated*

---

[8] See *The Supreme Court Practice 1973* Vol. 1, p. 351 and *Millensted* v. *Grosvenor House (Park Lane), Ltd* [1937] 1 K.B. 717; [1937] 1 All E.R. 736, C.A., where, however, discussion was not directed to the question of contempt.

[9] *Cf. The Wealdstone News and The Harrow News (Editor, Printer and Publisher)* (1925) 41 T.L.R. 508—where payment was under the Libel Act 1843, s. 2, but similar considerations would seem to apply to payments under Ord. 22. Presumably a judge would be no more than embarrassed by the knowledge and this would not be sufficient to constitute a contempt: above, p. 109.

[10] For a helpful discussion, see Goodhart, 'Newspapers and Contempt of Court' (1935) 48 Harv. L.R. 885, 895–898.

[11] (1912) 28 T.L.R. 202.

[12] *Ibid.*, at p. 203. See also *Russell* v. *Russell* (1894) 11 T.L.R. 38.

Engineering Union[13] provides a fairly extreme example of a criticism of a party being regarded as a deterrent to witnesses coming forward to give evidence on his behalf. Here one Hutchinson had applied for an injunction to restrain the AEU from removing him from his office as President of the union when the *Daily Worker* published an article bitterly attacking him for going beyond the union's own appeal structure to what it termed the 'capitalist judges'. The article suggested that members of the union 'will no doubt have no mercy on those who seek to upset working-class decisions in the capitalist courts'. Goddard, J. viewed such remarks as calculated to interfere with the administration of justice because of their potential effect upon both the litigant himself and, above all, on possible witnesses. As to the latter, he observed that he could conceive of nothing 'more calculated to make persons the plaintiff might desire to call as witnesses hesitate or refuse to give him their assistance'. 'If no mercy was to be shown to the litigant', Goddard, J. added, 'what was the probable fate that awaited those who assisted him?'

By way of contrast reference may be made to the more recent case of *Re Duncan, Deceased.*[14] In this case probate proceedings were pending to determine entitlement to the estate of Sir Oliver Duncan, the millionaire and grandson of the founder of the Pfizer pharmaceutical group, who died in Rome in 1964. The plaintiff was asking the court to pronounce against a will made in Rome in 1961 in which a certain Miss Fay was designated the universal legatee. It was contended that this will had been procured by fraud and improper pressure at a time when Sir Oliver was in a weak state of health. When proceedings were pending the *Evening Standard* published a column beneath the headline 'The Will of a Shadow?' in which Sam White, the journalist, made the following statements:

> (1) that Sir Oliver had left a huge sum to his Hungarian mistress (meaning Miss Fay) and nothing to his Hungarian wife: (Miss Fay denied that she was Sir Oliver's mistress and pointed out that Sir Oliver had left 4m. Swiss francs to his widow); (2) that an entry in a diary kept by Sir Oliver's Italian lawyer described him as being 'but a shadow of his former self' at the time of making the will: (Miss Fay was challenging the authenticity of the diary and asserting that the entry was forged).

It was contended on behalf of Miss Fay that these statements were likely to prejudice the fair trial of the action by, inter alia, discouraging witnesses from coming forward to support her case and colouring the evidence which they would otherwise have given. Latey, J. was, however, unimpressed with this contention and dismissed the application to commit the proprietors and editor with costs.

Tichborne v. *Mostyn, Tichborne* v. *Tichborne,*[15] was a case in which the disparagement was levelled at witnesses, rather than at a litigant. The background was that a person was claiming to be the eldest son of the late Sir James Francis Tichborne, and that he had recently returned to England to assert his title and position after an absence of fourteen years. The claimant contended that

[13] *The Times*, 25 August 1932. See also *Littler* v. *Thomson* (1839) 2 Beav. 129; 48 E.R. 1129; *Brodribb* v. *Brodribb & Wall* (1866) 11 P.D. 66; *Ilkley Local Board* v. *Lister* (1895) 11 T.L.R. 176; *Greenwood* v. *The Leather-Shod Wheel Co., Ltd* (1898) 14 T.L.R. 241; *Re Pall Mall Gazette, Jones* v. *Flower and Hopkinson* (1894) 11 T.L.R. 122.

[14] *The Times*, 20 May 1969. See Wintour, *Pressures on the Press* (1973), pp. 134–137.

[15] (1867) L.R. 7 Eq. 55n.

during his absence he had resided in Australia under an assumed name after having been shipwrecked on a voyage from Rio to New York and picked up at sea. When the cause was pending the *Pall Mall Gazette* published an article stating that it had been 'favoured with a perusal of the affidavits put in on the Plaintiff's behalf in this extraordinary case'. The article went on to comment:

> We have not space to enter into detail as to the statements of the thirty-four persons whose affidavits follow those of the claimant and Lady Tichborne. Many of them are important enough if the deponents can endure cross-examination in the witness-box; many are obviously false, absurd, and worthless, being those of persons who, never having seen the claimant before he left England, are nonetheless convinced that he is the person he claims to be.

When the publication was referred to Sir William Page Wood, V.C. he was satisfied that there had been an improper attempt to interfere with the administration of justice. Such a publication, he considered, could well 'affect the minds of persons who might be willing to give evidence in the case, and may prevent them from coming forward when they find that they will expose themselves to criticism of this description'.[16]

(c) *Effect on the parties and on other litigants.* Publications which abuse parties to proceedings may also be regarded as a contempt because of their likely effect upon the parties themselves, and upon litigants generally. Until recently the leading case in this regard was *Re The William Thomas Shipping Co., Ltd*[17] In this case a shipping company was suffering from the effects of the general economic depression and a receiver had been appointed on the application of the debenture holders. Sir Robert Thomas, the governing director and guarantor of the debenture stock, authorised local Liverpool newspapers to publish statements which were highly critical of the debenture holders' actions. It was suggested that they had 'smashed the goodwill and organisation of the business in a day', and that 'no one in shipping circles can understand this line of conduct'. No mention was made of the fact that the company was in a desperate financial position and could not possibly continue unless finance was immediately forthcoming. Hence an incomplete picture was presented to the newspapers' readers. The debenture holders reacted by seeking an order to commit Sir Robert Thomas and the publishers for contempt. When the case came before Maugham, J. he discounted the possibility of a Chancery judge being influenced, but nonetheless held that a contempt had been committed. His reasoning was that:[18]

> I think that to publish injurious misrepresentations directed against a party to the action, especially when they are holding up that party to hatred or contempt, is liable to affect the course of justice, because it may, in the case of a plaintiff, cause him to

---

[16] *Ibid.*, at p. 56n. See also *Felkin* v. *Herbert* (1864) 33 L.J. Ch. 294; *The Empire News (Editor), The Times*, 23 February 1932; *Re Doncaster and Retford Co-operative Societies' Agreement* (1960) L.R. 2 R.P. 129.
[17] [1930] 2 Ch. 368.
[18] *Ibid.*, at p. 376.

discontinue the action from fear of public dislike, or it may cause the defendant to come to a compromise which he otherwise would not come to, for a like reason.[19]

By way of contrast, he observed[20] that the position would have been different if,

Sir Robert Thomas had fairly stated the result of the evidence on which the Court made the order for the appointment of a receiver and manager, and had in a temperate manner expressed his opinion that another course ought to have been taken by the plaintiff.

The limits of permissible public pressure were further examined by the House of Lords in the *Sunday Times* case when commenting on the article of September 24, 1972 in respect of which the Attorney-General had declined to institute proceedings. This read in part as follows:[1]

Thirdly, the thalidomide children shame Distillers. It is appreciated that Distillers have always denied negligence and that if the cases were pursued, the children might end up with nothing. It is appreciated that Distillers' lawyers have a professional duty to secure the best terms for their clients. But at the end of the day what is to be paid in settlement is the decision of Distillers, and they should offer much, much more to every one of the thalidomide victims. It may be argued that Distillers have a duty to their shareholders and that, having taken account of skilled legal advice, the terms are just. But the law is not always the same as justice. There are times when to insist on the letter of the law is as exposed to criticism as infringement of another's legal rights. The figure in the proposed settlement is to be £3·25m., spread over 10 years. This does not shine as a beacon against pre-tax profits last year of £64·8 million and company assets worth £421 million. Without in any way surrendering on negligence, Distillers could and should think again.[2]

Taken as a whole the speeches in the House of Lords are far more favourable to the press when dealing with this issue than when dealing with the issue of prejudgment. Thus Lord Reid and Lord Cross both made clear their disagreement with the Attorney-General's contention that it was a contempt to do *anything* likely to bring pressure to bear on a party to proceedings.[3] Parties to litigation must, as Lord Reid put it, 'be protected from scurrilous abuse; otherwise many litigants would fear to bring their cases to court'.[4] But different considerations applied to fair and temperate criticism. This was quite permissible, even though it was both intended and likely to cause a party to forego his legal rights in whole or in part, or otherwise to modify his conduct.[5] Lord Cross agreed and he drew the distinction in the following terms:[6]

[19] Reliance was placed on *Kitcat* v. *Sharp* (1882) 52 L.J. Ch. 134; *Ilkley Local Board* v. *Lister* (1895) 11 T.L.R. 176. See also *The St. James's Evening Post Case* (1742) 2 Atk. 469, 471; 26 E.R. 683 *per* Lord Hardwicke, L.C.; *Vine Products, Ltd* v. *Mackenzie & Co., Ltd* [1966] Ch. 484, 496; [1965] 3 All E.R. 58, 61.

[20] [1930] 2 Ch. 368, 377. *Cf. Re South Shields Clearance Order 1931* (1932) 173 L.T. Jo. 76.

[1] See [1974] A.C. 273, 293; [1973] 3 All E.R. 54, 59.

[2] The passages which follow are reproduced with some minor modifications from an article by the author, 'Contempt of Court: The Sunday Times Case' [1975] Crim. L.R. 132, 136 *et seq.*

[3] The contention was based on a passage in the judgment of Buckley, J. in *Vine Products, Ltd* v. *Mackenzie and Co., Ltd* [1966] Ch. 484, 496; [1965] 3 All E.R. 58, 61.

[4] [1974] A.C. 273, 295; [1973] 3 All E.R. 54, 60.

[5] Such criticism might, however, be unlawful on the ground that it was likely to affect the mind of witnesses, jurors or magistrates: *ibid.*, at p. 298 and p. 63 respectively.

[6] [1974] A.C. 273, 326; [1973] 3 All E.R. 54, 87.

To seek to dissuade a litigant from prosecuting or defending proceedings by threats of unlawful action by abuse, by misrepresentation of the nature of the proceedings or the circumstances out of which they arose and such like is no doubt a contempt of court; but if the writer states the facts fairly and accurately and expresses his view in temperate language the fact that the publication may bring pressure—possibly great pressure—to bear on the litigant should not make it a contempt of court.

In the opinion of both Lord Reid and Lord Cross the article of September 24 had kept within the bounds of permissible pressure and did not constitute a contempt.[7]

Although Lord Diplock and Lord Simon both disagreed with this conclusion this need not be taken to suggest a difference of opinion as to the legality of a fair and temperate criticism, so much as a different assessment of the article itself. Thus Lord Diplock regarded the article as holding Distillers up to 'public obloquy' for their conduct.[8] As with Lord Reid he saw the attendant danger as lying 'in the inhibiting effect which it might have on all potential suitors if it were to become the common belief that to have recourse to the established courts of law for the ascertainment and enforcement of their legal rights and obligations would make them a legitimate target of public abuse'.[9] Similarly, Lord Simon agreed that the article was 'intended to interfere with the terms of settlement by holding Distillers up to execration'.[10] Since the passage in the article to which exception was taken has been set out above, readers may judge for themselves whether the epithets 'abuse', 'obloquy' and 'execration' can fairly be applied to it. Some may find the terms extravagant. From the standpoint of the general law the important factor is that the speeches as a whole are consistent with the view that fair and temperate public pressure is permissible where the sole complaint is that it is of a type which is likely to affect a party to the proceedings. It is only when threats or abuse are employed, or where there is an unfair and material misrepresentation of the circumstances surrounding the proceedings[11] that a contempt may be committed.

In so far as regard must be had to the likely effect of the publication on *litigants generally* it would seem that the temperament or resources of the individual litigant are not conclusive. The fact that his assets are so substantial as to make him immune from abuse, or that his temperament is such as to make him open to the pressure of moderate criticism, is not necessarily in point. Support for the opposing view is, however, to be found in the earlier judgment of Latey, J. in *Re Duncan Deceased*.[12] Here, it may be recalled, a certain Miss Fay was a party to probate proceedings instituted to determine the validity of a will made by Sir Oliver Duncan. In response to a submission that an article in the *Evening Standard* was likely to cause her to discontinue the action, Latey, J. is reported as saying:

---

[7] Lord Morris appears to have agreed: *cf.* [1974] A.C. 273, 306; [1973] 3 All E.R. 54, 70.

[8] [1974] A.C. 273, 313; [1973] 3 All E.R. 54, 76.

[9] *Ibid.* See also [1974] A.C. 273, 295; [1973] 3 All E.R. 54, 60 (Lord Reid).

[10] [1974] A.C. 273, 321; [1973] 3 All E.R. 54, 83.

[11] As in *Re The William Thomas Shipping Co., Ltd* [1930] 2 Ch. 368, above p. 133. Contrast *Re South Shields Clearance Order 1931* (1932) 173 L.T. Jo. 76.

[12] *The Times*, 20 May 1969, above, p. 132.

If the test were objective, it meant that one must look at the complainant as being neither oversensitive nor unduly thick-skinned. Especially where penal jurisdiction was invoked, it would be unreal to apply the purely objective test, ignoring personalities.

In the light of these considerations, Latey, J. concluded that it would be, 'fanciful to suppose that the article complained of would have the least influence on Miss Fay in the pending proceedings'.[13]

(iv) *Private threats and persuasion directed at courts, witnesses and parties.*

(a) *Courts and witnesses.* As was noted earlier when discussing contempt in relation to criminal proceedings, any attempt by threats, bribery, or other forms of improper persuasion to induce a juror, witness or judge to adopt a particular attitude with respect to a given case will constitute a contempt.[14] The same principles are applicable in civil proceedings. Indeed many of the leading examples noted earlier involve threats or persuasion aimed at influencing conduct in civil proceedings. Thus in *Re B (J.A.) (An Infant)*,[15] for example, the threat to expose the fact that a witness had had an illegitimate child if she gave evidence was made in the context of wardship proceedings. In such cases it seems clear that a contempt may still be committed even though the person offering the inducement was only threatening to exercise what would otherwise have been a legal right or privilege. Thus it would no doubt be a contempt for the chairman of a social club to threaten to expel a judge in accordance with the club rules unless he reaches a particular decision in a given case.[16] The same would be true of a threat directed against a witness.

Since juries are required to reach their decisions solely on the basis of evidence adduced in open court any attempt to exert influence outside these confines (or to exert improper pressure on a fellow juror) would constitute unlawful interference with the administration of justice. On the other hand, some forms of attempted persuasion directed at judges or witnesses would appear to be quite permissible. Thus if a High Court judge were faced with a claim involving the determination of a novel point of law, it is hoped that it would not be a contempt to publish an article in a legal journal or elsewhere arguing strongly in favour of one view or the other and with the intention that it should be brought to his notice.[17] Likewise it seems clear that attempts to influence a witness may in certain circumstances be quite permissible. So if it is known that A, an expert in a particular field, is to be called to give evidence in a case it can hardly be an offence for a colleague, B, to seek to persuade him that the proper view of (say) a book's literary merits is such and such. Submissions on points of law directed at judges, and forensic argument directed at expert witnesses, may be both intended, and perhaps likely, to affect the outcome of a case, but they can hardly be regarded as improper.

[13] For the Phillimore Committee recommendations, see below, p. 138.

[14] See above, p. 93 (jurors); p. 100 (witnesses); p. 105 (judges).

[15] [1965] Ch. 1112; [1965] 2 All E.R. 168. See also *Shaw* v. *Shaw* (1861) 2 Sw. & Tr. 517; 164 E.R. 1097, and cases cited above, p. 100, note 9.

[16] *Cf.* Lord Simon in *Att.-Gen* v. *Times Newspapers, Ltd* [1974] A.C. 273, 318; [1973] 3 All E.R. 54, 80.

[17] But see above, p. 130 for a discussion of whether prejudgments on issues of law constitute a contempt. *Quaere* also whether the position would be different if a copy of the article were sent to his chambers (a) by the disinterested author or (b) by a party?

(b) *Parties*. Broadly similar considerations apply to threats or persuasion directed at the parties to proceedings. Thus it is a contempt to seek to influence a party
by threats of physical harm, or by other forms of intimidation or by bribery. *Re
Mulock*[18] is a case in point. Here a certain Mrs Chetwynd was seeking a
dissolution of marriage when one Mulock sent her a letter threatening that if she
did not withdraw her suit he would, 'publish the full truth of the case, [and] a
statement of facts concerning yourself from before your marriage up to the
present time, borne out by irrefragable documents'. When the matter came
before Sir James Wilde, J.O., he said:[19]

> From the pressure of this threat Mrs. Chetwynd seeks protection, and she claims the
> right to approach this court free from all restraint or intimidation. It is a right that
> belongs to all suitors. . . . No one can doubt that the very offering of such a threat to a
> suitor in this Court, for such a purpose, is in itself, and quite independently of its
> subsequent fulfilment, a contempt of Court.

Mulock was accordingly found guilty of contempt and ordered to pay a fine of
£300.

Other cases present problems which are substantially more difficult to resolve.
They were highlighted in *Attorney-General* v. *Times Newspapers, Ltd*[20] by a
discussion of the position presented by the lawsuit involving Shylock and
Antonio in the play, *The Merchant of Venice*, where, it will be recalled, Shylock
was insisting on his pound of flesh. Lord Reid posed the following series of
questions:[1]

> Why would it be contrary to public policy to seek by fair comment to dissuade Shylock
> from proceeding with his action? Surely it could not be wrong for the officious
> bystander to draw his attention to the risk that, if he goes on, decent people will cease to
> trade with him. Or suppose that his best customer ceased to trade with him when he
> heard of his lawsuit. That could not be contempt of court. Would it become contempt
> if, when asked by Shylock why he was sending no more business his way, he told him the
> reason? Nothing would be more likely to influence Shylock to discontinue his action. It
> might become widely known that such pressure was being brought to bear. Would that
> make any difference? And though widely known must the local press keep silent about
> it?

Lord Diplock sought to deal with the problem of delimitation by distinguishing between public abuse and private persuasion. The former was a contempt
because of its inhibiting effect upon litigants generally. Thus it would have been
unlawful 'to hold either Shylock or Antonio to public obloquy on the Rialto
because he was seeking to enforce in a court of competent jurisdiction legal rights
to which he was entitled under the law as it existed at that time'.[2] Private
persuasion was, however, quite legitimate provided that it was 'unaccompanied
by unlawful threats'.[3] The threat to withdraw custom from Antonio or Shylock
as lender or borrower would not have constituted even a technical contempt.

[18] (1864) 3 Sw. & Tr. 599; 164 E.R. 1407.
[19] *Ibid.*, at p. 601. See also *Carroll* (1744) 1 Wils. K.B. 75; 95 E.R. 500; *Smith* v. *Lakeman* (1856) 26
L.J. Ch. 305.
[20] [1974] A.C. 273; [1973] 3 All E.R. 54.
[1] [1974] A.C. 273, 295–296; [1973] 3 All E.R. 54, 61.
[2] [1974] A.C. 273, 313; [1973] 3 All E.R. 54, 75–76.
[3] [1974] A.C. 273, 313; [1973] 3 All E.R. 54, 76.

While it may be accepted that private persuasion will constitute a contempt if it takes the form of unlawful threats (that is a threat to commit a crime, a tort or even a breach of contract), it is doubtful whether this can be regarded as a precondition of liability. Yet the Phillimore Committee appears to favour a similar dividing line. In any event it recommends that 'conduct directed against a litigant in connection with the legal proceedings in which he is concerned, which amounts to intimidation or unlawful threats to person, property or reputation should be capable of being treated as a contempt of court; but that conduct falling short of that should not be a contempt'.[4] It must be presumed that both Lord Diplock and the committee envisage the need for a threat which is 'unlawful' for reasons other than that it might constitute a contempt. Otherwise the purported limitation would beg the very point in issue.[5]

It is submitted, with respect, that it is not the law (nor should it be) that a threat to commit an otherwise lawful act unless a party modifies his conduct cannot constitute a contempt. Certainly any such limitation would be highly productive of anomalies. A may, for example, be threatened by B, a supplier, that he will no longer receive materials essential to his business if he proceeds with his action against C. On such facts the effectiveness of the threat will hardly depend on whether it is expressed in terms of breaking an existing contract, rather than in terms of refusing to renew a contract which has expired. Yet on the basis of Lord Diplock's approach a contempt could be committed in the former case, but not in the latter.[6] The same would be true of a case in which a father threatens to expel a daughter from home if she proceeds with an action against a third party, or where the threat is to reveal the discreditable past of a party and this could be justified in defamation proceedings.

Precedents for holding that an offence may be committed by a threat to do something one would generally be at liberty to do are to be found within other areas of the law. Blackmail affords a clear example.[7] Likewise within the law of contempt itself it is clear that the offence will be committed by victimising a witness for the evidence which he has given, and notwithstanding that the victimisation takes the form of doing something which would otherwise have been quite lawful. In the leading case of *Attorney-General* v. *Butterworth*,[8] for example, it was held to be a contempt to victimise a trade unionist by purporting to remove him from his post as delegate after securing the passage of the necessary resolutions. By the same token it has also been submitted that it may be a contempt to direct a threat or inducement at a judge or a witness even though

---

[4] Para. 62. The word 'intimidation' is presumably being used in its technical sense and thus requires a threat to commit an unlawful act: see Winfield, *Tort*, 9th ed., p. 463 and cases there cited.

[5] *Quaere*, however, whether the committee envisages that a similar limitation applies where the conduct is charged on indictment as an attempt improperly to interfere with the administration of justice?

[6] This would not constitute a tort of unlawfully interfering with business relations (see *Acrow Automation, Ltd* v. *Rex Chainbelt, Inc.* [1971] 3 All E.R. 1175, C.A.) unless the means employed by B were otherwise unlawful as constituting, for example, a contempt—which is, of course, the point in issue.

[7] *Cf. Thorne* v. *Motor Trade Association* [1937] A.C. 797 and, in general, Smith and Hogan, *op cit.*, Ch. 15, p. 464 *et seq.*

[8] [1963] 1 Q.B. 696; [1962] 3 All E.R. 626, below, p. 199.

the threat was to commit an act which would otherwise have been lawful.[9] The same must be true of threats directed at parties to the proceedings.

Lord Simon was the only other member of the House of Lords to express an opinion as to the proper approach in such cases. He clearly had reservations about Lord Diplock's view and preferred to attempt to draw the line in terms of whether the pressure was *justifiable*. That he did not equate the bounds of unjustifiable pressure with threats to commit otherwise unlawful acts may be seen from the following passage in his speech:[10]

> The justification for private pressure on a litigant might be such a common interest that fair, reasonable and moderate personal representations would be appropriate. Such common interest would not necessarily have to be monetary; a genuine unofficious and paramount concern for the real welfare of the litigant would, in my view, be sufficient. In contrast, merely by way of example, if parents are in dispute over the custody of a young child, it is in the public interest that such a dispute should (in default of agreement) be settled by impartial adjudication with the child's welfare as the first and paramount consideration: such public interest would be prejudiced if an adult child of the family were to say to one parent, 'Unless you instruct your solicitor to withdraw your case, I shall never speak to you again,' no less than by a public campaign which holds such parents up to odium.

The adult child would normally be at liberty to speak or not to speak to the parent as he chose, but the threat to exercise the liberty in the event of the parent continuing with the case would, in the opinion of Lord Simon, constitute a contempt. Lord Diplock would presumably disagree.

While it is submitted that the approach of Lord Simon is to be preferred it is clearly apt to introduce an element of uncertainty into the law. In the nature of things there can be no precise delimitation of the circumstances in which the directing of pressure at a litigant will be unjustifiable even though the result threatened is neither a crime, a tort, nor a breach of contract. That some attempts privately to induce a party to litigation to forego or compromise his rights, or otherwise to modify his position, are quite legitimate is obvious. Indeed such inducements typically accompany any attempt to settle a case out of court or, for that matter, any attempt by a legal adviser to persuade a client that it is not in his best interests to litigate. Likewise it is clear that if fair and temperate public criticism of the position adopted by a party is lawful[11] then the same must, *a fortiori*, be true of private criticism. In all such cases the party will only have been persuaded to modify his position by reference to considerations, such as the possibility of losing or the questionable morality of adopting a particular position, which are inherent in the process of litigation itself. No ulterior considerations will have been brought to bear on him.

In other cases the legality of the inducement may depend on how it arose. Thus in Lord Reid's example[12] the trader would be more likely to be held to be acting unjustifiably if he approached Shylock and threatened him with a future loss of custom, than if he simply went elsewhere, gave Shylock the reason when asked,

[9] See above, p. 136.
[10] [1974] A.C. 273, 319; [1973] 3 All E.R. 54, 81.
[11] See above, p. 133 *et seq.*
[12] See above, p. 137.

and added that he would return if, and only if, Shylock discontinued. In both cases the effect upon Shylock may be substantially the same, but the way in which it came about may be important. An analogy may again be found in the offence of blackmail where liability depends upon the accused making a demand, and where it is not sufficient that he accepts an offer to buy his silence.

Beyond this, pressure is more likely to be regarded as justifiable if it is motivated by a genuine desire to protect one's own interests, or the interests of a close associate, than if its origins are purely officious. To this extent, therefore, motives may be important.[13] This may explain the case of *Webster* v. *Bakewell Rural District Council*.[14] Here the yearly tenant of a cottage forming part of a settled estate was involved in a legal dispute with the local authority and was seeking an injunction to restrain it from removing soil from his roadside bank and from damaging his boundary wall. The tenant for life considered that the continuation of the dispute was prejudicial to her interests in the land and to her relationship with the authority. Her solicitor accordingly wrote to the yearly tenant in the following terms:

> Mrs. Thornhill is determined that this action shall not go forward and she is anxious to stop it with as little inconvenience to anybody as possible. She does not wish to take the extreme course of turning you out of the cottage so as to place you in such a position that you would have no locus standi in the matter, but she will not hesitate to do so if her wishes are not carried out. I hope however that you will not drive her to take this course.

Dismissing an application to commit the solicitor for contempt, Neville, J. considered that both the solicitor and the life tenant had acted quite lawfully by threatening that the tenancy would be terminated if the yearly tenant persisted in an action which the tenant for life regarded as injurious to her rights over the property. Taking a closely parallel example his Lordship said:[15]

> A weekly tenancy could be determined before any action in respect of the property could be tried, and I cannot see that there is anything to prevent a landlord exercising his legal rights in that way, if he does it honestly to protect the rights he has in the property.

The case is perhaps a borderline one, but it would seem that the interference was justifiable in the circumstances. The position might well have been quite different if an officious bystander had made a similar threat. A further example may be taken from the thalidomide case where considerable pressure by the parents in general was exerted on the five parents who refused to accept the £3·25 million proposal for a settlement. Such pressure from the parents who had a common interest in the matter may well have been justifiable, while pressure from an outsider might not have been.

In paragraphs 68–84 of its recent Working Paper, 'Offences Relating to the Administration of Justice', the Law Commission has also provisionally proposed

---

[13] See further below, p. 202 for the importance of motives where the contempt alleged is a victimisation of a witness etc.

[14] [1916] 1 Ch. 300.

[15] *Ibid.*, at p. 303.

that threats to exercise what would otherwise have constituted a legal right should be capable of giving rise to liability. This would be so where the person making the threat or demand did not believe that he had reasonable grounds for making it or did not believe that the use of menaces (any threat of action detrimental to or unpleasant to the person addressed) was a proper means of reinforcing the demand. Support for the views advanced above is also to be found in the recent decision of the Court of Appeal in *Kellett*.[16] Here it was held that D committed the offence of attempting to pervert the course of justice if in threatening to bring a slander action against certain neighbours he intended to induce them not to give evidence against him in divorce proceedings. This was so even though a threat to sue in slander is prima facie quite lawful, albeit one which was probably doomed to fail in the circumstances of the case since the neighbours' statements would presumably have been made on a privileged occasion.

(v) *Some further problems associated with civil proceedings*

(a) *Advertisements offering a reward for evidence.* Notwithstanding views expressed in an old 18th-century case,[17] it is now clear that advertisements offering rewards to persons coming forward to give evidence in a particular sense will normally be regarded as quite lawful. So much was established in *Plating Co.* v. *Farquharson*,[18] where a party to a dispute involving the alleged infringement of a patent published an advertisement offering a reward of £100 to anyone producing documentary evidence that nickel-plating was done before a certain date. The Court of Appeal dismissed the suggestion that such a promise of reward was a contempt as constituting a temptation to forgery, James, L.J. saying: 'I think these motions are a contempt of Court in themselves, because they tend to waste the public time.' Yet it would be unwise to assume that questions of contempt could never arise in such a case. Just as it should, in principle, be a contempt to offer a substantial sum to a known witness to give evidence in a particular sense[19] so also might it be a contempt to offer to pay a similar sum to a witness who will come forward to give evidence. If, for example, a newspaper had accused a politician of adultery and he had issued a writ for libel the promise of a reward of (say) £5,000 to anyone coming forward to give evidence in support of the allegation might reasonably be viewed as tending to interfere with the administration of justice. The tendency would be the more marked if payment were made contingent upon the failure of the action.

A contempt might also be committed if the advertisement prejudges the issue, disparages the opposing party or otherwise deters witnesses from coming forward for the opposing side. *Brodribb* v. *Brodribb & Wall*[20] was such a case. Here a co-respondent in a divorce action caused the following advertisement to be published in Bristol newspapers:

A notice having been served on me this day affecting my character and reputation, I take the earliest opportunity of giving the charges therein contained the most

[16] *The Times*, 21 June 1975, p. 14.
[17] *Pool* v. *Sacheverel* (1720) 1 P. Wms. 675; 24 E.R. 565.
[18] (1881) 17 Ch. D. 49.
[19] See further, above, p. 101.
[20] (1886) 11 P.D. 66.

unqualified denial, and I hereby offer a reward of one hundred guineas for such information as will lead to the discovery and conviction of the instigators of such charges.

On a subsequent motion for attachment Sir James Hannen, P. commented:[1]

> I must express my strong condemnation of his conduct, which is not in any way calculated to serve the interests of justice, and which, as tending to deter witnesses from coming forward to give evidence, is certainly a contempt of Court.[2]

(b) *Warnings in unfair competition cases.* A trading company which believes itself to be the victim of unfair competition, as through the infringement of a patent or trade-mark, may wish to safeguard its position by issuing warnings to the trade and to journals carrying advertisements of the rival concern. In the nature of things such warnings will frequently contain assertions as to the legal rights of the parties. When proceedings are pending to determine this very issue the possibility of committing a contempt must clearly be borne in mind.

In *J. & P. Coats* v. *Chadwick*[3] the plaintiffs were manufacturers of sewing cotton and they claimed that the defendants were infringing their trade mark, and so designing their goods as to pass them off as those of the plaintiff company thus benefiting unfairly from their goodwill. On the same day on which they issued their writ they also sent out a circular warning retail dealers and others in the trade. It read in part as follows: 'Being apparently unsuccessful in selling this class of goods with their own label, they have now adopted the device of imitating ours in order more readily to find purchasers for their thread.' The defendants replied by alleging that the circular was a contempt as being calculated to create a bias against them in the minds of those who received it, and to deter traders from coming forward to give evidence on their behalf. This contention was accepted by Chitty, J., who described the circular as, 'a strong, one-sided statement by one of the parties to the action on the merits of the case', which 'unhesitatingly imputes fraud and dishonesty to the Defendants'.[4] He concluded his judgment by saying:[5]

> I grant the injunction as asked, with costs, adding that I should not have intervened if the circular had amounted to a mere warning to the trade against infringement or imitation. The plaintiffs are at liberty to warn the trade as much as they like, notwithstanding the pendency of this action; but they are bound to refrain during its pendency from public discussion on the merits or demerits of the case.

The more recent case of *Carl-Zeiss-Stiftung* v. *Rayner & Keeler Ltd*[6] contains a full review of the earlier authorities and provides an example of a warning which was regarded as falling on the right side of the line. The case arose out of a complex dispute involving trade-marks and alleged passing-off and the facts in

---

[1] *Ibid.*, at p. 67.
[2] See also *Butler* v. *Butler* (1888) 13 P.D. 73; *Matthews* v. *Smith* (1844) 3 Hare 331; 67 E.R. 408; *Wilkinson* v. *Gordon* (1824) 2 Add. 152; 162 E.R. 250; *Re Cornish, Staff* v. *Gill* (1893) 9 T.L.R. 196. For discussion of payment to known witnesses in criminal proceedings, see above, pp. 101–102.
[3] [1894] 1 Ch. 347.
[4] *Ibid.*, at p. 349.
[5] *Ibid.*, at p. 350.
[6] [1960] 3 All E.R. 289.

broad outline were as follows. In 1955 Carl-Zeiss-Stiftung, which claimed to be a legal entity in East Germany, started a passing-off action against a firm of the same name which was said to be a legal entity in West Germany. Subsequently, in 1959, C.Z. Scientific Instruments Ltd., an agent in England marketing products of East German firms, began further proceedings to have certain trade-marks expunged from the register where they were currently associated with the West German company. While these actions were pending solicitors acting for the West German company wrote to the editor of a leading trade publication in the following terms:

Dear Sirs, It has been brought to our notice that you have published in your issue of the 10th instant an advertisement for Zeiss Binoculars on behalf of C.Z. Scientific Instruments, Ltd., of 12A Golden Square, W.1. We must inform you that our clients Carl-Zeiss-Stiftung, a body corporate having its principal place of business at Heidenheim a.d. Brenz Wurtenberg in the Federal Republic of Germany, are the registered proprietors of the trade mark No. 335738 being the words 'Carl Zeiss Jena' as depicted in the lenticular device shown in that advertisement, while C.Z. Scientific Instruments are the agents of an East German nationalised concern which calls itself VEB Carl Zeiss Jena, but which has no right to use the trade marks of which our clients are the proprietors. We think it right to warn you that our clients will take all legal steps available to them to protect their rights in their registered trade marks.

A similar letter was sent to a company in Bristol which sold cameras and optical instruments. It was contended on behalf of the East German company that these letters constituted a contempt as being likely to 'crystallise in the minds of the recipients a wrong and fanciful notion of what the position actually was'. Russell, J. did not, however, accept the submission. The only possible danger was that the letters might deter or discourage witnesses from coming forward to give evidence, and he did not feel that the necessary likelihood of such susceptibility to influence had been substantiated. A contempt had not, therefore, been committed.

The accepted distinction between a simple trade warning, which is permissible, and a public discussion of the merits of the case, which is not, is inevitably easier to state in the abstract than to apply in practice. The authorities would seem, however, to support the following propositions. In the first place, a trade warning may be quite lawful even though it states dogmatically that one side is entitled and the other is not. Indeed, as Russell, J. agreed in the *Carl-Zeiss-Stiftung* case, it is impossible to write a warning letter without making such an assertion.[7] Qualifying statements, such as 'the trademark which we *allege* to have been infringed', are not necessary. Secondly, Russell, J. also agreed that it is not necessary when writing such a letter to refer to the fact that proceedings are pending to determine the validity of the view which is advanced.[8] Thirdly, positive disparagement of the opposing party may colour an otherwise unobjectionable letter, especially if it imputes fraud or dishonesty to him.[9] Finally, it may be added that the general trend of the decisions culminating in the

[7] *Cf. ibid.*, at pp. 293–294.
[8] *Cf. ibid.*
[9] See, e.g., *J. & P. Coats* v. *Chadwick* [1894] 1 Ch. 347; *St. Mungo Manufacturing Co.* v. *Hutchinson, Main & Co., Ltd* (1908) 25 R.P.C. 356.

Carl-Zeiss-Stiftung case suggests a fairly robust approach on the part of the courts and an unwillingness to find that a contempt has been committed.[10]

(c) *Publishing details of the pleadings etc.* Pleadings in civil proceedings are designed to elucidate the points of contention and to set out the case which their proponents will subsequently seek to establish at the trial. In the nature of things they do not purport to set out both sides of the case. It was no doubt this consideration which prompted the statement in *Oswald* that: 'Printing, even without comments, and circulating the brief, pleadings, petition, or evidence of one side only, is a contempt.'[11] If this statement was intended to mean that such a publication is *necessarily* a contempt, it was not supported by the cases cited and does not represent the law.

Kitcat v. *Sharp*[12] is a case in which the publication of pleadings would have constituted a contempt. The plaintiff was a clergyman, who was seeking a declaration that he had been induced to take up certain shares by the defendant's fraudulent misrepresentations, and consequential relief from the transaction. The defendant responded by threatening to publish the statement of claim, together with his own disparaging comments, to other clergymen who were listed in the Clergy List. He reinforced his threat by adding, 'You deserve such treatment. Some years since I was done out of £1100 by a nobleman. I printed all his letters and my replies, and sent 4,000 copies (an immense sheet) to the nobility to show the man up.' Fry, J. granted an injunction to restrain the threatened publication which would have been a contempt as both abusing a party concerned in litigation, and prejudicing the public before the cause was heard.

Gaskell & Chambers, Ltd v. *Hudson, Dodsworth and Co.*[13] is perhaps the leading case on this particular aspect of contempt. Again it exhibited an unusual feature in that it was the agent of the defendant to an action of slander of title who had circulated the *plaintiff's* statement of claim to persons within the trade, together with accompanying disparaging remarks. These asserted that the action had only been begun because of the plaintiff's rabid jealousy, that a similar action had been brought and discontinued in the past, and that the defendant intended to contest 'this "cock and bull" claim to the uttermost degree'. In the ensuing contempt proceedings counsel for the plaintiff cited the passage in *Oswald* to which reference was made above, and maintained that the publication of the statement of claim, even without accompanying comments, was itself *necessarily* a contempt. Lord Hewart, C.J. dealt with this submission by saying:[14]

> In my opinion there is no case which goes near to establishing the proposition contended for on behalf of the applicants. It seems to me to be idle to speak of general rules in a context in which each case must be considered upon its own merits.

[10] See, e.g., *Easipower Appliances, Ltd* v. *Gordon Moore (Electrical) Ltd* [1963] R.P.C. 8; *Gaskell & Chambers, Ltd* v. *Hudson, Dodsworth & Co.* [1936] 2 K.B. 595; *Haskell Golf Ball Co.* v. *Hutchinson & Main* (1904) 21 R.P.C. 497. *Cf. Daw* v. *Eley* (1868) 7 Eq. 49; *Goulard & Gibbs* v. *Lindsay & Co.* (1887) 4 R.P.C. 189.

[11] *Contempt of Court*, p. 95.

[12] (1882) 52 L.J. Ch. 134. See also *Cheshire* v. *Strauss* (1896) 12 T.L.R. 291; *Re Cheltenham and Swansea Railway Carriage and Wagon Co.* (1869) L.R. 8 Eq. 580; *Bowden* v. *Russell* (1877) 46 L.J. Ch. 414 and cases cited in Oswald, *op. cit.*, p. 95, note (r).

[13] [1936] 2 K.B. 595.

[14] *Ibid.*, at p. 600.

The same refusal to countenance any such general rules is also evident in the judgments of Du Parcq and Goddard, JJ.[15] Furthermore, the Divisional Court also held that the comment accompanying the statement of claim did not, as had been submitted, constitute a contempt as tending to prejudice the public against the plaintiff, to deter witnesses from giving evidence on his behalf, or to discourage other persons from coming to the court for relief. The motion was accordingly dismissed.[16]

(d) *Gagging writs.* 'Gagging' writs may be said to cause the press and broadcasting agencies some of the most acute and practical problems within the whole of the law of contempt. A newspaper may, for example, have spent many months investigating a particular scandal which is a matter of legitimate public concern. It may be the fraudulent manipulation of an insurance company, a rigged 'antique ring', football bribery, or suspected corruption in the police force, in awarding local government contracts or in other areas. Such investigations have not infrequently provided information which has led to subsequent prosecutions and convictions. Newspapers ranging from the *Sunday Times* and *The Times*, to *The People* and the *News of the World* have been involved.

When it comes to publishing the results of its investigations the newspaper will be faced from the outset with the exigencies of the law of libel. Here it may be noted, in passing, that it is not sufficient under the present law that the newspaper reasonably believed the allegations to be true and their publication to be in the public interest.[17] It must establish that they were in fact true, which is a very different proposition. Given the high level of damages which are currently awarded in defamation cases, there is already a considerable disincentive against publishing.[18] As was noted earlier, a further disincentive arises from the fact that the police may be conducting parallel investigations and these may have reached the stage at which a criminal prosecution is imminent.[19] If this is so, and the newspaper ought to have realised the fact,[20] the publication of what is bound to be highly prejudicial matter may constitute a contempt as tending to prejudice the fair trial of the criminal proceedings.

A further and even more immediate problem will arise if the newspaper publishes one of a series of projected articles and this is followed by the issue of a writ for libel. To require the press in general, and the investigating newspaper in particular, to desist thereupon from further comment on the ground that it might prejudice the libel action would mean that a potential rogue had effectively purchased immunity from exposure at a very small cost. The immunity might, moreover, continue over a long period if the opportunities for delay afforded by the civil process were cynically manipulated to 'gag' the press. It is well settled that an injunction will not be granted to restrain the publication of a libel if the

---

[15] *Cf. ibid.*, at p. 601, and p. 603 respectively.

[16] See also *Fitzhugh, ex p. Livingston* (1937) 81 Sol. Jo. 258.

[17] Such a defence was recommended in the *Justice* report, *The Law and the Press* (1965), para. 119.

[18] *Cf.* Lord Francis-Williams speaking in the House of Lords debate on the *Justice* report: Hansard, H.L. Deb. Vol. 274, col. 1393, 25 May 1966.

[19] See above, p. 79.

[20] *Cf.* the Administration of Justice Act 1960, s. 11(1) and, in general, below, pp. 165–166.

defendant swears that he intends to justify his allegations.[1] To enable the same result to be achieved via the law of contempt would, as Du Parcq, J. recognised in *Gaskell & Chambers, Ltd* v. *Hudson, Dodsworth & Co.*[2] obviously be inconsistent with this rule. On the other hand, the person issuing the writ may not, in fact, *be* a rogue. He may genuinely intend to vindicate his reputation by proceeding with his action as soon as possible. If this is so, any future disparaging comments may be just as likely to prejudice the fair trial of the action as in any other case involving a jury. The problem lies in distinguishing between the two situations. and it is a problem to which there is no ready solution.

Daily Mail (Editor), ex parte Factor[3] is perhaps the leading case in point Over the period March 1926 to the end of July 1926 the *Daily Mail* had published a series of articles accusing one Jacob Factor of fraudulent dealings in shares. The object of the campaign, it was said, was to warn off potential investors in the companies he was floating. Factor had not reacted to these articles, but had left the country for America. In December 1927 a certain James Montgomery was convicted at the Old Bailey on charges involving fraud. The *Daily Mail* commented that on sending him to prison the presiding judge had, 'rid society for a time of a leader of the gang of share-pushing pests who, in association with the notorious Jacob Factor, have for several years been defrauding people all over Great Britain'. Factor, who had by then returned to the country, immediately issued a writ for libel. His complaint was carefully restricted to the allegation that he had been defrauding people *in conjunction with Montgomery*. It made no reference to the earlier and more general allegations that he had been defrauding people throughout the country. The *Daily Mail* replied by publishing a further article beneath the heading, 'Jacob Factor and the *Daily Mail:* A Writ for Libel', and which read in part as follows:

> The British public will be surprised to learn that Jacob Factor, the notorious share-pusher, who found England too hot for him after the *Daily Mail* exposure, is once again back in London. Through his solicitors . . . he has issued a writ against the *Daily Mail* claiming damages for libel. We thought we had succeeded in chasing this arch-swindler back to his haunts in America for good. . . . If Jacob Factor imagines that the issuing of the writ will muzzle us while he is engaged on some new deal he is labouring under a misapprehension.

Factor thereupon instituted contempt proceedings. In his defence the editor pleaded that he believed the sole purpose of the writ to be that of forestalling further exposure while Factor completed his fraudulent designs and left the country for good. The Divisional Court appears to have accepted this view. Having noted that no action had been taken over the earlier defamatory comments, and the very narrow terms within which the pending action had been confined, Lord Hewart, C.J. is reported as saying that: 'The Court found it impossible to believe that an action so framed could have been launched in order that a jury might vindicate Factor's character.'[4] The application to attach the editor was accordingly dismissed with costs.

[1] See *Bonnard* v. *Perryman* [1891] 2 Ch. 269; *Fraser* v. *Evans* [1969] 1 Q.B. 349; [1969] 1 All E.R. 8.
[2] [1936] 2 K.B. 595, 602.
[3] (1928) 44 T.L.R. 303.
[4] *Ibid.*, at p. 306.

Blumefeld, ex parte Tupper[5] was a case which raised similar problems. The *Daily Express* had published articles highly critical of a person calling himself 'Captain' Tupper, and accusing him of fomenting industrial unrest in South Wales with a view to plunging the country into civil war. Tupper issued a writ for libel, the *Daily Express* continued its criticism, and an application to attach the editor for contempt again followed. In delivering his judgment in the Divisional Court in favour of dismissing the application, Phillimore, J. emphatically discounted the idea that the issue of a writ accorded an automatic immunity. He pointed to the consequences of such a conclusion by saying:[6]

> But take the case of a vulgar cheat trying to get money by passing himself off as an old soldier or fraudulently collecting money on the pretence that it was for some missionary society. If some one once committed himself to the expression of an opinion as to this person it would only be necessary for him to issue a writ, and no one was to be allowed to say anything about him for fear it should prejudice the fair trial of the action.

Phillimore, J. did not believe that the law was responsible for any such absurd conclusion. According to his Lordship:[7]

> The court had to reconcile two things—namely, the right of free speech and the public advantage that a knave should be exposed, and the right of an individual suitor to have his case fairly tried. The only way in which the Court could save both was to refuse an unlimited extension of either right. It became, then, a question of degree.

The cases suggest that in attempting to achieve the right balance the paramount consideration is undoubtedly the motive which the court ascribes to the party issuing the writ. The fact that he has passed over a number of earlier defamatory comments may be taken to show a lack of any real concern to vindicate his character, as may the fact that his present complaint is cast in very specific and selective terms.[8] On the other hand there is force in Sir Henry Maddock's objection in the *Daily Mail* case that a failure to sue should not *always* be regarded as tantamount to an admission that the defamatory comment is justified. As he tartly commented in the course of his submissions: 'If every one who was criticised in the *Daily Mail* took action the Courts would require to be enlarged'.[9]

Another important consideration is the timing and area of circulation of the publication. Articles and statements published close to the hearing, as, for example, when the case has been set down for trial, and in an area from which jurors and witnesses are likely to come are probably more prejudicial than others.[10] Similarly a long delay may be taken as suggesting that the plaintiff does not intend to proceed with his libel action, and that he is instituting contempt proceedings for some ulterior motive. Thus delay on the part of Sir Oswald Mosley was clearly an important factor which led to the dismissal of the contempt proceedings in *Fox, ex parte Mosley*.[11] He had allowed nearly three years

---

[5] (1912) 28 T.L.R. 308.
[6] *Ibid.*, at p. 311.
[7] *Ibid.*
[8] *Cf. Daily Mail (Editor), ex p. Factor* (1928) 44 T.L.R. 303, above.
[9] *Ibid.*, at p. 306.
[10] *Cf. Blumenfeld, ex p. Tupper* (1912) 28 T.L.R. 308, 311 *per* Phillimore, J.
[11] *The Times*, 17 February 1966.

to elapse from the time when the BBC delivered its defence to a libel action which he had begun following references to him in a Panorama programme. When he then complained that further references in the *Radio Times* to his activities in the pre-war period were likely to prejudice this action, the Divisional Court not unreasonably took the view that he had no serious intention of proceeding with the action to judgment. In the meantime, however, he had caused substantial inconvenience to the BBC over a period of years.

A further important consideration is whether the publisher swears that he intends to justify the defamatory comments. This was the intention of the publishers in *Daily Mail (Editor), ex parte Factor*,[12] and *Blumenfeld, ex parte Tupper*,[13] and in both cases it was an important element leading to the failure of the contempt application. In *Higgins* v. *Richards*,[14] on the other hand, there was no indication that the *Neath News* intended to justify the defamatory comments which it had levelled at the local Chief Constable. This was no doubt one of the reasons why subsequent repetition of the comments after the writ had been issued led to a committal for contempt. The fact that the Chief Constable clearly intended to proceed with his action was equally important. The relevance of an intention to justify was further considered *obiter* in the recent case of *Thomson v. Times Newspapers, Ltd.*[15] Here the proprietors and editor of the *Sunday Times* were seeking to have a libel action dismissed for want of prosecution and claiming that the plaintiff had been guilty of an inordinate and inexcusable delay. The application failed, but Salmon, L.J. took the opportunity to comment on the problem of 'gagging' writs. He said:[16]

> It is a widely held fallacy that the issue of a writ automatically stifles further comment. There is no authority that I know of to support the view that further comment would amount to contempt of court. Once a newspaper has justified, and there is some prima facie support for the justification, the plaintiff cannot obtain an interlocutory injunction to restrain the defendants from repeating the matters complained of. In these circumstances it is obviously wrong to suppose that they could be committing a contempt by doing so. It seems to me to be equally obvious that no other newspaper that repeats the same sort of criticism is committing a contempt of court.

He went on to qualify these remarks by adding:[17]

> I appreciate that very often newspapers are chary about repeating criticism when a writ for libel has been issued because they feel they are running some risk of being proceeded against for contempt. Without expressing any final view, because the point is not before this court for decision, I think that in this they are mistaken.

The general encouragement to the press which was offered in this statement has been further strengthened by its being noted with approval by Lord Denning in *Wallersteiner* v. *Moir*[18] and by Lord Reid's remark in *Attorney-General* v.

---

[12] (1928) 44 T.L.R. 303.
[13] (1912) 28 T.L.R. 308.
[14] (1912) 28 T.L.R. 202, above, p. 131.
[15] [1969] 3 All E.R. 648, C.A.
[16] *Ibid.*, at p. 651. Widgery and Harman, LL.J. agreed with the judgment of Salmon, L.J.
[17] *Ibid.*
[18] [1974] 3 All E.R. 217, 230, C.A. See also Scarman, L.J.: *ibid.*, at p. 252.

Times Newspapers, Ltd that 'a gagging writ ought to have no effect'.[19] Yet the fact remains that there is no way in which a newspaper or television company can identify a 'gagging writ' in advance[20] or otherwise completely safeguard its position. They may move to have the proceedings dismissed for want of prosecution if there has been an inordinate and inexcusable delay, but this course is only open to the defendant to the original action and other newspapers may wish to comment. Likewise assurances may be sought from the Attorney-General's Department, but this will not prevent the 'rogue' himself from instituting contempt proceedings. If the Phillimore Committee recommendation is adopted and the law of contempt only begins to apply as from the time when the case is set down for trial then the problem will be effectively resolved.[1] If matters have gone thus far there is clearly every indication that the proceedings are genuine. The same would be true in a case in which substantial security had been given for costs.[2] Meanwhile the most that the press can do is to have regard to considerations such as those noted above and to the general atmosphere engendered by statements in the recent cases. It will be seen below that it is now unlikely that a general defence of counterbalancing public interest is available[3] should the court conclude that the subject of the comment was not in fact a rogue, and that he was genuinely intent on vindicating his reputation.[4]

2   PROCEEDINGS BEFORE TRIBUNALS

It was seen in an earlier chapter that the law of contempt has a limited application to tribunals of inquiry appointed under the 1921 Act and to certain other bodies which are not courts of law, but for which a specific statutory provision has been made.[5] The scope of the protection afforded by the law of contempt to tribunals of inquiry was discussed in the report of a committee sitting under the chairmanship of Lord Justice (now Lord) Salmon which was published in 1969.[6] Having noted the typical composition of such a body, the committee's conclusion was that comment on or statements about matters referred to a tribunal of inquiry should not be capable of amounting to a contempt on the basis that it was likely to influence the tribunal. As the committee explained:[7]

> No doubt comment may to some extent be embarrassing to a judge or to members of a Tribunal. The risk, however, of their being improperly influenced by such comment certainly ought to be—and we are quite satisfied is—minimal. We consider that the judges and the sort of people likely to be appointed members of a Tribunal of Inquiry

---

[19] [1974] A.C. 273, 301; [1973] 3 All E.R. 54, 65.
[20] *Cf.* Harold Evans, I.P.I. report, vol. 23, No. 2, p. 10 (February 1974).
[1] Para. 127. See, in general, above, p. 87.
[2] *Cf. Thomson* v. *Times Newspapers, Ltd* [1969] 3 All E.R. 648.
[3] See below, p. 150 *et seq.*
[4] Other English cases which have been concerned with possible 'gagging' writs include *Cronmire* v. *The Daily Bourse, Ltd* (1892) 9 T.L.R. 101; *Re Labouchere, Kensit* v. *The Evening News, Ltd* (1901) 18 T.L.R. 208; *Phillips* v. *Hess* (1902) 18 T.L.R. 400.
[5] See above, p. 33 *et seq.*
[6] Cmnd. 4078, June 1969.
[7] *Ibid.*, para. 26.

should have little difficulty in putting irrelevant and prejudicial matters out of their minds; nor, in our view, is there any real risk of their decision or report being influenced by a Press campaign or popular clamour.

This would certainly seem to be a realistic position to adopt for there is a close analogy in this respect between proceedings before a tribunal of inquiry and proceedings before a court staffed by senior judges. Indeed the chairman of a tribunal of inquiry would nowadays almost invariably be a judge of senior standing.

Even though it would seem to be right to discount the likelihood of a tribunal being improperly influenced, it does not necessarily follow that a contempt of the present category is incapable of being committed when proceedings are pending before the tribunal. It may, for example, be that a *prejudging* of the issues of fact which the tribunal has been established to elucidate will constitute at least a technical contempt if the ruling of the House of Lords in *Attorney-General* v. *Times Newspapers, Ltd*[8] is seen as applying to tribunals as well as to courts of law. Equally, it would no doubt be a contempt if improper threats or pressure were directed against a member of a tribunal of inquiry, if one of its members was publicly abused or vilified, or if there had been an *intention* to interfere with the deliberations of the tribunal in an improper manner.

In practice, however, the main danger would seem to lie in the possibility of contaminating the evidence which likely witnesses might be expected to give before the tribunal. As was noted in the last chapter, it was this danger which was seen by the prime minister and Attorney-General as being attendant upon the interviewing of witnesses on television at the time of the Aberfan disaster.[9] In particular it was feared that an interview might be so conducted as to lead potential witnesses to commit themselves in public to the expression of a particular point of view which they would find difficult to modify later. The Salmon Committee appears to have accepted that such a danger might indeed exist, and it recommended that it should be a contempt to say or do anything in relation to an interview or communication with a potential witness which was, 'intended or obviously likely to alter, distort, destroy or withhold' evidence from the tribunal.[10] Although this recommendation has not been specifically implemented, it would no doubt correspond with the present law.[11]

3   COUNTERBALANCING PUBLIC INTEREST

There is widespread agreement in this country as to the importance of preventing interference with the administration of justice in both criminal and civil proceedings. No responsible journalist would wish to see a slide towards trial by the news

---

[8] [1974] A.C. 273; [1973] 3 All E.R. 54—see above, pp. 126–130.
[9] See above, pp. 102–103 and sources there cited.
[10] See Cmnd. 4078, para. 32.
[11] See, e.g., cases such as *Hutchinson* v. *A.E.U., The Times*, 25 August 1932; *Littler* v. *Thomson* (1839) 2 Beav. 129; 48 E.R. 1129, discussed above, pp. 131–133. The principles established in such cases no doubt apply, *mutatis mutandis*, to hearings before tribunals of inquiry.

media and, apart from occasional lapses,[12] a high standard is generally maintained. But it must also be recognised that other conflicting interests may be present. Investigative journalism has played a valuable role in exposing questionable business activities[13] and outright corruption whether in the field of local government or elsewhere. Yet in performing this role there is a very real danger of coming into conflict with the law of contempt if police investigations are running on parallel lines and have reached a stage at which criminal proceedings are imminent. Moreover the problem for the news media will be posed in even more immediate terms if the person under investigation reacts to his exposure by issuing a writ for libel. Continued exposure from whatever source may then be regarded as prejudicial to the libel proceedings. It has been seen that recent cases have emphasised that a gagging writ should have no effect,[14] and they are important for the atmosphere they engender. But the protection is less than complete for the object of the attack may not, after all, be a rogue (no matter how reasonable the suspicion) and he may have issued the writ with the genuine intention of vindicating his character.

In all such cases an element of flexibility could be achieved through a general defence whereby it was open to a person against whom contempt proceedings had been instituted to show that the possibility of prejudice to a fair trial was offset by some other public interest advanced by the publication. In some of the cases involving 'gagging' writs there are indications that such a defence might have been recognised. Thus in *Daily Mail, ex parte Factor*, for example, Lord Hewart, C.J. is reported as saying that if half of what the *Daily Mail* had said about Jacob Factor were true, 'it was very much for the public benefit that his unmasking should not be delayed'.[15] Support for a defence along these lines was also to be found in the judgment of Lord Denning in *Attorney-General* v. *Times Newspapers, Ltd.*[16] Here the Court of Appeal's decision to lift the injunction was based, in part, on the view that the public interest in having the circumstances of the thalidomide case fully discussed outweighed the prejudice which discussion might cause to Distillers' case. The possibility of prejudice was not the end of the matter. It had to be balanced against the public interest advanced by full and open discussion. Scarman, L.J. agreed with Lord Denning. More recently in *Wallersteiner* v. *Moir*,[17] where the 'abracadabra' of *sub judice* had been called in aid to prevent shareholders from probing the affairs of a company, Lord Denning said that there must be a balancing of considerations and that, 'The shareholders of a public company should be free to discuss the company affairs at the company meetings. If a shareholder feels that there have been, or may be, abuses by those in control of the company, he should be at liberty to give voice to them'.[18]

---

[12] Some of which were the subject of critical comment in (1974) 124 New Law Jo. 1069–1070. See also *The Times*, 11 December 1974.

[13] As in the *Savundra* case, above, p. 79.

[14] See above, pp. 145–149.

[15] (1928) 44 T.L.R. 303, 307, adopting an expression used by Phillimore, J. in *Blumenfeld, ex p. Tupper* (1912) 28 T.L.R. 308.

[16] *Cf.* [1973] 1 Q.B. 710, 741; [1973] 1 All E.R. 815, 822.

[17] [1974] 3 All E.R. 217.

[18] *Ibid.*, at p. 231.

When, however, the *Sunday Times* case went to the House of Lords there was very little support for any such broad based defence. As Lord Cross pointed out it was admittedly only discussion of the specific issue of whether Distillers had been negligent in marketing the drug which was enjoined. Discussion of wider issues—such as the desirability of imposing strict liability on the supplier of drugs, or the suitability of the present method of assessing damages in personal injury cases—could continue unabated.[19] This was so even though it had, in the words of Lord Diplock, 'the indirect effect of bringing pressure to bear on a particular litigant to abandon or settle a pending action'.[20] Yet beyond this the general view which emerges is that publications which prejudge the issues, or which are likely to interfere with the administration of justice, are prohibited whatever the public benefit claimed for them.

Lord Simon dealt with the matter more systematically than the other members of the House of Lords. In his view the balance as between the protection of the due administration of justice and the freedom of the press to discuss and inform could not be drawn with reference to the specific facts of an individual case. A structured approach was required so that *pendente lite* the paramount public interest lay in protecting the administration of justice while at the conclusion of the case the balance shifted to allow full and free debate.[1] The only qualification was that ongoing discussion of matters of general public interest did not have to be suspended simply because particular litigation had intervened which might be prejudiced as an incidental, but unintended, by-product of such discussion.[2]

It may be said in passing that the logic behind this concession is difficult to discern. It stems from the judgment of Jordan, C.J. in a New South Wales case holding that newspaper criticism of a company's activities in fixing the price of bread might legitimately continue notwithstanding an intervening libel and conspiracy action brought by a third party against the company. Jordan, C.J. noted that, 'The fact that the articles complained of formed part of a series which began before the litigation had commenced, although not conclusive, goes to corroborate the evidence that any tendency to interfere with the litigation was unintentional'.[3] This may be true and it is also the case that an intent improperly to interfere will constitute an offence even though there is no likelihood of prejudice resulting. But it is difficult to appreciate why interference with the administration of justice will be more or less justifiable according to whether it was prompted by a particular event which later gave rise to proceedings, or whether it had already begun at a general level before the occurrence of that event. Moreover, Jordan, C.J. had earlier stated the principle in more general terms, saying:[4]

But the administration of justice, important though it undoubtedly is, is not the only matter in which the public is vitally interested; and if in the course of the ventilation of a question of public concern matter is published which may prejudice a party in the

---

[19] [1974] A.C. 273, 324; [1973] 3 All E.R. 54, 85.
[20] [1974] A.C. 273, 313; [1973] 3 All E.R. 54, 75.
[1] [1974] A.C. 273, 319–320; [1973] 3 All E.R. 54, 81–82.
[2] *Cf.* [1974] A.C. 273, 321; [1973] 3 All E.R. 54, 82.
[3] *Ex p. Bread Manufacturers, Ltd; Re Truth and Sportsman, Ltd* (1937) 37 S.R. (N.S.W.) 242, 251.
[4] *Ibid.*, at p. 249.

conduct of a law suit, it does not follow that a contempt has been committed. The case may be one in which as between competing matters of public interest the possibility of prejudice to a litigant may be required to yield to other and superior considerations.[5]

Adoption of the Phillimore Committee proposals for limiting the application of the law of contempt to the period after a suspect is charged, or a case set down for trial, would go a long way towards meeting the objection that the law is too restrictive.[6] But the committee rejected proposals for a general defence which would depend upon establishing that the public interest advanced by the publication was such as to offset the public interest in securing a fair trial.[7] It is submitted that it was wrong to do so. Admittedly such a defence would introduce an element of uncertainty into the law. Yet it is also the case that certainty must surely be acquired at too high a price if prejudicial comment published during the restricted *sub judice* period is necessarily to be designated a contempt.

A number of examples might be taken. The most obvious is perhaps the case envisaged in the 1959 *Justice* Committee report of a newspaper which seeks to protect the public by publishing a photograph of a dangerous criminal who is on the run.[8] The *Justice* Committee thought that it would be 'nothing short of folly' to regard such a publication as a contempt, and few would disagree. Yet in the absence of a defence of counterbalancing public interest a contempt would have been committed if proceedings were *sub judice* and the publication prejudicial to a fair trial.[9] Again, it might also be argued that the protection of the financial well-being of sections of the public might occasionally be sufficiently important to negative liability for contempt. Indeed it is cases of this nature which create most of the problems in practice for those who work in the field of investigative and financial journalism. For example, the Business News section of the *Sunday Times* frequently publishes stories setting out the past criminal record of persons currently promoting new business enterprises. Thus in August 1969 it reported that a certain Raymond Groome who was promising a high rate of return from a £100 company, Back Britain Investments, Ltd, had recently been sentenced to two years' imprisonment on charges of fraud. Then there was Michael Rush who 'peppered Britain with thousands of invitations to invest in a company called Diversified Mining Corporation' and who had just been released from a Canadian prison where he had spent four years on fraud charges; and Alex Herbage of the international investment fund market.[10] Beyond this it might be argued that discussion of matters of genuine international concern, such as Watergate or the massacre at My Lai, cannot sensibly be required to be suspended once a libel

---

[5] See also *Ex p. Dawson; Re Australian Consolidated Press, Ltd* (1958) 61 S.R. (N.S.W.) 573, 575 per Owen, J.; *Ex p. McRae; Re Consolidated Press, Ltd* (1954) S.R. (N.S.W.) 119, 125–126.

[6] See further above, p. 82 and p. 87.

[7] Paras. 143–145. The committee did, however, recommend a limited defence along the lines envisaged by Lord Simon: para. 142.

[8] *Contempt of Court* (1959), p. 11. See also *The Law and the Press* (1965), para. 43.

[9] For photographs as a contempt, see *Daily Mirror, ex p. Smith* [1927] 1 K.B. 845, above, p. 103. The situation would be more likely to arise under the present law whereby proceedings are probably *sub judice* once they are 'imminent', but it could still arise even if the Phillimore proposals for limiting the *sub judice* period were enacted.

[10] See respectively, *Sunday Times*, 3 August 1969 (Groome); 30 September 1973 (Rush); 9 August 1970 (Herbage). See also *the Savundra* case [1968] 3 All E.R. 439.

action has been set down for trial. The same must surely have been true of the thalidomide case had Distillers continued to market the product and had the *Sunday Times* published an article pointing to the causal connection between the drug and phocomelia.[11]

It would be unwise to seek to delimit the bounds of any such defence of public interest too closely. As the Law Commission has recently noted in a paper discussion the application of the defence to cases of breach of confidence:[12]

> The public interest is a developing concept which changes with the social attitudes of the times: many things are regarded as being in the public interest today which would not have been so regarded in the last century, or even twenty years ago . . . . If this fact is recognised, it seems to us that the only prudent course to follow is to frame the defence in terms which are flexible enough to enable each case to be judged on its individual merits. There is, of course, a substantial public interest in the preservation of confidences and the task of the court considering a defence of public interest would therefore be to balance this against the public interest in disclosing the information to which a confidence related.

The same arguments might be applied *mutatis mutandis* to contempt through prejudicing a fair trial, and the fact that the courts have had to decide as between competing claims in other areas[13] suggests that there would be no insuperable difficulty in a case of contempt.

4   PARLIAMENT AND THE SUB JUDICE CONVENTION[14]

The provision in Article 9 of the Bill of Rights whereby 'the freedom of speech, and debates or proceedings in Parliament ought not to be impeached or questioned in any court or place out of Parliament' precludes any control by the courts over parliamentary discussion of matters which are *sub judice*. As Lord Denning noted in *Attorney-General* v. *Times Newspapers, Ltd,*[15] referring to a House of Commons debate on the plight of the thalidomide children: 'It is plain that Parliament has the exclusive right to regulate its own proceedings. What is said or done within the walls of Parliament cannot be inquired into in a court of law.' Parliament has, however, long regulated its own internal affairs so as to restrict comment or debate when proceedings are *sub judice*.

In the case of criminal proceedings a Resolution of the House of Commons bans references to proceedings (whether during debate, in motions or in questions) from the time when a charge has been preferred through to the time when verdict and sentence have been pronounced.[16] The restrictions become operative once more when notice of appeal has been lodged. In certain respects this

---

[11] For further discussion, see Harold Evans, Granada Guildhall Lecture, U.K. *Press Gazette*, No. 425 (March 1974); *The Times*, 19 July 1973 (leading article).

[12] Working Paper No. 58, 1974, para. 93.

[13] As, e.g., breach of confidence and applications for an order of discovery.

[14] Erskine May, *Parliamentary Practice* (18th ed. 1971), pp. 416–417. For a recent short survey, see Drewry, 'Parliament and the Sub Judice Convention' (1972) 122 New Law Jo. 1158.

[15] [1973] 1 All E.R. 815, 823.

[16] The current Resolution dates from 23rd July 1963 and is set out in Hansard, H.C. Deb. Vol. 681, col. 1417.

Resolution is less restrictive than the law of contempt which curbs the press, but in other respects it is more restrictive. It is less restrictive in that parliamentary discussion is only curtailed as from the time when a charge has been preferred and not from the time when proceedings are 'imminent'.[17] Yet the parliamentary rule is more restrictive, as Mr Alexander Lyon, MP noted in a question to the Speaker in 1968,[18] in that it entails a complete ban on discussing a case once notice of appeal has been given. The press is not, in practice, subject to the same restraints in the post-trial period, for at this stage comment is unlikely to be regarded as prejudicial and thus as a contempt.[19] While it would seem right that parliamentary discussion should generally be curtailed in the interest of promoting the fair trial of criminal proceedings, the practice can have substantial accompanying disadvantages. Thus the police investigations and the eventual institution of proceedings against John Poulson, the architect, in 1973–74, resulted in a prolonged curtailment of any attempt to probe the extent of local government corruption through the traditional method of parliamentary debate and questions. In politically sensitive areas such as this the parliamentary rule places an immense premium upon the independence of the Law Officers of the Crown from the government of the day.

Turning to civil proceedings the points of distinction between the ambit of the law of contempt and of the parliamentary *sub judice* rule are broadly similar to those noted above. Thus while the law of contempt prohibits the prejudging of issues, and the publication of matter prejudicial to the fair trial of civil proceedings as from the time when a writ is issued or an equivalent step taken (and possibly even before),[20] the parliamentary rule forbids all reference to matters under adjudication, but only from the time when the case has been set down for trial or otherwise brought before the court. Before this time the Chair may, at its discretion, curtail discussion when it appears that there is a real and substantial danger of prejudice, but it is not otherwise bound by the terms of the rule to do so.[1]

On a number of occasions in recent years, parliamentary discussion has been curtailed in deference to the *sub judice* rule. Thus in March 1969 the Speaker reminded the House of Commons that members could not refer to an application by the Ford Motor Company for an injunction in a labour dispute when discussing Mrs Barbara Castle's White Paper, 'In Place of Strife'.[2] Similarly, in December 1970 members were warned that certain matters could not be discussed in a debate on the affairs of the Mersey Docks and Harbour Board when an application had been made to the High Court for the appointment of a

---

[17] For discussion of the application of the law of contempt when proceedings are 'imminent', see above, pp. 75–82. For the Phillimore Committee proposals, see above, p. 82.

[18] Hansard, H.C. Deb. Vol. 775, cols. 1384–1385, 18 December 1968.

[19] See, in general, above, pp. 107–112. But the press unlike parliament is technically subject to the restraints of the contempt power during the period in which it is open to an accused to appeal but he has not as yet done so.

[20] See above, pp. 85–86.

[1] See the report of the Committee on Procedure, H.C. 156 (1962–63), para. 10 which recommended this restriction on the scope of the rule. The recommendation was embodied in the Resolution of 23rd July 1963 (note 16 opposite).

[2] See Hansard, H.C. Deb. Vol. 779, col. 36 *et seq.*, 3 March 1969.

receiver.[3] More recently, the parliamentary *sub judice* rule created difficulties in October 1972 when Mr Jack Ashley, MP sought to introduce a motion critical of the conduct of the Distillers Company in the thalidomide case. The motion as originally drafted was ruled out of order, but the Speaker suggested an alternative form of words which did not, in his view, infringe the rule, and which was acceptable to Mr Ashley. This read as follows: 'That this House, deeply disturbed about the plight of thalidomide children calls upon Distillers (Biochemicals) Ltd., in dealing with these cases to face up to their moral responsibilities.' No doubt this was in order because it was the moral, as opposed to legal, responsibilites of Distillers which were to be canvased.[4]

During the British Rail pay dispute in 1972 it became apparent that an application of the *sub judice* rule to cases pending before the National Industrial Relations Court might effectively curtail parliamentary discussion in areas of crucial economic and political importance. Apart from the inherent disadvantages of such restraint, it would have been especially regrettable for two somewhat more specific reasons. In the first place, it would be highly incongruous that parliamentary discussion should be precluded even though the press could comment on proceedings before the court without any significant risk of infringing the law of contempt.[5] Secondly, the Act was notorious for the blurring of political and judicial roles in the section dealing with emergency procedures such as the 'cooling off' period and compulsory ballots. Lord Denning pointed to the dangers with characteristic insight in *Secretary of State for Employment* v. *ASLEF*. 'Here Mr Maurice Macmillan had applied to the National Industrial Relations Court for an order for a compulsory ballot in the railway pay dispute, it being part of his case that there were 'reasons for doubting whether the workers taking part in the industrial action are taking part in it in accordance with their wishes'. Upholding an order for a ballot in the Court of Appeal, Lord Denning observed:[7]

> If Parliament gives great powers to a Minister, these courts must allow them to him; but at the same time we will be vigilant to see that he exercises them in accordance with the law. This is especially the case where, as here, there is no immediate control by Parliament. The Minister applies to the court quickly before Parliament will have heard of his intentions. Pending the decision of the court, the matter is sub judice and his action is unable to be discussed. It is only after action has been taken that the matter may be raised in Parliament. So the courts must enquire closely to see that any action of the Minister is within his lawful authority.

[3] Hansard, H.C. Deb. Vol. 807, col. 1083 *et seq.*, 1 December 1970.

[4] Hansard, H.C. Deb. Vol. 843, cols. 463–464; *ibid.*, cols. 647–648, 19, 20 October 1972. It seems that the distinction between the moral and legal responsibilities of Distillers was first taken by Mr James Evans, legal adviser to Times Newspapers, Ltd. See Harold Evans, IPI Report, February 1974, p.9. A further recent example occurred on 19 June 1975 when the Speaker ruled that members could not discuss the Attorney-General's application for an injunction restraining publication of the Crossman diaries when the case was to be heard on 24 July: see *The Times*, 20 June 1975, p. 14.

[5] See, e.g., *Vine Products, Ltd* v. *Mackenzie & Co. Ltd* [1966] 1 Ch. 484; [1965] 3 All E.R. 58.

[6] [1972] 2 All E.R. 949, 962.

[7] *Ibid.*, at p. 963.

The Speaker having earlier ruled that the *sub judice* rule applied to cases pending before the National Industrial Relations Court,[8] the matter was referred to the Select Committee on Procedure. The committee duly reported and recommended that while the rule should continue to apply to criminal proceedings, proceedings under the Tribunals of Inquiry (Evidence) Act 1921, and in cases of defamation, it should not apply to other civil cases save at the discretion of the Chair and where it appeared that there was a real and substantial danger of prejudice to the proceedings.[9] Consideration of this proposal was postponed pending the report of the Phillimore Committee. Approval was, however, given to a somewhat narrower proposal introduced by Mr Robert Carr and which reads, in part, as follows:[10]

> That (1) notwithstanding the Resolution of 23rd July 1963 and subject to the discretion of the Chair reference may be made in Questions, Motions or debate to matters awaiting or under adjudication in all civil courts, including the National Industrial Relations Court, insofar as such matters relate to a Ministerial decision which cannot be challenged in court except on grounds of misdirection or bad faith, or concern issues of national importance such as the national economy, public order or the essentials of life; (2) in exercising its discretion the Chair should not allow references to such matters if it appears that there is a real and substantial danger of prejudice to the proceedings; . . .

The adoption of this proposal retains a continuing importance in spite of the demise of the National Industrial Relations Court.

---

[8] Hansard, H.C. Deb. Vol. 835, col. 761.
[9] See H.C. 298 (1971–72).
[10] Hansard, H.C. Deb. Vol. 839, col. 1589.

9 The Sub Judice Rule: Mens Rea and the Scope of Responsibility

1 MENS REA

(1) THE POSITION AT COMMON LAW

(i) *Mens rea not generally required*

Since contempt of court is a criminal offence general principles would require that a person should not be held liable simply on the ground that he had done something which *in fact* interfered with the administration of justice in a pending case. It should be necessary, rather, to show that in so interfering he acted with *mens rea*, that is, with intent or recklessness as to all the elements of the offence. The term 'recklessness' is used in this context to denote the state of mind of a person who consciously runs an unjustified risk of bringing about the proscribed consequences.[1] It has long been clear, however, that contempt through prejudicing proceedings which are pending or imminent is an exception to the general rule in this respect. If a person knowingly publishes material or indulges in some other conduct which, when viewed objectively, creates a substantial risk of prejudice, no further *mens rea* appears to be necessary to sustain liability. Certainly an intent to interfere with the due administration of justice, or a realisation that one is running this risk, is not essential.

Perhaps the clearest judicial statement to this effect is to be found in the judgment of Palles, C.B. in *Dolan*,[2] where it was said:[3]

> As to the law applicable to the case, there is no doubt. Actual intention to prejudice is immaterial. I wholly deny that the law of this Court has been that absence of an actual intention to prejudice is to excuse the party from being adjudged guilty of contempt of Court, if the Court arrives at the conclusion which I have arrived at, that there is a real danger that it will affect the trial.

Although this statement was made in the High Court of Ireland in a judgment dissenting as to the result of the case, there is no doubt that it represents the law in this country. Indeed it was expressly followed by the Divisional Court in *Odhams Press, Ltd, ex parte Attorney-General*, where Lord Goddard, C.J. said: 'The test is whether the matter complained of is calculated to interfere with the course of

---

[1] For a general discussion of *mens rea*, see Glanville Williams, *Criminal Law: The General Part,* 2nd ed., 1961, Ch. 2 and 5 especially; Smith & Hogan, *Criminal Law*, 3rd ed., 1973, Ch. 4, p. 42 *et seq.*
[2] [1907] 2 I.R. 260.
[3] *Ibid.*, at p. 284.

justice, not whether the authors and printers intended that result.'[4] The same view has also been taken in a number of leading Commonwealth cases.[5]

Although an intent to interfere with the due administration of justice is not, therefore, generally required as a precondition of liability, it is nonetheless of the utmost importance when a court turns to consider the question of punishment. This point was emphasised by Lord Parker, C.J., in delivering the judgment of the Divisional Court in *Thomson Newspapers, Ltd., ex parte Attorney-General*.[6] Having discussed the gravity of a contempt from the viewpoint of its likely effect upon a fair trial, his Lordship continued:[7]

> When one begins to look at it from the other angle of culpability, it is only right to say that the most serious contempts from that point of view are publications of matter done intentionally with the very object of prejudicing a fair trial. The court is quite satisfied that there can be no suggestion of that sort in the present case.[8]

It was this consideration which led the court to conclude that no separate penalty should be imposed on the editor of the *Sunday Times*.[9]

At the opposite extremity one has the case in which it is evident that the defendant has acted with the intention of interfering with the administration of justice, or with complete indifference as to whether or not such interference is caused. Such a state of mind will typically accompany a direct approach to a juror or witness as in the modern case of *Re B. (J.A.) (An Infant)*,[10] where the contemnor, Woodall, was committed to prison for four weeks. Happily, however, there are few modern English cases in which a court has ascribed such an intention or culpable disregard to persons concerned with the publication of newspapers, or with broadcasting. *Bolam, ex parte Haigh*[11] is the most notorious exception. Here the conduct of the *Daily Mirror* was such that Lord Goddard, C.J. concluded that: 'What had been done was not the result of an error of judgment but had been done as a matter of policy in pandering to sensationalism for the purpose of increasing the circulation of the newspaper.' The editior, Silvester Bolam, was imprisoned for three months and the proprietors fined £10,000.

(ii) *Ineffectual attempts to interfere with the administration of justice*

Intent may be relevant to the issue of liability in one exceptional case because it seems that when it is present an offence will be committed even though there is not the remotest risk of actual or potential prejudice occurring. The decision of the Court of Queen's Bench in *Skipworth's and the Defendant's Case*[12] is in point. The case followed upon statements made in a public speech at a time when one

---

[4] [1957] 1 Q.B. 73, 80; [1956] 3 All E.R. 494, 497.

[5] See, e.g., *Davis* v. *Baillie* [1946] V.L.R. 486; *Pacini* [1956] V.L.R. 544 (Vict. Sup. Ct).

[6] [1968] 1 All E.R. 268.

[7] *Ibid.*, at p. 270.

[8] See also *Dolan* [1907] I.R. 260, 284.

[9] [1968] 1 All E.R. 268, 270.

[10] [1965] Ch. 1112; [1965] 2 All E.R. 168. See also *Wellby* v. *Still* (1892) 8 T.L.R. 202.

[11] (1949) 93 Sol. Jo. 220, above, p. 95. See also *Higgins* v. *Richards* (1912) 28 T.L.R. 202, 203; *Surrey Comet, ex p. Baldwin* (1931) 75 Sol. Jo. 311.

[12] (1893) L.R. 9 Q.B. 230. See further above, pp. 96–97.

Castro or Orton was awaiting trial on a charge of perjury arising out of his claim to be entitled to the Tichborne estate. Blackburn, J. was clear that the words had been spoken with the express purpose of prejudicing the trial by attacking witnesses, and by attempting 'by vituperation' to prevent the Lord Chief Justice from presiding. On this basis he held that they constituted a contempt, even though he regarded the attempt as one 'which would be utterly ineffectual, and which no one, I think, who knows anything about it could ever imagine could be effectual at all'.[13]

The sufficiency of an intent to interfere with the administration of justice, no matter how ineffectual, is also apparent in cases in which an improper approach has been made to a judge. An example is provided by *Lechmere Charlton's Case*[14] where a barrister wrote letters to a Master and to the Lord Chancellor on the subject matter of a pending suit. Lord Cottenham, L.C. remarked that, 'although such a foolish attempt as this cannot be supposed to have any effect, it is obvious that if such cases were not punished, the most serious consequences might follow'.[15] The author was accordingly committed to the Fleet prison. Likewise in *Martin's Case*[16] an offence was committed when a bank note for £20 was sent to Hardwicke, L.C., although it can hardly have been thought that he was likely to be influenced by its receipt. Similar reasoning may also explain why anything in the nature of a deliberate campaign by the news media to influence an appellate judge in an improper manner will equally constitute an offence.[17]

(iii) *Cases imposing liability without fault*

The principle that *mens rea* is not generally essential to liability in this branch of the law of contempt has been reflected in a number of modern English cases where liability has been imposed quite irrespective of any requirement of fault at all. The law as stated in some of these cases has subsequently been amended by the Administration of Justice Act 1960, s. 11, which will be examined below.[18] Since this statutory reform has a strictly limited scope, it is necessary initially to examine the position at common law. The decision of the Divisional Court in *Evening Standard Co., Ltd, ex parte Attorney-General*[19] provides a convenient starting point for discussion.

The facts of the *Evening Standard* case have been set out more fully elsewhere.[20] Here it is sufficient to recall that prejudicial matter was published under the mistaken belief that it constituted a report of evidence given by a witness at the trial. In fact the statement in question had been made by a quite different witness at earlier committal proceedings, and had been held to be inadmissible at the trial itself. Although the court accepted that the reporter had made an honest mistake, and that the editor had no reason to suppose that the

---

[13] *Ibid.*, at p. 236. See also *Consolidated Press, Ltd.* v. *McRae* (1955) 93 C.L.R. 325, 329 *per* Taylor, J. *arguendo* (High Ct of Australia).

[14] (1837) 2 My. & Cr. 316; 40 E.R. 661. See also above, pp. 105–106.

[15] *Ibid.*, p. 342.

[16] (1747) 2 Russ. & M. 674; 39 E.R. 551.

[17] *Cf. Duffy, ex p. Nash* [1960] 2 Q.B. 188, 197; [1960] 2 All E.R. 891, 894, and above, pp. 110–111.

[18] On pp. 164–168.

[19] [1954] 1 Q.B. 578; [1954] 1 All E.R. 1026.

[20] See above, p. 120.

report was inaccurate, a contempt was still held to have been committed by both parties. No separate penalty was, however, imposed. The basis of the reporter's and editor's liability in this case will be examined critically later in the chapter.[1]

The imposition of liability without fault was subsequently extended to a different situation in *Odhams Press, Ltd, ex parte Attorney-General*[2] where contempt proceedings were instituted against the proprietors, editor and a reporter of *The People* newspaper following the publication of material which was admittedly prejudicial to the fair trial of a charge of brothel-keeping then pending against one Micallef. At the time of publication Micallef had already been arrested, charged and committed for trial. Nonetheless the defendants sought to plead by way of defence that they did not know that proceedings were pending against him, and that they had, moreover, taken steps to be kept informed about any developments. Although clearly of the opinion that there had been a want of reasonable care, the Divisional Court stressed that this was 'not a material or decisive question in the case except as to penalty'.[3] Liability was, in short, strict, at least with respect to this particular aspect of the offence. The earlier authorities had at most required the publisher to exercise 'prudence and caution'[4] and indeed some suggested that it was necessary to establish actual knowledge that the proceedings were pending.[5]

The decision in *Odhams Press Ltd* was followed in *Griffiths, ex parte Attorney-General*[6] where the several defendants included a firm which imported the American magazine *Newsweek*, together with the magazine's chief European correspondent and the distributors, W. H. Smith & Son. Unknown to all concerned a particular edition of *Newsweek* contained matter prejudicial to the fair trial of a murder charge then pending against Dr Bodkin Adams. In the resultant contempt proceedings the defendants sought to advance a defence of innocent dissemination such as is available to secondary publishers in defamation cases,[7] but without success. Delivering the judgment of the Divisional Court Lord Goddard, C.J. suggested that the defendants may well have been guilty of a failure to exercise reasonable care, 'having regard to what may be called the gossipy nature of this magazine and the wide interest that was evoked by the trial in question'.[8] He preferred, however, expressly to deny that a defence of innocent dissemination was available and to base his decision squarely on the ground of strict liability. A nominal fine was imposed on the importers, Rolls Publishing Co., and on W. H. Smith & Son, 'to emphasise the risk which is run by dealing in foreign publications imported here but which have no responsible editor or manager in this country'.[9]

[1] See below, pp. 169–170, 171–174.

[2] [1957] 1 Q.B. 73; [1956] 3 All E.R. 494.

[3] *Ibid.*, at p. 79 and p. 496 respectively.

[4] See *The St. James's Evening Post Case* (1742) 2 Atk. 469, 472; 26 E.R. 683; *Ex p. Jones* (1806) 13 Ves. Jun. 237; 33 E.R. 283.

[5] See *Metropolitan Music Hall* v. *Lake* (1889) 58 L.J. Ch. 513, at p. 516 *per* Chitty, J., *Re Marquis Townshend* (1906) 22 T.L.R. 341, 342, C.A. But *cf.*, however, *Grimwade* v. *The Cheque Bank* (1897) 13 T.L.R. 305.

[6] [1957] 2 Q.B. 192; [1957] 2 All E.R. 379.

[7] See *Emmens* v. *Pottle* (1885) 16 Q.B.D. 354, C.A.

[8] [1957] 2 Q.B. 192, 204; [1957] 2 All E.R. 379, 383.

[9] *Ibid.*

Similar principles were adopted in *Thomson Newspapers, Ltd, ex parte Attorney-General*,[10] where the contempt proceedings arose out of a publication in the *Sunday Times* which was prejudicial to the fair trial of Michael Malik, the black power leader. In this case the Divisional Court was, in the words of Lord Parker, C.J., 'quite satisfied that this newspaper, with a clean record of some 150 years, had devised, and the editor, Mr Harold Evans, had ensured was operated, an elaborate and reasonable system to avoid contempts of this sort, or indeed any contempt of court'.[11] Unfortunately the system broke down because the writer of the article failed to appreciate the dangers involved, and his attention was not drawn to them by the barrister employed to read the galley proofs. Although no separate penalty was imposed on the editor, Harold Evans, the main publishers, Times Newspapers, Ltd, incurred a £5,000 fine. It is difficult to appreciate what purpose this substantial fine was intended to serve. Reasonable precautions had admittedly been exercised and it is not easy to defend a law which requires a publisher to exercise an *unreasonable* amount of care.

(iv) *Possible limitations on strict liability*

In other cases it may still be possible to argue that an element of *mens rea* or negligence is required. Some support for this view is perhaps to be found in *Daily Mirror; ex parte Smith*,[12] where Lord Hewart, C.J. acknowledged that there was no general prohibition against publishing the photograph of a person involved in criminal proceedings, and continued:[13]

> But I am no less clear upon the point that there is a duty to refrain from the publication of the photograph of an accused person where it is apparent to a reasonable man that a question of identity may arise. If in these circumstances a newspaper prints a photograph it is taking a grave risk.

The natural inference is that a contempt would not be committed where a photograph is published in circumstances in which it would *not* be apparent to a reasonable man that a question of identity was likely to arise. But it has been suggested in a number of Commonwealth cases that this is not the law. Thus in *Attorney-General* v. *Noonan*[14] a contempt was held to have been committed even though the defendant had consulted a solicitor before publication and had been reliably informed that the prisoner intended to plead guilty. According to Henry, J., sitting in the New Zealand Supreme Court, the appropriate inquiry was into 'the likelihood of identity coming into question and not the defendants' belief in the likelihood of that question arising'. He added:[15]

> If this difference is kept in mind, the contents of the affidavit of the solicitor for the defendant company are irrelevant on this issue since the matter comes to be determined

---

[10] [1968] 1 All E.R. 268.
[11] *Ibid.*, at p. 270.
[12] [1927] 1 K.B. 845.
[13] *Ibid.*, at p. 850. See, in general, above, pp. 103–105.
[14] [1956] N.Z.L.R. 1021.
[15] *Ibid.*, at p. 1026.

on the facts existing at the time and not upon the information or belief of the defendants or the advice given to them or any of them by a solicitor.[16]

Further cases may be envisaged in which similar problems would arise. D might, for example, inform E of the past convictions of P, a person against whom he knew proceedings to be pending, without realising that E was involved in the case as a juror. Alternatively, he might communicate information to W, without realising that W was an actual or potential witness in the proceedings. On such facts general principles of criminal liability would suggest that D was not guilty of a contempt and it is to be hoped that the *Odhams Press* principle would not be applied.

Whatever may be the outcome of such cases it is submitted that, at the very least, D must be shown to have intended to engage in the conduct which was in fact prejudicial to the due administration of justice, or to have been reckless in this regard. Situations in which this limited requirement was absent would not occur very often. As an example one may cite a case in which D, a barrister, is discussing the best way to handle a defence to a charge with E, an accused. If D refers to E's previous convictions and his words are overheard by F, a juror, a person of whose presence D was unaware, E's trial may well be prejudiced. Yet D would not, it is submitted, have committed a contempt. Unlike the cases mentioned above where there was simply a mistake as to the *identity* of the person being addressed, D would not have intended to *publish* the information in any meaningful sense.

A lack of liability on such facts admittedly does not take one very far. A significant extension of the principle has, however, been advanced by Borrie and Lowe who apparently suggest that persons such as 'paper-boys and street-sellers and, perhaps, even the small retail shop' who are ignorant of the *contents* of a publication may properly be said to have had no intention to publish it.[17] The case of *McLeod* v. *St. Aubyn*[18] provides some support for this view. Here the appellant had made an overnight loan of his copy of the *Federalist* newspaper to the public library of St Vincent in the West Indies. Unknown to him it contained matter which was derogatory of the local chief justice and which scandalised the court. He was convicted before the Supreme Court of the island and successfully appealed to the Privy Council whose opinion was based on the proposition that: 'A printer and publisher intends to publish, and so intending cannot plead as a justification that he did not know the contents. The appellant in this case never intended to publish.'[19]

This proposition is, however, clearly untenable, for a person who knowingly sells, or lends, or delivers a newspaper or magazine to another person obviously intends to *publish* it. What he does not intend to do (being ignorant of the contents of the paper) is to publish matter which is prejudicial to a fair trial or, as the case may be, which scandalises the court. But this is an entirely different proposition. The position of innocent publishers of prejudicial matter under s. 11

---

[16] See also *Ex parte Auld; Re Consolidated Press, Ltd.* (1936) 36 S.R. (N.S.W.) 596, 598 (N.S.W. Sup. Ct); *Pacini* [1956] V.L.R. 544, 547 (Vict. Sup Ct).

[17] *The Law of Contempt* (1973), at p. 179.

[18] [1899] A.C. 549.

[19] *Ibid.*, at p. 562.

of the Administration of Justice Act 1960 will be discussed in more detail
below.[20] Here it is sufficient to make the point that the innocent disseminator
both intends to and does *publish* that which is objectively speaking prejudicial.
No doubt, as Lord Goddard, C.J. observed in *Griffiths*, 'the court would not
regard with favour applications against such persons to whom no real blame
would attach'.[1] But a decision not to impose a penalty, whether by way of fine or
committal, must not be confused with a decision that a person is entitled to be
acquitted. As in other areas of the law, the fact that the proceedings end in an
absolute discharge does not remove all possible objections to a conviction.[2]

(2) THE ADMINISTRATION OF JUSTICE ACT 1960, SECTION 11

(i) *Introduction*

The decisions in *Odhams Press, Ltd* and in *Griffiths* were both subjected to
criticism on the ground that they failed to achieve a satisfactory balance as
between the conflicting interests involved. As the *Justice* Committee observed in
their 1959 report, the effect of the former decision was that: 'The publication of
an article which is likely in fact substantially to prejudice the fair trial of any
pending proceedings which might be taking place in any [court] is contempt of
court, and therefore a criminal act, even though the alleged contemnor did not
know and even though he could not possibly have known of the pending civil
action or criminal proceedings.'[3] Likewise the decision in *Griffiths* produced a
situation in which, 'a mere distributor of a newspaper or other publication
commits a criminal offence if he distributes one containing such matter, although
he was not aware that it contained such matter, and although his lack of
knowledge was not due to any negligence on his part'.[4] The magnitude of the risk
thus imposed on secondary publishers may be gauged by reference to the fact that
at the time of the decision in *Griffiths*, W. H. Smith sold over three hundred
different foreign publications at Victoria station alone.[5] Neither could they take
comfort from the 'nominal' fine imposed in that case, since Lord Goddard, C.J.
had specifically warned that, 'should offences occur in the future similar leniency
may not be extended'.[6]

In the light of these considerations *Justice* recommended modifications in the
law and these were embodied in the Administration of Justice Act 1960. By s. 11
of the 1960 Act:

> (1) A person shall not be guilty of contempt of court on the ground that he has
> published any matter calculated to interfere with the course of justice in connection
> with any proceedings pending or imminent at the time of publication if at that time

---

[20] On pp. 166–167, 179.

[1] [1957] 2 Q.B. 192, 205; [1957] 2 All E.R. 379, 383, above, p. 161.

[2] See, e.g., *Ball and Loughlin* (1966) 50 Cr. App. Rep. 266 (dangerous driving) and *cf. Gosney* [1971]
3 All E.R. 220, C.A.

[3] *Contempt of Court*, p. 9.

[4] *Ibid.*, at p. 10.

[5] *Cf.* Glanville Williams, *Criminal Law—The General Part*, p. 249.

[6] See [1957] 2 Q.B. 192, 204; [1957] 2 All E.R. 379, 383.

(having taken all reasonable care) he did not know and had no reason to suspect that the proceedings were pending, or that such proceedings were imminent, as the case may be.

(2) A person shall not be guilty of contempt of court on the ground that he has distributed a publication containing such matter as is mentioned in subsection (1) of this section if at the time of distribution (having taken all reasonable care) he did not know that it contained any such matter as aforesaid and had no reason to suspect that it was likely to do so.

(3) The proof of any fact tending to establish a defence afforded by this section to any person in proceedings for contempt of court shall lie upon that person.

It is now proposed to examine the two limbs of this statutory defence in turn.

(ii) *Lack of knowledge that proceedings are pending or imminent: Section 11(1).*

The first limb of s. 11 is designed to amend the law as established in *Odhams Press, Ltd*[7] and to provide a defence to a publisher who, having exercised all reasonable care, neither knew, nor had any reason to suspect, that proceedings were pending or imminent,[8] as the case may be. By s. 11(3) of the Act the onus of proof of any fact tending to establish a defence under s. 11(1) is placed upon the publisher himself. In accordance with general principles he would be required to discharge this onus by proof on the balance of probabilities, that is by showing that it is more likely than not that the facts are as he alleges them to be. He would not be required to meet the higher standard of proof beyond reasonable doubt which is demanded of the prosecution.[9] On a strict and literal construction of s. 11(3), however, it would seem that while D must prove the relevant *facts* and, presumably, that they tend to establish a defence (as, for example, the fact that he contacted the police before publication), the onus, thereafter, is on the prosecution to show that D did know or have reason to suspect etc., or, alternatively, that he had failed to exercise reasonable care.[10] The wording of the subsection does not, in terms, require D to establish the contrary. Again, it may be said that although s. 11(1) only refers to one who 'did not know and had no reason to suspect' that proceedings were pending or imminent, general principles would equally suggest that the defence would not be available to one who *actually* suspected that such was the case, without having any *reason* to do so.[11] Neither would it be available to the publisher who deliberately chose to turn a blind eye to this possibility, for such wilful blindness may be equated with knowledge.[12]

For practical purposes the extent of the protection afforded by s. 11(1) will clearly depend on the spirit in which the standard of reasonable care is applied.

---

[7] [1957] 1 Q.B. 73; [1956] 3 All E.R. 494.

[8] The question of whether it is in fact sufficient for the purposes of the law of contempt that proceedings are imminent is discussed above, p. 75 *et seq.*

[9] See *Carr-Briant* [1943] 1 K.B. 607; [1943] 2 All E.R. 156.

[10] In accordance with the general principle laid down in *Woolmington* v. *D.P.P.* [1935] A.C. 462.

[11] *Cf. Harrison* [1938] 3 All E.R. 134.

[12] *Cf. Roper* v. *Taylor's Central Garages, Ltd* [1951] 2 T.L.R. 284, 288, *per* Devlin, J., and, in general, Smith and Hogan, *op cit.*, at p. 85. *Quaere* whether D might establish a defence if he had not exercised reasonable care, but would not have been any the wiser even if he had?: *cf. Dalloway* (1847) 2 Cox C.C. 273.

The fact that there is no central register of summonses issued or of committals for trial, and no manner in which the news media can ascertain with certainty whether a person has been arrested and charged, means that reasonable care will not always produce grounds for suspecting that proceedings are pending or imminent. It is obviously unlikely that the defence would succeed on facts such as those in *Odhams Press, Ltd*[13] itself, where the accused had been arrested, charged and committed for trial. Neither is it likely that the statutory defence would frequently be satisfied where a publisher wrongly assumes that proceedings have *ceased* to be pending and it is subsequently alleged that he has prejudiced a possible appeal,[14] or further proceedings which were still outstanding.[15] At this stage of criminal or civil proceedings it should normally be possible to obtain fairly precise information on all relevant matters.

On the other hand, the standard of reasonable care would be more readily satisfied at the opposite end of the spectrum when proceedings were no more than imminent. In civil cases, in particular, there may well be nothing to indicate that a writ is about to be issued. Likewise in criminal cases a reasonable mistake may similarly be made in the absence of any general announcement that a particular person is 'helping the police with their inquiries'.

The *Savundra*[16] case might have given some further indication of how the statutory defence would be interpreted had proceedings been taken against David Frost following his television interview with Savundra which was criticised in the Court of Appeal. Salmon, L.J. suggested that it must have been obvious to everyone at the time of the interview that Savundra was about to be arrested. Yet Frost stated in a letter to *The Times* that he had contacted the Board of Trade and the Fraud Squad, and had been assured that proceedings were not being contemplated.[17] This, it is submitted, must surely be consistent with the exercising of reasonable care. In practice it is known that the news media take steps to keep in close contact with investigating authorities whenever a contempt problem of this nature appears to arise. As a result of such contacts broadcasting agencies may decide at relatively short notice not to transmit an item,[18] while newspapers are faced with the additional problem of anticipating how far a case will have developed by the time the paper begins to appear on the stalls.

(iii) *Innocent dissemination: section 11(2)*

Substantially similar problems are posed by s. 11(2) of the 1960 Act which was designed to amend the law as established in *Griffiths*[19] and to provide a defence to the innocent distributor of prejudicial matter. The observations made when discussing s. 11(1) with respect to the incidence of the onus and the standard of proof, the knowledge of the defendant and the requirement of reasonable care also apply *mutatis mutandis* to s. 11(2). Again, however, the main practical

[13] [1957] 1 Q.B. 73; [1956] 3 All E.R. 494.
[14] See, e.g., *Grimwade* v. *The Cheque Bank, Ltd.* (1897) 13 T.L.R. 305.
[15] *Cf.* above, Ch. 7, p. 107, and p. 111.
[16] [1968] 3 All E.R. 439, above, p. 79.
[17] See *The Times,* 18 July 1968.
[18] This occurred, for example, when proceedings appeared to be imminent in the *Poulson* case.
[19] [1957] 2 Q.B. 192; [1957] 2 All E.R. 379.

difficulty lies in predicting the spirit in which the standard of reasonable care will be applied. Here it may be surmised that the secondary publisher will be required to take account of both the amount of interest aroused by a particular trial, and the nature, and volume and area of circulation, of a given newspaper or periodical. More care will be required when a *cause célèbre*—such as the 'Moors Murder Trial' or the 'Great Train Robbery'—is occupying the attention of the courts, than at a time of apparent inactivity. Similarly less care will be required when dealing with journals such as the *Times Literary Supplement* than with publications which have a reputation for investigating the seamier side of life.[20] Even in the case of such publications, however, it is probable that the publisher would not be required to acquaint himself with the contents of each and every edition before distribution. This is certainly not necessary in the analogous defence of innocent dissemination in libel proceedings.[1] Indeed were such a requirement to exist one would have again returned to a law imposing a *de facto* strict liability, thus defeating the whole purpose of the defence. As Mr Justice Brennan observed in the United States Supreme Court in *Smith* v. *California* when ruling on the constitutional propriety of an obscenity statute: 'If the contents of bookshops and periodical stands were restricted to material of which their proprietors had made an inspection, they might be depleted indeed.'[2]

(iv) *The limited nature of the statutory defence*

Although s. 11 of the 1960 Act has introduced a welcome element of reform into the law of contempt it has a strictly limited sphere of application. It only applies where a publisher makes a mistake on the issue of whether proceedings were pending or imminent, or where a distributor is ignorant as to the contents of a particular publication. In practice, moreover, the problem for the newspaper editor or programme producer is typically not that of a basic lack of knowledge as to how far proceedings have progressed. He may have detailed information on this point and still be left with the problem of deciding what inferences to draw. If he draws the wrong inference and decides to publish s.11(1) will not help him as he will have had 'reason to suspect' that proceedings were imminent at the time of publication. Indeed he may have actually suspected that they were imminent but decided that it was in the public interest to take a calculated risk.

Again, a publisher would not be protected if the facts of the *Evening Standard* case[3] were to recur and he mistakenly believed that the prejudicial matter constituted a report of evidence which had been led at the trial. No matter how reasonable the belief, the mistake would not have been as to the question of whether proceedings were pending or imminent. Nor, indeed, did the defence assist the editor and proprietors of the *Sunday Times* in *Thomson Newspapers, Ltd,*[4] although they had admittedly exercised reasonable care. Section 11(1) did not apply since the editor realised that proceedings against Malik were pending

---

[20] *Cf.*, e.g., the publications which gave rise to the contempt proceedings in *Bryan* [1954] 3 D.L.R. 631 (Ontario High Ct).

[1] See, e.g., *Emmens* v. *Pottle* (1885) 16 Q.B.D. 354, C.A.; *Bottomley* v. *Woolworth (F.W.) & Co., Ltd* (1932) 48 T.L.R. 521.

[2] 361 U.S. 147, 153 (1959). See also *Ewart* (1906) 25 N.Z.L.R. 709, 729 *per* Williams, J. (N.Z.C.A.).

[3] [1954] 1 Q.B. 578; [1954] 1 All E.R. 1026, above, p. 160.

[4] [1968] 1 All E.R. 268, above, p. 162.

but did not apparently appreciate that the prejudicial matter was being published. Being a primary publisher, rather than a secondary distributor, the paper fell outside the protection of s. 11(2) as well.

(v) *The Phillimore Committee proposals*

In discussing the mental element which should be required to ground liability for contempt the Phillimore Committee draws a distinction between contempt by publication and other cases.[5] Broadly speaking the committee believes that contempt by publication should continue to attract strict liability, but that in other cases an intent improperly to interfere with the administration of justice should be required. 'Publication' would be defined widely for this purpose to include printed matter, radio and television broadcasts, films, tape-recordings, dramatic performances and words addressed to a public meeting or to a private meeting to which the press was invited. Communications intended for 'private circulation' alone would not be covered.[6]

Although the committee is clearly right when it notes that for most practical purposes the publishers of prejudicial material will almost always have been negligent,[7] it is submitted that provision should be made for a general defence based on the exercise of reasonable care to cover the residue of cases. Such a defence already exists when the mistake is as to the issue of whether proceedings were pending or imminent and there is no reason why it should not be extended to other types of mistaken belief. Curiously, however, the committee does not really consider this possible half-way house between strict liability and liability dependent upon *mens rea*. It simply concludes that: 'A liability which rested only on proof of intent or actual foresight would favour the reckless at the expense of the careful. Most publishing is a commercial enterprise undertaken for profit, and the power of the printed or broadcast word is such that the administration of justice would not be adequately protected without a rule which requires great care to be taken to ensure that offending material is not published.'[8] This may be so, but the strict liability favoured by the committee goes further than is necessary for it would penalise the publisher who had exercised the greatest possible care. As in other areas of the law it is not a sufficient reply to assert that a substantial penalty is unlikely to be imposed.

2   THE LIABILITY OF PARTICULAR CLASSES OF INDIVIDUALS

Interference with the administration of justice may clearly be brought about in many different ways and by a correspondingly wide range of persons. In some cases there will be a readily identifiable defendant as, for example, a person who makes an improper approach to a juror or witness, or who makes a public speech

---

[5] Paras. 73-80.
[6] Para. 80.
[7] Para. 74. As the committee notes he is entitled to be judged in the light of the known or ascertainable facts at the time of publication and will not be prejudiced by wholly unforeseeable developments: *Lawson, ex p. Nodder* (1937) 81 Sol. Jo. 280.
[8] Para. 74.

which prejudices a fair trial.[9] In other cases, and especially those involving contempts committed through the production and distribution of newspapers and magazines, and through the medium of television, a wide range of different persons may be held responsible. It is now proposed to consider the basis and scope of the liability of persons falling into this latter category, and whom the cases show to be typically at risk.

(1) NEWSPAPER REPORTERS

Contempt generally envisages that prejudicial matter has been communicated to persons who are likely or intended to be affected by it. Hence a newspaper reporter who does no more than supply the material on which a prejudicial article is subsequently based ought not, in principle, to incur liability as a principal offender and on the basis that he has *published* the article. Support for this view is to be found in *Griffiths*,[10] where Eldon Griffiths, the chief European correspondent of the American magazine, *Newsweek*, was one of those charged. The magazine was compiled and edited in New York and the European edition was printed in Amsterdam whence copies were despatched by air to England. Griffiths stated in his affidavit that his typical role was that of collecting items of news and sending them by cable to New York where it was decided what use, if any, to make of them. He added that he took no part in the actual preparation of the magazine as such and that he did not write the offending article. In this state of the evidence, which appears to have gone uncontradicted, Lord Goddard, C.J. concluded that:[11]

> It does not seem to the court that responsibility for this article or for its publication can be imposed on the respondent Griffiths. *The offence is not the mere preparation of the article, but the publication of it during the proceedings.* It seems that the article was written in America, printed in Amsterdam and distributed by commercial houses in this country. It has never yet been held that a reporter who supplied to his editor or employer objectionable matter which the latter published is himself guilty of contempt.

While it is submitted that this analysis is correct, it must be conceded that Lord Goddard appears to have overlooked his own decision in the earlier case of *Evening Standard Co., Ltd.*[12] In this case the prejudicial article was based on material which a reporter, George Forrest, had sent in a telephone message to the *Evening Standard* office. Forrest had sent the message under the mistaken, but honestly held, belief that he was giving a report of evidence which he had heard a witness adduce in court during the trial. In the ensuing contempt proceedings the Divisional Court accepted that Forrest had made an honest, if careless, mistake. Yet he was nonetheless held to have committed a contempt although no separate penalty was imposed on him.

The precise basis of Forrest's liability was not clearly defined but, whatever it was considered to have been, the decision is far from satisfactory. He can hardly be regarded as a joint principal to the offence constituted by the publication of

[9] See, e.g., *Onslow's and Whalley's Case* (1873) L.R. 9 Q.B. 219.
[10] [1957] 2 Q.B. 192; [1957] 2 All E.R. 379.
[11] *Ibid.*, at p. 202, and at p. 382 respectively.
[12] [1954] 1 Q.B. 578; [1954] 1 All E.R. 1026, above, p. 160.

the prejudicial matter, for his telephone call to the office did not itself interfere with the administration of justice. It was the subsequent dissemination of the inadmissible evidence amongst the public at large, including members of the jury, which might have prejudiced a fair trial. On a correct analysis Forrest's liability was that of a secondary party to this offence.[13] As such it is submitted that he was wrongly convicted since liability as a secondary party requires *mens rea* in the sense of knowledge of all legally relevant facts, even in an offence which imposes strict liability upon a principal offender. An unreasonable failure to acquire such knowledge does not suffice.[14] Forrest, of course, lacked the necessary knowledge since it was accepted that he had acted under an honest mistake as to the source of his information.

The conclusion that he was wrongly convicted cannot moreover be avoided, as is apparently suggested by Borrie and Lowe,[15] by saying that he was liable in respect of a substantive offence of causing prejudicial matter to be published. Any such offence amounts to no more than an alternative, and somewhat inelegant, way of describing the liability of one who was a secondary party to a substantive offence of publishing. Unless one is to produce a different basis of liability by juggling with words it ought again to be interpreted as importing a requirement of *mens rea* in the sense described above.[16] It is doubtful, however, whether the same analysis can be applied to a reporter who is responsible for the writing of the prejudicial article for he can fairly be said to have *published* as a principal offender. Support for this view is perhaps to be found in the *Odhams Press* case[17] where those charged included Duncan Webb, an experienced crime reporter who had written the prejudicial article for the *People* newspaper. Webb was held liable, in spite of his honest mistake in failing to appreciate that proceedings were pending, and hence presumably as a joint principal. As a principal offender such a reporter would continue to be subject, to the same extent as his superiors, to the full rigours of strict liability, as modified by the 1960 Act.

(2) EDITORS

There is no doubt that in the English law of contempt a newspaper editor may be held liable as a principal offender to an offence constituted by the publication of prejudicial matter.[18] Many examples have already been noted. Here it is sufficient to recall the case of *Bolam, ex parte Haigh*[19] where Silvester Bolam, the editor of the *Daily Mirror,* was sentenced to three months' imprisonment following

[13] *Cf.* Smith and Hogan, *op cit.,* p. 605.

[14] See *Callow* v. *Tillstone* (1900) 19 Cox C.C. 576; *Johnson* v. *Youden* [1950] 1 K.B. 544, 546, and, in general, Smith and Hogan, pp. 109–110.

[15] See *The Law of Contempt* (1973), p. 199.

[16] The verb 'to cause' has not, however, been consistently interpreted as importing a requirement of *mens rea*: Smith and Hogan, *op. cit.,* p. 89 and cases there cited.

[17] [1957] 1 Q.B. 73; [1956] 3 All E.R. 494, above, p. 161. See also *Daw* v. *Eley* (1868) 38 L.J. Ch. 113; *Ex p. Hovell* (1869) 8 N.S.W.S.C.R. 163.

[18] For statutory provisions which expressly provide that an editor may be held liable in respect of the offence created by the statute, see Criminal Justice Act 1967, s. 3(5)(a)—reporting of committal proceedings; Judicial Proceedings (Regulations of Reports) Act 1925, s. 1(2)—reporting of indecent matter.

[19] (1949) 93 Sol. Jo. 220, above, p. 95.

grossly prejudicial references to a man called Haigh who was awaiting trial on a charge of murder.

Justification for thus imposing liability on an editor was advanced in a leading case in 1924, where Lord Hewart, C.J. was reported as saying:[20]

> Nobody who knew anything of the organization and management of a newspaper office could be ignorant of the fact that the work of newspapers was very often done in circumstances of great hurry by many different minds not always fully aware of what others might be doing. The result was a composite thing, but there must be central responsibility. It was impossible to say that men occupying responsible positions should be excused because they themselves were not personally aware of what was being done.

It now seems unlikely, however, that a separate penalty will be imposed on an editor whose ignorance in such circumstances is consistent with his having exercised reasonable care.[1]

(i) *The basis of an editor's liability*

The decision in *Evening Standard Co., Ltd*, in 1954 is important in determining the basis and scope of an editor's liability. In this case Lord Goddard, C.J. summarised the main submission advanced by counsel for the defendant proprietors and editor in the following terms:[2]

> Sir Hartley Shawcross said that, while his clients desired to abide by the well understood rule of journalism that the editor and proprietors of papers must in a case such as this take responsibility, he would suggest to the court that vicarious liability, as it is called, ought not in law to be visited upon them and that they ought not to be made vicariously liable for the mistake or misconduct of the reporter. I do not think that we can possibly agree with that submission.

The clear inference that the proprietors and editor were viewed as incurring a *vicarious* responsibility for the mistake of the reporter, Forrest, who had sent in the inaccurate telephone report, is strengthened by Lord Goddard's subsequent assertion that: 'I have already said that the principle of vicarious liability is well established in these cases and must be adhered to.[3] This assertion raises two distinct but related questions. The first is whether the offence does in fact import vicarious liability. The second is whether, on the assumption that it does, an editor can properly be held liable on this basis. Having discussed these two questions, it will be necessary to consider the practical consequences of regarding the editor as incurring a vicarious liability, as opposed to a primary liability as a joint principal.

(ii) *Is contempt an offence of vicarious liability?*

The general rule whereby an employer is vicariously liable for torts committed by his servants in the course of their employment has no parallel in the criminal law.[4]

---

[20] *Evening Standard, ex p. D.P.P.* (1924) 40 T.L.R. 833, 836.

[1] *Cf. Thomson Newspapers, Ltd.* [1968] 1 All E.R. 268.

[2] [1954] 1 Q.B. 578, 585; [1954] 1 All E.R. 1026, 1029.

[3] *Ibid.*, at p. 586 and p. 1030 respectively.

[4] See, in general, Glanville Williams, *Criminal Law—The General Part*, Ch. 7; Smith and Hogan, *op. cit.*, pp. 113–120.

Indeed there is no reason why it should. The law of tort is primarily concerned with compensating victims of civil wrongs, and vicarious liability operates to furnish such victims with defendants who are likely to be financially secure. Criminal law has different objectives, and the same justification for imposing liability on one who has not personally committed the *actus reus* of an offence with any necessary *mens rea* does not exist. The difference has, moreover, been recognised since the leading case of *Huggins* in the early 18th century, where Raymond, C.J. said: 'It is a point not to be disputed, but that in criminal cases the principal is not answerable for the act of the deputy, as he is in civil cases: they must each answer for their own acts, and stand or fall by their own behaviour.'[5]

Modern statutory offences have made inroads into this proposition, but this type of liability, which Lord Goddard himself once described as 'odious'[6] still has no more than a strictly limited role to play in common law crimes. Indeed public nuisance provides the only clear exception to the general rule,[7] and here the employers' liability can be explained on the basis that the proceedings are civil in all but name. The offence of publishing a criminal libel provides a further possible exception in that two old cases at *nisi prius* might be read as imposing vicarious liability on the proprietors of periodicals for libels published by their servants.[8] The cases are, however, of doubtful authority,[9] and are consistent with the view that the liability envisaged was personal or primary, rather than vicarious. The proprietors could, in other words, be said to have published the libels themselves, without their being any need to *impute* the employees' publication to them.

In the light of these considerations one might fairly expect any modern decision imposing vicarious liability for a common law offence to be convincingly supported by existing authority. Yet such authority was conspicuously absent. Certainly neither of the decisions cited by Lord Goddard substantiates his assertion that the principle of vicarious liability for contempt of court was well established. One such decision was *The St. James's Evening Post Case*.[10] As has already been observed, Lord Hardwicke's judgment in this case admittedly dispensed with the need for a full *mens rea* on the part of the defendant publisher, but it is by no means clear that it was intended to impose strict, let alone vicarious, liability.[11] The other decision, *Payne and Cooper*,[12] is not in point at all.

In the years which have passed since *Evening Standard Co., Ltd*[13] was decided there has been one further major development. This is the decision of the House of Lords in *Heatons Transport (St. Helens) Ltd* v. *Transport and General Workers' Union*.[14] The facts of this important case are discussed in some detail in

---

[5] (1730) 2 Stra. 883, 885; 93 E.R. 915, 917

[6] See *Gardner* v. *Akeroyd* [1952] 2 All E.R. 306, 311.

[7] See *Stephens* (1866) L.R. 1 Q.B. 702 and, in general, Glanville Williams, *op. cit.*, p. 268.

[8] *Cf. Gutch* (1829) M. & M. 432; 173 E.R. 1214; *Walter* (1799) 3 Esp. 21; 170 E.R. 524. See now Libel Act 1843, s. 7, and *Holbrook* (1877) 3 Q.B.D. 60; (1878) 4 Q.B.D. 42.

[9] See Glanville Williams, *op. cit.*, p. 68.

[10] (1742) 2 Atk. 469; 26 E.R. 683.

[11] See above, p. 161, note 4.

[12] [1869] 1 Q.B. 577.

[13] [1954] 1 Q.B. 578; [1954] 1 All E.R. 1026.

[14] [1973] A.C. 15, 78; [1972] 3 All E.R. 101.

a later chapter.[15] Here it is sufficient to note that the House of Lords held that the defendant union was liable for the acts of its shop stewards, who were regarded as having a continuing general authority as agents of the union to black certain hauliers' vehicles in support of union policy on containerisation, and in disobedience of an order of the National Industrial Relations Court. In the Court of Appeal Lord Denning, M.R. had taken the view that the union was not responsible for the acts of every servant or agent, but only for those who represented 'its directing mind and will, such as its committee and principal officers'.[16] The fact that he cited *Tesco Supermarkets, Ltd* v. *Nattrass,*[17] the leading case on the primary liability of corporations, in support of this view clearly indicates that he regarded the union's potential liability for breach of the order as being primary or original in nature. In the House of Lords, however, Lord Wilberforce, who delivered the joint opinion of the House, commented: 'Lord Denning, M.R. in his judgment referred to *Tesco Supermarkets, Ltd* v. *Natttrass* but with the greatest respect this does not bear on the present problem.'[18] In reversing the Court of Appeal and holding the union liable the House of Lords seems to have treated the case as one of true vicarious liability. Whilst this must clearly be taken to represent the law in cases of *civil* contempt as through the breach of a court order, it by no means follows that the same liability attaches to *criminal* contempt. As was explained above,[19] there are still some remaining differences between criminal and civil contempt of court. It may be that the imposition of vicarious liability is one of them. The better view, it is submitted, is that criminal contempt of court should not be regarded as an offence which imports vicarious liability.

(iii) *May an editor be held vicariously liable?*

To turn to the second question, it is clear that, even if contempt *were* an offence of vicarious liability, the decision in *Evening Standard Co., Ltd*[20] holding the editor liable on this basis for the mistake of the reporter is open to question on two further grounds. The first, which relates to the actual facts of the case, is that the liability of the reporter, Forrest, was, on a correct analysis, that of a secondary party and, it has been held, vicarious criminal liability cannot be incurred as a secondary party.[1] This point apart, vicarious liability almost invariably presupposes a relationship of master and servant, or an equivalent relationship such as principal and agent, or, perhaps, that which subsists between partners.[2] A reporter clearly does not stand in this relationship to an editor. Both are inferior and superior servants respectively of the proprietors employing them. The only apparent exception to this rule seems to arise in the case of a holder of a justices' licence who may be held responsible for the act of a fellow

---

[15] See below, p. 236.

[16] [1973] A.C. 15, 51; [1972] 2 All E.R. 1214, 1247.

[17] [1972] A.C. 153; [1971] 2 All E.R. 127, below, p. 176.

[18] [1973] A.C. 15, 109; [1972] 3 All E.R. 101, 117.

[19] See pp. 9–16.

[20] [1954] 1 Q.B. 578; [1954] 1 All E.R. 1026.

[1] *Cf. Ferguson* v. *Weaving* [1951] 1 K.B. 814; Smith and Hogan, *op. cit.*, p. 120 and cases cited.

[2] See *Booth* v. *Helliwell* (1914) 30 T.L.R. 529; *Rushton* v. *Martin* [1952] W.N. 258; *Mallon* v. *Allon* [1963] 3 W.L.R. 1053, 1060.

servant, although both are employed by a third party.[3] This may be explained on the ground that the relevant legislation is so drafted that it is the licensee *alone* who can commit the offence as a principal offender. Such a justification clearly does not apply to contempt of court where there is no corresponding obstacle to holding the proprietors liable.

It would seem, therefore, that the decision in *Evening Standard Co. Ltd* cannot be supported either in terms of existing authority or, still less, in terms of general principles. Nonetheless the decision does not stand entirely alone. It has, for example, been followed in Canada in *Steiner* v. *Toronto Star, Ltd*[4] where McRuer, C.J., sitting in the High Court of Ontario, regarded the point as having been settled beyond doubt.

(iv) *The practical consequences of imposing vicarious liability on an editor*

It remains to note the practical consequences which flow from imposing vicarious liability upon the editor of a newspaper. Here it may be said that since contempt of court is an offence which has been seen to embody a measure of *strict* liability, the consequences are less than they might otherwise have been. If an editor is to be held liable irrespective of any requirement of fault it might be thought unduly pedantic to insist that his liability is primary or personal, rather than truly vicarious. On the other hand the establishment of the correct basis of liability would be important in any case in which a degree of *mens rea* or negligence is an essential element of the offence. A possible example might arise were an editor to publish a photograph of an accused under a reasonable, but mistaken, belief that no question of identity was likely to arise at the trial. If liability is dependent on establishing negligence on such facts[5] the editor who has personally exercised reasonable care could be liable for the fault of a subordinate if (and only if) the offence imports vicarious liability.[6] The position is less clear in situations falling under s. 11(1) of the Administration of Justice Act 1960. This sub-section is expressed as providing a defence to the publisher who did not know or have reason to suspect that proceedings were pending or imminent, and who can establish facts consistent with his having exercised reasonable care. In view of the apparently explicit wording of the statutory defence it is hoped that it could not be circumvented by resort to the doctrine of vicarious liability. The concern should, in other words, be with the state of mind of the editor, and it should not suffice that one of his subordinates associated with the publication failed to exercise reasonable care or even, for that matter, knew that proceedings were pending.

Finally, it must be acknowledged that there is clearly a widely held belief that the ultimate responsibility of the editor for the contents of his newspaper is a necessary corollary of editorial independence. Charles Wintour has expressed this view in his book *Pressures on the Press* when discussing the decision of Clyde, L.J.G. in the Scottish *Daily Record* case in 1959.[7] Lord Clyde had acquitted the

---

[3] See *Goodfellow* v. *Johnson* [1966] 1 Q.B. 83; [1965] 1 All E.R. 941.

[4] (1956) 1 D.L.R. (2d) 297.

[5] See *Daily Mirror; ex p. Smith* [1927] 1 K.B. 845, 850. But see also the Commonwealth cases discussed above, p. 162.

[6] And, moreover, an editor is a person on whom vicarious liability may be imposed.

[7] See *Manchester Guardian*, 13 February 1959.

editor of the paper, and fined the chief assistant editor, who had been left in charge after the editor had gone home. Wintour commented:[8]

> In my view he was wrong to do so. As long as an editor is available for consultation, he should be held responsible for anything that appears in the newspaper he edits. If he is abroad on holiday, or so ill that he cannot speak on the telephone, then his nominated deputy should take over responsibility—but not otherwise. If the legal burdens were to be divided among various members of the staff according to their separate responsibilities, then the unique grip of an editor on the contents of his newspaper would be weakened, and far more errors could occur. Alternatively, the legal adviser would usurp the function of the editor, for other members of the staff might be less willing than an editor to challenge a legal opinion. In fact, although the present system imposes a considerable burden, I do not know of any individual editor who would wish to shed it.

Considerations such as these led the Phillimore Committee to conclude that the editor should continue to be held responsible for contempts appearing in the paper he edits.[9]

(3) NEWSPAPER PROPRIETORS

In cases of contempt by publication the proprietor of the newspaper in which the allegedly prejudicial matter is published will almost invariably be the primary target for contempt proceedings. While it is quite clear that such a person or body of persons may be held liable for contempt,[10] there is again some doubt as to the basis upon which liability is incurred. As in the case of editors, the source of the doubt is Lord Goddard's assertion in *Evening Standard Co., Ltd*[11] that the offence is one which carries vicarious liability. This suggestion is open to substantially the same objections as were canvased in the last section, and it is unnecessary to repeat them here. The only difference is that a newspaper proprietor—unlike an editor—is the master or employer of those employed on the newspaper. Hence this particular objection applies to the editor alone. Consequently one may say that *if* contempt were an offence carrying vicarious liability there would be no further difficulty in imputing (say) the editor's publication, together with any necessary *mens rea* or negligence, to the proprietors so as to hold the latter vicariously liable. In assessing the practical consequences which would flow from this basis of liability, a distinction must be drawn according to whether or not the proprietor is an incorporated body.

(i) *The unincorporated proprietor*

In the case of an unincorporated proprietor recognition that the offence does not carry vicarious liability would mean that the proprietor could only be held liable to the extent that he personally possessed any necessary element of *mens rea* or negligence demanded by the offence. As in the case of the editor discussed

---

[8] *Pressures on the Press* (1973), pp. 133–134.

[9] Paras. 147–149.

[10] See, e.g., *Thomson Newspapers, Ltd., ex p. Att.-Gen.* [1968] 1 All E.R. 268, where a £5,000 fine was imposed on the proprietors of the *Sunday Times; Odhams Press, Ltd., ex p. Att.-Gen.* [1957] 1 Q.B. 73; [1956] 3 All E.R. 494.

[11] [1954] 1 Q.B. 578, 585; [1954] 1 All E.R. 1026, 1029, above, p. 171.

above,[12] there could be no question of imputing *mens rea* or negligence to him. Presumably, however, the vast majority of proprietors nowadays are companies incorporated under the Companies Acts, even though one tends to think of individuals such as Lord Thomson and the late Lord Beaverbrook as the proprietors of their respective newspaper groups. Strictly speaking, however, it is not they, but the companies which they control which, as a matter of law, occupy this role. The position of these incorporated proprietors needs to be discussed in more detail.

(ii) *Incorporated proprietors*

(a) *The criminal liability of corporations.* In English law it has long been clear that a corporation may incur vicarious criminal liability to the same extent as a natural person.[13] If it is once decided that an offence carries vicarious liability, there is no difficulty in imputing the acts and mental state of a servant to a corporate master so as to hold the latter liable. In relatively recent years, however, the courts have accepted that a corporation may incur a potentially more extensive primary or original liability as well. Lord Reid has explained the rationale of this liability, as seen against the background of the artificial legal personality attributed to a corporation in English law, in the following terms:[14]

> A living person has a mind which can have knowledge or intention or be negligent and he has hands to carry out his intentions. A corporation has none of these; it must act through living persons, though not always one or the same person. Then the person who acts is not speaking or acting for the company. He is acting as the company and his mind which directs his acts is the mind of the company. There is no question of the company being vicariously liable. He is not acting as a servant, representative, agent or delegate. He is an embodiment of the company or, one could say, he hears and speaks through the persona of the company, within his appropriate sphere, and his mind is the mind of the company. If it is a guilty mind then that guilt is the guilt of the company. It must be a question of law whether, once the facts have been ascertained, a person in doing particular things is to be regarded as the company or merely as the company's servant or agent. In that case any liability of the company can only be a statutory or vicarious liability.

This *alter ego* doctrine, as it has been generally termed,[15] has been applied to common law, as well as to statutory offences,[16] and there is no inherent difficulty in regarding it as being applicable to criminal contempt of court. Before a person will be regarded as *being* the company for this purpose it must be shown that he occupies a very senior position in the corporate hierarchy. Typically he will be a managing director, a director, or some other person who is similarly placed to

---

[12] On p. 170 *et seq.*
[13] See, in general, Smith and Hogan, *op. cit.*, pp. 120–126; Glanville Williams, *op. cit.*, Ch. 22; Leigh, *The Criminal Liability of Corporations in English Law* (1969); R.S. Welch, 'The Criminal Liability of Corporations' (1946) 62 L.Q.R. 345.
[14] *Tesco Supermarkets, Ltd.* v. *Nattrass* [1972] A.C. 153, 170; [1971] 2 All E.R. 127, 131–132, H.L.
[15] In *Tesco Supermarkets, Ltd.* v. *Nattrass*, however, Lord Reid found the term misleading: *cf.* [1972] A.C. 153, 171.
[16] See *I.C.R. Haulage Co., Ltd.* [1944] K.B. 551; [1944] 1 All E.R. 691, C.C.A. (conspiracy to defraud). In the New Zealand case of *Morris* v. *Wellington City* [1969] N.Z.L.R. 1038 it was applied in a case of contempt by victimisation.

exercise a meaningful degree of control over the company's affairs. Persons lower down the ladder are not thus identified with the company,[17] and a company will be liable for their acts if, and only if, the offence is one of vicarious liability.

Applying these considerations to a newspaper company, it is submitted that an editor can fairly be said to act as the corporation. He has traditionally a large measure of independence and he is in day-to-day control of the publication he edits. Accordingly, it is quite possible to regard an incorporated proprietor as incurring liability through the editor in this way. While it is again submitted that this is the best approach to liability for criminal contempt, it is necessary to note the consequences for an incorporated proprietor of holding that the offence is one which carries vicarious liability.

(b) *The practical consequences of vicarious liability for incorporated proprietors.* Briefly stated the choice between these two differing bases of liability would have practical repercussions in a case in which it was only a person in a junior position in the corporate structure who could be said to have committed the *actus reus* of contempt with any necessary element of *mens rea* or negligence. On such facts the company would be liable if the offence was one of vicarious liability, but not otherwise. If, however, the individual was a person for whom the company was, in any event, liable under the *alter ego* doctrine, no practical consequences would be likely to ensue.

One can perhaps illustrate the point by taking the following example. Suppose that A, a newspaper reporter, writes an article knowing that proceedings against P are imminent but that E, his editor, having exercised all reasonable care, fails to appreciate that this is so. Assuming that contempt is *not* an offence of vicarious liability, the company would not be liable in respect of A's publication for he would occupy too junior a position for it to be identified with his acts. The position would be otherwise if the *Evening Standard* case was followed and vicarious liability was imposed.[18] If E, as editor, had himself failed to exercise reasonable care, the company would be liable in any event, for his publication and negligence would be regarded as *being* that of the company and the *alter ego* doctrine would apply. The Phillimore Committee believes that the imposition of ordinary vicarious liability is right in principle because 'the proprietors are ultimately responsible for the enterprise as a whole. It is they who seek to obtain profits or other benefits from publishing. Liability for contempt and other infringements of the law is the other side of the coin.'[19] There is no consideration in the report of whether the *alter ego* doctrine would provide a preferable basis for liability.

(4) DIRECTORS AND MANAGERS

A related question warranting brief discussion is the possibility of directors and managers of newspaper companies being held personally liable for contempt.

---

[17] Hence in the *Tesco* case a branch manager was not regarded as being so identified. *Cf. Moore* v. *I. Bresler, Ltd.* [1944] 2 All E.R. 515, which is a very borderline decision.

[18] Assuming that A may be said to *publish* the article and thus to commit the offence as a principal offender: cf. above, p. 170.

[19] Para. 153.

General principles would certainly suggest that such persons could not be held liable as principal offenders as they do not *publish* the articles in respect of which contempt proceedings are instituted. Their position is different in this respect from that of an editor who has an immediate day-to-day responsibility for publication. Nor should they be vicariously liable, if the offence is ultimately held to carry such liability, since it is the company, and not they, who is the master or employer of those employed on the newspaper.[20]

On the other hand, it would be consistent with general principles to hold a director or manager liable as a secondary party if he has the necessary *mens rea*. For this purpose it would have to be shown that he had consented to, or connived at, the publication of prejudicial matter. This is presumably what Lord Goddard, C.J. had in mind in *Bolam, ex parte Haigh*[1] where, in the context of a notoriously bad case, he is reported as having issued the following warning:

> Let the directors beware; they knew now the conduct of which their employees were capable, and the view which the court took of the matter. If for the purpose of increasing the circulation of their paper they should again venture to publish such matter as this, the directors themselves might find that the arm of that court was long enough to reach them and to deal with them individually.

If it were thought desirable to extend the liability of a director or manager for criminal contempt to cover negligent conduct, this could be done by enacting a provision which is now common form in statutes creating offences likely to be committed by corporations. The following form of words is typical:

> Where an offence . . . committed by a body corporate is proved to have been committed with the consent or connivance of, *or to be attributable to any neglect* on the part of, any director, manager, secretary or other similar officer of the body corporate or any person who was purporting to act in any such capacity, he as well as the body corporate shall be guilty of that offence and shall be liable to be proceeded against and punished accordingly.[2]

(5) PRINTERS

The person or body responsible for printing prejudicial matter which is subsequently circulated undoubtedly incurs a potential liability for contempt as a publisher and principal offender. Indeed in many of the earlier cases it was considered appropriate to proceed against the printer. The best known example is perhaps *The St. James's Evening Post Case*[3] where a Mrs Read, as printer of the newspaper, was committed to the Fleet prison for contempt, in spite of her lack of any personal knowledge of the contents of the paper. Nowadays proceedings against printers, as such, appear to be less common and separate penalties even rarer. This is, no doubt, attributable in part to the fact

---

[20] *Cf. Booth* v. *Helliwell* (1914) 30 T.L.R. 529, and cases cited above, p. 173, note 2.

[1] (1949) 93 Sol. Jo. 220, above, p. 95. See also *Mason, ex p. D.P.P., The Times,* 7 December 1932 (directors of printing company held liable); *Hutchison, ex p. McMahon* [1936] 2 All E.R. 1514 (manager of cinema ordered to pay the costs of the proceedings).

[2] *Cf.,* e.g., Prices and Incomes Act 1966, s. 22(5). Emphasis supplied. The Phillimore Committtee recommends that such a provision be adopted: para. 153.

[3] (1742) 2 Atk. 469; 26 E.R. 683. See also *Ex. p. Jones* (1806) 13 Ves. 237; 33 E.R. 283; *Re The American Exchange in Europe, Ltd.* (1889) 58 L.J. Ch. 706.

that a newspaper company will frequently print its publications itself, or print through a holding or subsidiary company. Thus in *Thomson Newspapers, Ltd*[4] the Attorney-General moved to commit Thomson Newspapers, Ltd as printers of the prejudicial article. But, 'having regard to the relationship between the parties', the Divisional Court did not think it necessary to impose any separate fine on this company, in addition to the fine of £5,000 imposed on Times Newspapers, Ltd as the body immediately responsible for publication.

(6) DISTRIBUTORS

Reference has already been made to the liability of distributors or secondary publishers.[5] It will be recalled that by the Administration of Justice Act 1960, s. 11(2), the distributor will no longer incur liability if he did not know, or have reason to suspect, that the publication contained prejudicial matter and he can establish facts consistent with his having exercised reasonable care. In *Griffiths, ex parte Attorney-General* Lord Goddard, C.J. conceded that a decision holding a large scale distributor, such as W. H. Smith, strictly liable for contempt might logically mean that 'every small newsagent or street seller who sells the paper would equally be liable'.[6] He added, however, that the courts would not view with favour applications against persons to whom no real blame would attach. Nowadays it may be assumed that innocent intermediaries at the lower end of the distribution network would typically satisfy the terms of s. 11(2) of the 1960 Act.[7] They would, no doubt, act reasonably in assuming that others higher up the chain had taken care to avoid disseminating prejudicial matter. The larger distributor or intermediary wholesaler might, however, continue to incur liability, especially when handling small-scale publications which were unlikely to have been carefully checked or, indeed, imported materials as in the *Griffiths* case itself.[8]

(7) TELEVISION AND RADIO BROADCASTS

When one considers the extent to which television and radio have superseded the printed word as popular media of communication, it is remarkable that there is virtually a complete lack of case law involving alleged contempts committed through them. Indeed it was only in 1972 that one had the first English decision in point which was fully reported, namely *Attorney-General* v. *London Weekend Television, Ltd*.[9] The case involved an application for an order of committal against the defendant programme contractors in respect of their screening of a recorded programme on the thalidomide tragedy and the alleged moral

[4] [1968] 1 All E.R. 268.
[5] See above, pp. 166–167.
[6] [1957] 2 Q.B. 192, 205; [1957] 2 All E.R. 379, 383.
[7] For a suggestion that such persons would not be liable because they do not intend to *publish*, see Borrie and Lowe, *Law of Contempt*, pp. 178–180, and above, p. 163.
[8] *Cf.* Phillimore Committee report, para. 154.
[9] [1972] 3 All E.R. 1146, D.C. For other cases, see *Fox, ex p. Mosley. The Times*, 17 February 1966, above, p. 147, *Re C (An Infant)*, *The Times*, 18 June 1969; *Pacini* [1956] V.L.R. 544 (Vict. Sup. Ct). See also *Hutchison, ex p. McMahon* [1936] 2 All E.E. 1514 (Gaumont British Distributors, Ltd. held liable in respect of film distributed by them and shown in cinemas).

responsibility of the Distillers Company. In the result the application failed, since the Divisional Court was not satisfied that the programme carried a serious risk of prejudice to the administration of justice. It is clear, however, that the defendants, as programme contractors within the independent television system, were rightly regarded as being subject to a potential liability for contempt in such circumstances. Parity of reasoning would also clearly suggest that the BBC would incur a similar liability in respect of programmes which it transmits. There is much more difficulty in predicting both the scope of this liability, and the attitude which a court would adopt if called upon to consider the personal liability of individual employees within the broadcasting networks. In the apparent absence of any cases directly in point, it is proposed to restrict discussion to two situations which are potentially fairly commonplace, but which nonetheless pose substantial problems for traditional legal analysis.

One possibility is that the prejudicial comment may be made in (say) a recorded current affairs programme. In such a case it is probable that the reporter presenting the item will be held liable as a principal offender if he was responsible for drafting the comment and is not merely reading it out. He would stand in a similar position to a person who makes prejudicial remarks in a public speech,[10] or in writing up a newspaper article.[11] Equally, it is thought, the programme producer or a person such as the ITN news editor may be held liable, for it is perhaps he who occupies a role in relation to the programme which corresponds most closely to that of a newspaper editor.[12] He may likewise be regarded as a principal offender. In the circumstances envisaged he has control over the programme to be presented and he can require the offending part to be cut.

The position of the producer's own superiors, such as the Head of current affairs, the Head of BBC 1, and the Director General of the BBC is less clear. Certainly they can be held liable as secondary parties if they know that the offending item is to be included and the BBC system of referring up doubtful matters is apt to fix them with this knowledge. It is probably also the case that they can be regarded as principal offenders in their own right and as persons in respect of whom the corporation would incur an original or primary liability under the *alter ego* doctrine.[13] As principal offenders they would presumably be liable (as was the editor of the *Sunday Times* in *Thomson Newspapers, Ltd*[14]) even though their failure to appreciate that a given programme contained a prejudicial item was consistent with their having exercised reasonable care. The Phillimore Committee recommends that the Independent Broadcasting Authority should specify who in any given company has editorial responsibility and should inform the company and that person accordingly.[15]

---

[10] Cf., e.g., *Onslows's and Whalley's Case* (1873) L.R. 9 Q.B. 219.

[11] Cf. *Odhams Press, Ltd., ex p. Att.-Gen.* [1957] 1 Q.B. 73; [1956] 3 All E.R. 494, above, p. 170.

[12] For the liability of a newspaper editor, see above, p. 170. See also the Criminal Justice Act 1967, s. 3(5)(c)—restrictions on reporting committal proceedings (above, p. 113), which also requires one to identify in the case of radio and television broadcasts the 'person having functions in relation to the programme corresponding to those of the editor of a newspaper or periodical'.

[13] See further, above, p. 176. Within the BBC the Director-General is acknowledged to be editor-in-chief: Phillimore Committee report, para. 151.

[14] [1968] 1 All E.R. 268.

[15] Para. 151. *Quaere* whether it should not rather be the company itself, as opposed to the IBA, which designates the person responsible?

As a second example one may take a case in which prejudicial comment is unscripted and is made in a live programme. Here the liability of all concerned will obviously depend upon the circumstances of individual cases. The interviewer would, no doubt, be held liable if he elicited the prejudicial remark and, *a fortiori*, if he made the remark himself. In this latter context the comments of Salmon, L.J. in the Court of Appeal in the *Savundra*[16] case are clearly in point. Here, it will be recalled, Emil Savundra had appealed to the Court of Appeal on the ground, inter alia, that his trial on charges of conspiring to defraud had been prejudiced by a television interview conducted by David Frost. The appeal was dismissed, but Salmon, L.J., who regarded the interview as having been conducted with the object of establishing Savundra's guilt, saw fit to issue the following warning:[17]

> This court hopes that no interview of this kind will ever again be televised. The court has no doubt that the television authorities and all those producing and appearing in televised programmes are conscious of their public responsibility and know also of the peril in which they would all stand if any such interview were ever to be televised in the future. Trial by television is not to be tolerated in a civilized society.

The terms of this warning suggest that the producer of such a programme, as well as the interviewer, stands liable to be convicted for contempt. This would appear to be correct in principle in the case of both a recorded programme, and a live programme in which the approved topic for discussion was likely to prompt such remarks. If, however, the interviewer made the remark unscripted in a live programme and in circumstances in which it could not have been anticipated, then the better view is that he alone should incur liability. Yet if contempt carries vicarious liability the programme contractor or the BBC would be liable, although the producer should not since he is not the reporter's employer or master.[18]

The Phillimore Committee discussed the problem outlined above and was prepared to see the doctrine of strict liability for contempt by publication extended to the extempore remark even when made by a guest or contributor.[19] This, with respect, is a remarkable suggestion, for it is tantamount to saying that criminal liability should be incurred through the wholly unforeseeable and uncontrollable acts of someone who is neither a servant, agent nor partner.[20]

---

[16] [1968] 3 All E.R. 439.
[17] *Ibid.*, at p. 441.
[18] But see, however, *Evening Standard Co., Ltd* [1954] 1 Q.B. 578 and, in general, above, p. 171.
[19] Para. 152.
[20] For further discussion of comments made in the course of television interviews, see above, pp. 102–103.

10 Scandalising a Court or Judge

I INTRODUCTION

(1) THE RATIONALE OF THE OFFENCE

It has long been clear that a contempt may be committed through publishing material, such as an accusation of bias or corruption, which interferes with the administration of justice by 'scandalising' a court or judge. There is no requirement that the comment be published *pendente lite*, or indeed that it be linked to any particular proceedings at all,[1] for the concern is with the broader issue of preventing the undermining of public confidence in the administration of justice.[2] An early example is provided by *Almon's* case.[3] Here the defendant had published a pamphlet accusing Lord Mansfield, the Lord Chief Justice, of having acted 'officiously, arbitrarily, and illegally'. He was brought before the Court of King's Bench on an application for a writ of attachment where Wilmot, J. explained why such conduct constituted a contempt by saying:[4]

> [It] excites in the minds of the people a general dissatisfaction with all judicial determinations, and indisposes their minds to obey them; and whenever men's allegiance to the laws is so fundamentally shaken, it is the most fatal and most dangerous obstruction of justice, and, in my opinion, calls for a more rapid and immediate redress than any other obstruction whatsoever; not for the sake of the Judges, as private individuals, but because they are the channels by which the King's justice is conveyed to the people. To be impartial, and to be universally thought so, are both absolutely necessary.

Similarly, in more recent years, Lord Denning has reiterated the substance of Wilmot J.'s views by saying:[5]

> The judges must of course be impartial: but it is equally important that they should be known by all people to be impartial. If they should be libelled by traducers, so that people lost faith in them, the whole administration of justice would suffer. It is for this reason that scandalising a judge is held to be a great contempt and punishable by fine and imprisonment.

---

[1] The contrary view was expressed by Hughes, 'Contempt of Court and the Press' (1900) 16 L.Q.R. 292, but is no longer tenable.

[2] *Cf.* also above, p. 135, where the same reasoning can be seen to have been employed to explain why the public abuse of a party to proceedings constitutes a contempt.

[3] (1765) Wilm. 243; 97 E.R. 94, discussed further, above, p. 20. See also *The St. James's Evening Post Case* (1742) 2 Atk. 469; 26 E.R. 683.

[4] (1765) Wilm. 243, 255.

[5] *The Road to Justice* (1955), p. 73. See also *Dunbabin, ex p. Williams* (1935) 53 C.L.R. 434, 442–443 *per* Rich, J. (High Ct of Australia).

Although this view had not gone unchallenged, especially in the United States,[6] the need for a criminal offence of this nature was accepted by the Phillimore Committee which concluded that it was not sufficient to leave it to the individuals concerned to institute defamation proceedings.[7] The committee proposed, however, that the offence should be charged on indictment, and not summarily as a contempt, and that proceedings should only be instituted at the instance of the Attorney-General.[8] Further recommendations of the committee are noted in the course of the chapter. Here it may be said that the general overall approach appears to represent a sensible compromise.

(2) THE SCOPE OF THE OFFENCE

(i) Which courts and tribunals may be 'scandalised'?

Although English cases appear to have been predominantly concerned with comments which have referred to superior courts of record, or the judges of such courts, there is little doubt that the offence may be committed by comments directed at inferior courts as well.[9] Indeed it may be thought significant in this respect that in a recent Canadian case a person has been held in contempt for imputing political bias to a magistrate.[10] By the same token it should also be remembered that certain statutory provisions extend the scope of the law of contempt to cover bodies which are not courts of law. Tribunals of Inquiry established under the 1921 Act are the most important example.[11] There is little doubt that the members of such a tribunal could be scandalised through (say) the imputation of corruption to them.[12]

(ii) Reference to a judge's conduct in his 'official capacity'

Because the law of contempt exists to protect public confidence in the administration of justice, the offence will not be committed by attacks upon the personal reputation of individual judges as such. As Professor Goodhart has put it:[13]

Scandalising the court means any hostile criticism of the judge as judge; any personal attack upon him, unconnected with the office he holds, is dealt with under the ordinary rules of slander and libel.

Similarly, Griffith, C.J. has said in the Australian case of *Nicholls* that:[14]

[6] Cf. *Bridges* v. *California*, 314 U.S. 252, 270–271 per Black, J.; *Evers* v. *State of Mississippi*, 131 So. 2d 653 (1961).

[7] Ch. 7, paras. 159–167.

[8] Paras. 163–164. See also para. 21. The Law Commission working Paper No. 62, 'Offences Relating to the Administration of Justice', agrees with the Phillimore Committee recommendations: see para. 114.

[9] Thus the decision in *Davies* [1906] 1 K.B. 32, above, p. 30, would presumably apply to this aspect of contempt no less than to contempts committed in relation to inferior courts *pendente lite*.

[10] *Re Borowski* (1971) 19 D.L.R. (3d) 537 (Manitoba Q.B.)—See also *Att.-Gen. for N.S.W.* v. *Mundey* [1972] 2 N.S.W.L.R. 887 (N.S.W. Sup. Ct)—below, p. 187.

[11] See The Tribunals of Inquiry (Evidence) Act 1921, s. 1(2)(c). See also Parliamentary Commissioner Act 1967, s. 9(1) and, in general, above, p. 33 *et seq.*

[12] Cf. *The Report of the Interdepartmental Committee on the Law of Contempt as it Affects Tribunals of Inquiry*, Cmnd. 4078 1969, para. 35.

[13] See 'Newspapers and Contempt of Court' (1935) 48 Harv. L.R. 885, 898.

[14] (1911) 12 C.L.R. 280, 285.

In one sense, no doubt, every defamatory publication concerning a judge may be said to bring him into contempt as that term is used in the law of libel, but it does not follow that everything said of a judge calculated to bring him into contempt in that sense amounts to contempt of Court.

Thus in *In the Matter of a Special Reference From the Bahama Islands*[15] the Privy Council advised that a contempt had not been committed through a publication in the *Nassau Guardian* concerning the resident Chief Justice, who had himself previously criticised local sanitary conditions. Though couched in highly sarcastic terms the publication did not refer to the Chief Justice in his official, as opposed to personal, capacity.[16] Thus while it might have been a libel it was not a contempt.

While this limitation is well established,[17] its full implications are less clear. It is at least arguable that a contempt might be committed if (say) a publication were to impute bias to a judge in his conducting of an official inquiry in an area with strong political overtones. It is doubtful whether such an imputation can be said to be 'unconnected with the office he holds' when it was that office itself, and the reputation for impartiality accompanying it, which was the very reason for the appointment to the inquiry. The point is not without importance in an age when senior judges are frequently invited to chair governmental inquiries and when the borderline between legal and political decisions is increasingly blurred. It would be unrealistic to assume that public confidence in the administration of justice might not be undermined by an accusation of bias in this extra-judicial capacity as much as by an accusation of bias in conducting a High Court action.[18]

2   EXAMPLES OF COMMENT WHICH SCANDALISES A COURT OR JUDGE

(1) SCURRILOUS ABUSE

The leading case of *Gray*[19] provides one of the few English examples of a contempt being committed through the publication of abusive comment levelled at an individual judge. Before the trial of one Wells on an obscene publications charge, Darling J., the presiding judge, warned the local Birmingham press that no privilege was afforded to them in respect of the publication of indecent matter which would be given in evidence. He added that he would make it his business to see that the law was enforced against anyone who chose to disregard his warning. The local press as a whole clearly felt that the warning was uncalled for, and reacted critically.[20] Gray, the editor of the *Birmingham Daily Argus*, went some-

---

[15] [1893] A.C. 138.

[16] *Cf. ibid.,* at p. 144 (Lord Watson).

[17] See also the passage cited from the judgment of Wilmot, J. in *Almon* (1765) Wilm. 243, 255; 97 E.R. 94, above, p. 182; *Helmore* v. *Smith* (No. 2) (1886) 35 Ch. D. 449, 455 *per* Bowen, L.J.; *McLeod* v. *St. Aubyn* [1899] A.C. 549, 561 *per* Lord Morris.

[18] If the inquiry took the form of a tribunal appointed under the 1921 Act the law of contempt would apply. See above, p. 33.

[19] [1900] 2 Q.B. 36, and (1900) 82 L.T. 534 where the article is reproduced in full.

[20] *Cf.* Walker-Smith, *The Life of Lord Darling,* at p. 121 especially.

what further than the others. The following day, after the trial had been concluded and Wells had been sentenced, he published an article beneath the heading 'A Defender of Decency' which read in part as follows:

> The terrors of Mr. Justice Darling will not trouble the Birmingham reporters very much. No newspaper can exist except upon its merits, a condition from which the Bench, happily for Mr. Justice Darling, is exempt. There is not a journalist in Birmingham who has anything to learn from the impudent little man in horsehair, a microcosm of conceit and empty-headedness, who admonished the Press yesterday.

When the matter was brought before the Divisional Court in London Lord Russell, C.J. had no hesitation in describing the article as 'personal scurrilous abuse of a judge as a judge'.[1] Gray, for his part, did not seek to argue that it was within the bounds of permissible criticism, but offered, rather, his apologies. He was fined the sum of £100 and ordered to pay a further £25 costs.

Vidal[2] provides a further example, although the contempt in this case was committed through a somewhat unusual means of communication. Here the defendant, dissatisfied as to the outcome of certain proceedings, and apparently believing the President of the Probate, Divorce and Admiralty Division of the High Court to be a party to a conspiracy to suppress evidence, paraded near the Law Courts carrying a sandwich-board which read: 'Is Judge Sir Henry Duke afraid to prosecute me? I accuse him to be a traitor of his duty and of defrauding the course of justice for the benefit of the Kissing Doctor.' He was sentenced to four months' imprisonment for what was described by the Divisional Court as 'scurrilous abuse of the worst description'.

The Canadian case of *Re Nicol*[3] provides an example of a contempt being committed through abusive comment directed at a *jury*. After William Gash had been found guilty on a charge of murder and sentenced to death by hanging, the *Vancouver Province* published an article written in the form of an allegory in which the author, Eric Nicol, pictured himself as being tried, in turn, before God for the murder of Gash. As part of his confession of guilt Nicol wrote:

> Although I did not myself spring the trap that caused my victim to be strangled in cold blood, I admit that the man who put the rope around his neck was in my employ. Also serving me were the 12 people who planned the murder, and the judge who chose the time and place and caused the victim to suffer the exquisite torture of anticipation.

Clyne, J. regarded this passage as calculated to lower the dignity of the Court and to destroy public confidence in the administration of justice. With reference to the description of the jury as persons who had planned a murder, the learned judge observed that it was not only insulting and contemptuous, but was also a type of comment which, if published with impunity, might deter future juries

---

[1] [1900] 2 Q.B. 36, 40.

[2] *The Times*, 14 October 1922. See also *McLeod* v. *St. Aubyn* [1899] A.C. 549, P.C.; *Fotheringham and Sun Publishing Co. Ltd.* (1970) 11 D.L.R. (3d) 353 (British Columbia Sup. Ct).

[3] [1954] 3 D.L.R. 690 (British Columbia Sup. Ct). See also *White* (1808) 1 Camp. 359 n.; 170 E.R. 985.

from bringing in verdicts of guilty.[4] This seems, with respect, to be a realistic position to adopt.[5]

(2) IMPUTATIONS OF BIAS AND IMPROPER MOTIVES

Publications imputing corruption to a judge, or suggesting that he has allowed his own religious, political, or racial views to influence his decision in a given case, are also likely to be regarded as a contempt. The leading English case is *New Statesman (Editor), ex parte D.P.P.*[6] Here, Dr Marie Stopes, an early advocate of birth control, had been involved in a libel action brought by the editor of the *Morning Post*. Damages totalling £200 had been awarded against her. The *New Statesman* thereafter published an article suggesting that Mr Justice Avory, who had presided over the action, had allowed his religious convictions as a Roman Catholic to prejudice his summing up. The article concluded by asserting: 'The serious point in this case, however, is that an individual owning to such views as those of Dr. Stopes cannot apparently hope for a fair hearing in a Court presided over by Mr. Justice Avory—and there are so many Avorys.' In the ensuing proceedings this was held to constitute a contempt and Lord Hewart, C.J. is reported as saying of the article that: 'It imputed unfairness and lack of impartiality to a Judge in the discharge of his judicial duties. The gravamen of the offence was that by lowering his authority it interfered with the performance of his judicial duties'.[7] Since the editor had made an unreserved withdrawal and apology the court refrained from making a committal order or imposing a fine.

The case of *Wilkinson*,[8] which came before a Divisional Court some two years later, provides an example of an imputation of *political* bias being treated as a contempt. In this case sentences of imprisonment of up to nine months were imposed upon persons responsible for publishing the *Daily Worker*. The offending passage, described by Lord Hewart, C.J. as a 'gross and outrageous contempt', read as follows:

> Rigby Swift, the judge who sentenced Comrade Thomas, was the bewigged puppet and former Tory M.P. chosen to put Communist leaders away in 1926. The defending counsel, able as he was, could not do much in the face of the strong class bias of the judge and jury.

In a more recent Canadian case[9] the Minister of Transport in the Province of Manitoba was similarly held guilty of contempt after imputing political bias to a magistrate during an interview which was being taped for a radio broadcast. The interview was subsequently broadcast and in it the minister sought to explain one of the magistrate's decisions by saying: 'The fact that he is a loyal Conservative and had been appointed by the Conservative Administration can't be overlooked'. He had also, it seems, referred to the magistrate as a 'bastard', and had

---

[4] [1954] 3 D.L.R. 690, 697.

[5] For the view that the violence and extravagance of the invective may sometimes *lessen* the risk of impairing public confidence in the administration of justice, see *Att.-Gen. of Quebec* v. *Hebert* [1967] 2 C.C.C. 111, 138 *per* Tremblay, C.J.Q. (Quebec Ct of Q.B.).

[6] (1928) 44 T.L.R. 301.

[7] *Ibid.*, at p. 303.

[8] *The Times*, 16 July 1930.

[9] *Re Borowski* (1971) 19 D.L.R. (3d) 537 (Manitoba Q.B.).

threatened to have him 'defrocked and debarred' if he heard a particular case. This latter threat was regarded by Nitikiman, J. as being 'unbelievably outrageous' in that it suggested to listeners that the judiciary was subject to dismissal at the pleasure of the executive. In so far as English law is concerned, it is known that the news media have been troubled in recent years by the possibility of committing a contempt by reporting (and thus publicising) accusations of political bias levelled by certain trade-union leaders and others at the National Industrial Relations Court.

More recently the imputation of racial bias has also formed the background to contempt proceedings in both Australia and in South Africa. In the Australian case of *Attorney-General for New South Wales* v. *Mundey*[10] the president of a trade union had been fined, together with another man, and bound over at Sydney quarter sessions following the infliction of damage upon goal posts. They had been protesting against the presence in Australia of the South African Rugby Union Football team. As the president left the court the secretary of the same union was asked by representatives of local television stations for his impression of the decision. He replied:

> Well, I think it's a miscarriage of justice . . . it showed that the judge himself was a racist judge. It shows you the extent to which racism exists within our society and it shows you what a tremendous problem we have, all Australians, to overcome this deeply ingrained racism. . . . I think the main purpose, the industrial action by the workers here this morning, the spontaneous action of workers walking off jobs, stopped the racist judge from sending these two men to jail; that's the real position.

An edited version of the statement was shown by at least one television station on its evening news. In a long and careful judgment Hope, J.A. held that a contempt by scandalising the court had been committed not because of the imputation of racial bias as such, but because of the suggestion that the judge had been overawed by the action of workers congregating in the vicinity of the court and that it was this alone which had caused him to refrain from imposing a prison sentence. It may be said, with respect, that Hope, J.A.'s refusal to accept that the allegation that the judge was a 'racist judge' was *itself* a contempt in the circumstances of the case shows a robust and commendable attitude to this branch of the law of contempt.

While there may be some measure of agreement that the public as a whole has an interest in proscribing the more extreme imputations of conscious religious, political, or racial bias to a judge, mild suggestions of unconscious bias would seem to stand on a different footing. For this reason the decision in *Colsey, ex parte D.P.P.*[11] is, by general consent, singularly difficult to defend. In this case the editor of the magazine *Truth* was fined £100 in respect of an article commenting upon a recent judgment of Slesser, L.J. The article suggested that he could hardly be 'altogether unbiased' when called on to deal with legislation which he had once helped to steer through parliament when a law officer in an earlier

---

[10] [1972] 2 N.S.W.L.R. 887 (N.S.W. Sup. Ct). The South African case of *S* v. *Van Niekerk* [1970] 3 S.A. 655 (T) is discussed below, p. 191. For further cases of general interest, see *Hinds, ex p. Att-Gen.* (1960) 3 W.I.R. 13 (Sup. Ct of Barbados); *Sommer* (1965) 1 C.C.C. 42 (Quebec Court of Q.B.).

[11] *The Times*, 9 May 1931.

Labour government.[12] It would seem most unlikely that an English court would adopt a similar attitude to such a seemingly innocuous publication today.

A contempt may also be committed where a general imputation of bias is levelled against a *court* as well as through an imputation which is referable to the conduct of a particular judge in a given case. The same is true of scurrilous abuse.[13] The Canadian case of *Murphy*[14] provides an example. Here an article in a newspaper run by students at the University of New Brunswick contained both an attack on the conduct of a particular judge in a specific case, and the following general accusation:

> The courts in New Brunswick are simply the instruments of the corporate elite. Their duty is not so much to make just decisions as to make right decisions (i.e. decisions which will further perpetuate the elite which controls and rewards them). Court appointments are political appointments. Only the naive would reject the notion that an individual becomes a justice or judge after he proves his worth to the establishment.

Delivering the judgment of the New Brunswick Supreme Court in the ensuing contempt proceedings, Bridges, C.J. held that the article was calculated to bring both the judge in question and the Courts of New Brunswick into contempt. The defendant publisher was accordingly found guilty. It may be doubted, with respect, whether it really serves a useful function to invoke the full panoply of the contempt power to deal with statements of this kind in a student newspaper with a limited circulation. Such a course seems likely to alienate students even further, and to reinforce the views which prompted the publication.

Although most instances of contempt by scandalising the court can be classified as either scurrilous abuse or an imputation of bias, the offence is potentially wider in scope than this. Indeed any course of conduct may amount to a contempt if it has the necessary tendency to destroy public confidence in the administration of justice. The recent Canadian case of *United Fishermen and Allied Workers' Union*[15] illustrates the point. Here the British Columbia Court of Appeal upheld convictions for contempt imposed on a trade union and its officers after they had publicly initiated a vote on whether the union should obey a court order. This conduct was regarded as a gross contempt in that it was calculated and intended to lower the prestige of the court by suggesting that it was a matter of choice as to whether its orders were obeyed. It is thought that an English court would adopt the same attitude if faced with a similar conduct.

(3) THE LEGALITY OF REASONED CRITICISM

By way of contrast it has long been clear that reasoned criticism of a judgment in a particular case, or of the administration of justice generally, is quite permis-

---

[12] For criticism, see, e.g. Goodhart (1935) 48 Harv. L.R. 885, 903–904; (1931) 47 L.Q.R. 315. It seems that Slesser L.J. did not want proceedings to be brought: see Slesser, *Judgement Reserved*, p. 256.

[13] *Cf. Dunbabin, ex p. Williams* (1935) 53 C.L.R. 434 (High Ct of Australia).

[14] (1969) 4 D.L.R. (3d) 289. See also *Att.-Gen.* v. *Blundell* [1942] N.Z.L.R. 287 (N.Z. Sup. Ct); *Glanzer* (1962) 38 D.L.R. (2d) 402 (Ontario High Ct); *Connolly* [1947] I.R. 213—Ireland; *Vidyasagara* [1963] A.C. 589, P.C., *Arrowsmith* [1950] V.L.R. 78; *Collins* [1954] V.L.R. 46—(Vict. Sup. Ct); *Re the Evening News* (1880) 1 N.S.W.L.R. 111 (N.S.W. Sup. Ct).

[15] (1968) 2 C.C.C. 257.

sible. Indeed a legal system could hardly hope to develop satisfactorily if it were not. Several well-known statements may be cited establishing the legality of such criticism of which the most important is to be found in Lord Atkin's opinion in the Privy Council in *Ambard* v. *Attorney- General for Trinidad and Tobago*.[16] In this case an article had been published in the *Port of Spain Gazette* criticising the apparent inequality of sentences imposed in two cases of attempted murder which had recently been before local colonial courts. The article was written in sober terms, and it called for a greater equalisation of the punishment with the crime committed. An unduly sensitive Supreme Court of Trinidad and Tobago held that such criticism constituted a contempt, but a different view was taken by the Privy Council on appeal. In an important and frequently cited statement affirming the legality of reasoned criticism Lord Atkin said:[17]

> But whether the authority and position of an individual judge, or the due adminis-
> tration of justice, is concerned, no wrong is committed by any member of the public
> who exercises the ordinary right of criticising in good faith, in private or public the
> public act done in the seat of justice. The path of criticism is a public way: the wrong-
> headed are permitted to err therein: provided that members of the public abstain from
> imputing improper motives to those taking part in the administration of justice, and are
> genuinely exercising a right of criticism, and not acting in malice or attempting to
> impair the administration of justice, they are immune.[18] Justice is not a cloistered
> virtue: she must be allowed to suffer the scrutiny and the respectful even though
> outspoken comments of ordinary men.[19]

Substantially the same point was made by the Court of Appeal in the more recent case of *Metropolitan Police Commissioner, ex parte Blackburn (No. 2)*.[20] The proceedings in this case arose from an article in the magazine *Punch* in which Mr Quintin Hogg had stated that the Gaming Act had been 'rendered virtually unworkable by the unrealistic, contradictory and, in the leading case, erroneous, decisions of the courts, including the Court of Appeal'. The article went on to suggest that the courts had seen fit to blame everyone but themselves for the resultant chaos, and would have done better to remember the golden rule for judges that silence was always an option. This mild criticism prompted Mr Raymond Blackburn, a private citizen who had earlier sought to enforce the gaming legislation, to institute contempt proceedings. Not surprisingly his application failed, but the case is of interest in that the Court of Appeal went out of its way to emphasize the importance of preserving the right to comment upon all matters of public interest, including the administration of justice. As Lord Denning, M.R. put it:[1]

> We do not fear criticism, nor do we resent it. For there is something far more important
> at stake. It is no less than freedom of speech itself. It is the right of every man, in
> Parliament or out of it, in the Press or over the broadcast, to make fair comment, even

---

[16] [1936] A.C. 322.

[17] *Ibid.,* at p. 335.

[18] *Quaere* whether the imputing of improper motives can ever be regarded as the genuine exercise of a right of criticism?

[19] See also *Gray* [1900] 2 Q.B. 36, 40 *per* Lord Russell, C.J.

[20] [1968] 2 Q.B. 150; [1968] 2 All E.R. 319.

[1] [1968] 2 Q.B. 150, 155.

outspoken comment, on matters of public interest. Those who comment can deal faithfully with all that is done in a court of justice. They can say that we are mistaken, and our decisions erroneous, whether they are subject to appeal or not. All we would ask is that those who criticise us will remember that, from the nature of our office, we cannot reply to their criticisms. We cannot enter into public controversy. Still less into political controversy. We must rely on our conduct itself to be its own vindication.

(4) FURTHER RELEVANT FACTORS

It is clearly not possible to view a given form of words in isolation and to say that they will either invariably amount to a contempt, or that they will never do so. All the surrounding circumstances must be taken into account in determining whether the necessary serious risk of impairing public confidence in the administration of justice is present.

Thus comment may well be viewed as relatively innocuous in one jurisdiction, and as scandalising the court in another.[2] Equally, within the same jurisdiction, it may be seen as likely to destroy confidence in the courts at one period of history and as unworthy of attention at another. By the same token a different response may well be warranted according to whether the comment relates to a contemporary case or to a case which is beginning to recede into history.[3] Again, the means of publication employed, and hence the likely audience, are relevant factors to be taken into account. Other things being equal one would expect statements in the popular press or on television to be more likely to ground liability than statements in the 'quality' press, specialist periodicals, or even books.[4]

On the basis of this last consideration the decisions in certain recent Commonwealth cases rest on very shaky foundations. In one such case, *Ex parte Attorney-General; Re Goodwin*,[5] the defendant to an action for malicious prosecution had been severely criticised by Goran, J., the presiding judge. He responded by writing to the Attorney-General and to the Registrars of a number of local District Courts within New South Wales questioning whether Goran, J. was a suitable person to be a judge and imputing ulterior motives to him. In the resultant contempt proceedings the Court of Appeal for New South Wales did not accept that the area of publication was insufficient to ground liability and a fine of $A2,000 was imposed. Although this decision finds support in other Commonwealth cases[6] it is difficult to reconcile with the accepted test of liability for contempt. No doubt the learned judge could have instituted proceedings for libel, but it can hardly be right to regard a limited publication to a group of District Court Registrars as being potentially destructive of public confidence in the administration of justice.[7]

[2] *Cf. McLeod* v. *St. Aubyn* [1899] A.C. 549, 561; *Hinds, ex p. Att.-Gen.* [1960] 3 W.I.R. 13 (Sup. Ct of Barbados).

[3] *Cf. Att.-Gen. of Quebec* v. *Hebert* [1967] 2 C.C.C. 111 (Quebec Ct of Q.B.).

[4] But see *S.* v. *Van Niekerk* [1970] 3 S.A. 655(T) discussed below, p. 191.

[5] (1969) 70 S.R. (N.S.W.) 413.

[6] See e.g., *Re Wiseman* [1969] N.Z.L.R. 55 (N.Z.C.A.) where the allegations were made in affidavits and a notice of motion; *Collins* [1954] V.L.R. 46 (Vict. Sup. Ct).

[7] For a case in which an abusive letter was sent to a judge himself, see *Freeman, The Times*, 18 November 1925.

3 MENS REA AND THE SCOPE OF LIABILITY

The general rules governing the scope of liability and the requirement of *mens rea* in criminal offences have been discussed in an earlier chapter on contempt through prejudicing pending proceedings.[8] Many of the conclusions which were then reached apply *mutatis mutandis* to contempts allegedly committed through scandalising a court or judge. It is necessary, however, to single out some points for special attention.

In the first place the balance of authority suggests that, as in the case of a contempt through infringing the *sub judice* rule, an actual intention to interfere with the administration of justice by scandalising the court is not required as an element of liability. Thus in *New Statesman (Editor), ex parte D.P.P.*[9] Lord Hewart, C.J. seemingly accepted that the defendant publisher had not intended to interfere with the performance of Avory, J's judicial duties when imputing religious bias to him. This did not, however, prevent liability from being imposed, together with an order to pay the costs of the proceedings. Further support for the view that *mens rea* in this sense is not required is to be found in Commonwealth cases.[10]

Support for the opposing view is to be found in the judgment of Claassen, J. sitting in the Transvaal Provincial Division in *S. v. Van Niekerk*.[11] This South African case is one of the most interesting to emerge in this area for many years. Van Niekerk, a senior lecturer in the Department of Law in the University of the Witwatersrand, had written an article entitled 'Hanged by the neck until you are dead', which was subsequently published in two parts in the *South African Law Journal*.[12] The article was in the form of a report based on a questionnaire which had been circulated to South African judges and advocates to find out their attitude to capital punishment. As one would expect, it was expressed in sober and responsible language, but it contained a passage which led to the institution of contempt proceedings. The offending passage which appeared immediately below an analysis of the replies to two questions read as follows:

> Whatever conclusion one may draw from the results of these two questions, the fact which emerges undeniably is that a considerable number of replying advocates, almost 50 per cent in fact, believe that justice as regards capital punishment is meted out on a differential basis to the different races, and that 41 per cent who so believe are also of the opinion that such differentiation is conscious and deliberate.

Without calling on the defence counsel to argue the contrary, Claassen, J. concluded that this passage might *objectively* speaking have constituted a contempt as imputing conscious racial bias to South African judges. This particular conclusion was, incidentally, viewed with alarm by academics and legal writers in

---

[8] See above, pp. 158 *et seq.*

[9] (1928) 44 T.L.R. 301, 303, above, p. 186.

[10] See, e.g., *Att.-Gen.* v. *Butler* [1953] N.Z.L.R. 944, 948 *per* Fair, J.; *Murphy* (1969) 4 D.L.R. (3d) 289, 294.

[11] [1970] 3 S.A. 655(T).

[12] See (1969) 86 S.A.L.J. 457, and (1970) 87 S.A.L.J. 60.

South Africa.[13] Yet Van Niekerk was nonetheless acquitted on the specific ground that he had not been shown to have published the article with *mens rea*. Claassen, J. spelt out the requirement which he took to be essential in the following terms:[14]

> I think that before a conviction can result the act complained of must not only be wilful and calculated to bring into contempt but must also be made with the intention of bringing the Judges in their judicial capacity into contempt or of casting suspicion on the administration of justice. For this type of intention it is sufficient if the accused subjectively foresaw the possibility of his act being in contempt of Court and he was reckless as to the result. . . . Subjective foresight, like any other factual issue, may be proved by inference.[15]

The Phillimore Committee has proposed that matter imputing improper or corrupt judicial conduct should only give rise to liability if published with the intention of impairing confidence in the administration of justice.[16] Pending the possible enactment of this proposal it is unlikely that an English court would insist upon intent or recklessness in this sense. But it may at least be hoped that strict liability would not be imposed upon a publisher who has acted under an honest and reasonable mistake. Yet an application of the decision in *Griffiths*[17] would indeed have this effect if a secondary publisher were to distribute matter which scandalises the court. Section 11(2) of the Administration of Justice Act 1960[18] could not be pleaded for it is limited in terms to matter which constitutes a contempt through interfering with the administration of justice in proceedings which are pending or imminent—that is, by infringing the *sub judice* rule. Such are the results of piecemeal law reform.

4 POSSIBLE DEFENCES

The points of similarity between the law of libel and scandalising the court prompts one to inquire whether the defences one associates with libel, such as justification and fair comment, are similarly available in a case of contempt. These are not questions which have been subjected to a detailed analysis in an English court. Hence any conclusions must necessarily be tentative.

(1) JUSTIFICATION

In criminal prosecutions charging the publication of a defamatory libel, s.6 of the Libel Act 1843 affords a defence to a person who can show that the facts as

---

[13] See, e.g., Milton, 'A Cloistered Virtue?' (1970) 87 S.A.L.J. 424. See also the criticism of the Council of the S.A. Society of University Teachers of Law, published in (1970) 87 S.A.L.J., at pp. 467–468.

[14] [1970] S.A. 655, 657.

[15] See Burchell and Hunt, *South African Criminal Law and Procedure* (1970) Vol. 1, pp. 110–111; Vol. 2, pp. 177, 181–187, for a discussion of other South African cases.

[16] Para. 164. The offence would only be punishable on indictment.

[17] [1957] 2 Q.B. 192; [1957] 2 All E.R. 379, above p. 161. See also *McLeod* v. *St. Aubyn* [1899] A.C. 549, P.C.

[18] See above, p. 164.

stated are true and that their publication is for the public benefit. In civil proceedings truth is itself a defence and the requirement of public benefit does not apply. In the New Zealand case of *Attorney-General* v. *Blomfield*[19] Williams, J. considered whether a similar defence might be available to a person charged with scandalising the court through imputing bias to a judge. The learned judge agreed that: 'If a person is charged with making imputations on a judge beyond the bounds of criticism and fair comment . . . it should certainly be open to the accused to bring forward evidence in justification, and to show whether and how far his imputations were justified.' He concluded, however, that: 'That has never been done and cannot be done in summary proceedings for contempt. The Court does not sit to try the conduct of the Judge.'[20]

The English case of *Vidal*[1] also suggests that the defence is not available. Here the defendant objected to the form of the proceedings, and maintained that he should have been prosecuted for publishing a criminal libel, when he would have pleaded that his allegation that Sir Henry Duke was a party to a conspiracy to suppress evidence was true. The objection was waved aside, and there is no suggestion that the Divisional Court thought it possible for him to raise the defence in contempt proceedings. Indeed his refusal to apologise led to his being imprisoned for four months. There are other pointers in the same direction. Thus it seems that justification was not available at *common law* as a defence to a charge of publishing a defamatory libel,[2] and this is a better indication of the position in contempt than the statutory defence afforded by the 1843 Act. Likewise it seems that justification is no defence to one who is charged with being in contempt of parliament by publishing derogatory matter.[3]

The Phillimore Committee, though clearly alive to the difficulties, recommended that it should be a defence to establish that the allegations are true and that their publication was for the public benefit. The committee suggested, however, that the public benefit requirement would be unlikely to be met unless the defendant had previously taken steps to submit the evidence of corruption or partiality to the Lord Chancellor.[4] By way of contrast the *Justice* Committee in their report *Contempt of Court* (1959) had concluded that such a defence should not be available, believing that the press was not the 'appropriate organ' for making such charges.[5] Although the point is unlikely to arise other than exceptionally, it is submitted that the view of the Phillimore Committee is to be preferred. The main objection to such a defence is that it might be abused by

[19] [1914] 33 N.Z.L.R. 545.

[20] *Ibid.*, at p. 563.

[1] *The Times,* 9 May 1931, above, p. 185.

[2] See *The Case De Libellis Famosis* (1606) 5 Co. Rep. 125a; 77 E.R. 250 and, in general, Holdsworth, *History of English Law* (2nd. ed.), Vol. VIII, p. 336, *et seq.*

[3] *Cf.* Erskine May, *Parliamentary Practice* (18th. ed., 1971), p. 161. Nor is the defence available on a charge of publishing a seditious libel: *Aldred* (1909) 74 J.P. 55 and, in general, *Archbold,* para. 3165. The fact that truth is not a defence to a contempt through infringing the *sub judice* rule (*cf. Skipworth and Castro's Case* (1873) L.R. 9 Q.B. 230, 234 *per* Blackburn, J.) is hardly in point for the issues are different.

[4] Para. 166. See also the Law Commission Working Paper No. 62, 'Offences Relating to the Administration of Justice', which agrees that such a defence should be available: para. 114.

[5] At p. 15. See also the report of the *Justice* sub-committee, *The Judiciary* (1972), para. 88.

someone intent on reopening the issue of liability via the backdoor by imputing a lack of impartiality to the presiding judge. But it is again doubtful whether this would occur frequently in practice.

In a related context it should also be noted that the rules of parliamentary procedure impose strict limitations upon the ability of a member of either House to question the conduct of an individual judge, or the judiciary generally. Such matters can only be raised on a substantive motion which admits of a vote and not during the normal course of debate.[6] This limitation was very much to the forefront in December 1973 during a debate in the House of Commons on the Industrial Relations Act. Before the debate began and against a background of criticism which had been levelled at Sir John Donaldson, the President of the National Industrial Relations Court,[7] the Speaker took the unusual course of citing Lord Atkin's well known statement in *Ambard's* case before going on to remind members that: 'Reflections on the judge's character or motives cannot be made except on a motion. No charge of a personal nature can be raised except upon a motion. Any suggestion that a judge should be dismissed can be made only on a motion.'[8] On several occasions during the debate the Speaker had to call for order with this ruling in mind as when a member made a statement which 'could only be construed as the imputation of political motive'.[9]

(2) FAIR COMMENT

In defamation proceedings it is a defence to establish that the words complained of represent fair comment on a matter of public interest. The defence only protects comment, as opposed to defamatory statements of fact, and it must further be shown that the comment is based on facts which are either substantially true or published on a privileged occasion. It seems that, 'where the comment imputes corrupt or dishonourable motives it will not be fair comment unless it is reasonably warranted by the facts'.[10] Subject to this apparent limitation, however, the defence only requires, thereafter, that the comment or observation be such that it might have been, and in fact was, published as the expression of an *honestly* held belief.[11] It is not necessary that it be a reasonable opinion; only that it was published in good faith, and not for an ulterior motive.

The decision of the High Court of Australia in *Nicholls*[12] is persuasive authority that a similar defence is available to a person charged with scandalising the court. In this case it was sought to commit the editor of *The Mercury* newspaper following the publication of an article which might have been read as imputing political bias to a judge of the Arbitration Court. In delivering the judgment of

---

[6] *Cf.* Erskine May, *op cit.* at pp., 361–362, 418.

[7] The criticism had as its immediate motivation the sequestration of funds from the AUEW in the *Con-Mech* case, discussed below, p. 241.

[8] See Hansard H.C. Deb. Vol. 865, col. 1092, 4 December 1969.

[9] *Ibid.*, col. 1144. Mr Ashton had pointed out that Sir John Donaldson had been President of the Conservative University Students Association, and President of the Inns of Court Conservative Association.

[10] See Clerk and Lindsell, *Torts* (13th. ed.), para. 1780; *Wason* v. *Walter* (1868) L.R. 4 Q.B. 73, 96.

[11] See *Merivale* v. *Carson* (1887) 20 Q.B.D. 275; *Thomas* v. *Bradbury, Agnew and Co., Ltd.* [1906] 2 K.B. 627; *Slim* v. *Daily Telegraph, Ltd.* [1968] 2 Q.B. 157.

[12] (1911) 12 C.L.R. 280.

the High Court dismissing the application Griffith, C.J., having stated that he did not so interpret the article, continued:[13]

> I am not prepared to accede to the proposition that an imputation of want of impartiality to a Judge is necessarily a contempt of Court. On the contrary, I think that, if any Judge of this Court or of any other Court were to make a public utterance of such character as to be likely to impair the confidence of the public, or of suitors or any class of suitors in the impartiality of the Court in any matter likely to be brought before it, any public comment on such an utterance, if it were a fair comment, would, so far from being a contempt of Court, be for the public benefit, and would be entitled to similar protection to that which comment upon matters of public interest is entitled under the law of libel.

This statement has been cited with approval and acted upon in subsequent Australian cases[14] and it seems fairly clear that a defence akin to the technical defence of fair comment may be pleaded in that country by a person charged with scandalising the court.

In English law there are certain strong pointers in the same direction, but it is perhaps less clear that the technical defence, as such, is available. Thus Lord Atkin's well known statement in *Ambard* v. *Attorney-General for Trinidad and Tobago*[15] seems to exclude imputations of improper motive from the range of permissible comment, and it is, of course, such imputations which carry the greatest danger of constituting a contempt.[16] In *Metropolitan Police Commissioner; ex parte Blackburn*[17] the Court of Appeal again emphasised the legality of fair comment on all matters of public interest including the administration of justice. This time there was no saving for imputations of improper motives, but perhaps too much significance should not be attached to this since Quintin Hogg's article did not contain any such imputations. On the other hand, Salmon, L.J. seemed to envisage that the publisher had to meet a standard of 'reasonable courtesy' as well as one of good faith,[18] and no requirement of this nature attaches to the defence of fair comment as such. Words in a judgment should not, however, be taken as the equivalent of a statutory definition, and it is submitted that the authorities should be interpreted as recognising that the defence exists in this country as in Australia. This conclusion is perhaps supported by the fact that Salmon, L.J. himself appears to have assumed that the defence is available, as is evidenced by the *Report of the Interdepartmental Committee on the Law of Contempt as it Affects Tribunals of Inquiry* of which he was the chairman. Here it is said that: 'In the most unlikely event, however, of there being just cause for challenging the integrity of a judge or a member of a Tribunal of Inquiry it could not be contempt of court to do so. Indeed it would be a public duty to bring the

---

[13] *Ibid.*, at p. 286.

[14] See, e.g., *Fletcher, ex p. Kisch* (1935) 52 C.L.R. 248, 257–258 (High Ct of Australia); *Brett* [1950] V.L.R. 226, 229 (Vict. Sup. Ct); *Foster, ex p. Gillies* [1937] St. R. Qd. 368, 378 (Queensland Sup. Ct), *Att.-Gen. for New South Wales* v. *Mundey* [1972] 2 N.S.W.L.R. 887, 910 (N.S.W. Sup. Ct). But *cf. McHugh* [1901] 2 Ir. Rep. 569.

[15] [1936] A.C. 322, 335, above, p. 189.

[16] The statement of Griffith, C.J. in *Nicholls*, above, specifically envisages imputations of partiality as being covered by the defence.

[17] [1968] 2 Q.B. 150 [1968] 2 All E.R. 319, above, p. 189.

[18] [1968] 2 Q.B. 150, 155.

relevant facts to light'.[19] The judgment of Griffith, C.J. in *Nicholls*[20] was cited in support of this proposition.

5   GENERAL CONSIDERATIONS AND CONCLUSIONS

Any attempt to assess the current limits of permissible criticism, and the extent to which these accord with that which is desirable, must inevitably be subjective and rely heavily on general impressions. Certainly there have been cases in which the press has commented on specific instances of what has seemed to be bad manners on the bench.[1] Thus when in 1967 a Divorce Commissioner called a pop singer (Miss Sandie Shaw) who was appearing before him 'a spoilt child who feels she is entitled to do anything to gain her own ends', the *Observer* remarked: 'The judges' bench is not a pulpit from which to pronounce on personal morality'.[2] Likewise a judge's handling of a particular case, or the sentence imposed, has been subjected to criticism. For example, Ludovic Kennedy in his book *The Trial of Stephen Ward,* whilst making it clear that he was not imputing conscious bias to Mr Justice Marshall, nonetheless left the reader in no doubt that he believed the judge's summing up to have been coloured by his background and upbringing.[3] More recently the *Daily Mirror* did not mince its words when discussing a sentence imposed in a baby-snatching case. It commented in a leading article:[4]

> Shocking. Atrocious. Unbelievable. That is the reaction of most people to the 21 month jail sentence on Jacqueline Paddon, the girl with a history of mental disturbance, who ran off with a friend's baby. . . . For the fifteen minutes until the baby was recovered, Doreen Walsh must have been distracted with worry. As the judge pointed out. But she still showed a degree of compassion that Mr. Justice Boreham at Chelmsford Crown Court did not match.[5]

Similar examples of critical comment are not difficult to find.

As against this there have been other instances in which the press has tended to overstate the restrictions imposed by the law of contempt. Thus in May 1966 Lord Gardiner, speaking as Lord Chancellor in a House of Lords debate, referred to the 'apparent impossibility of persuading newspapers that they are free to comment on the proceedings of courts of justice', and continued:[6]

> The law is not in any doubt. It is a free country. Anybody is entitled to express his honest opinion about a sentence and about the way in which the judge has conducted a

[19] Cmnd. 4078, June 1969, para. 36.

[20] (1911) 12 C.L.R. 280, 286, above, p. 195.

[1] See Abel-Smith and Stevens, *In Search of Justice* (1968), pp. 182–185; *Lawyers and the Courts* (1967), at p. 125 *et seq.*; the report of the *Justice* sub-committee, *The Judiciary* (1972), para. 85.

[2] *Observer*, 26 February 1967.

[3] (1963) Penguin Special, pp. 210–211 especially. See also Tony Palmer, *The Trials of Oz* (1971), p. 265 especially.

[4] 2 November 1972.

[5] Comment of a similar vein, but which regarded a sentence as too lenient, led to contempt proceedings in *Ex p. Att.-Gen.; Re Truth and Sportsman, Ltd.* (1961) 61 S.R.N.S.W. 484. The articles were regarded as a contempt on the ground that they prejudiced a pending appeal.

[6] See Hansard, H.L. Deb. Vol. 274, cols. 1438–39, 25 May 1966. See also Hansard, H.C. Deb. Vol. 776, col. 1725, 31 January 1969 (Sir Elwyn Jones, Q.C. Att.-Gen.).

case, though it is desirable that it should not overstep the bounds of courtesy and should not be a virulent personal attack on a judge. But, subject to that, the administration of justice is not, as Lord Atkin once said, a cloistered virtue, and anybody is entitled to express his honest opinion about it. I have tried for about thirty years to persuade newspapers that this is the law. They will not believe it.

It may be however that the message has got across in the intervening years for it was the view of the Phillimore Committee that: 'There is not much evidence that the press is unduly inhibited by this aspect of the law.'[7] Certainly this represents a more realistic assessment of the risks involved. Indeed there does not appear to have been a successful application for a committal in an English case in the post-war years, although there have been a number of Commonwealth cases.

[7] Para. 160.

11 Victimisation of Jurors, Witnesses and other Persons after the Conclusion of Proceedings

1 JURORS

A contempt will be committed where a person so acts as to victimise a juror for the part he has played in judicial proceedings. It does not matter that the proceedings in question have already terminated and are not, therefore, themselves capable of being prejudiced. So much was decided by the High Court in Ireland in the case of *Martin*.[1] Here one John Martin had been convicted of an offence when his brother, James, went to the home of the foreman of the jury and challenged him to mortal combat. The matter having been drawn to the attention of the Court, Martin was committed to prison for one month and required to enter into recognisances to keep the peace for seven years.[2]

2 WITNESSES

In a case which came before it at the end of the 19th century the House of Commons ruled that it was a breach of the privileges of the House to victimise a station master by the name of John Hood by dismissing him from his employment after he had given evidence before a select committee of the House. In the words of the Speaker such conduct was unlawful as being 'calculated to deter witnesses in giving evidence before this House or its committees'.[3] Within a matter of months parliament effectively transferred its jurisdiction in such cases to the ordinary courts by enacting the Witnesses (Public Inquiries) Protection Act 1892, which still forms part of the present law. By s. 2 of the Act a person commits an offence if he 'threatens, or in any way punishes, damnifies, or injures, or attempts to punish, damnify, or injure, any person for having given evidence upon any inquiry, or on account of the evidence which he has given upon any such inquiry'. The scope of the Act, however, was confined to inquiries begun 'under the authority of any Royal Commission or by any committee of either House of Parliament, or pursuant to any statutory authority'. Inquiries by any courts of justice were expressly excluded.[4]

---

[1] (1848) 5 Cox C.C. 356.
[2] See also *State of Illinois* v. *Vitucci*, 49 Ill. App. 2d 171; 199 N.E. 2d 78 (Appellate Ct of Illinois, 1964).
[3] (1892) H.C. Journal, at p. 167.
[4] *Cf.* the Witnesses (Public Inquiries) Protection Act 1892, s. 1.

The most natural explanation for the exclusion of courts of justice from the 1892 Act is that parliament must have assumed that the courts possessed an inherent power at common law to punish such conduct as a contempt.[5] Further pointers in the same direction are to be found in a number of 19th-century cases suggesting that threats directed at witnesses were contempts of court.[6] The cases are, however, susceptible of a restrictive interpretation for they concerned either threats or vilification offered at a time when proceedings were still pending, or threats offered to persons returning from court. It was only in 1962 in the case of *Attorney-General* v. *Butterworth*[7] that it was finally established beyond doubt that it was equally a contempt to punish or victimise a witness after the proceedings had finally terminated. At the hearing of a reference before the Restrictive Practices Court to consider an agreement between the Newspaper Proprietors' Association and the National Federation of Retail Newsagents, Booksellers, and Stationers (the RENA agreement), one Greenlees, a delegate and the honorary treasurer of the Romford branch of the Federation, had given evidence against the Federation's interests. Members of the committee of the Romford branch thereupon summoned him to appear before a number of meetings where, 'he was "hauled over the coals", required to explain his conduct, and condemned for it'.[8] At two subsequent meetings Butterworth, Boston, Etherton and other Federation officials secured the passage of resolutions purporting to remove Greenless from his position as delegate and honorary treasurer.

The Attorney-General applied to the Restrictive Practices Court for the officials' committal or attachment, but the application was dismissed following an extremely narrow interpretation of the authorities.[9] According to Russell, P., delivering the judgment of the court, such conduct, occurring as it did after the hearing had been concluded, was not capable of constituting a contempt. On appeal to the Court of Appeal, however, a different view was taken. Lord Denning, M.R. dealt with the somewhat equivocal nature of the earlier authorities in characteristically robust terms, and explained why such conduct was to be regarded as a contempt by saying:[10]

How can we expect a witness to give evidence freely and frankly, as he ought to do, if he is liable, as soon as the case is over, to be punished for it by those who dislike the evidence he has given? Let us accept that he has honestly given his evidence.[11] Is he to be liable to be dismissed from his employment, or to be expelled from his trade union, or to be deprived of his office, or to be sent to Coventry, simply because of that evidence which he has given? I decline to believe that he law of England permits him to be so

[5] *Cf.* Lord Denning in *Att.-Gen.* v. *Butterworth* [1963] 1 Q.B. 696, 721; [1962] 3 All E.R. 326, 330, C.A.

[6] See, e.g., *Littler* v. *Thomson* (1839) 2 Beav. 129, 131; 48 E.R. 1129 *per* Lord Langdale, M.R.; *Rowden* v. *Universities Co-operative Association, Ltd.* (1881) 71 L.T. Jo. 373; *Purdin* v. *Roberts* (1910) 74 J.P. Jo. 88.

[7] [1963]1 Q.B. 696; [1962] 3 All E.R. 326. See D.G.T. Williams (1962) 25 M.L.R. 723; Goodhart, (1963) 79 L.Q.R. 5.

[8] [1963] 1 Q.B. 696, 717 *per* Lord Denning, M.R.

[9] [1962] 1 Q.B. 534; [1962] 1 All E.R. 321.

[10] [1963] 1 Q.B. 696, 719.

[11] Suppose that the witness had already been convicted of perjury, would it be a contempt to victimise him then? And would it be a defence to a charge of contempt to prove that the evidence was perjured if there had been no such conviction?

treated. If this sort of thing could be done in a single case with impunity, the news of it would soon get round. Witnesses in other cases would be unwilling to come forward, they would hesitate to speak the truth, for fear of the consequences.

Similar views were expressed by Donovan and Pearson, LL.J.[12] and the Court was unanimous in holding that a contempt punishable on summary process had been committed by those of the respondents who had acted with the object of punishing Greenless. The case has been followed in a number of English[13] and Commonwealth[14] decisions, and must be taken to represent the law.

3   OTHER PERSONS

It would appear to be clear, in principle, that the same process of reasoning as was adopted by the Court of Appeal in *Attorney-General* v. *Butterworth*[15] may equally be applied, *mutatis mutandis*, to the victimisation of other persons concerned in judicial proceedings, as, for example, a judge,[16] counsel or solicitor,[17] or a party.[18] Although there is a paucity of authority indisputably in point[19] the underlying considerations are substantially the same as in a case in which it is a juror or witness who is victimised.

4   GENERAL CONSIDERATIONS

(1)   THE MEANS EMPLOYED

It would seem immaterial—at least for the purposes of the offence itself if not to the possibility of consequential relief[20]—what means are employed to punish the juror, witness etc. Violence or the threat of harm to person or property[1] would clearly be a contempt as in the recent case of *Moore* v. *Clerk of Assize, Bristol*,[2] where a fourteen-year-old schoolgirl was approached in a café by the brother of a person against whom she had given evidence earlier in the day. The brother who told her with his fist clenched and elbow on the table, 'You had better get out of here fast' was sentenced to three months' imprisonment for contempt. The Court

---

[12] *Cf.* [1963] 1 Q.B. 696, at p. 725 (Donovan, L.J.), and p. 728 (Pearson, L.J.).

[13] See *Chapman* v. *Honig* [1963] 2 Q.B. 502; [1963] 2 All E.R. 513; *Moore* v. *Clerk of Assize, Bristol* [1972] 1 All E.R. 58.

[14] See *Adams* v. *Walsh* [1963] N.Z.L.R. 158; *Morris* v. *Wellington City* [1969] N.Z.L.R. 1038 (N.Z. Sup. Ct); *Wright (No. 1)* [1968] V.R. 164 (Vict. Sup. Ct); *Re Samuel Goldman* [1968] 3 N.S.W.R. 325 (N.S.W. Sup. Ct).

[15] [1963] 1 Q.B. 696; [1962] 3 All E.R. 326.

[16] *Cf. Att.-Gen.* v. *Butterworth* [1963] 1 Q.B. 696, 722 *per* Lord Denning, *obiter*.

[17] *Re Johnson* (1887) 20 Q.B.D. 68, C.A.; *Re Samuel Goldman* [1968] 3 N.S.W.R. 325 (N.S.W. Sup. Ct).

[18] *Williams* v. *Lyons* (1723) 8 Mod. Rep. 189; 88 E.R. 138.

[19] Both *Re Johnson* and *Re Samuel Goldman, supra*, concerned threats which were offered in the precincts of the court or when the advocate was returning home. This may be thought relevant. But see Lord Denning in *Att.-Gen.* v. *Butterworth* [1963] 1 Q.B. 696, 722.

[20] See below, p. 203 *et seq.*

[1] See U.S.C., s. 1503.

[2] [1972] 1 All E.R. 58.

of Appeal refused to intervene on appeal. Other examples of alleged victimisation from the case law to date include dismissing a person from his post as delegate to a union,[3] dismissing an employee from his employment,[4] and giving a tenant notice to quit premises.[5] In principle any type of conduct actuated by a desire to victimise the juror or witness etc. for the part he has played in judicial proceedings should be sufficient.

(2) THE PUBLICITY ACCORDED TO THE VICTIMISATION

The danger primarily associated with the victimisation of witnesses is that it is likely to harm the administration of justice as a continuing process by making persons, generally, less willing to come forward to give evidence in future cases. It was this view of the rationale of the offence which prompted Donovan, L.J. to agree in *Attorney-General* v. *Butterworth* that:[6]

> [In] this kind of case it must be proved by the Crown that knowledge of the revenge taken upon one who has given evidence is likely to come to the knowledge of potential witnesses in future cases.

With reference to the facts of the case he added: 'I think that the Crown has proved that here as a matter of reasonable inference. The proceedings against Greenless were not all conducted in privacy.'[7] Pearson, L.J. committed himself to a similar opinion in *Chapman* v. *Honig*,[8] a case which is discussed in more detail below,[9] saying that it was 'possible to imagine a case in which there would be victimisation of a witness and yet there would be no contempt of court'.[10] In this latter case, however, both Lord Denning, M.R. and Davies, L.J. expressly disagreed with the suggestion that it was incumbent on the Crown to prove a likelihood of publicity.

Although there is a certain logic in the view of Donovan and Pearson, LL.J. it is singularly unlikely that it will come to represent the law. Apart altogether from the incongruous results which would be attendant upon the limitation,[11] it may be doubted whether it is necessary to give effect to the rationale of the offence. The witness who has been victimised will *himself* be deterred from giving evidence with the same freedom in future cases even if no one else will. It is not without significance, moreover, that in the most recent English case, *Moore* v. *Clerk of Assize, Bristol*,[12] Edmund Davies, L.J. specifically denied that the suggested requirement existed. In this case, as in the others, however, the point did not arise directly for decision and so the issue is still open for argument in a future case.

---

[3] See *Att.-Gen.* v. *Butterworth* [1963] 1 Q.B. 696. See also *Adams* v. *Walsh* [1963] N.Z.L.R. 158.

[4] *Morris* v. *Wellington City* [1969] N.Z.L.R. 1038. See also the incident involving the actress Dawn Addams as reported in *The Times*, 13 October 1972.

[5] *Chapman* v. *Honig* [1963] 2 Q.B. 502; [1963] 2 All E.R. 513, below, p. 203.

[6] [1963] 1 Q.B. 696, 726.

[7] *Ibid.*

[8] [1963] 2 Q.B. 502.

[9] On p. 203.

[10] [1963] 2 Q.B. 502, 519.

[11] *Cf. ibid.*, at pp. 511–512 (Lord Denning). See also *ibid.*, at p. 526 (Davies, L.J.).

[12] [1972] 1 All E.R. 58, 59, C.A.

(3) MENS REA

It has been noted in previous chapters that liability for contempt of court is not invariably dependent upon proof of *mens rea*.[13] So much was established in the leading case of *Odhams Press, Ltd., ex parte Attorney-General*.[14] When, however, the alleged contempt takes the form of a victimisation of a witness etc. the position is different. While it is not necessary in such a case to prove that the person allegedly in contempt intended to interfere with the administration of justice as such, it is apparently necessary to prove that he acted with the object of punishing the witness for the evidence he has given in the proceedings. Indeed it may be thought that such a requirement is built into the very notion of victimisation itself. If a person acts in a way adverse to the interests of another, but without the object of punishing him for the part he has played in the proceedings, that other will not have been victimised, though he may have been otherwise prejudiced.

This need to inquire into the motives of the person allegedly in contempt was accepted in *Attorney-General* v. *Butterworth* itself, where Lord Denning agreed that: 'The victimisation of a witness is only a contempt of court if it is done with the purpose of punishing him for having given evidence in the sense he did.'[15] In the majority of cases, no doubt, the alleged contemnor will have acted with mixed motives. In such a case, it was held, the court was not required to undertake a nice assessment of the weight of the respective motives or to isolate the predominant one for the purposes of determining liability. According to Lord Denning: 'If one of the purposes actuating the step is the purpose of punishment, then it is a contempt of court in everyone so actuated.[16] Applying these considerations to the facts of the case the Court of Appeal held that a contempt had been committed by the three respondents (Butterworth, Etherton and Bailey), whose predominant motive had been to punish Greenlees and they were ordered to contribute £200 each towards the costs of the proceedings. Equally, a contempt was held to have been committed by the three respondents who had been actuated in part, though not predominantly, by a desire to punish. They were ordered to pay £100 each towards the costs of the proceedings. The four remaining respondents with respect to whom there was no evidence of an intent to punish were acquitted.

The motivation behind the alleged contemnor's conduct in any given case is, of course, a question of fact to be determined in the light of all the available evidence. Professor Goodhart has written in a valuable note discussing the *Butterworth* case that it would not, for example, be a contempt for an employer to terminate his valet's employment on the ground that the effect of the evidence given by the valet in divorce proceedings was 'such as to make the relationship of employer and valet an impossible one'. Likewise, it is suggested, the result in the *Butterworth* case might itself have been different if in purporting to deprive Greenlees of his office the committee had been solely motivated by the con-

---

[13] See above pp. 158–168, 191–192 especially.
[14] [1957] 1 Q.B. 73; [1956] 3 All E.R. 494.
[15] [1963] 1 Q.B. 696, 723. See also *ibid.*, at p. 726 (Donovan, L.J.).
[16] [1963] 1 Q.B. 696, 723.

sideration that, 'his difference of opinion with the other members of the association made it impossible for him to act as their delegate'.[17] Yet this view cannot be accepted without reservation. In so far as the law of contempt is concerned with protecting the due administration of justice it may be that the inquiry should be directed to the 'victim's' reaction to the dismissal etc., rather than to the motives of the alleged contemnor as such.

(4) ARE DAMAGES RECOVERABLE AND RELATED PROBLEMS

As will be apparent from some of the cases discussed above, a contempt of the present category may be committed even though the means adopted would have been quite lawful in themselves were it not for the element of victimisation. A union official may clearly be removed from an honorary post by a resolution passed at a properly convened meeting, but if the object of the exercise is to punish him for having given evidence against the union an offence will have been committed. Similar considerations apply to the dismissal of a valet or other employee or, for that matter, to a case in which an irate father evicts an adult child from the family home as a punishment for having given evidence against him.

While it is quite clear that a contempt may, therefore, be committed even though D has done something which he would otherwise have been at liberty to do but for the element of victimisation, there are further related problems to which there is no such clear-cut solution. Thus it is necessary to inquire whether damages may be recovered by one who has been victimised and by way of compensation for the loss suffered. Secondly, there is the question of whether a court would be prepared to grant an injunction requiring D to desist from victimising P and, if so, in what circumstances. Finally, it is also necessary to inquire whether the act in question is effective to achieve its objective, notwithstanding that it amounts to a contempt of court.

Some of these problems were touched upon by the Court of Appeal in the case of *Chapman* v. *Honig*.[18] In this case Honig was the landlord of certain property in East London and he had been successfully sued in trespass by one of his tenants. Chapman occupied a flat in the same building and he had given evidence against Honig in the trespass action, though somewhat reluctantly and only after he had been subpoenaed. The following day he was served with a notice to quit the premises, but he ignored it and stayed on after the notice had expired. Some time thereafter Honig senior visited the premises and padlocked and stapled the doors. When Chapman returned home from work Honig sought somewhat disarmingly to explain his conduct to a police officer, who had also arrived on the scene, by saying: 'He gave evidence against me in court and you don't do that to landlords.' It was later found that in making this statement Honig senior was acting with the full authority of the son and as, in effect, his mouthpiece. Chapman was clearly made of stern stuff for he sought and was granted an injunction restraining Honig from trespassing on the premises or cutting off the electricity. However, the harassment had affected his wife's health and he was

---

[17] (1963) 79 L.Q.R. 5, at pp. 8–9.
[18] [1963] 2 Q.B. 502; [1963] 2 All E.R. 513.

eventually obliged to leave for her sake. He nonetheless pursued his action against Honig maintaining that the notice to quit was in contempt of court as being intended to victimise him and consequently, he claimed, was invalid. On this basis he sought damages in trespass and for breaches of the covenant of quiet enjoyment. Counsel for the landlord conceded (a) that if the notice had been served with a vindictive motive (as was later found to be the case) it was a contempt, and (b) that if there was a contempt of court the landlord was liable in damages. This latter concession was prompted by a *dictum* of Lord Denning in *Attorney-General* v. *Butterworth* where it was said: 'I would add that if the witness has been damnified by it [*sc*. the victimisation] he may well have redress in a civil court for damages.'[19] In the light of counsel's concession the county court judge gave judgment for the plaintiff, Chapman, for £50 damages for contempt of court, without finding it necessary to determine whether the notice to quit was in fact valid. It was from this judgment that the landlord appealed to the Court of Appeal.

Before the Court of Appeal the concession that damages were recoverable for contempt of court, as such, was allowed to be withdrawn. Thereafter a majority of the Court proceeded to allow the landlord's appeal and hold that an action for damages did not lie at least in the circumstances of this case. The reasoning which led to this conclusion was, in essence, as follows.

In the first place the majority held that the notice to quit was valid, notwithstanding that it amounted to a contempt because, in the words of Pearson, L.J.:[20]

> Common experience is that, when the validity of an act done in purported exercise of a right under a contract or other instrument is disputed, the inquiry is limited to ascertaining whether the act has been done in accordance with the provisions of the contract or other instrument. I cannot think of any case in which such an act might be invalidated by proof that it was prompted by some vindictive or other wrong motive. Motive is disregarded as irrelevant.

The view that the notice to quit was valid in the sense that it was effective to terminate the tenant's right of possession led to the finding that it was in this respect 'a lawful act'. Having adopted this premise, Pearson, L.J. concluded that:[1]

> The same act cannot be as between the same parties both a lawful exercise of a contractual right and at the same time unlawful as being tortious and giving rise to an action for damages. No such complication has yet existed in the law and it is not necessary or desirable to introduce it.

This conclusion would indeed follow from the premise, and yet it may be doubted whether the premise itself is correct. Certainly it is true that an act which is performed in accordance with the terms of a contract does not become unlawful as constituting a breach of contract solely because it is done with some ulterior motive in mind. Contractual rights may be exercised, as Pearson, L.J. put it, 'for a good reason or a bad reason or no reason at all'.[2] But it is surely a wholly

---

[19] [1963] 1 Q.B. 696, 719. *Cf.* also *ibid.*, at p. 721 where he reiterates the point.
[20] [1963] 2 Q.B. 502, 520.
[1] *Ibid.*, at p. 521.
[2] *Ibid.*, at p. 520. See *White & Carter (Councils), Ltd.* v. *McGregor* [1962] A.C. 413, H.L.

different proposition to say that what would otherwise have been a legitimate exercise of a contractual right is still lawful as between the parties notwithstanding that it constitutes a contempt of court. In his dissenting judgment Lord Denning held that the notice was invalid, and he took the view that this conclusion was essential if the tenant was to be accorded effective protection. As he put it:[3]

> If the landlord *victimises* a tenant by actually giving him notice to quit, the court must be able to protect the tenant by holding the notice to quit to be *invalid*. Nothing else will serve to vindicate the authority of the law. Nothing else will enable a witness to give his evidence freely as he ought to do. Nothing else will empower the judge to say to him: 'Do not fear. The arm of the law is strong enough to protect you.'

It should be added that this conclusion does not, of course, mean that the tenant would acquire a security of tenure which he did not otherwise possess. There would be nothing to prevent the landlord from serving a valid notice to quit which had not been motivated by a desire to punish the tenant on some future occasion. No doubt this would create a contingent difficulty of having to determine his motives at this time if the matter were again brought before the courts, but this would not be significantly more difficult than on the initial occasion.[4]

Chapman v. *Honig* should in fact have posed the problem of establishing the consequences for the civil law of holding an act illegal as a contempt by victimisation in a relatively straightforward form. It would have been quite possible to have held the notice invalid on the ground that, being intended to victimise the tenant, it was given in breach of an implied term of the contract. Thereafter damages for breach of the covenant of quiet enjoyment or in trespass might have been awarded. Similarly a dismissal from employment which constitutes a contempt by victimisation (as by the master of his valet) would, it is submitted, be in breach of contract notwithstanding that it was otherwise ostensibly carried out in accordance with the terms of the contract. Damages for breach of contract could be awarded thereafter. In both of the above cases, the underlying issue of whether damages may be claimed for a *contempt by victimisation as such* may well be avoided in practice.[5] The same would, no doubt, be true of the vast majority of other cases for the victimisation would generally take the form of a nominate and readily identifiable civil wrong.[6] In *Moore* v. *Clerk of Assize, Bristol*,[7] for example, there had clearly been an assault.[8] Realistic situations can, however, be

---

[3] [1963] 2 Q.B. 502, 513.

[4] The possibility of evading liability by serving a later notice was nonetheless a factor stressed by Pearson, L.J., and alluded to by Davies, L.J. in the second of the majority judgments: *cf.* [1963] 2 Q.B. 502, at p. 522, and p. 524 respectively.

[5] Yet it does not, of course, follow that damages for breach of contract would be quantified on the same basis as damages for contempt by victimisation.

[6] *Cf.* the judgment of Pearson, L.J. in *Chapman* v. *Honig* [1963] 2 Q.B. 502, 520.

[7] [1972] 1 All E.R. 58, above, p. 200.

[8] And in *Att.-Gen.* v. *Butterworth* [1963] 1 Q.B. 696 there might have been a remedy in the tort of conspiracy. If P were threatened *pendente lite* with dismissal if he gives evidence there would seem to be a remedy in the tort of intimidation, providing that this tort is seen as affording a remedy to the person threatened. See Heydon, *Economic Torts* (1973), pp. 53–54 and cases there cited for discussion of the scope of intimidation.

envisaged in which there would be no peg on which to hang a claim and in which the question would have to be squarely faced. A clear instance is provided by the case of a father who, with a view to victimisation, excludes an able-bodied adult child from the family home.

In an attempt to answer the question which would be thus posed it may be said that there is no general and all-embracing principle whereby a person may recover damages at common law to compensate himself for a loss on the ground that he has been injured by a criminal act. Perjury, for example, does not afford its victim any consequential relief in a civil action.[9] Equally, however, the fact that the claim would be a relatively novel one would not itself be a bar to relief. Indeed in *Chapman* v. *Honig* itself Pearson, L.J. did not entirely rule out the possibility of a civil remedy by way of damages for contempt by victimisation in an appropriate case.[10]

A somewhat stronger pointer in the same direction is to be found in the decision of the Court of Appeal in *Acrow (Automation), Ltd.* v. *Rex Chainbelt Inc.*[11] In this case it was held that D committed the tort of interfering with a business relationship with P by the use of *unlawful* means[12] in that his failure to supply equipment to P pursuant to directions given by a third party (X) assisted X to act in breach of an injunction. If, therefore, contempt by assisting another to act in breach of an injunction[13] is an unlawful act for the purposes of this newly recognised tort (and this of itself may be thought to provide support for the view that *Chapman* v. *Honig* was wrongly decided), it is not a big step thereafter to say that contempt by victimisation is *itself* a tort and that a person may recover damages if he suffers loss as a result of the victimisation. Ultimately, however, the case is open to argument either way.

The balance of the arguments, it is submitted, favours the granting of a remedy, not simply because this would assist the witness, but because in assisting the witness one is protecting the due administration of justice.[14] It would be small comfort to a witness who has been victimised, or to potential witnesses in future cases, to know that the contemnor has been committed to prison if consequential relief were not available to the witness himself. Such relief is available, moreover, to witnesses falling under the protection of the Witnesses (Public Inquiries) Protection Act 1892[15] and, as Lord Denning noted in *Chapman* v. *Honig*,[16] it would be anomalous if it were not equally afforded at common law to witnesses appearing before courts of justice. The same considerations clearly apply, *mutatis mutandis*, to jurors, judges and others.

---

[9] *Cf. Hargreaves* v. *Bretherton* [1959] 1 Q.B. 45.

[10] *Cf.* [1963] 2 Q.B. 502, 522.

[11] [1971] 3 All E.R. 1175.

[12] See, in general, Heydon, *Economic Torts* (1973), Ch. 3; Street, *The Law of Torts* (5th. ed., 1972), Ch. 19.

[13] For the liability in contempt of one who procures or encourages the breach of an injunction, see below, p. 247. On the substantive point decided in the *Acrow (Automation)* case, compare *Thorne R.D.C.* v. *Bunting (No. 2)* [1972] 3 All E.R. 1084.

[14] *Cf.* the principles whereby it is determined whether an individual has a personal remedy for breach of a statutory duty. But *quaere* whether this argument could be applied to contempt by infringing the *sub judice* rule where P has been denied a fair trial by a prejudicial publication?

[15] Sec. 4. See, in general, above, p. 198.

[16] [1963] 2 Q.B. 502, 514.

It is possible that the common law position must now be read subject to the Criminal Justice Act 1972, s.1(1). This empowers a court 'by or before which a person is convicted of an offence' to make a compensation order in favour of one who has suffered 'personal injury, loss or damage resulting from that offence'. There is, however, some doubt whether a committal for contempt is technically a 'conviction' for the purposes of this provision.

At one stage removed the courts may also be called upon to deal with issues such as the availability of an injunction in cases where (but for the conjectural question of whether contempt by victimisation is *itself* a civil wrong) no recognised civil wrong has been committed. Likewise it may be necessary to determine the legal status or effectiveness of the victimising act itself. As to injunctions, it is clear that they may issue to restrain an act which would be a contempt of court, but presumably the generally accepted limitations apply here, as elsewhere. On this basis an employer, for example, would not be restrained from dismissing an ordinary employee in order to victimise him.[17] Indeed Lord Denning conceded as much in *Chapman* v. *Honig*.[18] Equally, it would no doubt follow that where an injunction will not issue to restrain an act, the act, once committed, will be effective to achieve its objective. The employee would, in other words, have been effectively dismissed.[19] The position in other cases is perhaps less clear. In *Chapman* v. *Honig* the notice to quit would undoubtedly have been inoperative had its service been regarded as an unlawful act. Similarly in *Attorney-General* v. *Butterworth* the Court of Appeal clearly viewed the resolutions designed to remove Greenlees from his posts within the union as inoperative.[20] It may well be that future cases will show that this area of the law raises issues similar to the problem familiar to administrative lawyers of whether decisions taken in breach of the rules of natural justice are void or only voidable. The same difficulties with respect to collateral matters would appear to be discernible here, as they are there.

(5) THE PHILLIMORE COMMITTEE RECOMMENDATIONS

In its discussion of the matters covered in this chapter the Phillimore Committee makes two main recommendations. Firstly, the committee proposes that reprisals against witnesses or jurors after the termination of proceedings should be dealt with on indictment and not summarily as a contempt.[1] Secondly, it recommends that a court should have power to award compensation to the victim of the reprisal.[2] Both of these recommendations represent desirable changes or

---

[17] For the general rule, see *Page One Records, Ltd.* v. *Britton* [1967] 3 All E.R. 822; but *cf. Hill* v. *C.A. Parsons & Co., Ltd.* [1972] Ch. 305; [1971] 3 All E.R. 1745, C.A. The position would, no doubt, be otherwise where the employee occupies a special position affording protection as in cases such as *Malloch* v. *Aberdeen Corporation* [1971] 2 All E.R. 1278. See also *Ridge* v. *Baldwin* [1964] A.C. 40.

[18] *Cf.* [1963] 2 Q.B. 502, 513–514.

[19] For speculation as to the approach in quantifying the damage recoverable if damages were available for a contempt *as such*, see [1963] 2 Q.B. 502, at p. 514 (Lord Denning), and at p. 522 (Pearson, L.J.).

[20] [1963] 1 Q.B. 696.

[1] Para. 157. See also para. 21 and above, p. 6.

[2] Para. 158. The Committee only refers to reprisals against witnesses and jurors, but presumably the same principles should apply to other persons such as judges, parties, solicitors etc.

points of clarification in the law and they receive the approval of the recent Law Commission Working Paper, 'Offences Relating to the Administration of Justice'.[3]

[3] See para. 112 of the Working Paper.

12 Publicising Judicial Proceedings

1 INTRODUCTION

The general rule in English law is that judicial proceedings must be conducted in open court and that a fair and accurate report of such proceedings will not give' rise to liability in libel, contempt, or under any other heading.[1] The duty to administer justice in open court was clearly established by the decision of the House of Lords in the leading case of *Scott* v. *Scott,*[2] where it was held that the High Court had no power at common law to hear a nullity or other matrimonial suit in camera in the interests of public decency. In reaching this conclusion the House recognised that there were certain established exceptions to the general rule, which were 'the outcome of a yet more fundamental principle that the chief object of Courts of Justice must be to secure that justice is done'.[3] The exceptions arose in cases involving, for example, wards of court, persons of unsound mind, and trade secrets, where publicity would effectively prevent the achievement of this objective.

In this chapter it is proposed to consider the circumstances in which the publicising of judicial proceedings may exceptionally give rise to liability whether for a statutory offence or for contempt of court. The position with respect to the reporting of committal proceedings, and reports of criminal proceedings generally when they are not fair and accurate, has already been discussed in a previous chapter[4] and will not be dealt with again here. Discussion of the further limitations on publicity may be conveniently divided into two main headings according to whether the proceedings in question are heard in open court or in private.

2 PROCEEDINGS HEARD IN OPEN COURT

The general legality of publishing a fair and accurate report of judicial proceedings heard in open court has been qualified in two major respects by the enactment of provisions designed, respectively, to shield children from publicity and to prevent the publication of indecent matter. Although none of these

---

[1] For a survey of the limits to this proposition, see the Report of the Law Commission on *The Powers of Appeal Courts to sit in Private and Restrictions upon Publicity in Domestic Proceedings*, Cmnd. 3149, November 1966. See also *Halsbury*, Vol. 9, para. 20. For the requirement that the report be fair and accurate, see *Brook* v. *Evans* (1860) 29 L.J. Ch. 616.

[2] [1913] A.C. 417.

[3] *Ibid.*, at p. 437 *per* Viscount Haldane, L.C.

[4] See above, pp. 112–122.

provisions falls directly within the scope of the law of contempt, they have a sufficiently close affinity with the subject to be discussed here.

(1) PROVISIONS INTENDED TO SHIELD CHILDREN FROM PUBLICITY

By s. 49(1) of the Children and Young Persons Act 1933 as amended, it is provided that:

> [No] newspaper report[5] of any proceedings in a juvenile court shall reveal the name, address or school, or include any particulars calculated to lead to the identification, of any child or young person concerned in those proceedings, either as being the person against or in respect of whom the proceedings are taken or as being a witness therein, nor shall any picture be published in any newspaper as being or including a picture of any child or young person so concerned in any such proceedings as aforesaid:

The court or the Secretary of State may in any given case order that these requirements be dispensed with in relation to a child or young person where this is considered appropriate for the purpose of avoiding injustice to him.[6] A fine not exceeding £50 may be imposed in respect of each offence against the section.[7]

Section 39(1) of the 1933 Act contains further provisions designed to shield children from publicity which are in certain respects wider, and in others narrower, than the provisions of s. 49(1) noted above. By s. 39(1) as amended:

> In relation to any proceedings in any court the court may direct that
>
> (a) no newspaper report[8] of the proceedings shall reveal the name, address, or school, or include any particulars calculated to lead to the identification, of any child or young person concerned in the proceedings, either as being the person by or against or in respect of whom the proceedings are taken, or as being a witness therein;
>
> (b) no picture shall be published in any newspaper as being or including a picture of any child or young person so concerned in the proceedings as aforesaid,
>
> except in so far (if at all) as may be permitted by the direction of the court.

Again a fine not exceeding £50 may be imposed in respect of an offence against this provision.[9] It will be observed that unlike s. 49(1), s. 39(1) applies to any proceedings in any court[10] and not just to proceedings in a juvenile court.[11] On the other hand, s. 39(1) does not operate automatically but only where a court makes the necessary direction. In practice, however, it seems that the news media frequently refrain from identifying children or young persons in any proceedings in which identification would be adverse to their interests, and not only where they have been directed to do so, or where the case falls under s. 49(1).

---

[5] By the Children and Young Persons Act 1963, s. 57(4) the provision is extended to sound and television broadcasts.

[6] Cf. the proviso to s. 49(1) of the 1933 Act as amended by the Children and Young Persons Act 1969, s. 10(1)(c).

[7] Under s. 49(2) of the 1933 Act.

[8] Or sound or television broadcast: see Children and Young Persons Act 1963, s. 57(4).

[9] See Children and Young Persons Act 1933, s. 39(2).

[10] Presumably civil, as well as criminal, proceedings: see the Law Commission Report (above, n. 1), para. 46.

[11] Or on appeal from such a court (Children and Young Persons Act 1963, s. 57(2)).

(2) PROVISIONS INTENDED TO PREVENT THE PUBLICATION OF INDECENT MATTER

The Judicial Proceedings (Regulation of Reports) Act 1926 makes further inroads into the general proposition whereby proceedings in courts of law may be fairly and accurately reported. By s. (1)(a) of the Act it is unlawful to print or publish:

> . . . in relation to any judicial proceedings any indecent matter or indecent material, surgical or physiological details being matter or details the publication of which would be calculated to injure public morals.

Thus parliament has provided for the suppression of that which could not be suppressed at common law.

Further and more specific limitations in s. 1(1)(b) of the 1926 Act, as amended,[12] govern the reporting of matrimonial proceedings for dissolution of marriage; nullity; judicial separation; declarations as to legitimacy;[13] and of proceedings for discharge or variation of maintenance orders or for an order for financial provision, or for the discharge, variation or suspension of such an order.[14] With respect to such proceedings it is an offence to publish any particulars other than the following:

> (i) the names, addresses and occupations of the parties and witnesses; (ii) a concise statement of the charges, defences and countercharges in support of which evidence has been given; (iii) submissions on any point of law arising in the course of the proceedings, and the decision of the court thereon; (iv) the summing-up of the judge and the finding of the jury (if any) and the judgment of the court and observations made by the judge in giving judgment:[15]

In all of the above cases there is a saving for bona fide law reports and publications of a technical character intended for circulation among members of the legal or medical professions.[16] Prosecutions in respect of alleged offences against the Act can only be instituted with the consent of the Attorney-General,[17] and those found guilty are subject to a term of imprisonment not exceeding four months, or a fine not exceeding £500 or both.[18] It may be the case, however, that an injunction will issue to restrain the publication of matter other than that permitted by s. 1(1)(b) and which is likely to besmirch the reputation of a party to

---

[12] By the Domestic and Appellate Proceedings (Restriction of Publicity) Act 1968, s. 2(1), (3); Matrimonial Proceedings and Property Act 1970, ss. 20, 42(1), Sch. 2, para. 3 (see now the Matrimonial Causes Act 1973, Sch. 2, para. 7). The amendments stemmed from the Law Commission report on *The Powers of Appeal Courts to sit in Private and Restrictions upon Publicity in Domestic Proceedings,* Cmnd. 3149, November 1966, paras. 38–48 especially.

[13] Under the Matrimonial Causes Act 1965, s. 39, which provision is superseded by the Matrimonial Causes Act 1973, s. 45. S. 1(1)(b)(ii) of the 1926 Act was amended in such cases by the Domestic and Appellate Proceedings (Restriction of Publicity) Act, s. 2(3) to permit publication of a concise statement of the particulars of the declaration sought. The lack of a power to sit in private prior to 1968 is seen in *B. (otherwise P.)* v. *Att.-Gen.* [1965] 3 All E.R. 253.

[14] Now made under Part II of the Matrimonial Causes Act 1973, ss. 27, 31 especially. See also Sch. 2, para. 7 to the Act. Outstanding orders for maintenance or financial provision may have been made under earlier enactments, as, e.g., s. 22 of the Matrimonial Causes Act 1965.

[15] But note that s. 1(1)(a), above, would still apply when citing extracts from the summing up etc.

[16] See the Judicial Proceedings (Regulation of Reports) Act 1926, s. 1(4).

[17] *Cf. ibid.,* s. 1(3).

[18] *Ibid.* s. 1(2).

the proceedings.[19] Breach of such an injunction would constitute a civil contempt and the consent of the Attorney-General would not be needed for an application for a committal order. Neither would the statutory provisions as to punishment apply.

In magistrates' courts the Magistrates' Court Act 1952, s. 58(1) requires that reports in newspapers or periodicals[20] of domestic proceedings[1] be limited to the following details:

> (a) the names, addresses and occupations of the parties and witnesses; (b) the grounds of the application, and a concise statement of the charges, defences and counter-charges in support of which evidence has been given; (c) submissions on any point of law arising in the course of the proceedings and the decision of the court on the submission; (d) the decision of the court, and any observations made by the court in giving it.

As in the case of the 1926 Act there is a saving for publications of a technical character intended for circulation among members of the legal or medical profession,[2] and a provision whereby prosecutions for an alleged breach of the restrictions may only be instituted with the consent of the Attorney-General.[3] The maximum penalty for an offence under the Act is imprisonment for a term not exceeding four months, or a fine not exceeding £100, or both.[4]

3   PROCEEDINGS HEARD IN PRIVATE

(1) THE POSITION AT COMMON LAW

The general rule whereby justice must be administered in open court is subject to a substantial number of qualifications. Indeed the Law Commission has identified four overlapping sources from which a power to sit in private (whether in camera—that is in court but with the public including the press excluded—or in chambers) may be derived. These are:[5]

> (a) When this is permitted under an exception to the rule in *Scott* v. *Scott;*[6] (b) In interlocutory and administrative matters; (c) When the jurisdiction has been validly delegated to a single judge sitting in chambers; (d) Under express statutory provisions.

As a result of the Law Commission's recommendations the power has, moreover, been extended and made more generally available to appeal courts[7] which had

---

[19] See *Duchess of Argyll* v. *Duke of Argyll* [1967] 2 Ch. 302.

[20] But *semble* not radio or television broadcasts for which no specific provision is made.

[1] As defined in the Magistrates' Courts Act 1952, s. 56(1). See also *Halsbury* (3rd ed.) Vol. 25, para. 387.

[2] Sec. 58(4).

[3] Sec. 58(3).

[4] Sec. 58(2). See also the Magistrates' Courts Act 1952, s. 57(3) which permits the general public to be excluded during the taking of indecent evidence in domestic proceedings.

[5] See *The Powers of Appeal Courts to sit in Private and Restrictions upon Publicity in Domestic Proceedings*, Cmnd. 3149, para. 6.

[6] [1913] A.C. 417, above, p. 209. For a recent recommendation that there should be jurisdiction to hear a case in chambers when the paternity of an infant was in dispute, see *B. (L.A.)* v. *B. (C.H.)*, *The Times*, 18 February 1975 (Payne, J.).

[7] By the Domestic and Appellate Proceedings (Restriction of Publicity) Act 1968, s. 1.

hitherto, it seems, only been able to sit in private where the case could be heard in camera under an exception to the rule in *Scott* v. *Scott*.[8]

In 1959 the *Justice* committee examined the extent to which it was permissible to publish details of proceedings heard in private and discovered that there was a bewildering variety of statements purporting to represent the law.[9] At one extreme the view had been expressed that since proceedings in chambers were held in private: 'No report as to facts or parties in particular cases may be published. Any infringement of the ordinary rule . . . will continue to be a contempt of court.'[10] On the other hand, it was said in *Halsbury* that:[11]

> It is not a contempt to publish a report of or comments on proceedings which had been held in camera or in chambers, except where the reason for holding the proceedings in secret is that publicity would destroy the subject-matter of the suit, or where the court is exercising its parental jurisdiction over infants and persons of unsound mind.

This latter statement of principle is certainly more readily reconcilable with the decision of the House of Lords in *Scott* v. *Scott*,[12] where it was held that even if the High Court had had jurisdiction to hear a nullity suit in camera in the interests of public decency, the subsequent publicising of the proceedings would not have been a contempt. All that could be said with any degree of assurance, however, was that in cases involving wards of court the judge had a wide discretion to permit or forbid publicity, and that when the discretion was not explicitly exercised it would be a contempt to publish an account of the proceedings, but not an accurate summary of the *order* made.[13]

(2) THE ADMINISTRATION OF JUSTICE ACT, 1960

The Administration of Justice Act 1960 was intended to clarify the law in this area, though the extent to which it has in fact succeeded in doing so is perhaps open to doubt. By s. 12 of the Act it is provided that:

> (1) The publication of information relating to proceedings before any court sitting in private shall not of itself be contempt of court except in the following cases, that is to say
> (a) where the proceedings relate to the wardship or adoption of an infant or wholly or mainly to the guardianship, custody, maintenance or upbringing of an infant, or rights of access to an infant;
> (b) where the proceedings are brought under Part VIII of the Mental Health Act, 1959, or under any provision of that Act authorising an application or reference to be made to a Mental Health Review Tribunal or to a county court;
> (c) where the court sits in private for reasons of national security during that part of the proceedings about which the information in question is published;
> (d) where the information relates to a secret process, discovery or invention which is in issue in the proceedings;

---

[8] *Cf. Re Agricultural Industries, Ltd.* [1952] 1 All E.R. 1188, C.A.; *Re Green (a Bankrupt)* [1958] 2 All E.R. 57, C.A., and, in general, the Law Commission Report, at paras. 19–36 especially.
[9] See *Contempt of Court* (1959), pp. 16–20.
[10] Lord Hewart, C.J. in a Direction of 27 May 1932: see [1932] W.N. Misc. 185.
[11] *Laws of England* (3rd. ed.), Vol. 8, para. 15.
[12] [1913] A.C. 417.
[13] See *Re De Beaujeu* [1949] Ch. 230, 235; [1949] 1 All E.R. 439, 442 *per* Wynn-Parry, J.

(e) where the court (having power to do so) expressly prohibits the publication of all information relating to the proceedings or of information of the description which is published.

(2) Without prejudice to the foregoing subsection, the publication of the text or a summary of the whole or part of an order made by a court sitting in private shall not of itself be contempt of court except where the court (having power to do so) expressly prohibits the publication.

(3) In this section references to a court include references to a judge and to a tribunal and to any person exercising the functions of a court, a judge or a tribunal; and references to a court sitting in private include references to a court sitting in camera or in chambers.

(4) Nothing in this section shall be construed as implying that any publication is punishable as contempt of court which would not be so punishable apart from this section.

Subject to the effect of s. 12(4) of the Act to which reference is made below, the position may now be summarised as follows. In the first place, s. 12(1) makes it clear that the simple publication of information relating to proceedings which are held in camera or in chambers is not, of itself, and in all cases a contempt. This reaffirmation of the basic principle whereby publicity is prima facie lawful even in the case of proceedings conducted in private is to be welcomed. Secondly, sub-sections 12(1)(a)–(d) of the Act detail the specific instances in which the publication of such information *will*, of itself, constitute a contempt.[14] For example, s. 12(1)(c) refers to a case in which a court is sitting in private for reasons of national security, while s. 12(1)(d) covers a case where the information relates to a secret process, discovery or invention. It would seem from the observations of Lord Parker, C.J. when presiding over the trial of Nicholas Prager that when a court is sitting in camera for reasons of national security it would also be a contempt to *speculate* as to what might or might not be going on in the relevant period.[15] The same would, no doubt, be true of other cases falling within the ambit of s. 12(1)(a)–(d).

Thirdly, s. 12(1)(e) provides for cases falling outside s. 12(1)(a)–(d), where the court has a *residual* power to prohibit the publication of proceedings. Publication in such circumstances will constitute a contempt, but only where the necessary express prohibition has been made.[16] Such a power may be derived from statute—as, for example, under the Defence Contracts Act 1958, s. 4(3)[17]—or from the inherent jurisdiction recognised in *Scott* v. *Scott*[18] itself to forbid publication when it would defeat the object of the proceedings. Most instances of this inherent jurisdiction have now been catered for by the specific provisions of s. 12(1)(a)–(d), but the decision of the Court of King's Bench in the old case of

[14] Unless, it seems, an order permitting publication has been granted: *Re R (M.J.) (An Infant)* [1975] 2 All E.R. 749, below, p. 216. *Semble* that the contempt is *civil,* rather than criminal, in nature: see *Scott* v. *Scott* [1913] A.C. 417. On the distinctions between civil and criminal contempt, see above, pp. 7–19.

[15] See (1971) 121 New Law Jo. 548.

[16] Contrast the position in cases falling under s. 12(1)(a)–(d) where the prohibition operates automatically.

[17] *Cf.* also the Children and Young Persons Act 1933, s. 39(1), discussed above, p. 210. Is it a contempt under s. 12(1)(e) of the 1960 Act, as well as an offence under the 1933 Act, to publish in contravention of a direction made under s. 39(1)?

[18] [1913] A.C. 417.

Clement[19] might provide an example of a situation for which no such provision has been made. Generally, however, the position is unclear and it is regrettable that the scope of the residual power was not clarified in the 1960 Act itself.[20]

Fourthly, the wording of s. 12(1) with its reference to the 'publication of information relating to proceedings before any court' should be distinguished from that of s. 12(2) which refers to publication of the text or a summary of the whole or part of an *order* made by a court. The latter is permitted by s. 12(2)—in the sense that it is not, of itself, a contempt—unless the court expressly prohibits the publication of the order and it has the power to do so. As with the provision in s. 12(1)(e) above, the wording of the Act is such that there is no duty to comply with an order made without power until such time as it is quashed on an application for certiorari.[1] Unfortunately s. 12(2) does not detail the situations in which a court does have the power to make such an order. In *Re De Beaujeu*[2] Wynn-Parry, J. assumed *obiter* that such a power exists in wardship proceedings, but beyond this its precise scope is again unclear.

Fifthly, it should be noted that the general principle of legality established by s. 12(1) and s. 12(2) is a strictly limited one. In particular these sub-sections go no further than saying that a report of proceedings heard in private and of orders made therein *shall not of itself be contempt*, except to the extent specified. The inference is that if the report is not fair and accurate and it interferes with the due administration of justice, then a contempt may still be committed.[3] Moreover, even if the report is fair and accurate and permissible in terms of the law of contempt, it may still be unlawful for some other reason. It may, for example, constitute a libel, and there is authority for the view that in the law of libel no privilege attaches to reports of judicial proceedings heard in private.[4] Certainly the statutory defence afforded to newspapers and broadcasting authorities where defamatory matter is contained in a fair and accurate report of judicial proceedings is expressly limited to proceedings which are heard in public.[5]

Finally, reference may be made to s. 12(4) of the Act which provides that:

> Nothing in this section shall be construed as implying that any publication is punishable as contempt of court which would not be so punishable apart from this section.

The wording of this sub-section is not perhaps as clear as it might have been. Indeed it would appear to be open to two radically different interpretations. On one view it may be read as establishing that s. 12(1)–(3) contains, as it were, a complete and comprehensive code, and as saying that it is not permissible to

---

[19] (1822) 11 Price 68; 147 E.R. 404, above, p. 118.

[20] Does the power exist, for example, where persons other than the debtor are examined in private in bankruptcy proceedings as in the Poulson hearing (see the Bankruptcy Act 1914, s. 25(1) and the Bankruptcy Rules 1952, r. 8(2)), and it is known that the press has obtained details of the examination? See *Re Green* [1951] 2 All E.R. 57.

[1] For more general discussion of this point, see below, pp. 253–255.

[2] [1949] Ch. 230, 235; [1949] 1 All E.R. 439, 442.

[3] As in *Alliance Perpetual Building Society* v. *Belrum Investments, Ltd.* [1957] 1 All E.R. 635.

[4] See *Kimber* v. *Press Association* [1893] 1 Q.B. 65. See also *Scott* v. *Scott* [1913] A.C. 417, 452 *per* Lord Atkinson.

[5] See the Law of Libel Amendment Act 1888, s. 3, as amended by the Defamation Act 1952, s. 8. The defence is also worded so as not to authorise the publication of any 'blasphemous or indecent matter'.

imply that something further may constitute a contempt for which specific provision has not been made. The other possible interpretation, however, is that s. 12(4) means, rather, that the section is not to be taken as having *extended* the number of occasions on which a contempt would be committed, but is to be read subject to the existing law. On the latter interpretation the publicising of proceedings heard in private, or of orders made in such proceedings, would only be a contempt if it both fell within s. 12, and it would have been so punishable *apart from the section*, that is under the then existing law. This would mean, of course, that s. 12 would be the very reverse of a comprehensive code for there would be a constant need for reference back to the highly uncertain law as it was at the time when the Act came into force.

The former interpretation is the more convenient and seems on balance to represent the most natural reading of the sub-section. Had the second meaning been intended the draftsman would surely have omitted the words *any publication* in favour of a more specific reference to publications which would otherwise have been a contempt under the foregoing provisions of the section, that is s. 12(1)–(3). One hesitates, however, to be categorical on the point for at least one respected commentator has seemingly interpreted s. 12(4) as having removed the possibility that the Act might have extended the scope of the law of contempt in this area.[6] While it does indeed seem unlikely that s. 12 has extended the law of contempt, this would not, of course, *follow* from s. 12(4), unless the second of the two possible interpretations mooted above is taken to be correct. Recently, however, Rees, J. has held that the second interpretation is to be preferred and that regard must be had to the old law of contempt. He further held that notwithstanding s. 12(1)(a) of the 1960 Act it is open to a court to permit publication of information relating to wardship or adoption proceedings heard in private where this would advance the interests of justice and, more especially, where it would not harm any legitimate interest of the child.[7]

)

[6] *Cf.* D. G. T. Williams, 'The Administration of Justice Act 1960' [1961] Crim. L.R. 87, 100. See also Hansard, H.L. Deb. Vol. 222, col. 254, where Viscount Kilmuir, L.C. is reported as explaining the effect of the clause in terms which are susceptible to a similar interpretation.

[7] *Re R (M.J.) (An Infant)* [1975] 2 All E.R. 749.

13 Residual Categories of Contempt

1 OBSTRUCTING PERSONS OFFICIALLY CONNECTED WITH THE COURT OR ITS PROCESS[1]

(1) PROCESS SERVERS

According to *Oswald*, a contempt of court will be committed where a person so acts as to 'assault, illtreat, or threaten a process-server engaged in his duty',[2] and, no doubt, if he victimises such a person for having performed his duties. There is a wealth of old cases illustrating the point, of which the most famous is perhaps *Williams* v. *Johns*.[3] Here Lord Bathurst ordered the defendant to stand committed to the Fleet prison for contempt after he had responded to the issue of a subpoena by compelling the process server to eat it.[4] In other cases it has similarly been held to be a contempt forcibly to detain and to threaten to throw out of a window a person who had sought to serve a copy of a Chancery bill in a 'proper and respectful manner',[5] and to take a person by the throat and 'with foul epithets' to push him out of the door and down the steps.[6] It does not matter that in offering the threat or, in certain circumstances, refusing access,[7] the contemnor was frustrating process being served upon a third party, rather than upon himself.

A contempt will not be committed, however, unless the interference is really substantial and calculated to impede the service of process, or to make an equivalent obstruction such as preventing the effective execution of a writ of possession.[8] Minor obstruction will not suffice.[9] For this reason it seems most unlikely that a court would still react in the same way as in some of the old cases and hold in contempt one who, in the words of *Oswald*, uses 'insolent or indecent expressions, or oaths, or other violent or profane language on being served with any process.'[10] In one such case, a person was attached for his familiarity when,

---

[1] See, in general, *Halsbury*, Vol. 9, paras. 31–35.
[2] *Contempt of Court*, p. 85.
[3] (1773) Dick. 477; 21 E.R. 355; 1 Mer. 303n.; 35 E.R. 686.
[4] For other similar incidents, see Sir John Fox, 'The Practice in Contempt of Court Cases' (1922) 38 L.Q.R. 188, note 4; *Halsbury*, Vol. 9, para. 32.
[5] *Price* v. *Hutchinson* (1870) L.R. 9 Eq. 534.
[6] *Whitworth* v. *Duncan, The Times*, 14 January 1893, cited in Oswald, *op. cit.*, p. 85. See also *Lewis* v. *Owen* [1894] 1 Q.B. 102, and for a recent Australian example *Re Barnes* [1968] 1 N.S.W.R. 967 (N.S.W. Sup. Ct).
[7] Cf. *Danson* v. *Le Capelain and Steele* (1852) 7 Exch. 667 (prison governor); *Denison* v. *Harding* (1867) 15 W.R. 346 (keeper of a lunatic asylum).
[8] Cf. *Alliance Building Society* v. *Austen* [1951] 2 All E.R. 1068, and *The Supreme Court Practice 1973*, Vol. 1, p. 698.
[9] Cf. *Adams* v. *Hughes* (1819) 1 Brod. & Bing. 24; 129 E.R. 632.
[10] *Contempt of Court*, p. 84.

on being served with an order of the Master of the Rolls, he suggested that the judge should 'salute a certain part of his person.'[11] *Oswald* said of other cases that the language used was 'amusing, but not suitable for repetition, such is the prudery of a twentieth-century law book'.[12] He also doubted whether simple verbal abuse would constitute a contempt. The same must, *a fortiori*, be true of the present day.[13]

Liability for contempt must also clearly depend upon the process server being subsequently shown to have been acting within the scope of his powers at the time of the obstruction.[14] By way of example one may take a case in which P enters the house of D to serve civil process on a third party, X. Under the relevant substantive law P would be acting outside his powers, and so D would not commit a contempt in obstructing him, if permission to enter had not been granted, and either X was not in fact in the house, or the door of the house was broken open.[15] As in the analogous offence of obstructing a police officer in the execution of his duty,[16] D would, however, commit some other criminal offence (for example, an assault) if he used *excessive* force. Whatever may be the position in the law of contempt generally, D should not be held liable for a contempt of the present category in the absence of *mens rea*. Here the minimum requirement must be that he should know that P was a process server (or a person occupying a similar role) or that he was reckless in this regard. Preferably, it should be necessary to show an intent to obstruct him in his duties or recklessness as to whether or not he was so obstructed.

(2) RECEIVERS, LIQUIDATORS, SEQUESTRATORS ETC.

A receiver appointed by the court holds property as an officer of the court and interference with his possession will constitute a criminal contempt,[17] even though the order appointing him was improperly procured.[18] According to *Kerr:*[19]

> The rule is not confined to property actually in the hands of a receiver; for the court will not permit anyone, without its sanction and authority, to intercept or prevent payment

[11] *Witham* v. *Witham* (1669) 3 Ch. Rep. 41.

[12] See *op. cit.*, p. 84, note (o), and cases cited.

[13] *Cf. op. cit.*, p. 85, and *Weeks* v. *Whiteley* (1835) 3 Dowl. P.C. 536.

[14] For an outline of these powers, see *Halsbury* (3rd ed.), Vol. 34, para. 1205, *et seq.* The limited power to punish for contempt conferred on county courts by the County Courts Act 1959, s. 30 specifically provides for the person who, 'assaults an officer of a court *while in the execution of his duty*' (emphasis supplied). The High Court may itself punish such conduct in relation to county courts as a contempt: see *Edwards, ex p. Welsh Church Temporalities Commissioners* (1933) 49 T.L.R. 383 and, above, p. 30.

[15] See *Southam* v. *Smouth* [1964] 1 Q.B. 308; [1963] 3 All E.R. 104, C.A.; *Vaughan* v. *McKenzie* [1969] 1 Q.B. 557; [1968] 1 All E.R. 1154. See also *Re Clements and The Republic of Costa Rica v. Erlanger* (1877) 46 L.J. Ch. 375.

[16] Contrary to the Police Act 1964, s. 51.

[17] See, e.g., *Ames* v. *Trustees of the Birkenhead Docks* (1855) 20 Beav. 332; 52 E.R. 630 and cases cited below. The position will be otherwise where the receiver has not been appointed by the court, but appointed, rather, under a power contained in a debenture or trust deed.

[18] *Russell* v. *East Anglian Railway Co.* (1850) 3 Mac. & G. 104, 114; 42 E.R. 201; *Searle* v. *Choat* (1884) 25 Ch. D. 723, C.A.

[19] *The Law and Practice As To Receivers* (14th. ed., 1972), p. 146.

to the receiver of any property within the territorial jurisdiction of the court which he has been appointed to receive, although it may not be actually in his hands.

The same, or broadly similar, rules apply to liquidators appointed by the court in the winding up of a company,[20] and to sequestrators.[1]

There are clearly many ways in which a receiver's possession may be disturbed.[2] Some, such as the forcible taking of possession of property subject to the appointment,[3] are fairly obvious. Others pose problems which are not so easy to resolve. The leading case of *Helmore* v. *Smith (No. 2)*[4] illustrates the point. In this case a receiver and manager had been appointed to run a coal business in Piccadilly pending an appeal against an order dissolving the business. Helmore was a former employee who had been dismissed by the firm and who had subsequently set up in business on his own account. On leaving he had taken a list of the firm's customers with him and he later sent the customers a circular stating, in effect, that the old business had come to an end, subject to an appeal. The circular was clearly intended to solicit custom for his own business. It made no reference to the fact that the firm was still being carried on as a going concern by a manager appointed by the court in order to preserve the status quo until the matter had been finally determined. In an appeal to the Court of Appeal against an order committing him for contempt he argued, as Bowen, L.J. put it, that:[5]

> In all the reported cases of committal for interference with a receiver there has been some personal interference or an interference with the receipt of some definite, tangible thing, and that the sending out of this circular was merely such competition as the business would have been liable to experience in ordinary course; and it is contended that the business when under the management of a receiver and manager was no more entitled to protection from such fair competition than the business carried on by the original firm.

Dealing with this contention Bowen, L.J. agreed that: 'If the acts complained of merely amounted to such fair competition, the argument would be unanswerable.'[6] Both Bowen and Cotton, LL.J. did not, however, regard the circular as constituting 'fair competition'. They saw it rather as a libel on the business in that it suggested that it was in a poor financial state.[7] As such, Bowen, L.J. designated it, 'a wrongful act calculated to destroy property under the management of this Court'.[8] In the result Helmore's appeal was dismissed.

At least in the absence of a covenant by the employee not to solicit,[9] this case seems a very borderline one. The same is true of *Dixon* v. *Dixon*.[10] Here

[20] *Re Henry Pound, Son & Hutchins* (1889) 42 Ch. D. 402, C.A.; *Re Stubbs (Joshua), Ltd., Barney* v. *Stubbs (Joshua), Ltd.* [1891] 1 Ch. 475, C.A.; Companies (Winding-up) Rules 1949, S.I. 1949 No. 330, r. 78(2).

[1] *Pelham (Lord)* v. *Newcastle (Duchess)* (1713) 3 Swan. 289n.; 36 E.R. 867; *Angel* v. *Smith* (1804) 9 Ves. 335; 32 E.R. 632.

[2] See further, Oswald, *Contempt of Court*, pp. 75–76; Kerr, *op. cit.*, pp. 144–145.

[3] As in *Broad* v. *Wickham* (1831) 4 Sim. 511; 58 E.R. 191.

[4] (1886) 35 Ch. D. 449, C.A.

[5] *Ibid.*, at p. 456.

[6] *Ibid.*

[7] *Cf.* (1886) 35 Ch. D. 449, at p. 456 (Bowen, L.J.), and at p. 455 (Cotton, L.J.).

[8] *Ibid.*, at p. 457.

[9] And reliance was not placed on the fact that such a covenant might have been implied.

[10] [1904] 1 Ch. 161. Contrast *Re Gent* (1892) 40 W.R. 267.

a partnership had been dissolved by the court and a receiver and manager appointed to sell it as a going concern, when the defendant, who had been one of the partners, took an active part in establishing a rival concern within the same area to be carried on by his wife and sons. He informed some of the employees of the business that it was about to be sold, and managed to solicit three key employees to join him after giving the requisite notice. Swinfen Eady, J. regarded such conduct as an interference with the administration of justice and a contempt, saying:[11]

> In my judgment, tampering with employees and inducing them to leave a business that is being carried on under the direction of the Court with the view of taking employment at a business that is being started in opposition is an interference against which the receiver and manager is entitled to protection.

If this latter case is correctly decided then it is singularly difficult to know where the line is to be drawn. Certainly the receiver would have been prejudiced in the conduct of his affairs and in getting the best possible price for the business. But the same would be true of a case in which a large corporation opens a new supermarket near a grocer's shop which is likewise in the hands of a receiver and manager. Yet it could hardly be suggested that the corporation would commit a contempt in setting up the rival concern. In such cases it is submitted that the means adopted must be otherwise *unlawful* before there can be any question of committing a contempt. Leaving aside the possibility of contempt itself (which, of course, begs the question), there is nothing unlawful about suggesting to a man that he might like to work for another business after giving his employer proper notice.[12] *Dixon* v. *Dixon* must, it is accordingly submitted, be regarded as wrongly decided.

Finally, this aspect of contempt is as apt to produce problems in determining the mental element required to ground liability as any other. Notwithstanding the decision in *Odhams Press, Ltd,*[13] the minimum requirement should again be knowledge that a receiver has been appointed, or recklessness in this regard. Thereafter it would seem from the observations of Bowen, L.J. in *Helmore* v. *Smith*[14] that it is sufficient that the alleged contemnor intended to do something which was in fact likely to obstruct the receiver in an improper manner. It is probably not necessary that he should have intended to obstruct the receiver or, still less, that he should have intended to interfere with the administration of justice as such.

(3) SHERIFFS, BAILIFFS, THE ADMIRALTY MARSHAL AND OTHERS

It will likewise be a criminal contempt of court to assault or otherwise seek to frustrate a sheriff, his deputy, or a person occupying a similar role (such as a tipstaff) when he is carrying out a writ of execution, or of possession, or some

---

[11] [1904] 1 Ch. 161, 163.
[12] *Aliter* if a breach of contract had been induced, or some other unlawful means employed.
[13] [1957] 1 Q.B. 73; [1956] 3 All E.R. 494, above, p. 161.
[14] (1885) 35 Ch. D. 449, 457.

other order of the court. In *Lacon* v. *De Groat*[15] a writ had been issued directing a sheriff to give the plaintiff possession of a certain public house called the Duke of Wellington which was situated 'in one of the roughest parts of the East end of London'. One Woodhouse, who was acting on behalf of the defendant, refused to give up possession while the defendant himself was, it seems, active in inciting a drunken mob outside to kick and hammer on the doors. Woodhouse and the defendant were both committed for contempt, Pollock, B. saying that it was necessary to use a firm hand to repress such attempts to prevent the execution of process.

By the same token it is equally a contempt to interfere with a ship in the custody of the Marshal of the Admiralty or his deputy as by breaking arrest. Thus in *The Petrel*,[16] the ship, the *Petrel*, was under arrest when the master, mate and several others forcibly took possession and sailed her to Jersey where she was sold. When the matter was brought before Sir John Nicholl in the High Court of Admiralty he said of those involved in the breaking of arrest that:[17]

> They are charged with an offence of great enormity – a great breach of the law, and a great violation of the rights of property, a species of theft and piracy. All parties who conspired to effect this violence are guilty of contempt; it is not confined to those who actually carried off the vessel, but it included all who were privy to and assisted in the transaction.

While such incidents are hardly everyday occurrences the general principle remains. Thus in a modern case Hewson, J. fined the master of an Icelandic motor vessel which had broken arrest and sailed to Ireland.[18]

The above discussion is not intended to provide a comprehensive list of the various persons of whom it can be said that an interference with their official functions will constitute a contempt of court. Any such list would clearly be much wider. It would include persons such as High Court masters, official referees, county court registrars and, indeed, persons, such as messengers,[19] with an altogether less exalted role to play.[20] In one of the leading cases, *Re Johnson*, Bowen, L.J. expressed the principle in the following terms:[1]

> The principle is that those who have duties to discharge in a court of justice are protected by the law, and shielded on their way to the discharge of such duties, while discharging them, and on their return therefrom.

---

[15] (1893) 10 T.L.R. 24. See also *Alliance Building Society* v. *Austen* [1951] 2 All E.R. 1068; *Re Eichorn* [1961] V.R. 238 (Vict. Sup. Ct); and, in general, Oswald, *op. cit.*, pp. 77–78; *Halsbury*, Vol. 9, para. 35.

[16] (1836) 3 Hagg. 299; 166 E.R. 416.

[17] *Ibid.*, at p. 301.

[18] *The Jarlinn* [1965] 3 All E.R. 36. See also *The Selina Stanford, The Times,* 17 November 1908; *The Victor Pretol* (1898) 14 T.L.R. 244; *The Seraglio* (1885) 10 P.D. 120; *The Abodi Mendi* [1939] P. 178.

[19] *Cf. Elliot* v. *Halmarack* (1816) 1 Mer. 302; 35 E.R. 686; *Re Proud* (1841) 2 Mont. D. & G. 129.

[20] *Cf.* the County Courts Act 1959, s. 201, which defines an officer for the purposes of the Act as meaning, 'any registrar, deputy registrar or assistant registrar of that court, and any clerk, bailiff, usher or messenger in the service of that court;'.

[1] (1887) 20 Q.B.D. 68, 75.

2 INTERFERENCE WITH PERSONS UNDER THE SPECIAL PROTECTIVE JURISDICTION OF THE COURT

(1) WARDS OF COURT[2]

A contempt of court may also be committed by obstructing a court in the administration of the affairs of a person over whom it has a special protective jurisdiction. Wards of court provide the most important example both historically, and, with the current growth in the number of wardship cases,[3] at the present time.

The general position with respect to wards and contempt of court has been succinctly stated by Professor Bevan in the following terms:[4]

> When a minor is made a ward of court custody over him, in the wide meaning of that term, vests in the court, and it is therefore able to issue orders concerning various aspects of his upbringing. A parent or guardian of the ward is then subject to those orders and to general supervision by the court, just as a guardian, or any officer, appointed by it would be. Consequently, defiance of any order not only renders him liable to be deprived of powers, such as care and control, which still reside with him, but also constitutes contempt of court.

Similarly, of course, a third party, not being a parent or guardian, will equally commit a contempt if he defies the court or otherwise acts so as to frustrate its purpose. According to the leading case of *Wellesley* v. *The Duke of Beaufort*,[5] the contempt thus committed is criminal in nature,[6] or, at least, one which is accompanied by criminal incidents. So on the facts of the case it was held that a certain Mr Long Wellesley had been rightly committed to the Fleet prison for contempt after he had carried his infant daughter, who was a ward of court, from the house of the ladies in whose care she had been placed and refused thereafter to disclose her whereabouts. Because of the nature of the contempt he was not privileged from arrest by virtue of his membership of the House of Commons.[7]

In other cases the courts have likewise been called upon to treat as a contempt conduct ranging from the assistance in the removal of a ward from the jurisdiction,[8] to marrying,[9] attempting to marry,[10] or assisting in the marriage[11] of a

---

[2] See Borrie and Lowe, *The Law of Contempt* (1973), pp. 243–247; Oswald, *Contempt of Court*, pp. 80–81; *Halsbury*, Vol. 9, para. 36.

[3] *Cf.* Cross, 'Wards of Court' (1967) 83 L.Q.R. 200.

[4] *The Law Relating to Children* (1973), p. 422. See also Bromley, *Family Law* (4th. ed., 1971), p. 332 *et seq.*

[5] (1831) 2 R. & M. 639; 39 E.R. 538.

[6] This view is also supported by a series of old cases suggesting that criminal proceedings by way of indictment or information would be appropriate: see, e.g., *Pierson* (1739) Andr. 310; 95 E.R. 412; *Millet* v. *Rowse* (1802) 7 Ves. 419; 32 E.R. 169, and cases cited in the *English and Empire Digest*, Vol. 28(2), p. 926.

[7] See further, above, pp. 14–15.

[8] See, e.g., *Re J. (An Infant)* (1913) 29 T.L.R. 456.

[9] *Re H's Settlement* [1909] 2 Ch. 260; *Brandon* v. *Knight* (1752) 1 Dick. 160; 21 E.R. 230; *Cox* v. *Bennett* (1874) 31 L.T. 83.

[10] *Cf. Warter* v. *Yorke* (1815) 19 Ves. 451; 34 E.R. 584, where the attempted marriage was void.

[11] As, e.g., a parent or officiating clergyman: *cf. Long* v. *Elways* (1729) Mos. 249; 25 E.R. 378; *Hannes* v. *Waugh* (1713) 2 Eq. Cas. Abr. 754; 22 E.R. 639. See also *Re S (infants)* [1967] 1 All E.R. 202 (examination of ward by psychiatrist).

ward without obtaining the court's consent. By way of illustration of some of the difficulties which may arise one may cite the modern case of *Re Crump (An Infant)*.[12] Here a girl of eighteen had been made a ward of court at the instance of her parents and enjoined not to marry her cousin, K. She proceeded to marry the cousin, having, it seems, forged her parents' signature on a form of consent which she presented at the register office. Although the parents did not themselves wish to take any further action in the matter, the Attorney-General thought it right to move that they both be committed for contempt. This clearly placed Faulks, J. in a dilemma. As he rightly observed, 'to punish them severely would clearly fail to teach them not to commit the offence in future'. But, committal orders having been sought, 'it would therefore become known publicly that an order of the court has been deliberately flouted'. In the result the couple were committed to prison for twenty-eight days which was regarded as the shortest sentence not derisive of the authority of the court. It was hardly a good start to their married life, but criticism should, on the face of it, be directed at the initial decision to seek their committal rather than at the order eventually imposed.[13]

The cases also suggest that a contempt will be committed even though the alleged contemnor did not know that he was dealing with a ward of court, and so lacked an element of *mens rea* as to this crucial fact. Thus in *Herbert's Case*[14] H, who was an infant of eighteen and in the custody of a guardian appointed by the court, had been sent to the University of Oxford. It appears, in the words of the report, that, 'coming to town upon some occasion, he was drawn in to marry a common servant maid, older than himself, and of no fortune'. Philips, the parson who performed the ceremony, was ordered to appear before the Master of the Rolls where he sought to plead as a defence that he did not know that H was a ward of court. Sir Joseph Jekyll, M.R. dealt with the point by saying:[15]

> With regard to what is alleged by way of excuse, that the parson . . . had no notice of the infant's being a ward of the court; it is to be observed, that the commitment to the wardship to Sir Thomas Clarges was an act of the court, and in a cause then depending, of which every one at his peril is concerned to take notice, in the same manner as of a *lis pendens*. . . . If actual notice of the infant's being a ward of court were necessary, then these offences would be continually practised with impunity.

Similar conclusions were also reached in later cases involving both the marriage of a ward[16] and the removal of a ward from the jurisdiction without the consent of the court having been obtained.[17] While this dispensing with a requirement of *mens rea* appears therefore to be firmly established,[18] it is

---

[12] (1963) 107 Sol. Jo. 682.

[13] For other cases confirming that a ward may be personally committed for contempt, see *Re H's Settlement* [1909] 2 Ch. 260; *Re Leigh* (1888) 40 Ch. D. 290, 294. Nowadays the age of majority has been lowered to eighteen (see Family Law Reform Act 1969, s. 1). Marriage on attaining the age of majority would not, of course, be a contempt, for the court's jurisdiction in the matter would have ceased: see *Bolton* v. *Bolton* [1891] 3 Ch. 270.

[14] (1731) 3 P. Wms. 116; 24 E.R. 992.

[15] *Ibid.*, at pp. 117–118.

[16] *Cf. Nicholson* v. *Squire* (1809) 16 Ves. 259; 33 E.R. 983; *Re H's Settlement* [1909] 2 Ch. 260, 264.

[17] *Re J. (An Infant)* (1913) 29 T.L.R. 456, 457.

[18] It is also, of course, supported by the leading case at common law, *Odhams Press, Ltd., ex p. Att.-Gen.* [1957] 1 Q.B. 73, above, p. 161.

nevertheless hoped that the position will be re-examined in the future. There
is no sense in holding an offence to have been committed by a person who
lacks knowledge of the status of the person with whom he is dealing, and
whose interference with the protective jurisdiction of the court was no more
than a matter of bad luck.[19]

(2) OTHER CASES

It is not clear to what extent, if any, similar principles can be applied where a
guardian has been appointed to care for a child, but the child has not been made a
ward of court as such. Certainly there can hardly be any question of contempt
where the guardian has been appointed by a parental testament or deed. *Goodall
v. Harris*[20] is in point. Here one Henry Goodall had devised his real and personal
estate to his daughter and appointed a certain Charles Harris to be her guardian
during the period of her minority. Harris removed the girl from a boarding
school after the father's death and then, 'married her (she being then of the age of
nine years and three months) to his own son Francis Harris, who had no estate,
and was an apprentice to a peruke-maker'. It was sought thereafter to commit
Harris, but King. L.C. said:[1]

> The infant girl never having been under the care of the Court, nor committed by the
> Court to the custody of the defendant Harris. I do not think this an immediate
> contempt of the Court . . .; but then it is a very ill thing in the guardian to marry this
> child to his own son, and punishable by an information.[2]

Where it is the court which has appointed the guardian under the Guardianship
of Minors Act 1971,[3] it may however be possible to argue that interference with
his 'rights' over the child[4] could lead to a question of contempt[5] for children
generally are under the special protective jurisdiction of the courts.

Before the enactment of the Mental Health Act 1959 persons of unsound mind
were protected by the law of contempt in substantially the same way as infants.
Thus it was a contempt to marry such a person or to fail to produce him pursuant
to an order of the court.[6] The 1959 Act has, however, changed the general scheme
by designating certain acts in relation to persons of unsound mind criminal
offences[7] and by providing in s. 110(2) that:

> [any] act or omission in the course of [proceedings in the Court][8] which, if occurring in
> the course of proceedings in the High Court would have been a contempt of the Court,

---

[19] As, e.g., the airline pilot who has the misfortune to carry a ward of court out of the jurisdiction
without realising that he is doing so.

[20] (1729) 2 P. Wms. 561; 24 E.R. 862.

[1] *Ibid.*, at 562.

[2] *Sed quaere?*

[3] See ss. 3, 5.

[4] As to which see Eekelaar, 'What are Parental Rights?' (1973) 89 L.Q.R. 210.

[5] *Halsbury*, Vol. 9, para. 36 suggests that it is probably a contempt.

[6] See *Ash's Case* (1702) Prec. Ch. 203; 24 E.R. 99; *Re B. (An Alleged Lunatic)* [1892] 1 Ch. 459,
C.A., Oswald, *Contempt of Court*, pp. 79–80 and cases cited.

[7] See ss. 125–131 of the Act.

[8] That is, the Court of Protection in which the management of the property and affairs of mental
patients is vested.

shall be punishable by the judge in any manner in which it could have been punished by the High Court.[9]

This latter provision is clearly apt to cover the general range of contempts discussed in previous chapters—as, for example, a contempt by infringing the *sub judice* rule. It is less clear, however, that it is similarly apt to cover the residue of acts done in relation to persons of unsound mind which would have constituted a contempt before 1959 and for which no specific provision is made in the 1959 Act itself.

3 BREACH OF DUTY BY PERSONS OFFICIALLY CONNECTED WITH THE COURT OR ITS PROCESS[10]

It has already been seen that a contempt may be committed by obstructing persons officially connected with the court or its process when they are acting in the execution of their duties. Equally, however, such persons may *themselves* commit a contempt by an abuse of their position or a neglect to perform their duties. As a historical example reference may be made to an account in *Oswald* of how, in the days of assize courts, a certain High Sheriff at the Winchester Winter Assizes was fined 500 guineas by the presiding judge, 'for not being in attendance, he having gone without leave on a visit to Africa in search of a warmer climate, and notwithstanding that the Under-Sheriff was in attendance with the Sheriff's state carriage and usual retinue'. The fine was imposed because, 'it could not be left to the caprice of individuals to decide whether they would attend or not.'[11] The Sheriffs Act 1887 also contains a list of different types of misconduct on the part of a person being 'a sheriff, under-sheriff, bailiff, or officer of a sheriff' and of the penalties which may be imposed. These include letting a prisoner who is not bailable go at large,[12] and granting a warrant for the execution of a writ before actually receiving the writ.[13] It is also an offence under the 1887 Act to pretend to act as an under-sheriff, bailiff, or officer of a sheriff, or to take a fee or reward under colour or pretext of such office.[14]

Receivers and sequestrators may likewise commit a contempt as by making default in the payment of money due.[15] Similarly gaolers may incur liability to a fine under the Bankruptcy Act 1914, s. 124, on a refusal to receive a prisoner committed by the High Court sitting in bankruptcy. There is also a wealth of earlier authority indicating that judges of inferior courts may be dealt with for contempt for acting, unjustly, oppressively, or irregularly, in the execution of

---

[9] Committal is by the Lord Chancellor or a nominated judge after inquiry into the alleged act or omission: sec. 110(3).

[10] *Halsbury*, Vol. 9, paras. 39–46.

[11] *Contempt of Court*, p. 71, citing *Re Sir Alfred Tichborne, The Times,* 7 December 1892.

[12] S. 29(1)(c)—or, conversely, withholding a prisoner bailable after he has offered sufficient security: s. 29(2)(a).

[13] S. 29(2)(c).

[14] S. 29(6)—as amended by the Theft Act 1968, Sch. 3, Part I.

[15] See the Debtors Act 1869, s. 4, para. 3; *Re Gent, Gent Davis* v. *Harris* (1888) 40 Ch. D. 190; *Re Bell's Estate* (1870) L.R. 9 Eq. 172; *Re Grantham Wholesale Fruit etc. Merchants, Ltd.* [1972] 1 W.L.R. 559, and, in general, on the liabilities of receivers, see Kerr, *op. cit.,* Ch. 8.

their duty, or for disobeying writs issued by the High Court requiring them to proceed or not to proceed in matters before them.[16] Most of this jurisdiction would, however, be effectively superseded by modern statutory provisions whereby the Lord Chancellor is empowered to remove a judge of an inferior court from office for inability or misbehaviour.[17]

Solicitors, as officers of the Supreme Court, are subject, when acting in their capacity as solicitors,[18] to its inherent jurisdiction in disciplinary matters. This has been said to exist 'for the maintenance of their character and integrity.[19] They may be liable for contempt as through failure to comply with an order of the court to perform an undertaking,[20] or in respect of a wide range of breaches of discipline, including inexcusable negligence[1] and failure to act in the best interests of their clients. These are matters which are dealt with in detail in works such as Cordery on Solicitors,[2] and it is not intended to pursue them here. The Solicitors Act 1957 also contains provisions whereby it is an offence for an unqualified person to act as a solicitor,[3] or to pretend to be a solicitor or use any title implying he is qualified to act as such.[4] Again this is a matter which is dealt with in detail in Cordery.[5]

4 FORGING, ALTERING, OR ABUSING THE PROCESS OF THE COURT[6]

The forgery,[7] or alteration[8] of process may be treated as a contempt, at least if it is accompanied by an intent to defraud.[9] The same is true of the forgery of the signature of counsel[10] and of other serious abuses of process which interfere with the administration of justice. Thus in one 18th-century case it was regarded as a contempt to obtain a warrant to search certain property on the pretence that stolen goods were concealed there when the real object was to gain entry to carry out an arrest in aid of civil process.[11] A modern example is afforded by the case of

---

[16] See Halsbury, Vol. 9, para. 46; Oswald, op. cit., pp. 73–74, and cases cited.

[17] See, e.g., Courts Act 1971, s. 17(4)—(circuit judge); County Courts Act 1959, s. 8(1)—(county court judge).

[18] See Silver (Geoffrey) and Drake v. Baines [1971] 1 All E.R. 473.

[19] Cf. Sittingbourne and Sheerness Railway Co. v. Lawson (1886) 2 T.L.R. 605, 606 per Lord Esher, M.R.

[20] See, e.g., United Mining and Finance Corpn., Ltd. v. Becher [1910] 2 K.B. 296. It is unclear whether the contempt thus committed is criminal or civil. See, in general, Halsbury, Vol. 9, para. 76.

[1] See, e.g., Re A Solicitor [1972] 2 All E.R. 811.

[2] See 6th ed., 1968, pp. 158–182 especially.

[3] S. 18(1). Such conduct constitutes a contempt (s. 18(2)(a)), and may also be punished by a maximum statutory penalty of £50 and costs (s. 18(2)(c)).

[4] S. 19. This offence is punishable by a maximum fine of £50. Further offences are contained in ss. 20–21.

[5] Op. cit., Ch. 4. See also Davies v. Davies, Re Watts (1913) 29 T.L.R. 513.

[6] Halsbury, Vol. 9, para. 38.

[7] Re Hungerford & Aylmer (1663) Sanders' Ch. Orders, 317.

[8] Re Jacobs, The Times, 13 June 1874.

[9] Cf. Re Taylor [1912] A.C. 347, P.C. See, in general, Oswald, op. cit., p. 82.

[10] Fawcett v. Garford (1789) not reported, but referred to in Oswald, op. cit., at p. 62.

[11] See Anon (1758) 2 Keny. 372; 96 E.R. 1214.

Weisz, ex parte Hector MacDonald, Ltd.[12] Here W claimed to have won some £380 in a gambling transaction with a firm of bookmakers, which sum could not be recovered in a court of law because of the provisions of the Gaming Act, 1845. He nonetheless instructed a firm of solicitors to institute proceedings apparently in the belief that the threat of attendant publicity might induce the bookmaker to pay. A writ was accordingly issued and it was indorsed in very general terms as being a claim in respect of the balance due on an account stated. Solicitors acting for the bookmakers applied for particulars of the debt or claim, but these were not forthcoming. Contempt proceedings were subsequently instituted against W's solicitor and were based on the contention that the indorsement on the writ was wholly fictitious and designed to conceal from the court the true nature of W's claim. The Divisional Court accepted that this was so and delivering the judgment of the court Goddard, L.C.J. said:[13]

> This was simply a naked action for the recovery of money alleged to have been won by betting which the Gaming Act, 1845, prohibits. Such an action is, therefore, an abuse of the process of the court, but it is not necessarily a contempt to bring it. But to attempt to deceive the court by disguising the true nature of the claim is a contempt.

Consistently with this statement of principle the Divisional Court held that the solicitor who had attempted to deceive the court had committed a contempt, but the client, W, who did not know of the terms of the indorsement, had not. It was not sufficient to constitute a contempt that he knew that proceedings did not lie to recover a gaming debt and was using the process of the court for an ulterior motive.

This latter point is of some importance for it suggests that a court today is most unlikely to treat a simple abuse of the process of the court as a contempt. An additional element of deceit, or some other reason for regarding the conduct before the court as a substantial interference with the administration of justice, will be required. Abuse taking the form of a pleading or indorsement which discloses no reasonable cause of action or defence, or which is scandalous, frivolous or vexatious, can normally be dealt with simply by striking it out or amending it.[14]

A number of examples may be cited to give some indication of the range of liability. In *Re Elsam*,[15] for instance, it was held to be a contempt for an attorney to present a fabricated case to the court for the purpose of obtaining an opinion on a point of law. More recently contempts have also been held to have been committed by a party who deliberately presented falsehoods in a divorce petition;[16] by a solicitor who used the threat of contempt proceedings to extort money from a newspaper;[17] and by a barrister who was instrumental in procuring the making of an affidavit which he knew to be false and which he then read to

---

[12] [1951] 2 K.B. 611; [1951] 2 All E.R. 408.
[13] *Ibid.*, at p. 617.
[14] See R.S.C. Ord. 18, r. 19 comprehensively annotated in *The Supreme Court Practice 1973*, Vol. 1, pp. 298–307.
[15] (1824) 3 L.J. O.S. K.B. 75.
[16] *Apted* v. *Apted and Bliss* [1930] P. 246.
[17] *Newton* (1903) 19 T.L.R. 627.

the court.[18] Equally it is a contempt to seek to pass oneself off as a creditor in bankruptcy proceedings,[19] or as a creditor or a contributory in the winding up of a company.[20] It has also been suggested that it is a contempt to use the court's process as a vehicle for disseminating a libel as by circulating copies of a statement of claim containing statements which are defamatory.[1]

5   FURTHER POSSIBLE CASES OF CONTEMPT

(1)   DIVULGING THE CONFIDENCES OF THE JURY ROOM

Although a juror is not required to swear on oath that he will keep the deliberations of the jury secret, it would generally be accepted that it would be improper for him to divulge them, or for a third party to seek to persuade him to do so. In *Ellis* v. *Deheer*[2] Bankes, L.J. was prepared to envisage that something more than impropriety might be involved for he said:[3]

> I may say that I saw the other day with astonishment and disgust the publication in a newspaper of a statement by the foreman of the jury in an important criminal trial as to what took place in the jury room after the jury had retired. I do not think it necessary to express any opinion as to whether such a publication amounts to a contempt of Court, but I feel confident that anyone who read that statement will realize the importance of maintaining the rule.[4]

Although this rather tentative suggestion does not appear to have been followed up in a subsequent English case,[5] the view that such a publication would constitute a contempt is certainly quite tenable. The maintenance of secrecy concerning deliberations in the jury room is viewed as apt to promote the due administration of justice. Hence the publicising of such deliberations may be regarded as satisfying the broad test of liability for contempt.[6]

(2)   PREVENTING ACCESS BY THE PUBLIC TO COURTS OF LAW

The general rule applicable to English and Commonwealth courts alike is that justice must be administered in open court with the press and the public entitled

---

[18] *Linwood* v. *Andrews and Moore* (1888) 58 L.T. 612. See also above, p. 55.

[19] *Cf.* Bankruptcy Act 1914, s. 14(4).

[20] *Cf.* Companies Act 1948, s. 235(7).

[1] *Cf. Gaskell and Chambers, Ltd.* v. *Hudson, Dodsworth & Co.* [1936] 2 K.B. 595, 603–604 *per* Goddard, J. For the publication of pleadings generally, see above, p. 144.

[2] [1922] 2 K.B. 113.

[3] *Ibid.*, at p. 118.

[4] Warrington, L.J. expressed his concurrence with the view that this would be a 'grave impropriety' (*ibid.*, at p. 119) while Atkin, L.J. preferred not to express an opinion on whether it would be a contempt: *ibid.*, at p. 121.

[5] The statements of Bankes and Warrington, LL.J. were cited in *Thompson* [1962] 1 All E.R. 65, 66–67, but the case does not take one any further. For an earlier and similarly inconclusive case, see *Armstrong* [1922] 2 K.B. 555, 568–569 *per* Lord Hewart, C.J. For discussion of an unreported Australian case, *Ex p. Hartstein* (1971), see (1972) 46 A.L.J. 369. See also *Dyson* [1972] 1 O.R. 744 (Ontario High Court).

[6] See Enid Campbell (1962) 36 A.L.J. 119, at pp. 124–125 especially, and Andrews (1962) 25 M.L.R. 345. See also Devlin, *Trial By Jury* (1956), at pp. 46–48, doubting whether disclosure is a contempt.

to be present.[7] In the Australian case of *Ex parte Tubman; Re Lucas*[8] it was argued that as a corollary of this rule a contempt will be committed if members of the public are denied access to the courts. Here some one hundred persons were to appear before petty sessional courts in Sydney on charges arising out of anti-Vietnam war demonstrations, and a large crowd had gathered outside. Lucas, a senior police officer, was directed by the Chief Stipendiary Magistrate to take such measures as appeared appropriate to prevent disorderly conduct and to facilitate the business of the courts. Acting on this instruction he cleared the vestibule of the court telling those present to wait outside. The magistrate hearing the 'demonstration' cases later directed persons without seats to leave the court. Eventually one half of the public seating accommodation was occupied by members of the general public, the remaining half being taken up by police who had been concerned in the arrests.

A subsequent application to commit Lucas and another police officer for contempt was dismissed on the ground that, having regard to the reasonable anticipation of all concerned and the statutory and inherent powers vested in magistrates, no unauthorised exclusion of the public from the court or its precincts had been established. The Court of Appeal for the Supreme Court of New South Wales was prepared to envisage, however, that in appropriate circumstances a contempt might be committed by an improper exclusion of the public. As Asprey, J.A. put it:[9]

> I have no doubt that, when the proceedings of a court are to be administered as a forum open to the public, any person who, without lawful authority or justification, prevents or attempts to prevent not only parties, their legal representatives or witnesses but also members of the public who are desirous of being present at those proceedings from entering the court or its precincts could be adjudged guilty of contempt of court.

While this would appear to be correct in principle, it would no doubt be extremely difficult in practice to show that anyone concerned with the maintenance of order had acted without the necessary lawful authority or justification.

(3) SERVICE OF PROCESS IN THE PRECINCTS OF THE COURT

In the 18th-century case of *Cole* v. *Hawkins*[10] it was held to be a contempt to serve process in the precincts of the court upon a person who was a party to proceedings. This case must, however, be regarded as being of doubtful authority in view of the subsequent decision of the King's Bench Division in *Jones; ex parte McVittie*.[11] Here one Eric McVittie had shown himself to be singularly adept at avoiding attempts to execute a judgment debt against him. In all he had disobeyed a bankruptcy notice, ignored an order for the payment of the debt by instalments, and evaded attempts to serve some four or more judgment sum-

---

[7] See *Scott* v. *Scott* [1913] A.C. 417 and, in general, above, p. 209. For a recent discussion of what constitutes an 'open court' for the purposes of the Magistrates' Courts Act 1952, s. 98(4), see *Denbigh Justices, ex p. Williams and Evans* [1974] 2 All E.R. 1052.

[8] [1970] 3 N.S.W.R. 41 (N.S.W. Sup. Ct).

[9] *Ibid.*, at p. 51.

[10] (1738) Andrews 275; 95 E.R. 396.

[11] [1931] 1 K.B. 664.

monses. Eventually it became known that he would be in the Manchester Assize Court on a certain day when he would be involved in a case as a plaintiff. Jones, the solicitor who had acted for the plaintiff in the original action, accordingly went to the Assize Court and served a judgment summons on him while he was waiting in the corridor outside the court for the case to come on for trial. McVittie responded by seeking a writ of attachment against Jones and in the circumstances of the case it is hardly surprising that the application was dismissed with costs. MacKinnon, J. regarded the application as being 'impudent' and 'farcical' and thought that the supposed rule was entirely obsolete, dating as it did from the time when arrest was freely used as an aid to civil process.[12] Lord Hewart, C.J. was perhaps less categorical on this point and was prepared to envisage that there might be circumstances in which service of process within the precincts of the court constituted a contempt.[13] This does, however, seem most unlikely.[14]

(4) DISCLOSING THE IDENTITY OF WITNESSES

A further instance of contempt arose from the recent trial for blackmail of Janie Jones in April 1974. As is common in such cases two of the chief prosecution witnesses who, it was claimed, were being blackmailed by Miss Jones on account of their unusual sexual proclivities, were referred to throughout the proceedings as Mr Y and Mr Z. After listening to submissions Judge King-Hamilton Q.C., the presiding judge, had ruled 'that it would not be right for the full names to be given and for this reason I adhere to the decision [taken by the examining magistrates] that they, the witnesses, should be referred to by letters'. This attempt to conceal their identity was frustrated when Paul Foot published an article in the *Socialist Worker* with the names and addresses of the persons said to be Mr Y and Mr Z. In resultant contempt proceedings the Divisional Court held that the offence had been established on the grounds that the publication was (i) an affront to the authority of the court, and (ii) calculated to interfere with the due course of justice 'by destroying the confidence of witnesses in potential future blackmail proceedings'.[15] Both Mr Foot and the company publishing the paper were fined £250.

Although there is force in the view that the administration of justice is as much prejudiced by such disclosures as by the victimisation of witnesses after the trial,[16] it would nonetheless seem preferable to enact a specific statutory provision to cover the point.[17] Meanwhile it would seem that liability depends upon establishing the following points. First the judge must have made an order

[12] *Cf. ibid.*, at p. 671.

[13] *Cf. ibid.*, at p. 670.

[14] See also *Ex p. Brantschen, The Times*, 7 December 1970 cited by Borrie and Lowe, *op. cit.*, p. 225; *Re Tole, ex p. Tole* (1933) 50 W.N. (N.S.W.) 216 (N.S.W. Sup. Ct). It is clear that the service is in any event *valid: Poole* v. *Gould* (1856) 25 L.J. (Ex.) 250. It has been held by the Committee for Privileges of the House of Commons that it is a contempt of the House to serve a copy of a writ on a member within the precincts of the House when parliament is sitting: see *The Times*, 23 February, 1973.

[15] *Socialist Worker Printers and Publishers Ltd., ex p. Att.-Gen.* [1975] 1 All E.R. 142, 151 *per* Lord Widgery, C.J.

[16] *Att.-Gen.* v. *Butterworth* [1962] 3 All E.R. 326, above, p. 199 was relied on heavily by both the Attorney-General and the Divisional Court.

[17] The Phillimore Committee so recommends: para. 141, note 72.

against disclosure. A simple request would probably not suffice,[18] but it is not apparently necessary that the order should be explicitly directed to non-disclosure outside the confines of the court. Indeed the order in the instant case was clearly not so directed, possibly because the judge considered that he had no jurisdiction to make such an order. Secondly, there must *in fact* have been jurisdiction to make the order in question.[19] Such jurisdiction was held to exist in the present case, but Lord Widgery, C.J. doubted, *obiter*, whether there was likewise jurisdiction to prohibit publication of the name of a complainant in (say) a case of rape.[20] Thirdly, there must have been a disclosure in breach of the order. Here disclosure through the press or television would clearly suffice. Whether a more limited disclosure, as to the employer or wife of the witness, would equally suffice is unclear. Certainly it might be as damaging to the witness as widespread publicity.[1] Finally, it is submitted that the person making the disclosure must have known of the order or have been reckless as to its existence. It is unthinkable that an ordinary private individual who happened to recognise a witness should be held liable in the absence of such knowledge. A journalist might, however, be under a duty to ascertain that no such order had been made.

[18] Thus Lord Widgery, C.J. said of such a request or invitation that 'it may very well be that it has no legal effect at all.': *ibid.*, at p. 145. The statement is less categorical than might have been expected.

[19] *Cf.* [1971] 1 All E.R. 142, 149. Yet the general rule, discussed further below, p. 253, is probably that there is a duty to obey an order made without jurisdiction until such time as it is quashed by an application for certiorari.

[20] *Ibid.*, at p. 151. Would it be a contempt, as well as a statutory offence, to disclose the identity of a child or young person contrary to the provisions of the Children and Young Persons Act 1933, s. 49(1) and s. 39(1)? The point is important because the penalty for contempt is at large. The 1933 Act is discussed above, p. 210.

[1] *Cf.* Professor J. C. Smith in [1974] Crim. L.R. 712.

14   Civil Contempt of Court

The general nature of civil contempt of court or, as it is sometimes termed, contempt in procedure, and the methods available for dealing with it, have both been outlined in earlier chapters, as have the main features which distinguish civil contempt of court from criminal contempt of court.[1] In this final chapter it is proposed to consider this aspect of the law of contempt in more detail. Since the law has long treated disobedience of an order requiring payment of a sum of money differently from disobedience of other orders, the chapter as a whole has been divided into two main parts reflecting this division.

1   DISOBEDIENCE OF AN ORDER OTHER THAN AN ORDER FOR THE PAYMENT OF A SUM OF MONEY

(1) EXAMPLES OF CONTEMPT

(i) *Disobedience of judgments requiring an act to be done*

R.S.C. Ord. 45, r. 5(1) contains the general provision whereby sanctions for civil contempt may be directed against a person required by a judgment or order of the High Court to do an act within a specified time, who 'refuses or neglects to do it within that time or, as the case may be, within that time as extended or abridged'. There are numerous examples of such judgments or orders and it is not proposed to attempt to provide a comprehensive list here. A person may, for example, fail to comply with an order to answer interrogatories or for the discovery or production of documents.[2] It is here that the coercive power of the law of contempt is especially important, notably as an aid in bankruptcy proceedings,[3] and in inquiries into the affairs of companies[4] and charities.[5] Alternatively, there

---

[1] See above, Ch. 2, pp. 7–19.

[2] See, e.g., *Price* v. *Price* (1879) 48 L.J. Ch. 215; *Thomas* v. *Palin* (1882) 21 Ch. D. 360; *Eccles & Co.* v. *Louisville and Nashville Rail Road Co.* [1912] 1 K.B. 135, C.A.; *Re Bramblevale* [1970] Ch. 128; [1969] 3 All E.R. 1062. Separate provision is made for failure to comply with an order for discovery or inspection of documents in Ord. 24, r. 16(2)–(4) and for failure to comply with an order for interrogatories in Ord. 26, r. 6(2)–(4). But the situation is covered by the general provision of Ord. 45, r. 5 and the Phillimore Committee report suggests (para. 180) that the separate provisions might be revoked. See further *Halsbury*, Vol. 9, para. 68.

[3] See Bankruptcy Act 1914, ss. 22, 48, and the Bankruptcy Rules 1952, r. 83 and, in general, Oswald, *Contempt of Court*, pp. 105–106; *Halsbury*, Vol. 9, para. 72; *Williams on Bankruptcy* (18th ed., 1968), pp. 120–121, 415–416, and p. 640.

[4] See, e.g., Companies Act 1948, s. 167; *Re Pergamon Press, Ltd.* [1971] Ch. 388, and, in general, *Palmer's Company Law* (21st. ed. 1968), Ch. 69, p. 684 especially; *Halsbury*, Vol. 9, para. 73.

[5] See *Halsbury*, Vol. 9, para. 74; Charities Act 1960, ss. 6(3), 7(1), 41; *Tudor on Charities* (6th ed. 1967), pp. 571–575, 628–629.

may be a failure to comply with an order of prohibition, certiorari, or mandamus[6] as by a local authority which refuses to obey an order requiring the payment of a sum of money to a central fund,[7] or the implementation of a statutory provision. Thus it was that in February 1973 Clydebank Town Council was fined £5,000 at the Court of Session in Edinburgh for failure to obey a court order requiring it to prepare a scheme for rent increases in accordance with the provisions of the Housing Finance Act 1972.[8] By the same token a failure to comply with a writ of habeas corpus directing the delivery up of a person who has been unlawfully detained will also constitute a contempt,[9] as will disobedience of a custody order requiring the handing over of a child,[10] or of an order directing the specific performance of a contract,[11] or the delivery up of goods.[12] Other 19th century cases have concerned alleged contempt through disobedience of orders requiring money to be reinvested;[13] copyholds to be surrendered;[14] letters patent to be delivered up for cancellation;[15] an inventory to be delivered;[16] and negotiable securities to be delivered up or deposited.[17] Equally it may be a contempt to fail to comply with an order requiring money to be paid into court as security.[18]

One general point must be emphasised with respect to such positive or mandatory orders. This is that the power to commit for contempt will only be used in an extreme case and where it is necessary to make the order effective. In the vast majority of cases enforcement will be through an appropriate writ, such as a writ of delivery for goods, or of possession for land,[19] and it is, of course, a criminal contempt to obstruct or impede the execution of such a writ.[20] Moreover the Judicature Act 1925, s. 47 empowers the High Court to order, inter alia, that a conveyance, contract or other document be executed by a person nominated by the court itself in place of the party who has neglected or refused to comply. In

---

[6] See, e.g., *Mungean* v. *Wheatley* (1851) 6 Exch. 88; *R* v. *Leicester Guardians* (1899) 81 L.T. 559; *R.* v. *Worcester Corporation* (1903) 98 J.P. 130.

[7] As in *R.* v. *Poplar Borough Council (No. 2)* [1922] 1 K.B. 95, C.A.

[8] See *The Times*, 14 February 1973. Individual councillors at Clay Cross in Derbyshire were surcharged by district auditors on their failure to comply with the Act: see *Asher* v. *Lacey* [1973] 3 All E.R. 1008. See also *Asher* v. *Secretary of State for the Environment* [1974] 2 All E.R. 156, C.A.

[9] *Thompson, R.* v. *Woodward* (1889) 5 T.L.R. 565, 601; *Rowe* (1894) 11 T.L.R. 29. This is classified in *The Supreme Court Practice 1973*, Vol. 1, p. 764 as a *criminal* contempt.

[10] *Stark* v. *Stark and Hitchins* [1910] P. 190, 192, C.A. See also *B (B.P.M.)* v. *B (M.M.)* [1969] P. 103.

[11] *C.H. Giles & Co., Ltd.* v. *Morris* [1972] 1 All E.R. 960.

[12] *Bettinson* v. *Bettinson* [1965] Ch. 465; [1965] 1 All E.R. 102. For an unusual example, see *The Times*, 1 March 1968 (refusal to hand over a cat).

[13] *Re Newberry* (1835) 4 Ad. & El. 100; 111 E.R. 725. See also *Midgley* v. *Midgley* [1929] 3 W.W.R. 121.

[14] *Vaughan* v. *Dix* (1896) 40 Sol. Jo. 728; subsequent proceedings: *ibid.*, p. 846.

[15] *Newton* (1845) 5 L.T.O.S. 261; *Steiner* (1852) 18 L.T.O.S. 267.

[16] *Edwards* v. *Martyn* (1850) 2 Rob. Eccl. 285; 163 E.R. 1320.

[17] *Brucklebusch* v. *Cousins* (1888) 5 T.L.R. 137; *Harvey* v. *Morris (No. 2)* (1874) 23 W.R. 40.

[18] *Jones* v. *Jones* [1912] P. 295; *De La Pole (Lady)* v. *Dick* (1885) 29 Ch. D. 351 and cases cited in English and Empire Digest, Vol. 16, paras. 462–470.

[19] See *Halsbury*, Vol. 9, para. 67. The procedure in the rare case in which committal or sequestration is considered necessary is set out in *The Supreme Court Practice 1973* at p. 679 (land), and p. 682 (goods).

[20] *Cf.* above, p. 219.

Danchevsky v. *Danchevsky*[1] the Court of Appeal stressed that this power should always be employed in preference to coercion through committal.[2]

A somewhat more general power is to be found in R.S.C. Ord. 45 r. 8 which states that:

> If an order of mandamus, a mandatory order, an injunction or a judgment or order for the specific performance of a contract is not complied with, then, without prejudice to its powers under section 47 of the Act and its powers to punish the disobedient party for contempt, the Court may direct that the act required to be done may, so far as practicable, be done by the party by whom the order or judgment was obtained or some other person appointed by the Court, at the cost of the disobedient party, and upon the act being done the expenses incurred may be ascertained in such manner as the Court may direct and execution may issue against the disobedient party for the amount so ascertained and for costs.

As the wording of this rule itself makes clear, the ability to order that the act be done by an appointed person does not derogate from the power of the court to punish the disobedient party for contempt. It does, however, render the contempt power that much less essential than would otherwise have been the case.

(ii) *Disobedience of judgments prohibiting the doing of an act*

Just as a contempt may be committed by failing to comply with the terms of an order requiring an act to be done, so also may it be committed where a person disobeys a judgment or order requiring him to desist or abstain from doing an act.[3] Again it is not proposed to attempt to furnish an exhaustive list of the types of prohibitory or negative injunctions breach of which may constitute a contempt. Recent examples of contempt applications which have followed upon alleged breaches have, however, included injunctions restraining a man from molesting his former wife;[4] a father from communicating with his child;[5] a ward of court from associating with a particular man;[6] a landlord from harassing his tenants;[7] the obstruction of a right of way;[8] the causing of a nuisance by noise;[9] the remaining on land belonging to Warwick Corporation and the giving of a circus performance there,[10] together with several examples from the field of industrial relations which will be examined in more detail below.[11] Equally it

---

[1] [1974] 3 All E.R. 934, C.A.

[2] This case also decided that a county court possesses the same power under the County Courts Act 1959, s. 74.

[3] See R.S.C. Ord. 45, r. 5(1)(b).

[4] *Vaughan* v. *Vaughan* [1973] 3 All E.R. 449, C.A.

[5] *Re An Infant, The Times,* 13 January 1954.

[6] *Re Crump (An Infant)* (1963) 107 Sol. Jo. 682, above, p. 223.

[7] *Jennison* v. *Baker* [1972] 2 Q.B. 52; [1972] 1 All E.R. 997.

[8] *Knight* v. *Clifton* [1971] Ch. 700; [1971] 2 All E.R. 378. See also *McIlraith* v. *Grady* [1967] 3 All E.R. 625.

[9] *Worthington* v. *Ad Lib Club, Ltd.* [1965] Ch. 236; [1964] 3 All E.R. 674.

[10] *Warwick Corporation* v. *Russell* [1964] 2 All E.R. 337.

[11] See below, pp. 236–242.

would be a contempt to flout an injunction enjoining the publication of a libel or of matter which would have constituted a contempt of court.[12]

An injunction may also be granted in aid of the criminal law where the penalties are so low as to render effective enforcement of the law otherwise impossible. The case of *Attorney-General* v. *Harris*[13] provides a leading example. Here the several defendants had habitually put up flower stalls near the entrance to the Southern Cemetery in Manchester and in so doing had partially obstructed the footpath. The business was clearly sufficiently successful to enable it to absorb the maximum penalty of 40 shillings provided by the Manchester Police Regulation Act 1844. Indeed the first defendant, Robert Harris, had been convicted and fined in respect of breaches of the Act on some 142 occasions, while his wife, Audrey, had registered some 95 convictions. This did not, however, deter them from continuing to ply their trade. Acceding to the Attorney-General's application for an injunction to restrain the defendants from continuing to flout the law, Sellers, L.J. said:[14]

> It cannot, in my opinion, be anything other than a public detriment for the law to be defied, week by week, and the offender to find it profitable to pay the fine and continue to flout the law. The matter becomes no more favourable when it is shown that by so defying the law the offender is reaping an advantage over his competitors who are complying with it.[15]

The decision to grant the injunction meant, of course, that continued recalcitrance could be met thereafter by theoretically unlimited terms of imprisonment for contempt which was clearly a much more effective deterrent.

It may be argued that ideally parliament should increase the statutory penalty in such a case, and that circumventing the limited fine by resorting to the injunction is inherently objectionable. Yet it is doubtful whether this is an entirely realistic view given the current pressures on parliamentary time. In any event there are some circumstances in which immediate compliance would be clearly essential and where injunctive relief is particularly appropriate to secure this end.[16]

(iii) *Breach of undertakings*

It frequently happens that the defendant undertakes to comply with the terms of the order or injunction which is sought with the result that the court finds it unnecessary to enjoin him to do that which he is in any event seemingly willing to do. If, however, there is a subsequent failure to comply with the undertaking on the faith on which the court considered it unnecessary to make a formal order (or

---

[12] Committal for civil contempt would accordingly have been the ultimate sanction in *Att.-Gen.* v. *Times Newspapers, Ltd.* [1974] A.C. 273 in the unlikely event of the order enjoining publication having been disobeyed.

[13] [1961] 1 Q.B. 74; [1960] 3 All E.R. 207.

[14] *Ibid.*, at p. 86.

[15] See also *Att.-Gen.* v. *Sharp* [1931] 1 Ch. 121.

[16] As in *Att.-Gen.* v. *Chaudry* [1971] 3 All E.R. 938 (carrying on a hotel without adequate fire escapes, maximum statutory penalty £20 plus £5 for each day during which the offence continues). See also *Att.-Gen.* v. *Melville Construction Co., Ltd.* (1968) 67 L.G.R. 309 (proposed cutting down of trees subject to a preservation order).

the opposing party to press for it) the consequences will nonetheless be the same
as on a breach of an injunction. The position in this respect was clearly explained
by Brightman, J. in *Biba, Ltd* v. *Stratford Investments, Ltd* in the following
terms:[17]

> It is a common practice for a plaintiff in these sort of proceedings to accept an
> undertaking offered by a defendant as a substitute for the imposition of an injunction. I
> think that it would be a pity to disturb that practice by giving a lesser quality to an
> undertaking than to an injunction.[18]

Again there is no lack of modern authority to illustrate the point. Thus in recent
years contempt applications have followed upon alleged breaches of undertakings not to infringe patent rights[19] and registered trade marks,[20] and not to
enforce or give effect to restrictions in an agreement which had been found by the
Restrictive Practices Court to be contrary to the public interest.[1] Several of the
cases in point are of assistance in resolving the problems which arise where it is a
corporate body which is allegedly in breach of an order or undertaking, and they
will be examined in more detail below.[2]

(iv) *Contempt in labour disputes*[3]

The granting of injunctions in cases involving labour disputes, and the imposition of fines and of committal orders for contempt on breach thereof, is by no
means a modern phenomenon either in this country or, still less, on the North
American continent.[4] Such cases have, however, come to the forefront in this
country in recent years with the opposition of the trade union movement to the
Industrial Relations Act 1971 and to the National Industrial Relations Court.
This is a convenient point at which to outline the facts of some of the leading
cases, which retain their general interest in spite of the repeal of the Act and the
abolition of the court.

(a) *The Heatons Transport Case:*[5] The origins of the *Heatons Transport* case are
to be found in the long-standing fear of insecurity of employment in the docks
and, in particular, in the modern practice of containerisation. Because of this

---

[17] [1972] 3 All E.R. 1041, 1045.

[18] See also *Halsbury*, Vol. 9, para. 75; *The Supreme Court Practice 1973*, Vol. 1, p. 685; Oswald,
Contempt of Court, p. 108. For breach of undertakings by solicitors, see above, p. 226, and, in general
Cordery on Solicitors, (6th. ed., 1968), p. 164 *et seq.*, Borrie and Lowe, *The Law of Contempt* (1973),
p. 335 *et seq; Halsbury*, Vol. 9, para. 76.

[19] *Cf. Hoffman La Roche & Co., Att.-Gen.* v. *Sieczko* [1968] R.P.C. 460, 466, C.A.

[20] *Biba, Ltd.* v. *Stratford Investments, Ltd.* [1972] 3 All E.R. 1041. See also *Steiner Products, Ltd.* v.
Willy Steiner, Ltd. [1966] 2 All E.R. 387; *Ronson Products, Ltd.* v. *Ronson Furniture, Ltd.* [1966] 2 All
E.R. 381.

[1] *Re Garage Equipment Associations Agreement* (1964) L.R. 4 R.P. 491. See also *Re Galvanized
Tank Manufacturers' Association's Agreement* (1965) L.R. 5 R.P. 315; *Re The Agreement of the
Mileage Conference Group of the Tyre Manufacturers' Conference, Ltd.* [1966] 2 All E.R. 849.

[2] On pp. 250–252.

[3] For a recent survey, see Davies and Anderman, 'Injunction Procedure in Labour Disputes'
(1973) 2 Industrial Law Jo. 213; (1974) 3 Industrial Law Jo. 30.

[4] See, e.g., *U.S.* v. *United Mine Workers of America*, 330 U.S. 258 (1947).

[5] *Heatons Transport (St. Helens), Ltd.* v. *Transport and General Workers' Union* [1973] A.C. 15;
[1972] I.C.R. 308; [1972] 3 All E.R. 101.

practice, work which had once been the traditional preserve of the dock-worker—notably the storage and the loading and unloading of cargo—has been replaced by the 'stuffing' and 'stripping' of containers, which is performed in depots outside the area of the docks and without using dock labour.[6] With a view to protecting the interests of dockers and road haulage drivers alike, a committee of shop stewards at Liverpool, who were all members of the TGWU,[7] drew up an agreement which was accepted by a number of road haulage companies in the area, but rejected by some others including Heatons Transport. Heatons were blacked, but responded by obtaining an interim order from the National Industrial Relations Court enjoining the TGWU 'to refrain both themselves and by their officers, servants and agents from continuing to take such action and any other action of a like nature in relation to the complainants'.

The shop stewards were informed of the terms of the order by the national and local officers of the union, but the blacking continued. On a subsequent complaint to the National Industrial Relations Court the union was fined £5,000 for contempt, but the fine was suspended for a period of fourteen days to enable the union to appear before the court and to explain its conduct. This it declined to do and the fine was thereafter ordered to be paid. The committee was subsequently contacted by the regional secretary of the union at the instance of the general secretary repeating 'the advice previously conveyed' that the industrial action should stop. The advice was, however, ignored and the blacking continued. Thereupon a further and substantial fine of £50,000 was imposed on the union and threats that the totality of its assets might be sequestered pending compliance were issued. Having decided to depart from its earlier policy of not appearing before the National Industrial Relations Court, the TGWU then sought a review of the contempt orders. The change of mind was welcomed by the court which proclaimed that: 'A new chapter has begun. Justice, the public interest and the promotion of good industrial relations all point to the desirability of making a fresh start.'[8] The orders were affirmed after full argument, but in the circumstances it was not thought appropriate to make yet further orders in respect of the blacking which, it was alleged, was still continuing. Sir John Donaldson, P. concluded the judgment of the court by saying:[9]

> Now that we have reconsidered and affirmed our decisions after the fullest argument on behalf of the union, it is for the union to obey. The task of the leadership will not be easy, for the fog of argument has hidden the vital difference between objecting to a law and disobeying it. But no further time must be lost. We shall adjourn the matter for 21 days and shall take no further action if by the end of that period the union is in compliance with the law. If it is not, we shall be forced again to assert our authority and in unmistakable manner. It is our hope and our belief that that situation will not arise.

The TGWU appealed thereafter to the Court of Appeal, which allowed the appeal on the ground that the shop stewards, as agents of the union, were acting outside the scope of their authority in continuing to black the complainants

[6] For a brief, but graphic, description, see the judgment of Lord Denning in the Court of Appeal: [1973] A.C. 15, 39–40; [1972] 2 All E.R. 1214, 1238–1239.

[7] The committee was 'unofficial' in the sense that no provision was made for it in the union rules; but it operated from the union's headquarters: see [1973] A.C. 15, 105.

[8] [1973] A.C. 15, 28; [1972] I.C.R. 308, 321 (N.I.R.C.).

[9] [1973] A.C. 15, 33; [1972] I.C.R. 308, 326.

notwithstanding the advice to the contrary.[10] On a subsequent appeal to the House of Lords the orders of the National Industrial Relations Court were then restored following a single unanimous judgment delivered by Lord Wilberforce.[11]

In essence the view of the House of Lords was that the shop stewards had a general implied authority as agents of the union to take industrial action in support of its policy on containerisation, and such authority could only have been withdrawn by a communication which the agent would understand as forbidding him to do that which he had previously been authorised to do. In the circumstances of the case the House agreed with the National Industrial Relations Court that no such communication had been made.[12] Since the shop stewards' disobedience of the order had been neither 'casual nor accidental and unintentional',[13] the union was to be regarded as liable in respect of it.

(b) *The Chobham Farm and Midland Cold Storage Cases.*[14] At the same time as the *Heatons' Transport* case was before the courts in the summer of 1972 so also were the *Chobham Farm* and the *Midland Cold Storage* cases. The scene had shifted from Liverpool to London, but containerisation was again the underlying issue. In the first of the cases, *Churchman* v. *Joint Shop Stewards' Committee of the Workers of the Port of London,*[15] employees at the Chobham Farm container depot in East London sought and were granted interim injunctions restraining the defendant committee and three of its members, Bernard Steer, Vic Turner and Alan Williams, from picketing the depot and otherwise indulging in unfair industrial practices contrary to s. 96 of the Industrial Relations Act 1971. The object of the picketing was to replace the complainants and their fellow employees with registered dock labour, and it was accompanied by threats to black any firm on a national basis if it crossed the picket lines. The National Industrial Relations Court directed that all breaches of its order should be reported to it,[16] and on June 13, 1972 notice of an intention to report alleged breaches was duly given. The respondents, who had at no time appeared before the court, were notified by letter and on the following day (June 14) the court sat to hear the report. It was evidently satisfied that breaches of the order had occurred and Steer, Turner and Williams were duly committed to prison for contempt. The court acted of its own motion and not at the request of the complainants.[17] It directed, however, that warrants for the arrest and detention of the men were not to issue until Friday, June 16, at 2 pm to give them time to make representations to the court, or to appeal to the Court of Appeal. Failing such action they were to be imprisoned over the weekend and brought before the court on the following Monday.

[10] [1973] A.C. 15, 37; [1972] I.C.R. 308, 330; [1972] 2 All E.R. 1214, 1237.

[11] [1973] A.C. 15, 78; [1972] I.C.R. 308, 371; [1972] 3 All E.R. 101.

[12] *Cf.* [1973] A.C. 15, 111; [1972] I.C.R. 308, 404.

[13] See further, below, pp. 244–247.

[14] See P. L. Davies (1973) 36 M.L.R. 84.

[15] See *The Times*, 15 June 1972 (N.I.R.C.); [1972] I.C.R. 222; [1972] 3 All E.R. 603, C.A. For further description of the background to the case, see the *Sunday Times*, 18 June 1972, p. 17.

[16] See further, below, p. 265.

[17] See further, below, p. 265.

The men did not themselves make any move, but the Official Solicitor, whose role it is to attend to the interests of all persons committed to prison for contempt[18] and who had received the papers from the secretary to the court, appealed to the Court of Appeal on their behalf.[19] This action was taken against a background of mounting industrial unrest fanned by the considerable publicity which was inevitably being given to the case. In a brief, but important, judgment the Court of Appeal allowed the Official Solicitor's appeal on the ground that the evidence before the National Industrial Relations Court was insufficient to support the committal order. In particular the court was not satisfied that the men had received the necessary notice of the terms of the order or that they were in breach of it.[20] The committal orders were accordingly set aside, the immediate crisis passed, and the dispute was later settled by negotiation.[1] Some, however, were left with the indelible impression that there was something seriously amiss with a law which, for whatever reason, could precipitate a local employment dispute into a nationwide industrial crisis.

Relief was, as it transpired, shortlived for the point of conflict then shifted to the Midland Cold Storage depot where picketing had likewise been continuing over the preceding weeks. Again the object was to secure the replacement of the existing employees by registered dock workers, and to this end hauliers were threatened with blacking if they entered the depot. On a complaint by the company to the National Industrial Relations Court interim orders were granted against seven individual dockers (including Steer and Turner) restraining them from continuing to threaten to black vehicles entering the depot.[2] The picketing continued, whereupon the company then sought an injunction and declaratory orders in the Chancery Division of the High Court[3] believing, presumably, that an order from this court outside the Industrial Relations Act would be more likely to be obeyed. The application was refused by Megarry, J. on the ground, inter alia, that the substance of the complaint lay within the jurisdiction of the National Industrial Relations Court and it was for the plaintiffs to enforce the remedy which had been granted there. Such a conclusion seems to have been inevitable for the granting of parallel orders would clearly have seriously undermined the standing of the former court. Midland Cold Storage then returned to the National Industrial Relations Court, which committed five of the dockers, including Steer and Turner, to prison for contempt.

This time the committal orders were put into effect, the men were duly imprisoned, and widespread industrial conflict again became the order of the day. The imprisonment was, however, relatively shortlived for on the very day on which the Official Solicitor applied to the court for the discharge of the men the House of Lords handed down its decision in the *Heatons' Transport* case. One

---

[18] See further, below, pp. 258–259.

[19] The speculation over the weekend over the circumstances leading to the Official Solicitor's intervention prompted Lord Denning to make a statement in the Court of Appeal on Monday, 19 June 1972: see [1972] I.C.R. 222, 229–230; [1972] 3 All E.R. 603, 609. See also Hansard, H.C. Deb. Vol. 840, cols. 1173–1175, 10 July 1972, for parliamentary questions.

[20] See below, pp. 242–244 for further discussion of the requirements of notice and proof of breach.

[1] See *The Times*, 22 June 1972; *Financial Times*, 23 June 1972 and Davies, *op. cit.*, p. 86.

[2] *Midland Cold Storage, Ltd.* v. *Turner* [1972] I.C.R. 230.

[3] *Midland Cold Storage, Ltd.* v. *Steer* [1972] I.C.R. 435; [1972] 3 All E.R. 941.

effect of this decision was to make it clear that the primary method of enforcement contemplated by the Industrial Relations Act was by taking action against the funds of organisations (such as the TGWU) rather than against individuals.[4] On this basis Sir John Donaldson, P. felt able to discharge the men after they had been in prison some four to five days although they had at no time approved the Official Solicitor's application on their behalf or given any assurances as to their future conduct.[5] The decision to release them was not made any easier by the fact that it was such an eminently convenient outcome to the case, or by the fact that there had been suggestions, which Sir John Donaldson found it necessary to refute, that the government had in some way placed pressure on the court to secure that result.

(c) *The Goad Case. Goad* v. *Amalgamated Union of Engineering Workers (Engineering Section)*[6] is another important case involving contempt through disobedience of the orders of the National Industrial Relations Court. Here Mr James Goad, a quality control inspector at a CAV, Ltd. plant at Sudbury in Suffolk, had been granted an order that he should not be 'arbitrarily or unreasonably' excluded from meetings of the local branch of the Amalgamated Union of Engineering Workers (AUEW). He was in conflict with the union because he had some years previously refused to take part in an unofficial strike and it was the union's case that he was not a member. The AUEW did not appear before the court in pursuance of its policy of non-cooperation with the Industrial Relations Act and its institutions and even though it might have had a perfectly good defence to Goad's claim. Within a month two shop stewards, claiming to have been acting on instructions from the union's head office, had excluded Goad from a further branch meeting to which he had sought entry. Goad then applied to the court for relief. The court adjourned the hearing and ordered the union to attend through 'one or more fully authorised representatives' to assist in determining whether the exclusion was indeed in breach of its earlier order. This was the first time that such an order for attendance had been made and it was disobeyed. At the adjoured hearing a £5,000 fine was imposed on the union, but although Sir John Donaldson clearly appears to have treated the non-attendance as 'simple lawbreaking' and as a contempt,[7] it seems that the fine related solely to Goad's exclusion from union meetings.[8] The union refused to pay the fine which was subsequently collected by sequestrators.[9] The following month Goad was

---

[4] See [1973] A.C. 15, 98.

[5] See *The Times*, 28 July 1972.

[6] See *Goad* v. *A.U.E.W.* [1972] I.C.R. 429 and, for further proceedings, *Goad* v. *A.U.E.W. (No. 2)* [1973] I.C.R. 42; *Goad* v. *A.U.E.W. (No. 3)* [1973] I.C.R. 108. For further discussion of the background to the case, see Innis Macbeath, *The Times*, 15 December 1972.

[7] *Cf.* [1973] I.C.R. 42, 45. See also [1973] I.C.R. 108, 111. Since the Court did not have the power to order a party to attend *qua* party on pain of committing a contempt if he did not, it must be assumed that the union was ordered to attend *qua* witness under the Industrial Court Rules, 1971, r. 64(1): see Rideout, *The Practice of the National Industrial Relations Court* (1973), pp. 44–45.

[8] See *The Times*, 9 November 1972.

[9] For some of the problems which this generated, see *Eckman* v. *Midland Bank, Ltd.* [1973] I.C.R. 71, discussed below, p. 262.

again refused admission to a union branch meeting and he applied once more to the court for relief. This time the union was 'invited' to attend the hearing, declined to do so, and was fined a further £50,000 for its continuing disobedience of the order relating to Goad's access to branch meetings. The size of the fine reflected the fact that the disobedience was part of a declared and deliberate policy on the part of the union to defy the court.[10] It was subsequently collected by sequestration. As for Goad he had been sent home on full pay after his fellow employees had made it clear that they did not wish to work with him. He was later reported as having suggested that one way out of the deadlock might be through his agreeing to drop his attempts to enter union meetings in consideration of CAV, Ltd. paying him the sum of £30,000.[11]

(d) *The Con-Mech case:* The AUEW policy of disobeying orders of the National Industrial Relations Court was again the immediate cause of the contempt proceedings in *Con-Mech (Engineers), Ltd.* v. *AUEW (Engineering Section).*[12] Here the complainant's factory at Sheerwater, Woking, had refused to recognise the AUEW as the sole bargaining unit at the plant, not being satisfied that this was what was wanted by the employees as a whole. A strike was then called and the company was granted an order referring the question of recognition to the Commission on Industrial Relations. An interim order restraining the union from indulging in unlawful industrial action was also granted. On a subsequent motion for contempt for breach of this latter order, the court, acting of its own motion,[13] ordered sequestration of union assets to the value of £100,000. A fine of £75,000 was imposed on the union some twelve days later to be recouped out of the assets which had been sequestered.

It was unfortunate for a variety of reasons that the most convenient source available to the sequestrators happened to be a loan made by the union to Hebburn UDC from its 'political', as opposed to its 'general', fund. It being impossible thereafter to transfer funds from the 'general' to the 'political' account to make good the deficiency the latter account was accordingly diminished. The seizure set in train a series of events which included an early day motion signed by over 180 Labour MPs calling for a select committee 'to consider the presentation of a Humble Address to the Crown praying for the dismissal of Sir John Donaldson';[14] an official Labour party motion noting the 'regrettable involvement of the National Industrial Relations Court in matters of political controversy' and calling for a repeal of the Industrial Relations Act;[15] an after-dinner speech by Sir John Donaldson defending the position of the Court and the sequestrators;[16] renewed criticism leading to a speech by Lord

---

[10] *Cf.* [1973] I.C.R. 108, 112.

[11] See *The Times*, 9 November 1972.

[12] [1973] I.C.R. 620.

[13] See further, below, p. 265.

[14] The terms of the motion are set out in *The Times*, 4 December 1973, p. 1.

[15] For the House of Commons debate on this motion, see Hansard, H.C. Deb. Vol. 865, col. 1092 *et seq*, 4 December 1973.

[16] Extracts from the speech were reproduced in (1973) 123 New Law Jo. 1111.

Hailsham, the Lord Chancellor, criticising the unofficial early day motion and calling for the rule of law to be upheld;[17] and a contention that this speech was a breach of the privileges of the House of Commons.[18]

(2) GENERAL CONSIDERATIONS: PRACTICE, PROCEDURE AND POWERS OF THE COURTS

(i) *The High Court, Court of Appeal and courts of equivalent status*

Ord. 45, r. 5(1) provides that a judgment or order requiring a person to do or abstain from doing any act may be enforced by one or more of the following means, that is to say,

> (i) with the leave of the Court, a writ of sequestration against the property of that person;
> (ii) where that person is a body corporate, with the leave of the Court, a writ of sequestration against the property of any director or other officer of the body;
> (iii) subject to the provisions of the Debtors Acts, 1869 and 1878, an order of committal against that person or, where that person is a body corporate, against any such officer.

These powers and the further power to fine a contemnor will be examined in more detail below. Initially, however, several points of a more general nature require to be discussed.

(a) *The need for sufficient notice of the terms of the order.* In all cases it must be shown that the person against whom it is sought to apply the sanction of the law of contempt had sufficient prior notice of the terms of the judgment or order which it is alleged he has disobeyed. The ways in which this requirement of notice may be satisfied are set out in R.S.C. Ord. 45, r. 7.[19]

The general rule is that personal service of a copy of the judgment or order is required.[20] Likewise in the case of a judgment or order against a corporate body enforcement will only be possible against an individual director or officer if he has been personally served.[1] So that the consequences of disobedience may be clearly appreciated Ord. 45, r. 7(4) also requires that the copy of the judgment or order should be indorsed with a notice stating that non-compliance will render the party liable to process of execution to compel obedience.[2] The general need for personal service may, however, be dispensed with in appropriate circumstances. Thus Ord. 45, r. 7(6) provides that in the case of a judgment requiring a person to

---

[17] See *The Times*, 4 December 1973, p. 4.

[18] See Hansard, H.C. Deb. Vol. 865, col. 1089 *et seq.*, 4 December 1973. The saga continued with a subsequent refusal of the AUEW to pay £47,000 compensation to Con-Mech in respect of unfair industrial practices; the total sequestration of union assets (with a saving for its real property and superannuation fund); threats of widespread industrial action, and the issuing of instructions to the sequestrators to accept payment through an offer made by anonymous donors who were seeking to prevent damage to the economy: see *The Times*, 10 April 1974; 4, 9 May 1974.

[19] See *The Supreme Court Practice 1973*, Vol. 1, pp. 687–691., *Halsbury*, Vol. 9, para. 61.

[20] Ord. 45, r. 7(2). See further *Halsbury*, Vol. 9, para. 64.

[1] Ord. 45, r. 7(3)(a)(b). Where a specified time is fixed for doing the act required the order must have been served within that time or any extension thereto: *Iberian Trust, Ltd.* v. *Founders Trust and Investment Co., Ltd.* [1932] 2 K.B. 87. For the position of directors and officers generally, see below, pp. 250–252.

[2] The appropriate wording is set out in *The Supreme Court Practice 1973*, Vol. 1, pp. 689–690. See also *Halsbury*, Vol. 9, para. 62.

abstain from doing an act the process of the law of contempt may be employed against one who has not been personally served if the court is satisfied that he had notice of the order either (a) by being present when it was made,[3] or (b) by being notified of its terms, whether by telephone, telegram,[4] or otherwise.[5] In other words personal service is little more than a convenient way of establishing notice where the order is couched in negative or prohibitory terms.[6] This provision has no application, however, to positive or mandatory orders requiring an act to be done. Here personal service is necessary,[7] subject to the proviso that the court has a general power under Ord. 45, r. 7(7) to dispense with service where it considers it just to do so, as where there is an attempt to evade service.[8] Parallel provisions also operate where there has been a failure to comply with the terms of an undertaking, as opposed to an order or judgment. Indeed this is as one would expect for the equivalence of an order and an undertaking has been frequently emphasised.[9]

(b) *Proof of the breach of the order or undertaking:* Apart from the requirement of notice, process for civil contempt will also depend upon proving a breach of the order or undertaking which has been made or given. This really has two facets, namely (i) the existence of the breach and (ii) the proof thereof.

The necessity of determining whether there has been a factual breach of an order or undertaking on the part of the body or person brought before the court clearly demands that the terms of the order itself be expressed in clear and unambiguous language. In so far as possible that person should know with complete precision what it is he is required to do or to abstain from doing. The requirement of clarity has been admirably stated in a leading American case, where it was said of an injunction that:[10]

> [It] should be as definite, clear and precise in its terms as possible, so that there may be no reason or excuse for misunderstanding or disobeying it; and, when practicable, it should plainly indicate to the defendant all of the acts which he is restrained from doing, without calling on him for inferences or conclusions about which persons may well differ.[11]

In the nature of things the degree of clarity and specificity which is capable of being achieved will vary according to the subject matter of the proceedings. An injunction enjoining entry on a particular piece of land lends itself to clarity and

---

[3] *Cf. Husson* v. *Husson* [1962] 3 All E.R. 1056.

[4] *Re Bryant* (1877) 4 Ch. D. 98.

[5] *Cf. Avory* v. *Andrews* (1882) 51 L.J. Ch. 414. See also *Halsbury*, Vol. 9, para. 65.

[6] See *United Telephone Co.* v. *Dale* (1884) 25 Ch. D. 778; *D.* v. *A. & Co.* [1900] 1 Ch. 484. See also Ronson Products, Ltd. v. Ronson Furniture, Ltd. [1966] Ch. 603, and *cf. Mckeown* v. *Joint Stock Institute Ltd.* [1899] 1 Ch. 671.

[7] *Re Tuck, Murch* v. *Loosemore* [1906] 1 Ch. 692.

[8] Provision is also made for substituted service by Ord. 65, r. 4.

[9] See, e.g., *Biba, Ltd* v. *Stratford Investments, Ltd.* [1972] 3 All E.R. 1041, and above, p. 235.

[10] *Collins* v. *Wayne Iron Works*, 227 Pa. 326; 76 A. 24, 25 (1910) cited in Spry, *Equitable Remedies* (1971), p. 338 to which reference should be made for a more detailed treatment. For further American cases, see *U.S.* v. *Joyce*, 498 F. 2d 592 (1974) and, in general, American Jurisprudence 2d, Vol. 17, s. 52, pp. 54–55.

[11] See also *Redland Bricks, Ltd.* v. *Morris* [1970] A.C. 652, 666; [1969] 2 All E.R. 576, 580 (Lord Upjohn).

precision more readily than does an injunction restraining the commission of a nuisance by noise, or the harassment of a person, where questions of degree are necessarily involved. In all such cases, however, it is the duty of the person enjoined to comply with the order absolutely as from the time it becomes operative.

Turning to the related question of proof of breach, the application for a committal order or for a writ of sequestration must be supported by an affidavit reciting what the respondent is alleged to have done in breach of the judgment or order.[12] A copy of the notice of motion and of the accompanying affidavit must generally be served on the respondent personally,[13] although personal service may be dispensed with in exceptional circumstances as where service is being evaded.[14] As to the quantum of proof required, it is a very demanding one, being pitched at the level normally associated with criminal proceedings. Hence breach of the order and sufficient notice of its terms must be proved beyond reasonable doubt.[15]

These requirements have recently been emphasised by the Court of Appeal in *Churchman* v. *Joint Shop Stewards' Committee of the Workers of the Port of London,* where Lord Denning said:[16]

> The notice which is given to the accused must give with it the charges against them with all the particularity which this court or the High Court here ordinarily demands before depriving a person of his liberty. He must be given notice of any new charge and the opportunity of meeting it. Even if he does not appear to answer it, it must be proved with all the sufficiency that we habitually require before depriving a man of his liberty.

With reference to the actual facts of the case, which have been set out above,[17] the Court of Appeal was not satisfied that the evidence went anywhere near to meeting the stringent requirements for proof of a breach which it demanded. Equally, the facts of the case suggest that several of the alleged breaches would have occurred before the respondents, Steer, Turner and Williams, were served with the order and before a point at which it was clear beyond reasonable doubt that they had obtained knowledge of its substance from another source. Such conduct ought clearly to be discounted in so far as a direct proof of a breach is concerned, although it might possibly be relevant as tending to throw light on their later conduct.

(c) *Mens rea: intent and inability to comply:* A further problem is that of whether it is sufficient to support an application for contempt that D did *in fact* fail to comply with the terms of an order or undertaking, or whether it is necessary,

---

[12] *Cf.* Ord. 52, r. 4(1) and Ord. 46, r. 5(2). In both instances the application will be by motion in the Division in which the judgment or order was obtained.

[13] Ord. 52, r. 4(2) and Ord. 46, r. 5(2).

[14] Ord. 52, r. 4(3) and Ord. 46, r. 5(3). An order may also be made for substituted service under Ord. 65, r. 4.

[15] *Cf. Re Bramblevale, Ltd.* [1970] Ch. 128; [1969] 3 All E.R. 1062, and, in general, above, pp. 8–9, and cases there cited.

[16] [1972] I.C.R. 222, 229; [1972] 3 All E.R. 603, 608.

[17] On p. 238.

rather, to show that the failure was accompanied by a particular intent or mental element.[18]

In this context the wording of the Rules of the Supreme Court is clearly important. By Ord. 45, r. 5(1) of the rules which are currently in force it is provided that an order or judgment may be enforced by sequestration or committal where D (being either a natural person, a body corporate, or a director thereof) either (i) *refuses or neglects* to comply with a positive order, or (ii) *disobeys* a prohibitory order. This form of words differs from that which is to be found in the old Rules of the Supreme Court which were in force until October 1 1966, and which required a judgment or order against a corporation to have been *wilfully* disobeyed before the process of the law of contempt could be employed.[19]

Although support could be found for the view that the requirement that the disobedience be 'wilful' demanded something akin to contumacy,[20] it is doubtful whether this ever truly represented the law.[1] In *Stancomb* v. *Trowbridge U.D.C.*,[2] for example, where alleged breaches of an injunction restraining the fouling of a stream were in issue, Warrington, L.J. expressed the opinion that the word 'wilfully' was only intended to exclude 'casual or accidental and unintentional acts'.[3] This interpretation has been accepted in a number of subsequent cases,[4] and has recently been approved by the House of Lords in *Heatons Transport, Ltd.* v. *Transport and General Workers Union.*[5] Here there had been no question of contumacious or insulting behaviour on the part of the defendant union. Yet its disobedience of the order of the National Industrial Relations Court was not casual or accidental and unintentional. On this basis, it was held, fines and conditional orders for sequestration could be imposed. As Lord Wilberforce observed in delivering the judgment of the House, any effect which might be attributed to the omission of the word 'wilfully' from the Rules of the Supreme Court now in force cannot be in favour of the party who has disobeyed the order.[6]

It would seem, therefore, that liability for civil contempt will only be negatived where the act alleged to constitute a contempt is *itself* accidental and unintentional. This would be the case where, for example, D has installed an adequate system to prevent the commission of a nuisance by noise, or through

[18] *Mens rea* is clearly required to the extent that D must be shown to have had notice of the substance of the order itself (see above, p. 242). Likewise the order may, of course, be so drafted that a factual breach will be made dependent upon an element of intent.

[19] See Ord. 42, r. 31. But Ord. 43, r. 6 (refusal or neglect) did not contain the word 'wilful'.

[20] See *Worthington* v. *Ad Lib Club, Ltd.* [1965] Ch. 236; [1964] 3 All E.R. 674.

[1] The possible meanings of the word 'wilful' as used in this context are canvassed by Moskovitz, 'Contempt of Injunctions, Civil and Criminal' (1943) 43 Col. L.R. 780, 793.

[2] [1910] 2 Ch. 190.

[3] *Ibid.*, p. 194, referring to *Fairclough* v. *Manchester Ship Canal Co.* [1897] W.N. 7; 41 Sol. Jo. 225. This case was also cited by Stirling, J. in *Worthington* v. *Ad Lib Club, Ltd.* (above), but the inferences which he drew were different.

[4] See, e.g., *Steiner Products, Ltd.* v. *Willy Steiner, Ltd.* [1966] 2 All E.R. 387, 390–391; *Re the Agreement of the Mileage Conference Group of the Tyre Manufacturers' Conference, Ltd.* [1966] 2 All E.R. 849, 861–862; *Knight* v. *Clifton* [1971] 1 Ch. 700, 713, 721; [1971] 2 All E.R. 378, 386, 393, C.A.

[5] [1973] A.C. 15; [1972] 3 All E.R. 101, above, p. 236.

[6] [1973] A.C. 15, 109; [1972] 3 All E.R. 101, 117.

the emission of noxious fumes or an effluent, and the system suddenly fails. On such facts it is doubtful whether D could be said to have disobeyed a court order prohibiting the nuisance if he seeks to prevent the continuing escape as quickly as possible. On the other hand, it would not be sufficient to negative liability if the facts were rather that D, having obtained and acted upon professional advice, believed his conduct to be in compliance with the terms of the order when such was not in fact the case. Similarly, it has been held that a contempt may still be committed even though legal advice has been obtained and followed.[7] In both instances D would have intended to do that which was objectively speaking a breach of the order or undertaking, and the fact that he has exercised all due care will go to mitigation alone.[8]

A somewhat different problem is presented by the person who claims that he is simply *unable* to comply with the terms of an order or undertaking, whether through a lack of funds or for some other reason. In the nature of things this problem is more likely to arise in the case of a mandatory order than in the case of a prohibitory order. It was touched upon by the Court of Appeal in *Lewis* v. *Pontypridd, Caerphilly and Newport Railway Co.*[9] Here the defendant company pleaded a lack of funds to excuse its non-compliance with a judgment requiring it to make a junction to connect the plaintiff's works to its own line. Lord Esher, M.R. dealt with the submission by saying: 'If from the time when the judgment was given they had always been unable, through want of funds, to do the work, probably they could not be said to have wilfully disobeyed the judgment. But it was necessary for the directors to make that out.'[10] On the facts of the case it could not be established that all possible economies had been made to enable the junction to be built and the orders for writs of attachment against the directors were upheld.[11] The view that liability for contempt will not be incurred where a lack of funds creates a genuine inability to comply with the order has been accepted in some American cases.[12] A genuine inability to comply with the terms of an order may equally arise for other reasons, as where D is called upon to deliver up documents and he claims that he does not have them in his possession or control. In *Re Bramblevale Ltd*[13] the Court of Appeal quashed a committal order where it had not been proved that the relevant documents were in the defendant's possession at the time of the Registrar's order calling on him to deliver them up. Equally, it is thought, a contempt would not be committed where the disability arises after the order has been made but before the time has elapsed for complying with it. Again there is support for this view in American

---

[7] See *The Mileage Conference Group* case [1966] 2 All E.R. 849, 862 (R.P.C., Megaw, P.).

[8] The position would appear to be the same in the United States: see American Jurisprudence 2d, Vol. 17, s. 53, p. 55 and cases there cited.

[9] (1895) 11 T.L.R. 203.

[10] *Ibid. Cf. R* v. *Poplar Borough Council* [1922] 1 K.B. 95 where disobedience of an order of mandamus requiring a rate to be levied was not excused by pleading that the borough was too poor to support it.

[11] Is a person who is subject to such an order required to seek or to remain in the most financially rewarding employment open to him?

[12] See 30 A.L.R. 154–155 for cases for and against the proposition.

[13] [1970] 1 Ch. 128; [1969] 3 All E.R. 1062.

cases which place the onus of proving the disability on the defendant and require him to establish that it was not brought about by any fault on his part.[14] It is doubtful, however, whether there is any justification for punishing one whose inability to comply is brought about by nothing more than carelessness, and is not deliberately induced.[15]

(d) *Who may be held liable?* In many cases there will be no particular difficulty in determining who is to be held liable in respect of the breach of an order or undertaking. If, for example, D is ordered not to molest or associate with a particular person and he acts in breach of the injunction then clearly he will be the person immediately responsible for such breach. In other cases, however, difficult problems are raised, notably in determining the liability of one who assists another to act in breach of an order, or in cases in which the order has been issued against a corporation, or some other organisation or body of persons. Some of these problems can be discussed at this point.

(i) *Assisting or procuring the breach of an order or undertaking.* There is no doubt that if a person (D2) actively assists another person (D1) to break an order or undertaking he will himself commit a contempt. What is perhaps less clear is the nature of the contempt committed by D2, and the scope of the liability of one who is not himself immediately subject to the order or undertaking. *Seaward* v. *Paterson*[16] is the leading case. It concerned a promoter who had arranged boxing matches on residential premises in London and thereby knowingly assisted the lessee to disobey an order enjoining him from committing a nuisance. In the course of his judgment in the Court of Appeal upholding the promoter's committal for contempt, Lindley, L.J. distinguished between: 'A motion to commit a man for breach of an injunction, which is technically wrong unless he is bound by the injunction'[17] and 'a motion to commit a man for contempt of court, not because he is bound by the injunction by being a party to the cause, but because he is conducting himself so as to obstruct the course of justice'.[18] The inference to be drawn from this distinction and the incidents which Lindley, L.J. considered accompanied it is that the liability of the promoter was considered to be as for a *criminal* contempt of court. In *Scott* v. *Scott*,[19] however, Lord Atkinson denied that this was so, and himself suggested that it would be absurd if a criminal contempt were to be committed by one who was *not* personally prohibited from doing the act in question, while no more than a civil contempt was committed by one who was. Subsequent English cases have served to confirm the liability of one who actively assists in the breach of an injunction without finding it necessary to state categorically whether the contempt thus committed is

---

[14] See, e.g., *State ex rel. Cook* v. *Cook*, 66 Ohio St. 566, 64 N.E. 567 (1902—Sup. Ct Ohio) and American Jurisprudence 2d Vol. 17, s. 51, pp. 53–54 and cases there cited. See also Dobbs, 'Contempt of Court: A Survey' (1971) 56 Cornell L.R. 183, 265–267.

[15] As, e.g., where D's inability to hand over goods or documents stems from a fire or accident caused by his own negligence but where there is no question of their having been intentionally destroyed.

[16] [1897] 1Ch. 545, C.A.

[17] *Cf. Iveson* v. *Harris* (1802) 7 Ves. 251, 256; 32 E.R. 102 *per* Lord Eldon, L.C.

[18] [1897] 1 Ch. 545, 555.

[19] [1913] A.C. 417, 458–459.

criminal or civil in nature.[20] On the whole though it would seem that, notwithstanding the force of Lord Atkinson's objection, the person rendering assistance commits a criminal contempt.[1]

The mental element upon which such liability depends, and indeed the scope of the liability itself, are not matters which have been explored in detail in the English cases. It is submitted, however, that some assistance may be derived from the principles which govern the liability of one who procures or encourages another to commit a criminal offence, even if the analogy is not a precise one.[2] On this basis it must clearly be shown that the person rendering assistance knew of all legally relevant circumstances and, in particular, of the substance of the order. In *Seaward* v. *Paterson*[3] it was not regarded as essential that the promoter should have actually seen a copy of the order restraining the lessee from committing a nuisance, and suggestions that the position may be different in the case of a mandatory order are surely without foundation.[4] Indeed it is difficult to see how a court could identify in advance all those who might subsequently assist in the breach of the order so as to be able to serve a copy upon them.[5] Whether some ulterior intent to defeat the course of justice is also required to ground liability is unclear. It would seem, however, that it is unnecessary and that it is sufficient to show that the defendant voluntarily rendered a positive act of assistance with knowledge of all legally relevant circumstances.[6]

Similar difficulties exist in determining when sufficient assistance or encouragement will have been offered to support a finding of contempt. Here it is submitted that an analogy may again be drawn with the position in the criminal law. Indeed in *Seaward* v. *Paterson* itself the leading case of *Coney*[7] was cited as authority for the view that a mere spectator would not have committed a contempt although the promoter and the 'master of ceremonies' did. *Thorne Rural District Council* v. *Bunting (No. 2)*[8] is also in point. In this case a father (W) had entered into an undertaking to withdraw his application under which certain land in the West Riding of Yorkshire was registered as provisional common land pending the determination of the Commons Commissioners. W complied with his undertaking, but the land was not de-registered since the original application had been made not by W alone, but by W jointly with his wife (J) and his son (N). J and N had not sought to have the register vacated. The council then sought to

---

[20] See, e.g., *Elliot* v. *Klinger* [1967] 3 All E.R. 141; *Phonographic Performance, Ltd.* v. *Amusement Caterers (Peckham), Ltd.* [1964] 1 Ch. 195; [1963] 3 All E.R. 493; *Acrow (Automation), Ltd.* v. *Rex Chainbelt Inc.* [1971] 3 All E.R. 1175. See also *Johnston* v. *Moore* [1965] N.I. 128.

[1] This is also the view advanced in Oswald, *Contempt of Court*, p. 107, and in Fox, *The History of Contempt of Court* (1927), p. 45.

[2] The analogy is not precise because (i) a contempt in procedure is not a criminal offence and (ii) it will be suggested below that the party who renders assistance is better viewed as a principal offender in his own right, rather than a secondary party.

[3] [1897] 1 Ch. 545.

[4] The view is advanced in Borrie and Lowe, *The Law of Contempt* (1973), p. 324.

[5] Since no such difficulty exists in identifying the person enjoined no inferences may be drawn from the requirement of personal service upon him (see above, p. 242).

[6] *Cf. National Coal Board* v. *Gamble* [1959] 1 Q.B. 11; [1958] 3 All E.R. 203 and, in general, Smith & Hogan, *Criminal Law* (3rd ed. 1973), at p. 97 *et seq.*

[7] (1882) 8 Q.B.D. 534.

[8] [1972] 3 All E.R. 1084.

commit J and N for contempt on the ground that they had wilfully and deliberately failed to assist W in carrying out his undertaking. It is hardly surprising that the application failed for J and N had not themselves given any undertaking with respect to the land in question, and it would have been quite wrong to have held them in contempt for failing to withdraw their application when they were not under otherwise an obligation to do so. As Russell, L.J. observed.[9]

> I do not see myself why, for example, a gratuitous undertaking in proceedings by A can be said to put B and C in the position of obligation to take a step which they were not bound to take in law; and that is what this case amounts to.

While this conclusion seems to be clearly correct on the facts of the case, it must not be thought that a contempt is always incapable of being committed through nonfeasance, that is, a simple failure to act. It is, for example, clear that a third party may commit a contempt by refusing to hand over goods to a sequestrator on demand[10] or, it has been held, by failing to renew an agreement to deliver goods to P, thus assisting D to act in breach of an injunction.[11]

A further reason for holding that the wife and son were not in contempt was explained by Buckley, L.J. in the following terms:[12]

> It is well established that a stranger to an action who aids and abets a breach of an undertaking or an injunction by a party to an action is himself particeps criminis[13] and guilty of contempt of court. . . . But here there is no breach of an order or undertaking which either of the respondents to this motion is aiding or abetting. Mr. Bunting, the father, . . . is not in breach. There is no breach to which either the mother or the son can be a party.[14]

This raises a question of general importance, namely whether a third-party stranger can only be held liable where there has been a breach of the order (or undertaking) on the part of the person enjoined.

This limitation has the attraction of providing some clearly defined boundaries to the scope of contempt. But it may be regarded as productive of anomalies. It would presumably mean, for example, that D would not commit a contempt where he openly incited E to flout a court order but E decided to comply. Equally, and to adapt an example discussed in *Jennison* v. *Baker*,[15] it would mean that D would not commit a contempt if, knowing of the terms of an injunction enjoining E not to kill P's cat, he killed the cat himself before E had the opportunity of deciding whether to obey the order or not. If it were thought desirable to hold D liable for a criminal contempt of court on such facts this could be done without any great violation of principle. Certainly a person may be held liable for the inchoate offence of incitement where he incites another to commit a *crime*,

---

[9] *Ibid.*, at p. 1088.
[10] *Cf. Eckman* v. *Midland Bank, Ltd.* [1973] I.C.R. 71; [1973] 1 All E.R. 609.
[11] See *Acrow (Automation), Ltd.* v. *Rex Chainbelt Inc.* [1971] 3 All E.R. 1175.
[12] [1972] 3 All E.R. 1084, 1088.
[13] This is not strictly speaking correct since it is not a crime in which he is *particeps*.
[14] See also *Ronson Products, Ltd.* v. *Ronson Furniture, Ltd.* [1966] Ch. 603, 615; [1966] 2 All E.R. 381, 384 (Stamp, J.).
[15] [1972] 2 Q.B. 52; [1972] 1 All E.R. 997, C.A.

although the crime is not in fact committed.[16] There is no obvious reason why incitement to disobey a court order should not constitute a contempt (or be charged on indictment as an attempt to interfere with the due administration of justice) even though it is unsuccessful. Admittedly a conviction for aiding and abetting an offence does appear to depend upon there being a principal offender.[17] But this should not be viewed as decisive of the matter for although there has been a tendency to speak of the third party as aiding and abetting the contempt, it is submitted that his liability is, on a true analysis, that of a principal offender. The essence of the wrong committed by the promoter in *Seaward* v. *Patterson* is that he interfered with the administration of justice as a principal in his own right.[18]

The main drawback to such an approach is, of course, that it envisages a liability which is virtually open ended whereby injunctions are effectively good against all who have knowledge of their substance.[19] Such an extensive liability may be quite unacceptable. In any event it would appear to be clear that under the present law there is no requirement that the person enjoined be brought before the court along with the person who is alleged to have procured or assisted in the breach. On any view it should be sufficient to establish that a breach had *in fact* occurred.

(ii) *Corporations, their directors, officers and servants*. The basic position on an alleged breach of an order by a corporate body may be stated quite simply. By RSC, Ord. 45, r. 5(1)[20] it is provided that enforcement may be by a writ of sequestration against the corporate property or, subject to the requirements of notice having been met,[1] by a writ of sequestration against the property of 'any director of other officer', or by his committal. It is also clear that the same rules apply to undertakings and that a corporate body may be fined and ordered to pay the costs of the proceedings. Two problems of a general nature require to be discussed, namely (i) the persons for whose acts the corporate body may be held responsible, and (ii) the position of individual directors and servants.

As to the former problem, the terms of the enjoinder or undertaking will normally restrain the defendant 'by his servants, agents or otherwise' from doing the prohibited act.[2] It would seem that this form of words will be implied even if it is not expressly adopted.[3] In *Heatons Transport, Ltd* v. *Transport and General*

---

[16] If it is committed his liability is for aiding and abetting.

[17] See, e.g., *Morris* v. *Tolman* [1923] 1 K.B. 166; *Thornton* v. *Mitchell* [1940] 1 All E.R. 339 and, in general, Smith & Hogan, *op. cit.*, at pp. 105–109. The proposition in the text should now be read subject to the decision in *Cogan and Leak*, *The Times*, 10 June 1975, C.A., holding that D1 may be convicted as a secondary party to the offence of rape though D2, the alleged principal offender, was acquitted.

[18] See also *Lord Wellesley* v. *Earl of Mornington* (1848) 11 Beav. 181; 50 E.R. 786; *St. John's College, Oxford* v. *Carter* (1839) 4 My. & Cr. 497; 41 E.R. 191 (where, however, the person enjoined was present and giving tacit assent to the act of the third party). If D is to be regarded as a secondary party, rather than a principal offender, it may be argued that the limits to the liability of secondary parties to criminal offences need not be imported wholesale into the liability of a secondary party to a civil contempt.

[19] See Gregory, 'Government by Injunction' (1898) 11 Harv. L.R. 487, 510.

[20] See above, p. 242.

[1] As to which, see above, p. 242.

[2] See *Marengo* v. *Daily Sketch and Sunday Graphic, Ltd.* [1948] 1 All E.R. 406, H.L.

[3] Spry, *Equitable Remedies* (1971), p. 339.

Workers' Union Lord Denning, M.R. took the view that the defendant union, which had been enjoined in such terms to refrain from blacking, was nonetheless only responsible for 'those who represent its directing mind and will, such as its committee and principal officers'. In his opinion it was not responsible 'for every servant and every agent'[4]*Tesco Supermarkets, Ltd* v. *Nattrass,*[5] the leading case delimiting the original or primary liability of corporate bodies, was cited as authority for this proposition. In the House of Lords, however, it was clearly established that no such limitation existed, and that the union was responsible, rather, for the acts of its agents, including shop stewards, within the scope of their authority.[6] The only limit to this doctrine of full vicarious liability for civil contempt would appear to be the traditional one that the servant or agent must have been acting within the course of his employment, or the scope of his authority.[7] Equally it has been held that a company will commit a contempt through a failure to comply with an undertaking of which it has formal notice even though none of the individual directors or officers of the company was aware that the undertaking was being broken.[8] The implication, and it is not an unreasonable one, is that the directors as a body must take steps to ensure that the order or undertaking is being observed.[9] Natural persons and other non-incorporated employers will, no doubt, also be liable for the acts of their servants and agents within the course of their employment.

The position of the individual servants, agents and directors themselves will depend in part on the terms of the order or undertaking. When, as would normally be the case, it enjoins or binds the defendant 'by his servants or agents etc.', it is clear (subject to what is said below) that it is the defendant alone who can be held in breach. A servant or agent can only be held in contempt if, with knowledge of all legally relevant facts, he assists or procures the breach within the principles discussed in the previous section. The directors and other officers of a body corporate stand, however, on a different footing. As Ord. 45, r. 5(1) makes clear, they may be held liable in contempt even though they do not render active assistance in procuring the breach, and provided only that they have notice of the substance of the terms of the order or undertaking.[10] At least in the case of prohibitory orders or undertakings personal service on the director is not required,[11] although the position may be otherwise where the order or

---

[4] [1973] A.C. 15, 51; [1972] I.C.R. 308, 344.

[5] [1972] A.C. 153.

[6] *Cf.* [1973] A.C. 15, 109; [1972] I.C.R. 308, 402.

[7] Presumably the 'course of employment' and 'scope of authority' tests are to be applied in the same way as in the law of tort: as to which, see, in general, Atiyah, *Vicarious Liability in the Law of Torts* (1967), part V.

[8] See *Re Garage Equipment Association's Agreement* (1964) L.R. 4 R.P. 491 (R.P. Ct, Megaw, J.).

[9] *Cf. Re Galvanized Tank Manufacturers' Association's Agreement* (1965) L.R. 5 R.P. 315.

[10] A 'director' is defined in the Companies Act 1948, s. 455(1) to include 'any person occupying the position of director by whatever name called' and an 'officer' is defined to include, 'a director, manager or secretary'. *Semble* that a 'manager' means someone who manages the affairs of the company *as a whole*, and that it does not include a branch manager: see *Registrar of Restrictive Trading Agreements* v. *W. H. Smith & Son, Ltd.* [1969] 3 All E.R. 1065, C.A.

[11] See *Ronson Products, Ltd.* v. *Ronson Furniture, Ltd.* [1966] Ch. 603; [1966] 2 All E.R. 381 and Ord. 45, r. 7(3)(a); Ord. 45, r. 7(6), 7(7).

undertaking is mandatory in form.[12] This would be in accordance with the distinction which applies to prohibitory and mandatory orders generally, and which was noted earlier in the chapter.[13] While the net result is that individual directors or officers may incur a wide-ranging liability for civil contempt even though they were not personally enjoined, the extent to which they were personally at fault will of course be reflected in the order made against them.[14]

By way of contrast, an order which is directed against 'the defendant its directors officers servants and agents' would appear to seek to subject to a personal enjoinder all who fall within these several categories, and this whether the defendant is a corporate body or a private individual. It would seem wrong, however, that a person should be subjected to an injunction unless he was before the court as a party to the proceedings, and it has been so held by the House of Lords.[15] The High Court of Australia has, however, made an order in these terms in recent years[16] while American cases afford examples of injunctions being directed against an even wider category of persons. In *Clemmons* v. *Congress of Racial Equality,*[17] for example, the enjoinder referred to 'the defendants and their officers, agents, servants, employees, and attorneys, and those persons in active concert or participation with them'. Although the overall effect of this latter form of words would appear to be little more than that of subjecting to a personal enjoinder those who would otherwise have been held liable for assisting or procuring the breach, it is not likely to be approved in this country.

(iii) *Successors in office and in title.* In some American cases it has been held that injunctions bind not only those who are specifically designated in them, but also their successors in office and, it seems, successors in title to real property. Thus in one case an injunction restraining a named person as dean of admissions in a university faculty was regarded as binding on his successor in office who had knowledge of the decree.[18] *Avery* v. *Andrews*[19] appears to be the only English case to come near to adopting this approach. Here an injunction had been issued restraining the named trustees of a friendly society from dividing certain money among the members of the society. The trustees retired, new trustees were appointed, and knowing of the terms of the order they proceeded to share the money out among the members who included the old trustees. On an application to commit the trustees for contempt, it was argued that the new trustees were not parties to the original action, nor the servants or agents of the persons against

---

[12] See *Ronson's* case [1966] Ch. 603, 614–615; *Att.-Gen.* v. *Wheatley & Co., Ltd.* (1903) 48 Sol. Jo. 116; *McKeown* v. *Joint Stock Institute, Ltd.* [1889] 1 Ch. 671.

[13] See above, pp. 242–243.

[14] See *Biba, Ltd.* v. *Stratford Investments, Ltd.* [1972] 3 All E.R. 1041. For the position of directors as shareholders, see *Northern Counties Securities* v. *Jackson* [1974] 2 All E.R. 65.

[15] In *Marengo* v. *Daily Sketch and Sunday Graphic, Ltd.* [1948] 1 All E.R. 406. See also *Iveson* v. *Harris* (1802) 7 Ves. 251, 256; 32 E.R. 102 *per* Lord Eldon, L.C.

[16] See *Beecham Group. Ltd.* v. *Bristol Laboratories Pty., Ltd.* (1967) 118 C.L.R. 618. See also Spry, *op. cit.,* p. 339.

[17] 201 F. Supp. 737 (1962). See also *Bullock* v. *U.S.,* 265 F. 2d 683 (6th. Cir., 1959); the Federal Rules of Civil Procedure, r. 65(d), and, in general, Note, 'Binding Nonparties to Injunctive Decrees' (1965) 49 Minn. L.R. 719.

[18] *Lucy* v. *Adams,* 224 F. Supp. 79 (N.D. Ala. 1963) affd. 328 F. 2d 892 (5th. Cir., 1964).

[19] (1882) 51 L.J. Ch. 414.

whom the injunction had been granted. Kay, J., however, viewed the entire transaction as one in which there had been a ruse to get rid of the order of the court, and he committed the new trustees and one of the old to prison for contempt.[20] The precise basis of their respective liabilities was not analysed. It might possibly be argued that it was the *old* trustees who were in breach of the order by acting through the agency of the new trustees, and that the latter were committed for assisting in (or aiding and abetting) the breach. It is more likely, though, that it was the *new* trustees as successors in office who were regarded as subject to the enjoinder and in breach of it, and the old trustees as having procured the breach. *Avery* v. *Andrews* is admittedly a fairly extreme case, and it is doubtful whether English law recognises any general principle whereby successors in office are regarded as subject to enjoinders which bind their predecessors. Any such principle would be difficult to reconcile with the *in personam* nature of injunctive relief.[1]

Still less is it likely that successors in title to real property can be regarded as bound by an injunction relating to the use of the property even if it is so worded as to purport to cover them and they have notice of its terms.[2] Neither is it likely that we would subscribe to the so-called *in rem* injunction theory which has been developed in some courts in the United States.[3] Under this theory an injunction may be effectively drafted to restrain anyone from using property for a particular purpose on pain of committing a contempt.[4] This would seem to be judicial legislation under another name.

(e) *Void and erroneous orders.* In *Oswald* on Contempt it is said that:[5]

> An order irregularly obtained cannot be treated as a nullity, but must be implicitly obeyed, until by a proper application it is discharged, and the case is the same where the order is alleged to have been improvidently made.

The balance of English authority clearly supports this view. Thus in *Fennings* v. *Humphrey*, for example, Lord Langdale, M.R. dealt with a contention that the original order had been erroneously granted by saying:[6]

> It is clear that a party who is served with an order may be guilty of a contempt for disobedience in a case in which the order ought not to have been made. He is not to determine for himself, but ought to come to the Court for relief, if advised that the order is invalid.

---

[20] *Cf. Busch* v. *Simms Manufacturing Co., Ltd.* (1909) 25 T.L.R. 419 where a company reconstruction was carried out in good faith and the new independent company was not bound by an injunction directed against the old.

[1] Yet if an injunction is obtained as against A, B and C as governors of a school should it be necessary to obtain a fresh injunction as against E and F when they replace B and C as governors?

[2] But *quaere* whether an analogy might be drawn with the *Tulk* v. *Moxhay* doctrine? For some American cases, see e.g., *Wilcox* v. *Ashford*, 131 Neb. 338, 268 N.W. 81 (1936) where the injunction was expressed as covering S. and 'all persons claiming through or under him'; *Hindi* v. *Smith*, 73 N.M. 335, 388 P. 2d 60 (1963).

[3] See Dobbs, 'Contempt of Court: A Survey' (1971) 56 Cornell L.R. 183, 257–260.

[4] *Cf.*, e.g., *State* v. *Terry*, 99 Wash. 1, 168 P. 513 (1917)—use of premises for the purposes of prostitution; *Silvers* v. *Traverse*, 82 Iowa 52, 47 N.W. 888 (1891)—use of premises for sale of liquor.

[5] At p. 107. See also *Halsbury*, Vol. 9, para. 55.

[6] (1841) 4 Beav. 1, 7; 49 E.R. 237, 239.

Likewise in *Woodward* v. *The Earl of Lincoln*[7] Lord Nottingham, L.C. said, in response to a submission that an injunction should not have been granted, that 'whatever the mistakes be, the subject must obey below and dispute here, for a contempt is not to be justified'.[8]

There would seem to be little doubt that this is the best approach in a case in which the court is possessed of jurisdiction of persons and subject matter and any irregularity is a purely technical one. When, however, there is an irregularity of substance, or a lack of jurisdiction to make the order, then it is open to argument whether public policy requires that the order be obeyed until it is quashed on an application for certiorari. The judgment of Viscount Haldane, L.C. in *Scott* v. *Scott*[9] gives some measure of support to those who would argue that there is no such duty. It was his opinion that the fact that an order to hear a case in camera in the interests of public decency was made 'under a mistaken impression as to the law' was of itself sufficient to dispose of the appeal.[10] It would seem, however, that the decision in *Scott* v. *Scott* ultimately turned on the fact that it was not, in any event, a contempt in the circumstances of the case to publish a fair and accurate report of the proceedings.

As was noted in an earlier chapter,[11] the Administration of Justice Act 1960, s. 12 has now superseded the common law in the area covered by *Scott* v. *Scott*. It has, moreover, done so in a way which is apt to create situations in which void orders may be lawfully disobeyed. Thus s. 12(2) of the Act provides that the publication of the text, or of a summary, of the order of a court sitting in private 'shall not of itself be contempt of court except where the court (having power to do so) expressly prohibits the publication'. The clear implication is that an order prohibiting publication which is made without the necessary power may be lawfully disobeyed. The same result follows from the wording of s. 12(1)(e) of the Act which relates to the publication of the proceedings themselves.[12]

American cases provide some support for the view that a void or erroneous order must be generally obeyed and this even in a case in which the injunction is of doubtful constitutional legality. *Walker* v. *City of Birmingham*[13] is one of the leading cases. Here an Alabama court had granted an injunction restraining the petitioners from participating in or encouraging street parades or processions without a permit as required by a city ordinance. Their request for a permit had earlier been denied. On a subsequent breach of the injunction the Supreme Court ultimately upheld sentences for contempt, and this even though the injunction and the ordinance on which it was based were both, at best, 'subject to substantial

---

[7] (1674) 3 Swan. 626; 36 E.R. 1000.

[8] See also *Drewry* v. *Thacker* (1819) 3 Swan. 529, 546; 36 E.R. 963, 967; *Blake* v. *Blake* (1844) 7 Beav. 514; 49 E.R. 1165; *Chuck* v. *Cremer* (1846) 2 Ph. 113; 41 E.R. 884; *Russell* v. *East Anglian Railway Co.* (1850) 3 Mac. & G. 104; 42 E.R. 201, and cases cited in the *English and Empire Digest*, Vol. 16, pp. 55–56.

[9] [1913] A.C. 417, 439. See further above, p. 209.

[10] See also *Socialist Worker Printer and Publisher Ltd., ex p. Att.-Gen.* [1975] 1 All E.R. 142, above, p. 230. For the position where a magistrates' court order is made without jurisdiction, see *Halsbury*, Vol. 9, para. 86 and cases there cited.

[11] See above, p. 215.

[12] For a case in which a person was wrongly committed on 'breach' of an order which had lapsed, see *Hennie* v. *Hennie*, *The Times*, 25 November 1972.

[13] 388 U.S. 307 (1967).

constitutional question' in terms of the First and Fourteenth Amendments.[14] In a vigorous dissenting judgment holding that the petitioners had been warranted in flouting an injunction which was at variance with the Constitution, Douglas, J. noted: 'if a person must pursue his judicial remedy before he may speak, parade, or assemble, the occasion when protest is desired or needed will have become history and any later speech, parade or assembly will be futile or pointless.'[15] Notwithstanding the force of this objection, it would seem that in the United States there is a duty to obey the order unless it is 'transparently invalid or had only a frivolous pretence to validity'.[16]

(f) *Powers of the court.* It is now proposed to consider the powers of the High Court, the Court of Appeal and of courts of equivalent status for dealing with a contempt in procedure. Discussion may be conveniently arranged under the following headings: (i) committal; (ii) fines; (iii) sequestration; (iv) costs.

(i) *Committal.* The procedure on an application for a committal order is laid down in R.S.C. Ord. 52 which applies to civil as well as to criminal contempt. Since the general scheme of Ord. 52 has already been noted in an earlier chapter[17] it is unnecessary to cover the same ground in detail here. In broad outline, the application will be by motion which will generally be moved before a single judge of the Division of the High Court which granted the original order[18] after notice of motion and a copy of the supporting affidavit have been served on the respondent in person.[19] Service may be dispensed with by the court[20] where, for example, the respondent is seeking to evade service.[1] A committal order may be made on an *ex parte* application in exceptional circumstances.

An example of an *ex parte* committal is provided by the case of *Warwick Corporation* v. *Russell.*[2] Here the respondent had been restrained by injunction from giving circus performances on land belonging to Warwick Corporation. He was informed of the terms of the injunction by the Town Clerk, served with a copy of the order, and warned of the consequences of breaking it. He nonetheless gave a performance the same evening, and proposed to give a second performance in accordance with his original plans the following day. In these

---

[14] 388 U.S. 307, 317.

[15] *Ibid.* at 336.

[16] *Cf. ibid.*, at 315. For further cases and discussion, see *Shuttlesworth* v. *City of Birmingham*, 382 U.S. 87 (1965); *U.S.* v. *United Mine Workers' of America*, 330 U.S. 258 (1947); *U.S.* v. *Seale*, 461 F 2d 345, 361–362 (1972); *U.S.* v. *Deleon*, 498 F 2d 1327 (1974); Cox, 'The Void Order and the Duty to Obey' (1948) 16 Univ. of Chicago L.R. 86; Watt, (1947) 14 Univ. of Chicago L.R. 409; Chafee, *Some Problems of Equity* (1950), p. 364.

[17] See above, pp. 30–33.

[18] See R.S.C. Ord. 52, r. 1(3), r. 4(1). On disobedience of a prerogative order or of a writ of habeas corpus issued out of a Divisional Court of the Queen's Bench Division the motion will be moved before a Divisional Court of that Division after an initial *ex parte* application for leave to apply: see Ord. 52, r. 1(2)(a)(i), r. 2, r. 3(1) and, in general, above, p. 30 and p. 32.

[19] Ord. 52, r. 4(2), r. 3(3).

[20] Ord. 52, r. 4(3), r. 3(4)—whether at the hearing of the motion or on an *ex parte* application. Substituted service may also be ordered: see *ibid* and Ord. 65, r. 4.

[1] See *The Supreme Court Practice 1973*, Vol. 1, p. 767 and cases there cited.

[2] [1964] 2 All E.R. 337.

circumstances the corporation moved *ex parte* for a committal order without notice of the motion having been served. Buckley, J. granted the order, saying:[3]

> In the present case it seems to me that the breach of which the respondent has already been guilty was as flagrant and contumacious as it could be. Not only that, but he is threatening a further breach of the order which, if he were to commit it successfully, would result in his having given the two performances . . . which he advertised and in his thus having achieved the whole of his purpose notwithstanding the order of the court. Although in this case the breach of which the corporation complain does not create any immediate serious danger to life or limb or anything of that kind,[4] which would be a ground on which the court might make a committal order on an *ex parte* application, yet . . . this is a proper case in which to grant the relief asked. Of course, anyone committed in such circumstances can always at any time and on the shortest possible notice apply to the court for the order to be discharged.[5]

According to Lane, J. in *Egan* v. *Egan*,[6] a committal order made on an *ex parte* application should contain a proviso that the person committed should apply for release three days after being received into custody, this period being the minimum necessary for practical purposes. The contemnor should also be shown the order before he is arrested or shortly after he is placed in custody.

The term of imprisonment and applications for discharge. As was seen in an earlier chapter, committal for civil contempt may be for either an indefinite period or for a fixed term, the former course being more appropriate where it is intended to coerce the contemnor into compliance and the latter where it is intended to punish him for past disobedience.[7] The operation of the committal order may also be suspended for such period, or on such terms and conditions, as may be specified, and it has been held that where this form of order is employed the court still retains a general discretion to do what is just in the circumstances in the event of a further breach. The committal order does not have to be automatically activated in its original form.[8] Provision may also be made for the committal order to lie in the office for a specified period to give the contemnor time to comply and thus obviate the need to execute the order. Equally, the court may decide not to employ the power of committal, but to issue an injunction restraining the respondent from committing a future contempt. This is, however, a matter for the court itself and it is not open to a party to ask for an injunction on a contempt application.[9]

---

[3] *Ibid.*, at p. 338.

[4] *Cf. Hipgrave* v. *Hipgrave* [1962] P. 91; [1962] 1 All E.R. 75 (husband attempting to run wife over with car); *Egan* v. *Egan* (1971) 115 Sol. Jo. 673 (husband assaulting wife in breach of a non-molestation order). Contrast *Hennie* v. *Hennie, The Times,* 25 November 1972, where there was no urgency and the granting of an *ex parte* application was criticised by the Court of Appeal.

[5] Committal on an *ex parte* application may also be appropriate where a person has taken an infant out of the jurisdiction in defiance of a court order or broken an undertaking to return the infant: see *Gordon* v. *Gordon* [1903] P. 141; *O'Donovan* v. *O'Donovan* [1955] 3 All E.R. 278.

[6] (1971) 115 Sol. Jo. 673. See also the Phillimore Committee report, para. 182.

[7] See above, pp. 10–11.

[8] *Re W. (B.) (An Infant)* [1969] 2 Ch. 50; [1969] 1 All E.R. 594.

[9] *Cf. Elliot* v. *Klinger* [1967] 3 All E.R. 141, 144 *per* Stamp, J. An injunction may, however, be sought in separate proceedings: see *Acrow (Automation), Ltd.* v. *Rex Chainbelt Inc.* [1971] 3 All E.R. 1175, C.A.

The period which the contemnor actually spends in prison will naturally depend upon a variety of considerations. Some points of a general nature may, however, be made. In the first place, where the committal is for a *fixed* term the contemnor must be released at the very latest at the expiration of that term, although he may be released earlier. Secondly, one may say that to the extent that the purpose of committal is to coerce the contemnor, rather than to punish him, he may expect to be released *ex debito justitiae* once he has complied with the order and so purged his contempt.[10] Thirdly, the court is empowered by RSC Ord. 52, r. 8(1) to hear an application for the discharge of the offender at any time, and this irrespective of whether he has been committed for a fixed term or for an indefinite period.

The response which is likely to be adopted on an application for release will depend upon the totality of the circumstances. Regard will be had to, for example, the reasons for the original committal, the period already spent in prison, the character and apparent intentions of the contemnor, and the likely consequences of a future or continuing breach. A contemnor who, for instance, resolutely refuses to comply with an order for the delivery up of documents will not in practice be imprisoned for more than a matter of months, for neither the consequences of non-compliance, nor the need to mark the authority of the court, would warrant this.[11] Yet different considerations may apply where an order prohibiting the molestation of a person or the causing of a nuisance is concerned. Here the court has to balance the need for protecting the public against the principle that a person should not be deprived of his liberty for longer than is necessary. According to Devlin, L.J. in *Yager* v. *Musa*,[12] the appropriate way of dealing with a person who repeatedly violates such an order is to treat him in the same way as a criminal court treats a persistent offender, that is by subjecting him to increasingly longer periods of imprisonment until obedience is secured. Thus on the facts of the case a man who had formed a wholly unreciprocated obsession for a girl, and who persisted in contacting her, was ordered to be released by the Court of Appeal on a specified date some three months later by which time he would have been in prison for eight months in all. For earlier violations of the same order he had already spent two separate periods of three and five months in prison. In such a case the contemnor's undertakings as to his future conduct clearly become less convincing with each breach. Yet it is only by releasing him that a court is ultimately able to test his sincerity.

Yager v. *Musa* also established that while it is open to a court dealing with an application for discharge to fix a future date for release, it may not make an order denying the contemnor liberty to apply for an earlier release. Neither, as the Court of Appeal was later to decide in *Vaughan* v. *Vaughan*,[13] is it proper for the original committal order itself to purport to debar the contemnor from making an application for release until a specified future date. The contemnor must be allowed to retain a general liberty to apply, at least unless he can be said to be abusing the process of the court.

---

[10] See above, pp. 10–11.
[11] *Cf. Re Barrell Enterprises* [1972] 3 All E.R. 631.
[12] [1961] 2 Q.B. 214; [1961] 2 All E.R. 561.
[13] [1973] 3 All E.R. 449. See also *Danchevsky* v. *Danchevsky* [1974] 3 All E.R. 934.

The Official Solicitor.[14] In recent years attention has been focused upon the role of the Official Solicitor to the Supreme Court of Judicature whose extensive range of duties includes that of watching over the interests of persons committed to prison for contempt. Before 1963 the Official Solicitor and his predecessors (the Solicitor to the Suitors' Fund and the Official Solicitor to the High Court of Chancery) were subject to duties of visitation, and of reporting upon contempt prisoners, under the Court of Chancery Act 1860. With the repeal of the 1860 Act his terms of reference and responsibilities now derive from a direction of the Lord Chancellor of 29 May 1963, which provides as follows:[15]

> I The Right Honourable Edward Baron Dilhorne do hereby direct that the Official Solicitor to the Supreme Court of Judicature do review all cases of persons committed to prison for contempt of court, do take such action as he may deem necessary thereon and do report thereon quarterly on the 31st day of January, the 30th day of April, the 31st day of July and the 31st day of October in every year.

It was in pursuance of this direction that the Official Solicitor successfully appealed to the Court of Appeal in the *Chobham Farm* case,[16] and then later applied to the National Industrial Relations Court for the release of the imprisoned dockers in the *Midland Cold Storage* case.[17] In both cases the action was taken without the request or approval of the dockers themselves, thus illustrating the independent status of the office.

The duty to review all cases of committal for contempt is facilitated by prison regulations. These require the Official Solicitor to be notified whenever a person is received into prison on committal by the Supreme Court, or by any of the superior courts, or on committal by a county court for an indefinite term or for a fixed term in excess of six weeks.[18] Likewise it is open to a judge in making a committal order, or on hearing a contempt application, to cause the Official Solicitor to be notified so that he may take any steps which appear appropriate. In the majority of cases the duty to review can be satisfactorily discharged by ensuring (with the assistance of prison legal aid officers) that the contemnor is placed in contact with solicitors with a view to arranging an appeal or an application for discharge. In some cases, however, a more active role will be adopted and the Official Solicitor will himself apply to the court, through counsel, for the discharge of a contemnor. Such cases might occur where, for example, the form of the committal order was itself invalid as in *Vaughan* v. *Vaughan*,[19] or where a person is committed for breach of an order which has lapsed, as happened in *Hennie* v. *Hennie*.[20] Similarly, an active role may also be considered appropriate where it is apparent that the contemnor will steadfastly

---

[14] I am indebted to Mr. Norman Turner, the Official Solicitor, for his assistance. Responsibility for any inaccuracies is, of course, mine alone. An outline of the Official Solicitor's duties is to be found in *The Supreme Court Practice 1973*, Vol. 2, p. 960.

[15] See the report of *Churchman* v. *Joint Shop Stewards' Committee* [1972] 3 All E.R. 603, 604; [1972] I.C.R. 222, 223.

[16] *Churchman* v. *Joint Shop Stewards' Committee* (above), see further, above, p. 238.

[17] *Midland Cold Storage, Ltd.* v. *Turner, The Times*, 28 July 1972.

[18] But not less than six weeks. The Phillimore Committee recommends (para. 190) that this lacuna be filled and that provision should be made for notification in all cases.

[19] [1973] 3 All E.R. 449.

[20] *The Times*, November, 1972.

refuse to comply with the court order whether through simple obstinacy, high principle, a search for martyrdom, or because he maintains that he is unable to do so.[1] In virtually all such cases there will come a time when further imprisonment can no longer be justified, and when the Official Solicitor's intervention will be both warranted and generally welcomed. In other cases he may also intervene where private solicitors are reluctant to act, as for one who has been repeatedly in breach of a court order; where medical reports indicate that the contemnor is in need of hospital care and is unfit to be kept in prison; or where his assistance is sought by a judge, perhaps to argue a legal point which appears to be open to a contemnor who is applying in person.

The number of cases referred to the Official Solicitor in the course of a year is detailed in the Civil Judicial Statistics, and in recent years has been as follows:

Year ending December 31	Contempt cases pending at commencement of year	New references during year	Disposed of during year	Pending at end of year
1968 (Cmnd 4112)	9	94	97	6
1969 (Cmnd 4416)	6	124	124	6
1970 (Cmnd 4721)	6	144	143	7
1971 (Cmnd 4982)	7	179	182	4
1972 (Cmnd 5333)	4	213	210	7
1973 (Cmnd 0000)	7	308	286	29

(ii) *Fines.* It has been seen in an earlier chapter that English courts have now accepted that a fine is a permissible outcome to civil contempt proceedings whether the proceedings are against a corporate body or against an individual.[2] As with committal orders the fine may probably be suspended so that it would only become operative in the event of a future breach.[3] Similarly a decision as to the appropriate level of the fine may be postponed to give the contemnor time for further consideration of his position, and sequestration of assets up to a given amount ordered in the meantime. This was the course adopted by the National Industrial Relations Court in the *Con-Mech* case.[4] Again the amount of the fine

[1] As in *Re Barrell Enterprises* [1972] 3 All E.R. 631.
[2] See above, pp. 11–12.
[3] In the United States it seems that a fine imposed as for a civil contempt *must* be suspended: see *Doyle* v. *London Guarantee Accident Co.*, 204 U.S. 599 (1907).
[4] *Con-Mech (Engineers) Ltd.* v. *A.U.E.W.* [1973] I.C.R. 620, above, p. 12 and pp. 241–242.

will be determined by similar considerations to those which apply to committal orders. Hence account will be taken of the effect of the breach, and of whether it is an isolated occurrence or one of a series reflecting a policy of non-compliance. Likewise account will be taken of the contemnor's financial resources. Thus in both the *Heatons' Transport* case[5] and *Goad* v. *AUEW*[6] the defendant union was fined the modest sum of £5,000 in respect of the first breach of the court order and a more substantial sum of £50,000 in respect of a subsequent breach. Even this latter sum was, however, relatively small when set alongside the total assets of the respective unions, and the level of the fines imposed in some cases in the United States.[7]

(iii) *Sequestration*. The writ of sequestration provides a further means of dealing with contempt of court which closely parallels the process of committal with the important difference that whereas the one operates against the person of the contemnor, the other operates against his property. The writ itself is directed to not less than four sequestrators or 'commissioners' chosen by the plaintiff in the action, and it authorises and commands two or more of them,

> to enter upon and take possession of all the real and personal estate of the [contemnor] and to collect, receive and get into your hands the rents and profits of his real estate and all his personal estate and keep the same under sequestration in your hands until the [contemnor] shall [pay into Court to the credit of the said action or matter the sum of £x or as may be] and clear his contempt and our said Court make other order to the contrary.[8]

In its extreme form the writ thus binds all the real and personal property of the contemnor, denying him the ability to dispose of it or to enjoy it without let or hindrance. As such it is clearly a drastic method of coercing a contemnor into compliance which will not be granted lightly. Indeed, according to the commentary in the *Supreme Court Practice*, sequestration is rarely used in the High Court other than against the property of a body corporate or of a director or officer of such a body, or in the Family Division where it issues to enforce orders in matrimonial cases.[9] When used as an aid to securing compliance with a court order (other than an order for the payment of money) the writ does not envisage the forfeiture or the subsequent sale of the property seized, except to the extent that this is necessary to defray the sequestrators' costs and only then with leave of the court. In other cases, however, sequestration may be used for the more limited purpose of enforcing the payment of a fine for contempt, which has itself been imposed in respect of non-compliance with a court order and where it appears that the fine would not be paid voluntarily. In such a case sequestration would not extend to the totality of the contemnor's assets, but would be limited to a sum sufficient to pay the fine and the costs of execution. *Goad* v. *AUEW (No.*

---

[5] *Heatons Transport, Ltd* v. *T.G.W.U.* [1973] A.C. 15, above, p. 236.

[6] [1973] I.C.R. 42; *Goad* v. *A.U.E.W. (No. 3)* [1973] I.C.R. 108, above, p. 240.

[7] Thus in *U.S.* v. *United Mine Workers of America*, 330 U.S. 258 (1947) the defendant trade union was fined $700,000 for disobedience and a further suspended fine of $2,800,000 was imposed to become payable in the event of future non-compliance.

[8] *Atkin's Court Forms* (2nd ed.), Vol. 19, p. 234.

[9] See *The Supreme Court Practice 1973*, Vol. 1, pp. 699–700.

2)[10] is a case in point. Here the order of the National Industrial Relations Court fining the defendant union £5,000 for its initial contempt provided that if the fine was not paid by a specified date writs of sequestration should issue to be executed, 'only to the extent and for the purposes herein or as hereinafter ordered'. As Sir John Donaldson, P. subsequently commented,[11] the effect of the limitation appended 'was that at all material times the writs were only to be executed to the extent necessary to recover the amount of the fine and the costs of execution'.[12]

Procedure. The procedure on an application for a writ of sequestration is essentially the same as on an application for an order of committal. The same requirements with respect to notice of the terms of the judgment or order, penal indorsement, proof of breach, and service of the notice of motion and accompanying affidavit apply. The writ itself may only be issued with the leave of the Court.[13] The application for the writ will almost invariably be moved at the instance of the aggrieved party for it is he who will typically have the primary interest in ensuring that the original judgment or order is enforced. The position is less clear, however, where sequestration is employed to assist in the enforcement of a fine for contempt the purpose of which was wholly or predominantly punitive. In such a case any incentive to apply for the writ may well be lacking. Sir John Donaldson, P. has said that in the *Goad* case the complainant and his solicitors were obliged to send out the writs of sequestration whether the complainant wished to or not, because the court had ordered him to do so.[14] Yet it is by no means clear that the National Industrial Relations Court (or indeed any other court) had the power to require a complainant to adopt a positive course of action on pain, presumably, of *himself* committing a contempt if he neglected or refused to do so. Procedural expedients designed to remove an impediment in the law, and to avoid placing a party in a position of appearing to hound an opponent, clearly cannot be allowed to extend the scope of the substantive law of contempt. In the subsequent case of *Con-Mech* v. *AUEW*[15] the National Industrial Relations Court changed its procedure and decided that it had an inherent jurisdiction to issue writs of sequestration *of its own motion* and without an initial application being made. It proceeded to order sequestration of the defendant union's assets to the value of £100,000. The ability so to act in cases of civil contempt is by no means clearly established. Yet it seems reasonable to assume that it exists now that the courts have accepted that civil contempt may invite a response which is avowedly punitive and in no way designed to benefit the complainant.[16] It remains to be seen whether the High Court itself will adopt the

[10] [1973] I.C.R. 42, above, p. 240.

[11] In *Eckman* v. *Midland Bank Ltd.* [1973] 1 All E.R. 609, 611; [1973] I.C.R. 71, 74.

[12] The Phillimore Committee recommends (para. 188) that the usual machinery for enforcing fines for contempt under the Fines Act 1833 and the Queen's Remembrancer Act 1859 be replaced by a simple system of recovery under the Criminal Justice Act 1967.

[13] See R.S.C. Ord. 45, r. 5, 7; Ord. 46, r. 5 and accompanying annotations in *The Supreme Court Practice 1973*, Vol. 1, pp. 683–690,699–702.

[14] The statement was made in *Eckman* v. *Midland Bank, Ltd.* [1973] 1 All E.R. 609, 611; [1973] I.C.R. 71, 74.

[15] [1973] I.C.R. 620.

[16] See above, pp. 7–8.

same procedure, or, indeed, whether it will purport to place a duty to proceed on the litigant at whose instance the original judgment or order was made.

The effect of the writ and the position of third parties. The issue of the writ binds both the real[17] and personal property[18] of the contemnor, including choses in action, but does not, of itself, create a charge on the property in favour of the person at whose instance it was issued. A charge on land requires that the writ be registered under the Land Charges Act 1925, whilst a charge on personal property requires an order of the court.[19]

As to the choice of assets called in to satisfy a limited sequestration in aid of enforcing payment of a fine, this is a matter for the sequestrators themselves. There is no question of their having to seek the court's approval of their choice. Indeed it is doubtful whether a court has jurisdiction either to grant or to withhold such approval. This point was of some significance at the time of the *Con-Mech* case when the sequestrators caused a political furore by calling in part of a loan made from the 'political' fund of the Amalgamated Union of Engineering Workers to the Hebburn UDC.[20]

The position and the duties of third parties faced with a claim by the sequestrators has been examined in recent years by Sir John Donaldson, P. in *Eckman* v. *Midland Bank Ltd*[1] and by Brandon, J. in *Bucknell* v. *Bucknell*.[2] The former case arose out of the refusal of the Midland Bank and of Hill Samuel & Co., as bankers for the Amalgamated Union of Engineering Workers (Engineering Section), to comply with the demands of the sequestrators in the *Goad* case. The latter had been charged with the duty of collecting the original £5,000 fine and the costs of execution from the union's assets. In carrying out their duties under the writ the sequestrators had required the bankers to (i) verify by affidavit the balances on the union's accounts with them and all deeds, documents of title etc. held by them on behalf of the union, and (ii) pay to them from the union's accounts the sum of £5,000 and a further £275 to cover the costs of execution. The banks had declined to comply with this demand unless required to do so by a specific court order directed to them individually. They pointed to the special confidential relationship between a bank and its customers based on commercial custom and practice, and argued that the writ *entitled* a third party to transfer possession of property to the sequestrators, but did not itself *oblige* them to do so. Hence the application by the sequestrators to the National Industrial Relations Court for such an order.

The order was duly granted against Hill Samuel & Co., where the union had a sufficient credit balance to meet the sequestrators' requirements, and indeed it was not resisted. Analysing the duties of third parties holding the contemnor's assets, Sir John Donaldson's conclusion was essentially the same as that reached by Brandon, J. in the earlier case of *Bucknell* v. *Bucknell*. Both were of the

[17] *Re Lush* (1870) L.R. 10 Eq. 442.
[18] *Dixon* v. *Rowe* (1876) 35 L.T. 548. For further details, see *Supreme Court Practice 1973*, Vol. 1, p. 701; Borrie and Lowe, *Law of Contempt*, pp. 346–347.
[19] *Supreme Court Practice 1973*, Vol. 1, pp. 700–701 and cases there cited. The leading case is *Re Pollard* [1903] 2 K.B. 41, at pp. 47–48 especially.
[20] See further, above, p. 241.
[1] [1973] 1 All E.R. 609; [1973] I.C.R. 71.
[2] [1969] 2 All E.R. 998.

opinion that the third party was obliged to comply with the sequestrators' demands, unless there were special circumstances warranting his insistence upon a specific court order to protect his position. Sir John Donaldson amplified the point in the following terms:[3]

Counsel for the banks has asked that we define the duty of banks and other third parties in relation to their dealings with a contemnor's property following the issue of writs of sequestration. We do not think that we can do this exhaustively, but in our judgment it at least extends to the following: (i) The third party is completely unaffected unless and until he knows of the issue of the writ of sequestration. (ii) The only duty which arises out of mere knowledge that a writ of sequestration has been issued is a duty to refuse to take any action the object of which is known by the third party to be the frustration of the object of the writ. Thus, in the absence of express instructions from the sequestrators banks can continue to honour cheques and stockbrokers can sell securities on the authority of the contemnor, unless they know that the transactions are exceptional and designed to obstruct or prevent the sequestration. If they have any doubts they can protect themselves by reporting the facts to the sequestrators. (iii) A demand by sequestrators for disclosure of property held for account of the contemnor not only may but must be answered promptly, fully and accurately. The duty of disclosure extends to revealing, on request, that no such property is held, or, if it has been but is no longer held, when, in what manner and to whom it was disposed of. If there is doubt as to the contemnor's title or the property is or may be subject to a charge, the full facts must be given to the sequestrators, who are as much entitled to the information as is the contemnor. (iv) If sequestrators require the transfer of possession of property which is or may be held for account of the contemnor or (which is the same) that the property be held to their order, the requirement must be strictly complied with unless (a) someone other than the contemnor has or may have an interest in the property;[4] e.g. the bank itself has a charge on securities possession of which is demanded by the sequestrators or money is held on the joint account of the contemnor and others or there is notice of a trust in favour of others; or (b) there is doubt whether the property is liable to sequestration;[5] in these exceptional cases it is the duty of the third party to explain the reasons for its failure to comply with the sequestrators' demand in order that the sequestrators may decide whether or not to seek a specific order from the court.

Although such exceptional circumstances were not present (at least in the case of Hill Samuel & Co.), neither of the defendants was regarded as having acted unreasonably in resisting the sequestrators' demands and they were not required to pay the costs of the motion. The sequestrators were accordingly left to recoup their costs from the sequestrated funds—a result which is perhaps less than fair to the contemnor who has no control over the source against which the sequestrator chooses to act. This point apart, it would seem, with respect, that the overall conclusion of Sir John Donaldson and of Brandon, J. in *Bucknell* v. *Bucknell* is clearly correct. To allow the third party to insist upon a specific court order being directed against him on each occasion, and to deny that there was a general duty to afford the sequestrator active cooperation in the absence of such an order, would go a long way towards effectively frustrating the whole process of sequestration.

[3] [1973] 1 All E.R. 609, 616; [1973] I.C.R. 71, 80–81.
[4] *Cf. Craig* v. *Craig* [1896] P. 171.
[5] *Cf. Fenton* v. *Lowther* (1787) 1 Cox Eq. Cas. 315; 29 E.R. 1182.

Discharge of sequestration. As to the discharge of the writ the basic position is clearly set out in the *Supreme Court Practice (1973)* where it is said:[6]

> Where the person whose property has been sequestered has purged his contempt, an order may be obtained on motion or summons for the discharge of the sequestration, and directing the sequestrators to withdraw from possession, and to pass their final accounts, and, after retaining their costs, charges and expenses, and any payments properly made by them, to pay the balance to him, and for the discharge therefrom of the sequestrators from all liability in respect of their office.

Nowadays, at least, it seems safe to assume that even when the contempt has not been purged by complying with the original order the process of sequestration will not be allowed to continue indefinitely, any more than will the process of committal.

(iv) *Costs.* Until relatively recent years it was generally assumed that on an application based on alleged contempt in procedure it was not possible to order that the respondent pay the costs of the proceedings unless he had been found to have committed a contempt.[7] In *Knight* v. *Clifton,*[8] however, the Court of Appeal held that this assumption was inconsistent with the general provision in the Supreme Court of Judicature (Consolidation) Act, 1925, s. 50(1), whereby the court or judge is accorded 'full power to determine by whom and to what extent the costs are to be paid'. At the same time the Court equally made it clear that the power to award costs against a successful defendant should only be exercised in exceptional circumstances as, for example, when he had deceived the plaintiff into believing that an injunction or undertaking had been breached.[9] The more usual outcome will be for the application to be dismissed with costs (unless it fails on purely technical grounds when the costs may be allowed to lie where they fall)[10] for, as it is said in *Oswald:* 'the extreme course of applying to commit or attach should not be resorted to unless the circumstances of the case justify that course'.[11] Conversely, where the defendant is held to be in contempt, but there are mitigating circumstances, it may well be that an order that he pay the costs of the proceedings, coupled with the usual apologies and undertakings, will be seen as the most appropriate outcome. In such a case it is possible for the party moving the court to be given a complete indemnity to cover costs as between solicitor and client.[12] Costs as between solicitor and client cannot, it seems, be given to the respondent if the motion fails.[13]

---

[6] Vol. 1. p. 702.

[7] See, e.g., Halsbury, *Laws of England* (3rd ed.), Vol. 8, para. 72; Oswald, *Contempt of Court,* p. 215, citing *Re Emmerson, Rawlings* v. *Emmerson* (1887) 57 L.J.P. 1.

[8] [1971] Ch. 700; [1971] 2 All E.R. 378, C.A.

[9] *Cf. ibid.,* at p. 713 and p. 386 respectively.

[10] *Cf. Oswald,* p. 215. No order was made in respect of the costs of the motion in *Eckman* v. *Midland Bank, Ltd.* [1973] 1 All E.R. 609 where the application was successful but the defendants were regarded as having acted reasonably.

[11] See *Contempt of Court,* p. 215. See also *Knight* v. *Clifton* [1971] Ch. 700, 714; [1971] 2 All E.R. 378, 386–387 *per* Russell, L.J.

[12] *Plating Co.* v. *Farquharson* (1881) 17 Ch. D. 49; *Steele* v. *Hutchings* [1879] W.N. 18; *Oswald,* p. 216.

[13] *Plating Co.* v. *Farquharson,* above. *Halsbury,* Vol. 9, para. 105.

(g) *Developments in the National Industrial Relations Court.* At several stages in the present chapter reference have been made to decisions on procedural and other matters in the National Industrial Relations Court. The decisions are still of general interest in spite of the demise of that court for it may be that they are applicable to superior courts generally.

One such development was the assumption in *Churchman* v. *Joint Shop Stewards' Committee of the Workers of the Port of London* that the Court was entitled to act *ex mero motu*, that is, of its own motion, in committing a contemnor, and that it did not have to wait until the machinery of the law of contempt was activated by a complainant.[14] This view was, in effect, both repeated and developed in *Con-Mech (Engineers), Ltd* v. *AUEW*.[15] Here Sir John Donaldson, delivering the judgment of the Court, announced a change in procedure whereby complainants would not, in future, 'be required formally to ask the court to take action against the alleged contemnor as is customary in notices of motion to commit for contempt of court'.[16] The Court would, he added, issue writs of sequestration of its own motion.

The assumption of jurisdiction so to act was seen as being justifiable both in terms of preventing the authority of the court from being undermined by complainants (who might themselves be subject to industrial pressures) declining to act, and in terms of giving effect to the general recognition that a fine or committal for contempt may be legitimately intended to serve a punitive function.[17] It may be said, with respect, that both strands of this argument are sound. The public as a whole clearly has an interest over and above that of the complainant in ensuring that orders of the courts as for the time being established are not openly flouted. Equally it is clear that a fine which is imposed in civil contempt proceedings as a punitive response, rather than as an aid to coercion, may well afford the complainant little incentive to see that payment is enforced through sequestration. Yet there would be general agreement that enforcement remains necessary in the public interest.

Other suggestions and procedural developments associated with the National Industrial Relations Court are much more questionable. This is particularly true of the duty which the court purported to place upon a complainant of keeping it informed of any breaches of orders granted at his behest. The alleged duty was referred to by Sir John Donaldson in *Heatons Transport, Ltd* v. *TGWU* in the following terms:[18]

> We regard it as the duty of any person who obtains an order of this court to bring to the court's attention any alleged disobedience of that order. In later cases we have included a direction to this effect in the order itself. As a result, possible penalties for disobedience of the court's orders will not be available as bargaining counters and the

---

[14] In the Court of Appeal Lord Denning commented: 'I do not say that the court was not entitled to act as it did. It may be that in some circumstances the court may be entitled, on sufficient information being brought before it, to act on its own initiative in sending a contemnor to prison': [1972] I.C.R. 222, 229; [1972] 3 All E.R. 603, 608.

[15] [1973] I.C.R. 620.

[16] *Ibid.*, at p. 626.

[17] *Cf. Jennison* v. *Baker* [1972] 2 Q.B. 52; [1972] 1 All E.R. 997, C.A., and above, p. 8 and below p. 268.

[18] [1972] 2 All E.R. 1214, 1230.

complainant will incur the minimum of odium in bringing allegations of disobedience to the attention of the court.

In the subsequent *Con-Mech* case a further reason was given, namely that: 'Complainants will necessarily still be involved in the duty of reporting breaches of the court's orders because the court at present has no machinery for supervising compliance with such orders.'[19]

The inevitable corollary of any such duty must presumably be that the complainant would himself commit a contempt by failing to report breaches of which he was aware. A duty must be backed by a sanction if it is to be at all meaningful. On this basis it is submitted, with respect, that no such duty exists. The scope of the substantive law of contempt clearly cannot be extended in this way, even though the extension might have both promoted harmony in industrial relations and acted as a substitute for the lack of any formal machinery for supervising compliance. The Phillimore Committee has, however, recommended that a court should have the power to require breaches to be reported to it.[20]

On a related point the view was also expressed in *Eckman* v. *Midland Bank, Ltd*[1] that the National Industrial Relations Court had the power to require a complainant to sue out a writ of sequestration on pain, presumably, of committing a contempt if he did not. Again, it seems most unlikely that any such power existed. Likewise the apparent suggestion in *Goad* v. *AUEW (No. 3)*[2] that a contempt will be committed by a refusal to comply with an order to attend the court can only be correct if the order is understood as being directed to the defendant *qua* witness. There was no apparent basis for a power to order a person to attend *qua* party to the proceedings.[3]

(h) *The position of the party in contempt.* There is a general rule of uncertain scope whereby a party in contempt may be disentitled from taking any further steps in the same proceedings, at least where the opposing party takes objection and applies for the proceedings to be stayed.[4] The rule does not, however, prevent him from seeking to set aside the order on which the alleged contempt was founded,[5] from seeking discharge on the ground that he has purged his contempt,[6] nor, in appropriate cases, from defending himself when an accusation is made against him.[7] As Lord Denning has explained, the rule originated in canon law and was adopted by the ecclesiastical courts and the chancery courts.[8]

---

[19] [1973] I.C.R. 620, 626.

[20] Para. 171.

[1] [1973] I.C.R. 71, 74; [1973] 1 All E.R. 609, 611.

[2] [1973] I.C.R. 108, 111.

[3] See further Rideout, *The Practice and Procedure of the National Industrial Relations Court* (1973), p. 45.

[4] *Semble* that he may proceed in the original cause if the defendant does not apply to stay the proceedings: see Oswald, *Contempt of Court*, p. 248; *Ricketts* v. *Mornington* (1834) 7 Sim. 200; 58 E.R. 813; *Wilson* v. *Bates* (1838) 3 My. & Cr. 197, 204; 40 E.R. 900, 902. See further, *Halsbury*, Vol. 9, para. 106.

[5] *Gordon* v. *Gordon* [1904] P. 163, C.A.

[6] *Chuck* v. *Cremer* (1846) 2 Ph. 113; 41 E.R. 884.

[7] *Gordon* v. *Gordon* [1904] P. 163; Oswald, *op. cit.*, p. 247, note 1 and cases there cited.

[8] See *Hadkinson* v. *Hadkinson* [1952] P. 285, 295.

In practice it appears to have been applied and discussed in divorce cases in which a party has taken a child out of the jurisdiction in defiance of a court order and has then sought to take further steps in the same proceedings.

Hadkinson v. *Hadkinson*[9] was such a case. Here a wife had been granted custody of her child but enjoined not to take it out of the jurisdiction without the consent of the court. On her decree nisi being made absolute she remarried and took the child with her to Australia without obtaining leave. The father then sought and was granted an order directing her to return the child within the jurisdiction, and it was against this order that the mother sought to appeal to the Court of Appeal. A preliminary objection having been taken by counsel for the father, the Court of Appeal declined, at its discretion, to hear her since she was in contempt of the earlier order in a way which impeded the course of justice. As Lord Denning observed:[10]

> So long as the boy remains in Australia, it is impossible for this court to enforce its orders in respect of him. No good reason is shown why he should not be returned to this country so as to be within the jurisdiction of this court. He should be returned before counsel is heard on the merits of this case, so that, whatever order is made, this court will be able to enforce it.

The decision not to hear the mother may be assumed to have had the desired effect for the child was later brought back within the jurisdiction at which time the mother's appeal was allowed.[11]

(ii) *County courts*

Thus far discussion has been directed towards the contempt powers of the High Court, Court of Appeal and courts of equivalent status. The position with respect to county courts is governed by the County Courts Act 1959 and the County Court Rules 1936. By s. 74 of the 1959 Act it is provided that:

> Every county court, as regards any cause of action for the time being within its jurisdiction, shall in any proceedings before it (a) grant such relief, redress or remedy or combination of remedies, either absolute or conditional; and (b) give such and the like effect to every ground of defence or counterclaim equitable or legal (subject to the provisions of section sixty-five of this Act); as ought to be granted or given in the like case by the High Court and in as full and ample a manner.

Ord. 25, r. 67 of the County Court Rules makes provision for the enforcement of such orders in the following terms:

> Orders in the nature of an injunction and all orders within the competence of the court which, if they were made in an action or matter in the High Court, could in that court be enforced by attachment or committal, may be enforced, by order of the judge, by attachment.

---

[9] See above, note 8.
[10] *Ibid.*, at p. 298.
[11] The disability only applies within the *same* proceedings: *Bettinson* v. *Bettinson* [1965] 1 All E.R. 102. See also *Daniell, Chancery Practice*, 8th. ed., Vol. 1, p. 786; Oswald, *op. cit.*, p. 248; *Clark* v. *Dew* (1829) 1 Russ. & M. 103; 39 E.R. 40; *Taylor* v. *Taylor* (1849) 1 Mac. & G. 397; 41 E.R. 1318. See also *Short* v. *Short* (1973) 7 S.A.S.R. 1 (Sup. Ct South Australia).

The limits of the jurisdiction of a county court judge to grant an injunction fall outside the scope of the present work. Here it is important to note that although the County Court Rules contemplate imprisonment for an indefinite term after arrest by attachment as the sole mode of enforcement[12] it is not the function of these rules to remove any powers which might otherwise exist. Accordingly it has recently been held by the Court of Appeal in *Danchevsky* v. *Danchevsky*[13] that a county court has the power to imprison for a fixed term, and to direct under s. 47 of the Supreme Court of Judicature (Consolidation) Act 1925 that the conveyance of property be executed by a third party.[14] Parity of reasoning would likewise suggest that a county court may fine for contempt under its inherent jurisdiction. This lesser penalty is available in the High Court—without there being any specific statutory provision or rule of the Supreme Court in point—and the same would probably be true of the county courts. Likewise, it would seem from *Danchevsky* v. *Danchevsky* that it is at least arguable that sequestration might issue as a means of enforcing an injunction or other relevant order, It is doubtful, however, whether a county court would have any jurisdiction to proceed as against a stranger to the injunction who had procured its breach, for this appears to be a criminal contempt.[15] Yet in such a case an application might be made to a Divisional Court of the Queen's Bench Division calling in aid the decision in *Davies, ex parte Hunter*[16] where it was held that the Queen's Bench Division has power to punish interference with the administration of justice in inferior courts generally.

The limits of the jurisdiction of a county court judge to punish for contempt were likewise explored in *Jennison* v. *Baker*.[17] Here a landlord was in breach of a county court injunction restraining her from evicting her tenants or from interfering with their reasonable enjoyment of the premises. On an appeal to the Court of Appeal against an order imprisoning her for contempt, Simon Goldblatt submitted that, while the High Court might itself have imprisoned for contempt, a county court judge could not do so once it appeared that the complainant was no longer actively seeking the benefit of the injunctive relief. Imprisonment in such circumstances could, he noted, only operate as a punishment for a past wrong and not as coercion towards future compliance. Although the argument was, in the words of Edmund-Davies, L.J., 'brilliantly developed', it did not meet with success. In the view of the Court of Appeal, liability to subsequent attachment remained an essential part of the original remedy even in a case in which the benefit of the remedy was no longer sought.[18] This was so in the High Court and it followed that the same was true of a county court, which is empowered by s. 74 of the 1959 Act to grant the same remedies as the High Court and 'in as full and ample a manner'.

---

[12] See Ord. 25, rr. 67, 68 and 70 and forms 195, 196; *Halsbury*, Vol. 10, paras. 561–566.

[13] [1974] 3 All E.R. 934.

[14] See further, above, pp. 233–234.

[15] See above, p. 247. Inferior courts may only punish for a criminal contempt committed in the face of the court itself, above, p. 29.

[16] [1906] 1 K.B. 32, above, p. 30.

[17] [1972] 2 Q.B. 52.

[18] See also *Martin* v. *Bannister* (1879) 4 Q.B.D. 212; 4 Q.B.D. 491.

As for the procedure leading to the issue of a warrant of attachment, the position is governed by Ord. 25, r. 68 of the County Court Rules. This provides that at the time when an order 'in the nature of an injunction' is drawn up the registrar shall issue a copy of the order indorsed with a notice indicating the consequences of non-compliance,[19] which will then be served on the respondent personally.[20] In the event of non-compliance with the injunction the registrar will then, on the application of the applicant, issue a notice calling on the respondent to show cause why he should not be attached for contempt.[1] Personal service upon the respondent is again required. Thereafter, r. 68(3) provides that if, on the day fixed for the hearing, the judge is satisfied that the respondent has failed to obey the order (or, should the respondent fail to appear, that he has been served with an indorsed copy of the order and of the notice) then he may order a warrant of attachment to issue.[2] A copy of the order for the issue of the warrant must be served on the respondent either before or at the time when the warrant is executed, unless the judge makes an order to the contrary.[3]

(iii) *Magistrates' courts.*

Magistrates' courts possess a limited statutory power to fine or imprison in respect of breaches of their own orders. By the Magistrates' Courts Act 1952, s. 54(3) it is provided that:

> Where any person disobeys an order of a magistrates' court . . . to do anything other than the payment of money[4] or to abstain from doing anything, the court may (a) order him to pay a sum not exceeding one pound for every day during which he is in default; or (b) commit him to custody for a specified period or until he has sooner remedied his default: Provided that a person shall not by virtue of this section be ordered to pay more than £20 or be committed for more than two months in all for disobeying one or more orders to do or abstain from doing the same thing.

In *B. (B.P.M.)* v. *B. (M.M.)*[5] a Divisional Court of the Probate, Divorce and Admiralty Division of the High Court consisting of Sir Jocelyn Simon, P. and Baker, J. had occasion to consider the limits of a magistrates' court's powers under this section. A father had been in breach of an order of the Gravesend magistrates granting him limited access to his children and the magistrates had committed him to prison for two months, the sentence being suspended for one year. On appeal to the Divisional Court it was held that the justices had no power to suspend a term of imprisonment for contempt whether under the Criminal Justice Act 1967, s. 39 or otherwise. Furthermore, on the strict construction of s. 54(3) which was appropriate, committal for a fixed term of two

---

[19] As in Form 140 of the County Court Forms.

[20] See C.C.R., Ord. 25, r. 68(1).

[1] C.C.R., Ord. 25, r. 68(2). See also Form 194 for the wording of the notice.

[2] For the wording of the order for the warrant, see Form 195. This form must set out the particular matter of the contempt which the respondent has committed or the order will be bad: see *McIlraith* v. *Grady* [1967] 3 All E.R. 625, C.A. For the form of the warrant itself, see Form 196.

[3] C.C.R., Ord. 25, r. 68(4). For enforcement of undertakings by solicitors in the county court, see the County Courts Act 1959, s. 195; C.C.R., Ord. 25, r. 69; *Cordery on Solicitors* (6th ed.), pp. 164–171.

[4] As to which, see below, p. 273. Recalcitrant witnesses who refuse to answer a question etc. may be imprisoned for up to seven days; Magistrates' Courts Act 1952, s. 77(4).

[5] [1969] P. 103; [1969] 1 All E.R. 891.

months was also regarded as being beyond the justices' powers. According to Sir Jocelyn Simon, the correct form of the order was, rather, that the father stand committed for his disobedience until he had caused the child to be handed over to the mother at a designated time and place, such imprisonment not to exceed two months or such lesser period as might appear to be justified.[6] On the basis of such an order the father would have been entitled to be released on compliance, and the period of two months (or the shorter period designated in the order) would have simply indicated the maximum term of imprisonment in the event of non-compliance. Imprisonment could, in short, have been employed for coercive or remedial purposes, but not as a form of punishment for past disobedience.[7]

It is submitted, with respect, that this is the correct approach in interpreting the sub-section, even though the actual decision itself is less than fully satisfactory. In particular it appears to have been based on the original wording of the 1952 Act ('commit him to custody until he has remedied his default'), and not on the wording as amended by the Criminal Justice Act 1961, s. 41(1) and schedule 4, as set out above. Where a fine is concerned, the correct form of order would be that the defendant pay a specified sum not in excess of £1 for each day in default, the total not to exceed £20 in all. In the result the Divisional Court in *B. (B.P.M.)* v. *B. (M.M.)* decided that it was unnecessary to send the father to prison, although it was empowered to make any order which might have been made by the court below.

In certain circumstances disobedience of an order made by justices acting within their jurisdiction may be punished on indictment as a common law misdemeanour.[8] Thus in *Robinson,*[9] for example, it was held that an indictment would lie for refusing to obey an order of quarter sessions calling on the defendant to keep and maintain his two infant grandchildren. Delivering the opinion of the Court of King's Bench, Lord Mansfield distinguished between those statutory offences in which breach of an order might be punished on indictment, and those in which the statutory procedure and penalty alone was available. According to Lord Mansfield:[10]

> The true rule of distinction seems to be, that where the offence intended to be guarded against by a statute, was punishable before the making of such statute prescribing a particular method of punishing it, there such particular remedy is cumulative, and does not take away the former remedy: but where the statute only enacts 'that the doing any act not punishable before, shall for the future be punishable in such and such a particular manner,' there it is necessary that such particular method, by such Act prescribed, must be specifically pursued; and not the common law method of an indictment.

Consistently with this distinction it was subsequently held in *Hall*[11] that neglect by a parish overseer of the poor to perform his duties under the Registration Act

---

[6] *Cf. ibid.*, at p. 114.

[7] Contrast the position in the High Court and in county courts as seen in *Jennison* v. *Baker* [1972] 2 Q.B. 52.

[8] See *Russell on Crime* (12th. ed.) Vol. 1, pp. 314–316; *Halsbury*, Vol. 9, para. 86.

[9] (1759) 2 Burr. 799; 97 E.R. 568.

[10] *Ibid.*, at 805.

[11] [1891] 1 Q.B. 747, 765 (Charles, J.).

of 1843 was not punishable on indictment since it was not 'antecedently punishable by a common law proceeding'. Whilst it is readily understandable that the enactment of a new offence should not be viewed as increasing the number of common law misdemeanours, it is less clear that an existing misdemeanour should continue to be regarded as extant once a statutory provision has been enacted covering the same ground. The apparent absence of modern cases suggests, however, that the point is of little practical significance.

2 DISOBEDIENCE OF AN ORDER FOR THE PAYMENT OF A SUM OF MONEY[12]

In the early part of the 19th century the imprisonment of debtors at the instance of their creditors without even the need for an intervening court order was a notoriously common occurrence. The number of persons so imprisoned decreased with the establishment of a system of execution operating through the county court structure set up in 1846, but it was not until the Debtors' Act 1869 that radical changes were effected in the law.

Section 4 of the 1869 Act contains the general provision abolishing imprisonment for debt with a saving for certain exceptional cases. The section provides that:

> With the exceptions herein-after mentioned, no person shall, after the commencement of this Act, be arrested or imprisoned for making default in payment of a sum of money. There shall be excepted from the operation of the above enactment:
>
> 1. Default in payment of a penalty, or sum in the nature of a penalty, other than a penalty in respect of any contract:
> 2. Default in payment of any sum recoverable summarily before a justice or justices of the peace:
> 3. Default by a trustee or person acting in a fiduciary capacity and ordered to pay by a court of equity any sum in his possession or under his control:
> 4. Default by an attorney or solicitor in payment of costs when ordered to pay costs for misconduct as such, or in payment of a sum of money when ordered to pay the same in his character of an officer of the court making the order:
> 5. Default in payment for the benefit of creditors of any portion of a salary or other income in respect of the payment of which any court having jurisdiction in bankruptcy is authorised to make an order:
> 6. Default in payment of sums in respect of the payment of which orders are in this Act authorised to be made:[13]
>
> Provided, first, that no person shall be imprisoned in any case excepted from the operation of this section for a longer period than one year; and, secondly, that nothing in this section shall alter the effect of any judgment or order of any court for payment of money except as regards the arrest and imprisonment of the person making default in paying such money.

By the Debtors Act 1878, s. 1, the court was subsequently given a discretion to grant or refuse an application for attachment in cases falling under the third and

---

[12] See, in general, *Halsbury*, Vol. 9, paras. 77–84.

[13] A further exception was created by the Crown Proceedings Act 1947, s. 26(2) to cover the non-payment of death duties or purchase tax.

fourth of the above exceptions. It is these two exceptions covering, respectively, defaults by trustees and persons acting in a fiduciary capacity and defaults by attorneys or solicitors, which created most of the early difficulties of interpretation. In view of the apparent lack of recent cases and of the adequate treatment of the section elsewhere, it is not proposed to discuss the scope of the exceptions created by s. 4 any further.[14]

Further provisions covering the non-payment of a sum of money are to be found in the Debtors Act 1869, s. 5, as amended by the Administration of Justice Act 1970, s. 11. Section 5 provides for the committal of a contumacious debtor who can be shown to have, or to have had, the means to pay the debt,[15] but to have refused or neglected to do so. Subject to this limitation, however, the section, as originally enacted, enabled a court to commit 'for a term not exceeding six weeks, or until payment of the sum due, any person who makes default in payment of any debt or instalment of any debt due from him in pursuance of any order or judgment of that or any other competent court'. Whilst the impecunious debtor was protected, the debtor who had had the means to pay remained liable to a maximum term of six weeks' imprisonment to coerce him into compliance.

The scope of this general provision has, however, been subsequently limited so that the power is now exercisable only[16]

(a) by the High Court in respect of a High Court maintenance order; and
(b) by a county court in respect of—(i) a High Court or a county court maintenance order; or (ii) a judgment or order which is enforceable by a court in England and Wales and is for the payment of any of the taxes, contributions or liabilities specified in Schedule 4 [to the Administration of Justice Act 1970].[17]

In cases falling outside these limits committal by the High Court or by a county court is no longer possible and the creditor is restricted to enforcement through execution against the debtor's property, or through an attachment of earnings order. This latter order will be directed to the person who appears to the court to have the debtor in his employment instructing him to make periodical deductions from the debtor's earnings, and to pay the amounts so deducted to the collecting officer of the court.[18] By the Attachment of Earnings Act 1971, s. 3(4) it is further provided that where proceedings are taken in the High Court or a county court for the enforcement of a maintenance order by committal, the court may make an attachment of earnings order in lieu of committing the debtor. Such an order to

---

[14] Further discussion of the scope of s. 4 may be found in, e.g., *The Supreme Court Practice 1973*, Vol. 1, pp. 672–675; *Halsbury*, Vol. 9, para. 79 (trustees), para. 80 (attorney or solicitor); *Lewin on Trusts* (16th. ed., 1964), pp. 682–685; *Cordery on Solicitors* (6th. ed., 1968), pp. 177–182. For non-compliance with orders for the payment of a sum of money into court, see *Halsbury*, Vol. 9, para. 84.

[15] See the Debtors Act 1869, s. 5(2).

[16] See the Administration of Justice Act 1970, s. 11.

[17] The Crown debts referred to are income tax or any other liability recoverable under the Taxes Management Act 1970, s. 65, 66 or 68, contributions under the National Insurance Act 1965, s. 3 or 4, the National Health Service Contributions Act 1965, s. 1, or the National Insurance (Industrial Injuries) Act 1965, s. 2, and redundancy fund contributions under the Redundancy Payments Act 1965, s. 27: Administration of Justice Act 1970, Sch. 4; Finance Act 1972, Sch. 28, Part VIII: see *Halsbury*, Vol. 3, title Bankruptcy, para. 254, note 2.

[18] See the Attachment of Earnings Act 1971, s. 6. If the employer fails to comply he is liable on summary conviction to a maximum fine of £25: *ibid.*, s. 25(3).

secure payments may not, however, be made unless it appears that the debtor's failure to comply with the maintenance order was due to his wilful refusal or culpable neglect.[19] A county court is similarly empowered to make an attachment of earnings order on an application for committal in respect of disobedience of a judgment for the payment of Crown debts.[20]

Broadly parallel provisions now restrict the power of a magistrates' court to commit for non-payment of a sum of money. By the Magistrates' Courts Act 1952, s. 64, a magistrates' court could commit on default in paying 'a sum adjudged to be paid by a conviction or order of a magistrates' court'. A warrant for committal could issue either as an alternative to levying distress against the goods of the defaulter, or on the levying of distress appearing to be insufficient to make good the default.[1] The main limitation to this power of committal was that, as with s. 5 of the 1869 Act, committal for the non-payment of a civil debt was only possible where the court was satisfied that the defaulter had had the means to pay and had refused or neglected to do so.[2] The Administration of Justice Act 1970, s. 12(2) has, however, restricted the power of committal on default in paying a judgment debt (while leaving unaffected the power to commit for non-payment of a sum adjudged to be paid by a conviction) so that it is now only exercisable in respect of a default under:

(a) a magistrates' court maintenance order;
(b) an order for the payment of any of the taxes, contributions or liabilities specified in Schedule 4 to [the 1970] Act; or
(c) an order (in this Act referred to as a 'legal aid contribution order') under section 76 of the Criminal Justice Act 1967 (now Legal Aid Act 1974, s.32: contribution by legally assisted person to the cost of his defence in a criminal case).

On an application for committal on a failure to comply with a maintenance order, the Attachment of Earnings Act 1971, s. 3(4)(b), empowers a magistrates' court to make an attachment of earnings order in lieu of committal. Such an order may also be made under s. 1(3) of the 1971 Act in cases corresponding to those detailed in s. 12(2) of the 1970 Act as set out above, where the order is sought by the appropriate persons listed in s. 3 of the 1971 Act. It seems, however, that it is only in the case of a maintenance order that a magistrates' court may attach the earnings of the defaulter, rather than commit him, where it is his committal which has been sought under the 1952 Act.

---

[19] See s. 3(5) of the 1971 Act.
[20] *Ibid.*, s. 3(6). For general discussion of the problems of enforcement, see the Report of the Committee on the Enforcement of Judgment Debts, Cmnd. 3909, 1969 under the chairmanship of Mr Justice Payne.
[1] Magistrates' Courts Act 1952, s. 64(2).
[2] See s. 73(1) of the 1952 Act. The maximum period which a defaulter may be kept in prison is set out in the Third Schedule to the 1952 Act. In respect of a civil debt the term is limited to six weeks: Magistrates' Courts Act 1952, s. 64(3), Sch. 3, para. 4.

Index